AF765597

IIC STUDIES

Studies in Industrial Property and Copyright Law

Volume 26

·HART·
PUBLISHING

OXFORD AND PORTLAND, OREGON
2007

Published by the Max Planck Institute for Foreign and International Patent, Copyright and Competition Law, Munich

Editors

Professor Dr Josef Drexl
Professor Dr Reto Hilty
Professor Dr h.c. Joseph Straus

IIC STUDIES

Studies in Industrial Property and Copyright Law

Dr Christopher Heath and Professor Kung-Chung Liu
(editors)

Copyright Law and the Information Society in Asia

A joint project by The Max Planck Institute, Munich,
The Academia Sinica, Taipei & The IP Academy Singapore

HART PUBLISHING
OXFORD AND PORTLAND, OREGON
2007

Published in North America (US and Canada) by
Hart Publishing
c/o International Specialized Book Services
920 NE 58th Avenue, Suite 300
Portland, OR 97213-3786
USA
Tel: +1 503 287 3093 or toll-free: (1) 800 944 6190
Fax: +1 503 280 8832
E-mail: orders@isbs.com
Website: www.isbs.com

© Hart Publishing 2007

The editors and contributors have asserted their right under the Copyright, Designs and Patents Act 1988, to be identified as the authors of this work.

All rights reserved. No part of this publication may be reproduced, stored in a retrieval system, or transmitted, in any form or by any mean, without the prior permission of Hart Publishing, or as expressly permitted by law or under the terms agreed with the appropriate reprographic rights organisation. Enquiries concerning reproduction which may not be covered by the above should be addressed to Hart Publishing at the address below.

Hart Publishing, 16C Worcester Place, Oxford, OX1 2JW
Telephone: +44 (0)1865 517530 Fax: +44 (0)1865 510710
E-mail: mail@hartpub.co.uk
Website: http://www.hartpub.co.uk

British Library Cataloguing in Publication Data
Data Available

ISBN-13: 978- 1-84113-654-7
ISBN-10: 1-84113-654-9

Typeset by Compuscript Ltd, Shannon
Printed and bound in Great Britain by
Lightning Source UK Ltd

Contents

Contents

Acknowledgement

Based on a co-operation agreement signed in 1999, the Academia Sinica in Taipei and the Max Planck Institute for Foreign and International Patent, Copyright and Competition Law in Munich held their third conference on "New Paradigms of Copyright Law in the Information Society" in June 2004 in Taipei. As was the case with the previous two conferences on well-known marks (1999) and technology transfer (2001), the six topics of this conference were dealt with in comparative fashion. This approach is reflected in the way the chapters are structured in this book: A comparative analysis followed by country reports of nine Asian jurisdictions updated as of 1 January 2006.

The editors are grateful for the contributions written by both academics and practitioners in the region or familiar therewith, many of whom have already been on board for one of the previous publications of the Max Planck Institute's Asian Series edited by Kluwer Law International.

Apart from the Academia Sinica and the Max Planck Institute, financial assistance for the conference and publication was provided by the IP Academy in Singapore.

The manuscripts were thankfully checked for format and language by Ms. Lim Li from the IP Academy in Singapore.

The Editors

Introductory Preface

Christopher Heath and Kung Chung Liu

The book takes a look at the six most important topics currently discussed for copyright law in the information society and for each topic provides an in-depth introduction that compares the approaches taken in Europe and the US. Subsequently, these issues are analysed in the context of nine Asian jurisdictions: China, Taiwan, Hong Kong, Japan, Korea, Singapore, Malaysia, Thailand and the Philippines.

Chapter 1 - The Expansion of Copyright Law and its Social Justification
Introduction by Reto Hilty, Max Planck Institute, Munich

In the last decade, copyright law has been expanded vertically and horizontally. Vertically in that it covers subject matters that previously were not deemed copyrightable at least in those countries that require a certain threshold of creativity. Examples would be computer programs and databases. Horizontally, because copyright law has been strengthened in various ways: The protection period has been extended, additional rights of rental and lending have been given to owners of certain categories of rights, and new rights have been added to the catalogue (right of making available, etc.). All this has significantly tipped the balance in favour of copyright owners, but not necessarily in favour of society at large. On the contrary, such over-protection may have led to imbalances in the framework of copyright law as an incentive to stimulate creative works.—The Country reports indicate how these issues are perceived in their home countries, particularly in view of the "digital divide" between developing and developed countries.

Chapter 2 - Internet Trade, Digital Works and Parallel Imports
Introduction by Christopher Heath, European Patent Office, Munich

Issues of exhaustion and parallel importation have become highly politicised in the last decade. A good number of countries have erected barriers against the parallel importation of copyrighted goods, e.g. Taiwan and the US, as has Europe. In addition, more copyrighted works have been endowed with inexhaustible rights of rental and lending, e.g. film works. At the same time, Internet trading has become an important economic factor. How then is Internet trade affected by the above-mentioned mechanisms of rights owners to enforce their rights against parallel importers and distributors of films works (e.g. video tapes) in the digital environment, and, vice versa, can rules limiting parallel importation and distribution of film works still be effectively enforced in a digital environment? And has this issue already been addressed in court cases and legislation?

Chapter 3 - The Collective Exercise of Copyrights
Introduction by Kung Chung Liu, Academia Sinica, Taiwan

Collective exercise of copyrights has more than ever become a crucial instrument of copyright management and enforcement, even a possible alternative for extensive criminalization of copyright infringements that is now taking place on a worldwide scale. And yet the concerted actions by the collecting societies may incur market power and antitrust concerns. Country reports should indicate how the collecting societies have developed in their home countries in terms of members, market shares, revenues, and how their laws are dealing with the collective exercise of rights respectively, such as if there are control of royalty fees, compulsory management of copyrights, and exemption from cartel prohibition.

Chapter 4 - The Law on Anti-Circumvention and Digital Rights Management
Introduction by Andy Sun, National Chenchi University, Taipei, Taiwan and Zhi Wei, Peking University, Beijing

Measures against the manufacture and distribution of programmes or devices meant to overcome or circumvent copyright management systems (or, less euphemistically, systems to prevent the copying of works) are required by the WIPO Copyright Treaties that in this respect represent clear elements of TRIPS plus protection. While such programmes or devices may well have unlawful purposes in allowing users the copying of works beyond what copyright law actually allows, this is not necessarily so: After all, copyright limits allow the copying for purposes of fair use. Such limitation could be successfully overridden by right owners in installing technical means, while users would not be able to purchase programmes or devices that would allow them to exercise their lawful rights. The country reports address how this friction has been solved by national law, if at all.

Chapter 5 - Copyright Contracts, Public Policy and Antitrust
Introduction by Estelle Derclaye, University of Nottingham

This topic is complementary to the previous one. While in case of anti-copying devices, the means to prevent copying (lawful or unlawful) are technical, the same result may be achieved by way of contract, e.g. through shrink-wrap and click-wrap licences. There are two main questions to be addressed: are such contracts valid under contract law and if so, are they nevertheless valid under copyright law? As amatter of fact, copyright contracts overriding limits to copyright can lead to a number of public policy issues, namely if such clauses can be made binding especially to consumers. The question is to what extent the limits of copyright law are principles of public policy that may not be overridden by contractual provisions and thus whether, if at all, copyright limits can be compromised to meet commercial needs.

Chapter 6 - Contributory and Vicarious Liability for Copyright Infringement
Introduction by Andy Sun, National Chenchi University, Taipei, Taiwan

Modern copyright law often encounters the difficulty that enforcement would require suing private consumers, e.g. in cases of performances in karaoke bars or downloading of songs or film works. While possible, this looks impracticable in many cases. A more promising alternative thus looks to sue the managers of karaoke bars, the manufacturers of machines, the writers of copying programmes or the Internet service providers. Prominent cases have been reported from the US (Napster), Japan (File Rogue) and Korea (Soribada). The country reports address the laws and cases on these issues in their countries.

The country reports that follow each introduction were prepared by experts in the respective jurisdictions and cover the following countries:

(1) China: Wei Zhi (Peking University, Beijing)
(2) Taiwan: Kung-Chung Liu (Institutum Iurisprudentiae, Academia Sinica, Taipei) and John Juo-Fan Lee
(3) Hong Kong: Gabriela Kennedy (Lovells, Hong Kong)
(4) Japan: Christopher Heath (European Patent Office, Munich) and Peter Ganea (Max-Planck Institute for Intellectual Property Law)
(5) Korea: Byung-il Kim (Inha University, Incheon)
(6) Singapore: Ng-Loy Wee Loon (National University of Singapore; IP Academy, Singapore)
(7) Malaysia: John Chong (Mindvault, Kuala Lumpur)
(8) Thailand: Rutorn Nopakun (Domnern Somgiat & Boonma Law Office Ltd, Bangkok)
(9) The Philippines: Alex Fider (Angara Abello Concepcion Regal & Cruz, Manila)

About the Authors and Editors

John Chong is Director and Principal Consultant of Mindvault Sdn Bhd. He holds Bachelor of Economics, Bachelor of Laws and Master of Laws degrees from Monash University, and is a qualified Malaysian lawyer. He is currently president of the Licensing Executives Society (Malaysia) and is an Honorary Member of the Association of Legal Scholars of the Centre for International Legal Studies.
E-mail: john@mindvault.com.my

Estelle Derclaye is a lecturer in law at University of Nottingham where she teaches intellectual property law. She studies law at the Universities of Liège, Leuven (Diplôme d'études spécialisées en droit européen) and the George Washington University (LLM). In November 2005, she obtained her PhD for her doctoral thesis on the legal protection of databases at the University of London (Queen Mary). Prior to joining the University of Nottingham in 2006, Estelle worked as an associate in an international law firm in Brussels specialising in intellectual property law and was previously a lecturer at the Universities of Leicester and London (Queen Mary). She has also been a visiting lecturer at several universities and a fellow (Stipendiatin) at the Max-Planck Institute for Intellectual Property, Competition and Tax Law (Munich).
E-mail: Estelle.Derclaye@nottingham.ac.uk and ederclaye@hotmail.com

Alex Ferdinand S. Fider is a Partner at the law firm of Abello Concepcion Regala & Cruz (ACCRA LAW) in Manila, the Philippines. He was admitted to the Philippine bar in 1987. He obtained his Bachelor of Laws from the University of the Philippines in 1986 and Master of Laws from Queen Mary College, University of London in 1990. He is the Monitor of the Intellectual Property Department of ACCRA LAW and specializes in intellectual property law, franchising and licensing, technology transfer arrangements and enforcement of intellectual property rights. He is the President of the Licensing Executive Society of the Philippines.
E-mail: asfider@accralaw.com.

Peter Ganea, Dr. phil., studied Japanese studies, Chinese studies and economics at the Universities of Munich and Hokkaidô. He has been co-head of the Asian Department of the Max Planck Institute for Patent, Copyright and Competition Law in Munich since 2000.
E-mail: p.ganea@ip.mpg.de

Christopher Heath (1964) studied at the Universities of Konstanz, Edinburgh and the LSE. He lived and worked in Japan for three years, and between 1992 and 2005 headed the Asian Department of the Max Planck Institute for Patent, Copyright and Competition Law in Munich. Christopher Heath is a Member of the Boards of Appeal at the European Patent Office in Munich and editor of the

Max Planck Institute's Asian Intellectual Property Series published by Kluwer Law International.
E-mail: cheath@epo.org

Reto Hilty studied mechanical engineering at Swiss Federal Institute of Technology Zurich (ETH Zurich); first intermediate diploma (1980); Study of law, University of Zurich, School of law; doctorate in law, Zurich (1989). Head of department and member of board of directors at Swiss Federal Institute of Intellectual Property, Berne. Postdoc in civil, intellectual property, competition and media law, University of Zurich (2000). Full professor for technology and information law at Swiss Federal Institute of Technology Zurich (ETH Zurich). Since January 2002 Director at the Max Planck Institute for Intellectual Property, Competition and Tax Law and Scientific Member of the Max Planck Society. Additional positions: full professor of law at University of Zurich, professor of law at Ludwig-Maximilians-University of Munich.
E-mail: Hilty@ip.mpg.de

Gabriela Kennedy is a partner of Lovells in Hong Kong practising in the Intellectual Property and TMT Group. She handles all aspects of intellectual property work including enforcement, licensing and registration work. She has handled a number of high profile cases in Hong Kong including a copyright case that went to the Court of Final Appeal in 1997. Her practice also includes all aspects of information technology, e-commerce and telecommunications work. Gabriela has written extensively on issues concerning e-commerce, intellectual property, information technology and telecommunications law for various publications. She is a member of the editorial board of the Computer Law and Security Report and was the Hong Kong editorial adviser of the now defunct IP Asia.
E-mail: gabriela.kennedy@lovells.com.

Byung-Il Kim is a graduate of Yonsei University, Seoul. He was a Max-Planck Research Fellow between 1994 and 1999 and holds a PhD from Munich University. Currently, Dr. Kim holds a chair as associate professor at Inha University, Inchon.
E-mail: hobyung1@dreamwiz.com

John Juo-Fan Lee holds a bachelor's degree from the National Taiwan University, and master degrees from Soochow Law School and Harvard Law School. He was a visiting researcher at Harvard Law School, worked as attorney-at-law in two Taiwanese law firms and was Legal Counsel of the General Counsel Office, Department of National Defense, ROC(Taiwan). Currently, he is a Legal Researcher, Scientific and Technology Law Center, Institute of Information Industry, Taiwan.
E-mail: johnlee@iii.org.tw

Kung-Chung Liu holds both a bachelor's and master's degree from the National Taiwan University. He was a Max-Planck Research Fellow between 1987 and 1991, and holds a PhD from the University of Munich. In 1992, he became an

assistant Research Fellow at the Institute for Social Sciences and Philosophy (Jurisprudence Division), Academia Sinica, in 1996 an Associate Research Fellow, and since 2002, he has been Research Fellow and conjunct professor of law at the Graduate School of Intellectual Property, National Chen Chi University. He is also a Consultant for the Taiwan Institute of Economic Research. In February 2006, Professor Liu was appointed by the Premier for a term of three years as Commissioner of the National Communications Commission.
E-mail: liukc@gate.sinica.edu.tw.

Rutorn Nopakhun is a Director in Domnern Somgiat & Boonma Law Office Ltd., a law firm specialising in intellectual property laws in Bangkok, Thailand. He holds a Bachelor of Law from Chulalongkorn University and a Master of Comparative Law from Southern Methodist University and is a licensed attorney-at-law in Thailand. He has worked in the field of intellectual property laws for 17 years, handling mostly IP enforcement work.
E-mail: rutorn@dsb.co.th

Andy Sun M.C.L., the George Washington University Law School, J.D., University of Maryland School of Law. The author is an Associate Professor at the Graduate Institute of Intellectual Property and the Graduate Institute of Interdisciplinary Laws, National Chengchi University, Taipei, Taiwan. He is also the Executive Director of the Asia Pacific Legal Institute, a non-profit organization chartered in Washington, D.C. and dedicated to the legal cooperation and exchange between the U.S. and East Asia.
E-mail: asun@apli.org and asun@nccu.edu.tw

Haochen Sun is a research scholar at the Faculty of Law, National University of Singapore. He was a Max Planck scholarship fellow in 2005 and is currently enrolled as an LLM student at Harvard Law School.
E-mail: hsun@law.harvard.edu

Ng-Loy Wee Loon holds a LLB from the National University of Singapore and a Master's degree from London University. She is an Associate Professor at the Faculty of Law, National University of Singapore. Currently, she is the Director of its LLM (IP & Technology Law) programme. In 2003—2004, she was also the Deputy Director of the IP Academy (Singapore).
E-mail: lawngwl@nus.edu.sg

Zhi Wei holds an bachelor degree from the South-west Institute of Political Science and Law, a master degree from the People's University of China and a doctoral degree from Munich University. Dr. Wei is currently an Associate Professor at the Law School of Peking University, Arbitrator of the Beijing Arbitration Commission and part-time attorney-at-law at the Tonghe-Tongzheng Law Office.
E-mail: weishejiao@hotmail.com

1
The Expansion of Copyright Law and its Social Justification

RETO M. HILTY*

In the last decade, copyright law has been expanded vertically and horizontally. Vertically, in that it covers subject matters that previously were not deemed copyrightable at least in those countries that require a certain threshold of creativity. Examples would be computer programs and databases. Horizontally, because copyright law has been strengthened in various ways: The protection period has been extended, additional rights of rental and lending have been given to owners of certain categories of rights, and new rights have been added to the catalogue (right of making available, etc.). All these have significantly tipped the balance in favour of copyright owners, but not necessarily in favour of society at large. On the contrary, such over-protection may have led to imbalances in the framework of copyright law as an incentive to stimulate creative works.—The Country reports indicate how these issues are perceived in their home countries, particularly in view of the "digital divide" between developing and developed countries.

A: Introduction

I. Where everything began...

At the very beginning—around 1886, when the Berne Convention for the Protection of Literary and Artistic Works (Berne Convention)[1] as the first international instrument for copyright protection was established—copyright faced a set of challenges spawned by the following kinds of illegal exploitation of works:

— the unauthorized *performance* of protected works, particularly in the fields of literary and musical works[2]; and
— the unauthorised *manufacture* and *dissemination of* copies of protected works, particularly based upon the reprinting of books[3].

---

* The author wishes to thank Haochen Sun, LL.B., LL.M., Research Fellow at the Max Planck Institute for Intellectual Property, Competition, and Tax Law, for his invaluable support, especially in document enquiry and analysis.

[1] Berne Convention for the Protection of Literary and Artistic Works, September 9, 1886, revised 24 July 1971, 828 U.N.T.S. 221.

[2] See e.g., Berne Convention, Art. 11(1)(i).

[3] See *Sam Ricketson*, The Berne Convention for the Protection of Literary and Artistic Works: 1886–1986 (London: Centre for Commercial Law Studies, Queen Mary College, 1987) at 17–19 ("[U]nauthorized reproduction and use of foreign works were, for a long time, established features of European cultural and social life, and continued to be so for a considerable period after the adoption of national copyright laws by most countries.... The prevention of this international piracy was the principal reason for the gradual development of international copyright relations during the nineteenth century").

The main thrust of international copyright law then was the regulation of *commercial activities* using protected works. Against this backdrop, the idea of copyright reflected an increasingly accepted notion that intangible goods should be accorded similar proprietorial rights as their tangible counterparts[4], should be vested with some entitlement against third parties[5]. Nevertheless, the justification for copyright protection in Continental Europe was initially linked with the person who in fact creates the work concerned[6]. This author-centred aspect of copyright law is still animated today in the theory of the "droit d'auteur" approach, even if in practice it is of no more than marginal importance in comparison with those commercial aspects of copyright which have shaped copyright from the outset[7].

The ongoing advance of technology has consistently opened up new dimensions to the concept of copyright. By 1889, it was possible to record motion pictures on light-sensitive strips of celluloid and the first cinematographic device was

---

[4] See e.g., *Trotter Hardy*, Not So Different: Tangible, Intangible, Digital, and Analog Works and Their Comparison for Copyright Purposes, 26 U.Dayton L.Rev. 211 (2001).

[5] This perception of property right in intellectual products largely stems from the Lockean Labor Theory. About three hundred years ago, John Locke laid the foundation of this theory by stating that: "Though the Earth, and all inferior Creatures be common to all Men, yet every Man has a Property in his own Person. This no Body has any Right to but himself. The labour of this Body, and the Work of his Hands, we may say, are properly his. Whatsover he then removes out of the State that Nature hath provided, and left it in, he hath mixed his Labour with, and joyed to it something that is his, and thereby makes it his Property.... [I]t hath by this labour something annexed to it, that excludes the common right of other Men". John Locke, *Two Treaties on Government*, Book II, ch. V (1690). See also, *Stephen M. Stewart*, International Copyright and Neighboring Rights (London: Butterworths, 1989) at 4 ("The property in the work is justified by the fact that the right owner has created or made it"). For an excellent critique of Labour Theory, see *William Fisher*, Theories of Intellectual Property, in New Essays in the Legal And Political Theory of Property 168 (Stephen R. Munzer ed., 2001); *Seana Valentine Shiffrin*, Lockean Arguments for Private Intellectual Property, in New Essays in the Legal And Political Theory of Property 168 (Stephen R. Munzer ed., 2001); *Justin Hughes*, Philosophy of Intellectual Property, 77 Geo. L.J. 287 (1988); *Wendy Gordon*, A Property Right in Self—Expression: Equality and Individualism in the Natural Law of Intellectual Property, 102 Yale L. J. 1533 (1993); *Alfred Yen*, Restoring the Natural Law: Copyright as Labor and Possession, Ohio St. L. J. 517 (1990); *Peter Drahos*, A Philosophy of Intellectual Property (Brookfield, Vt.: Dartmouth, 1996) at 41–72.

[6] See *Jane C. Ginsburg*, A Tale of Two Copyrights: Literary Property in Revolutionary France and America, 64 Tul. L. Rev. 991, 992 (1990) ("[P]ost—revolutionary French laws and theorists portray the existence of an intimate and almost sacred bond between authors and their works as the source of a strong literary and artistic property right").

[7] *Ulrich Loewenheim*, in Loewenheim, Handbuch des Urheberrechts (Munich: Beck, 2003) at § 1 No. 4–7; *Haimo Schack*, Urheber—und Urhebervertragsrecht (Tübingen: Mohr Siebeck, 3rd ed. 2005), at No. 2 et sec.; critical *Reto M. Hilty*, Urheberrecht in der Informationsgesellschaft: Wer will was von wem woraus?—Ein Auftakt zum "zweiten Korb", 47 ZUM 983–1006 (2003). On the differences between the droit d'auteur and the copyright system *see Alain Strowel*, Droit d'auteur and copyright (Brussels: Bruylant et al., 1993) passim; for a historical view *see Jane C. Ginsburg*, A Tale of two Copyrights: Literary Property in Revolutionary France and America, 64 Tul.L.Rev. 991 (1990).

patented in 1895[8]. With the arrival of this technology—along with phonographic recordings—one crucial matter of fact occurred: it was no longer necessary for works to be performed live on every occasion. On the contrary, films and music could be recorded and, in consequence, be presented at any time and place should the supporting technology be available. Undoubtedly, this kind of "canned technology" has robbed the copyright holder of the chance of a clear overview of where his works had been and were being used for commercial purposes. This advance of technology represents the first turning point for copyright law since the exploitation of protected works, could for the first time be carried out free of the constraints posed by the time-and-space limits of the former technologies. At that time, the potentially uncontrollable mass production and dissemination of works came to fruition[9].

Accordingly, new exclusive rights were vested in right holders, e.g. the rights of reproduction[10] and communication[11]. More importantly, responding to the need to enforce the then existing bundle of exclusive rights and in particular to the outcries for adequate compensations for the commercial use of protected works, *collecting societies* were established and they engineered to act on behalf of the right holders against mass distribution and exploitation of their works without compensation[12].

---

[8] The Frenchman Louis Lumiere is considered the inventor of the first motion picture camera in 1895. It is reported that early in 1895, "Lumiere and his brother were the first to present projected, moving, photographic, pictures to a paying audience of more that one person." See The History of the Motion Picture: Who Invented Cinema, the Camera, or Film?, available at http://inventors.about.com/library/inventors/blmotionpictures.htm. Moreover, one should also note that in 1896, the American Mutoscope and Biograph company produced the first projection of moving images onto a screen. See *Edward Samuels*, The Illustrated Story of Copyright (New York: Thomas Dunne Books/St. Martin's Press, 2000) at 57.

[9] See *Jane C. Ginsburg*, Copyright and Control over New Technologies of Dissemination, 101 Colum.L.Rev. 1613, 1614 (2001): "Before mass market audio and video recording equipment, copyright owners also controlled access to works made publicly available through performances and transmissions, because the public could not see or hear the work without attending a licensed live performance, or viewing or listening to it through licensed media. With the arrival of these technologies, the *de facto*, and often the *de jure*, balance substantially shifted to users".

[10] See Berne Convention, Art. 9 (1). Moreover, Article 9 (3) specifically prescribes that "Any sound or visual recording shall be considered as a reproduction for the purposes of this Convention".

[11] See e.g., Berne Convention, Arts. 11(ii) and 11bis (1) (ii).

[12] Between the end of the 19th century and the first decade of the 20th century, collective societies "were formed in nearly all European countries and in some other countries as well". See WIPO, Collective Management of Copyright and Related Rights (Geneva: 2000) at 19.

In 1926, delegates from 18 collective societies founded the International Confederation of Societies of Authors and Composers (CISAC) in France. According to Article 5 of the Statutes of the CISAC, this organisation is concerned, *inter alia*, with setting up "effective machinery for the collection and distribution of copyright royalties and [assuming] full responsibility for the operations attaching to the administration of the rights entrusted to it". As of 2004, CISAC numbers 207 authors' societies from 109 countries and indirectly represents more than 2 million creators within all the artistic repertoires: music, drama, literature, audio—visual works, graphic and visual arts. For an introduction of the CISAC, readers can visit its official website at www.cisac.org/ (last visits of all websites on 1 May, 2005).

Until then, confrontations in the arena of copyright law had primarily occurred among commercial entities within or relating to the copyright industry. The ease with which those "canned" works could be replayed enabled an explosive increase in the number of commercial uses of copyrighted works. Hence, although the primary copyright principle is that private consumption of a work (such as reading a book or listening to a concert or music CD) should be free, copyright began to catch up with the great mass of consumers, albeit in a rather indirect way. From the fifties in Continental Europe, commercial usage was "charged" with copyright levies—an extra payment that was consequentially reflected in the price of the associated product. Ultimately the private consumer paid (however unwittingly)—through the higher price of a ticket or a service (as, for example, at the hairdressers with background music) or through a levy on reproduction equipment, such as CD writers or devices that permit copying (i.e. in Germany)[13].

Nonetheless, it has never been proclaimed that copyright, as a form of private property rights, is absolute and permanent in nature. In our society, people, without exception, need to "stand on the shoulders of giants" to create anything new[14]. At the same time, a proper degree of individual needs for personal well-being should be fully respected and thus legal regulations, albeit with various prohibitions, should permit the consumption of works for the purposes of self-entertainment[15] which do not harm the right holders' economic and moral interests. Imbued with the need to sustain the long-term social development fostered by the legitimate uses of works, the law therefore carves out a set of limitations and exceptions on copyright. The public at large, from the very beginning of the history of copyright law, has been left with considerable room to have access to, and use of, works by availing themselves of the privileges derived from the limitations carved out by copyright law. In such a way, copyright law purports to maintain the equilibrium of legal protection of works of authorship in a

---

[13] See e.g., *Karsten* M. *Gutsche*, Equitable Remuneration for Authors in Germany—How the German Copyright Act Secures their Rewards, 50 J.Copyright Soc'y U.S.A. 257 (2003).

[14] See *Campbell v. Acuff—Rose Music*, 510 U.S. 569, 575 (1994) ("[I]n truth, in literature, in science and in art, there are, and can be, few, if any, things, which in an abstract sense, are strictly new and original throughout. Every book in literature, science and art, borrows, and must necessarily borrow, and use much which was well known and used before."). *William* M. *Landes*, *Richard* A. *Posner*, The Economic Structure of Intellectual Property Law (Cambridge, MA: Harvard University Press, 2003) at 66–67 ("Creating a new expressive work typically involves borrowing or building on material from a prior body of works, as well as adding original expression to it."); *Laddie*, Copyright: Over—strength, Over—regulated, Over—rated?, 5EIPR 253, 259 (1996) ("The whole human development is derivative. We stand on the shoulders of the scientists, artists and craftsmen who preceded us. We borrow and develop what they have done; not necessarily as parasites, but simply as the next generation. It is at the heart of what simply we know as progress. When we are asked to remember the Eighth Commandment, 'thou shalt not steal', bear in mind that borrowing and developing have always been acceptable").

[15] *Joseph Liu*, Copyright Law's Theory of the Consumer, 44 B.C. L. Rev. 397 (2003) (discussing users' right in this respect).

manner conducive of the promotion of social well-being in the long run. As Landes and Posner have pointed out, "[s]triking the correct balance between access and incentives is the central problem in copyright law"[16].

Historically, this balance-oriented objective has been interwoven into the fabric of copyright law. Early in 1709, the mother of modern copyright law—the Statute of Anne—replaced the self-interested guild control of copyright and sought to secure public welfare, by recognizing the need for enlightenment and boldly proclaiming a new purpose for the protection of original works—"the encouragement of learning"[17]. Throughout the three hundred years following the adoption of the Statute of Anne, copyright laws in various jurisdictions have inherited this tradition and endeavoured to maintain the balance of competing interests. Arguably, the necessity for societal development motivated the framers of the U.S Constitution to mandate Congress to promote the progress of science and the useful arts by securing to authors for limited periods an exclusive right in their writings[18]. At the international level, the Agreement on Trade-Related Aspects of Intellectual Property Rights (TRIPS Agreement)[19], highlights the very need to embrace a balance-oriented approach to the protection of intellectual property, in general, and copyright in particular[20]. Akin to the TRIPS Agreement, the WIPO Copyright Treaty (WCT)[21] recognises the primary importance of the "need to maintain a balance between the rights of authors and the larger public interest, particularly in education, research and access to information"[22].

Therefore, in pursuit of public interest[23], the concept of copyright to this day is based on the premise that private enjoyment of a work—including such enjoyment in schools or certain internal business concerns—should be a privilege[24].

---

16 *William Landes and Richard Posner,* An Economic Analysis of Copyright Law, 18 J. Legal Stud.325, 326 (1989).

17 See *Mark Rose*, Authors and Owners: The Invention of Copyright (Cambridge, Mass.: Harvard University Press, 1993) at 42; *Lyman Ray Patterson*, Copyright in Historical Perspective (Nashville: Vanderbilt University Press, 1968) at 147.

18 See U.S. Const. Art. I, § 8, cl. 8

19 Agreement on Trade—Related Aspects of Intellectual Property Rights, April 15, 1994, Marrakesh Agreement Establishing the World Trade Organization, Annex 1C, Legal Instruments—Results of the Uruguay Round vol. 31, 33 I.L.M. 81, Art. 28.1 (1994).

20 Article 7 of the TRIPS Agreement provides: "The protection and enforcement of intellectual property rights should contribute to the promotion of technological innovation and to the transfer and dissemination of technology, to the mutual advantage of producers and users of technological knowledge and in a manner conducive to social and economic welfare, and to a balance of rights and obligations".

21 WIPO Copyright Treaty, December 20, 1996, 36 I.L.M. 65.

22 Preamble of the WCT.

23 See *Gillian Davies*, Copyright and the Public Interest (London: Sweet & Maxwell, 2nd ed. 2002) at 27–232 (examining in detail about the concept of public interest in various national copyright laws); *Diane Leenheer Zimmerman*, Copyright in Cyberspace: Don't Throw Out the Public Interest with the Bath Water, 1994 Ann. Surv. Am. L. 403.

24 Robert Burrell & Allison Coleman, Copyright Exceptions: The Digital Impact (New York: Cambridge University Press, 2005) (arguing that "all modern copyright systems provide for circumstances in which copyright will not be infringed by the unauthorized reproduction or presentation of a copyright work") at 4.

The background to this lies in the awareness of a "social obligation" of copyright. This obligation places limits on the assertion of exclusive rights. In accordance with the principle of guaranteeing access to information and culture, copyright, as indicated above, is subject to limitations and exceptions dedicated to balancing the divergent interests of right holders and users. Hence, it would not be bold to assert that "[i]f all property is subject to the legal balance between the exclusive owner and the public, then [copyright law] is merely the realm in which the balancing is most explicitly acknowledged"[25].

II. … and how it got out of hand

Historically, copyright law has consistently shown that it is a daunting task to strike a proper balance between the competing interests of right owners and the public at large. Copyright law, as Benkler has posited, "is defined by constant tensions between exclusive private rights on the one hand and the freedom to read and express oneself as one wishes on the other hand"[26]. When the advances in technology facilitate the diversification of the ways to exploit works of authorship, a plethora of balance-distorting challenges have arisen from the increasing ease with which works can be illegally used. Behind this copyright-and-technology interface lies a twofold question: how far should legislators extend the scope of exclusive rights accorded to right holders while carving out limitations on such ever-expanding rights? Furthermore, central to the endeavour of seeking the answers to this question are the twin goals of providing sustained incentives to right holders as well as promoting the public interest in the unfettered flow of information and knowledge.

The recent leap forward in digital technology and its accompanying overhaul of the copyright system have further exacerbated the difficulty of striking such a balance in the framework of copyright law. On the one hand, it is the advance in digital technology that, for the first time, enhances users' ability to have access to, and use of, works to an unprecedented degree. The newly developed technology allows various categories of works to be digitally combined at a high technical level in order to create interactive multimedia products[27]. Thanks to digital technology, works can be disseminated over the Internet with no loss of quality and reproduced at virtually no marginal cost. It goes without saying that the possibilities for exploitation of works has increased exponentially. For example, a small number of music CDs or DVDs suffice to develop a sizeable market in pirate copies. Individuals, too, can swap protected works at will via the internet and pass

---

[25] *Jon M. Garon*, Normative Copyright: A Conceptual Framework for Copyright Philosophy and Ethics, 88 Cornell L. Rev. 1278, 1309 (2003).

[26] *Yochai Benkler*, Through the Looking Glass: Alice and the Constitutional Foundations of the Public Domain, 66 Law & Contemp. Prob. 173, 175 (2003).

[27] *Irini A. Stamatoudi*, Copyright and Multimedia Products: A Comparative Analysis (Cambridge: Cambridge University Press, 2002) at 21–24 (discussing the relationship between digitisation and multimedia products); *Julián Rodríguez Pardo*, Copyright and Multimedia (The Hague; London: Kluwer Law International, 2003).

these on to parties entirely unknown to them—with no central control over the exchange of data, making it practically impossible to keep track of what is going on. This magical change is epitomised by the recent proliferation of peer-to-peer (P2P) networks on which a vast amount of works have been and are being disseminated[28].

On the other hand, an unprecedented overhaul of copyright law both at the international and national levels it has also been witnessed recent years. By the power of that new technology, the private enjoyment of works—tolerated without difficulty for the past hundred years—has suddenly been thrust into the limelight. Even worse: the entertainment industry has likewise suddenly recognised free private or other privileged use as a new threat to its economic existence[29].

Reactions to these developments were not long in coming. The entertainment industry's lobbying groups, dominated largely by American enterprises, have excelled in bundling their economic interests[30]. It convinced the world community

---

[28] A P2P network concerns "a network that relies on computing power at the edges (ends) of a connection rather than in the network itself. P2P networks are used for sharing content like audio, video, data or anything in digital format." See Wikipedia, peer-to-peer, available at http://en.wikipedia.org/wiki/Peer_to_peer. Its advantage largely lies in the fact that "the bandwidth of all clients can be used, so the total bandwidth—and usually the available download bandwidth for the average user—grows with the number of nodes, instead of all clients having to share the bandwidth of one server, where adding more clients could mean slower data transfer for all users." See ibid. The increased and wider use of P2P networks, in fact, has fundamentally altered the landscape of information sharing and in particular information production. It has been argued that P2P networks have resulted in a peer-based, rather than individual- or firm-based, mode of information production. See *Yochai Benkler*, Coase's Penguin, or, Linux and the Nature of the Firm, 112 Yale L.J. 369 (2002).

[29] The International Intellectual Property Alliance (IIPA) "estimates that copyright piracy around the world inflicts approximately $20-$22 billion in annual losses to the U.S. copyright industries (and this estimate does not include internet piracy)". See *IIPA*, Copyright & Trade Issues, available at www.iipa.com/copyrighttrade_issues.html. According to the Motion Picture Association of America (MPAA), the U.S. motion picture industry is estimated to suffer losses in excess of $3 billion annually in potential worldwide revenue due to piracy. See MPAA, Anti-Piracy, available at www.mpaa.org/anti-piracy/. Moreover, Recording Industry Association of America reports that the music industry "loses about $4.2 billion to piracy worldwide". See *RIAA*, Anti-Piracy, available at www.riaa.com/issues/piracy/default.asp.

[30] See *Pamela Samuelson*, The U.S. Digital Agenda at WIPO, 37 Va. J. Int'l L. 369, 374 (1997) (pointing out that the U.S. copyright-based industries "not only successfully lobbied the Clinton administration, persuading it to moderate or abandon parts of its digital agenda at WIPO, they also attended WIPO-sponsored regional meetings to acquaint other states with their concerns about the draft treaties, and went to Geneva in large numbers to participate informally in the diplomatic conference as observers and lobbyists"); *UK Commission on Intellectual Property Rights*, Integrating Intellectual Property Rights and Development Policy, at 101, available at www.iprcommission.org/graphic/documents/ final_report.htm ("Representatives from these industries have stressed to us the importance of copyright laws and strong protection against unauthorized copying to encourage investments in creativity and innovation, as well as in product and technological development").

that existing copyright should be supplemented with new powers for the right holders[31]. As a result, after years of status quo since the 1971 revision of the Berne Convention[32], 1996 saw two new supplementary agreements reached at the international level: the WIPO Copyright Treaty (WCT)[33] and the WIPO Performances and Phonograms Treaty (WPPT)[34]. These Treaties established, inter alia:

(1) a new "right of making available to the public"[35]. In other words, the right to prohibit others from making works publicly available via communications networks; and
(2) in acknowledgement of the meanwhile legendary words of Charles Clark that "the answer to the machine is in the machine"[36], the legal protection for the integrity of technological measures designed to prevent unauthorized access to as well as use of works[37].

Though these new standards have been introduced into international copyright law, the WCT and the WPPT have merely laid the foundations, rather than the ceiling, for the members from which such new standards will be implemented into municipal copyright laws. In other words, these two Treaties have left considerable room for members to define the content and scope of the new forms of protection, subject to the minimal standards set forth in the WCT and the WPPT. For example, Article 11 of the WCT[38] is silent as to the extent to which the legal protection of technological measures afforded by national copyright law would be deemed "adequate" and "effective". Neither does it make crystal clear whether "preparatory activities", including the manufacture and trafficking of

---

[31] See *WIPO*, Basic Proposal for the Substantive Provisions of the Treaty on Certain Questions Concerning the Protection of Literary and Artistic Works to Be Considered by the Diplomatic Conference, (WIPO Doc. CRNR/DC/4 , August 1996) at para. 0.05 ("While introducing certain provisions on 'traditional issues', the proposed Treaty also includes solutions to urgent questions raised by the technological developments.... The proposed Treaty is therefore part of a series of simultaneously published draft Treaties which could be characterised as 'Global Information Infrastructure Treaties' in the field of copyright and rights related to copyright").

[32] See e.g., *Jane Ginsburg*, Berne Without Borders: Geographic Indiscretion and Digital Communications, Stephen Stewart Memorial Lecture, Intellectual Property Institute, London (2001), 2002 I.P.Q. 111 (concluding that to "complete the task of creating supranational substantive copyright rules" is one of the ways to address the issues for digital copyright protection that the Berne Convention fails to comprehensively deal with).

[33] WIPO Copyright Treaty, 20 December 1996, 36 I.L.M. 65.

[34] WIPO Performances and Phonograms Treaty, 20 December 1996, 36 I.L.M. 76.

[35] WCT, Art. 8; WPPT, Arts.10 and 14.

[36] *Charles Clark*, "The Answer to the Machine is in the Machine", in The Future of Copyright in a Digital Environment (The Hague: Kluwer Law International, 1996, P. Bernt Hugenholtz ed.) at 139–146.

[37] WCT, Art. 11; WPPT, Art. 18.

[38] Article 11 of the WCT provides: "Contracting Parties shall provide adequate legal protection and effective legal remedies against the circumvention of effective technological measures that are used by authors in connection with the exercise of their rights under this Treaty or the Berne Convention and that restrict acts, in respect of their works, which are not authorized by the authors concerned or permitted by law".

circumvention-enabling devices, should be prohibited by national copyright laws, and if so, how such a ban should properly be laid down.

However, under sustained pressure from the entertainment industry's powerful lobbying efforts, these international requirements have been rapidly implemented in the United States such that much higher standards of protection have been set out[39]. With the enactment of the Digital Millennium Copyright Act (DMCA)[40] in 1998, the United States has taken the lead in furnishing stringent legal protection through technological measures. The essence of the DMCA-type anti-circumvention regulations lies in the anti-trafficking provision aimed broadly at prohibiting the manufacture and distribution of devices that:

— are primarily designed or produced to circumvent; or
— have only limited commercially significant purpose or use other than to circumvent; or
— are marketed for use in circumventing[41].

Three years later the EU adopted the Directive on the Harmonization of Certain Aspects of Copyright and Related Rights in the Information Society (Information Society Directive)[42] and thereby committed member states to implement equivalent protection by incorporating into their respective national copyright systems[43] the essence of the DMCA-type anti-circumvention regulations.

Moreover, such stringent anti-circumvention regulations have been, and are being, extended to the countries that have entered into bilateral free trade agreements (FTAs) with the United States[44]. One can easily find that recently

---

[39] See *Pamela Samuelson*, Intellectual Property and the Digital Economy: Why the Anti-Circumvention Regulations Need To Be Revised, 14 Berkeley Tech. L.J. 519, 523 (1999) ("Clinton Administration officials, bowing to the wishes to Hollywood and its allies, opted instead to support an unpredictable, overbroad, and maximalist set of anti-circumvention regulations").

[40] Digital Millennium Copyright Act, Pub. L. No. 105–304, 112 Stat. 2860 (1998).

[41] See 17 U.S.Const. §§ 1201(a)(2)(A)–(C).

[42] Council Directive 2001/29/EC of the European Parliament and of the Council of 22 May 2001 on the Harmonization of Certain Aspects of Copyright and Related Rights in the Information Society, 2001 O.J. (L 167) 10.

[43] The E.U. Information Society Directive borrows the three tests embodied into the DMCA to outlaw the manufacture and distribution of circumvention devices. Article 6.2 of the Directive provides: "Member States shall provide adequate legal protection against the manufacture, import, distribution, sale, rental, advertisement for sale or rental, or possession for commercial purposes of devices, products or components or the provision of services which:

(a) are promoted, advertised or marketed for the purpose of circumvention of, or
(b) have only a limited commercially significant purpose or use other than to circumvent, or
(c) are primarily designed, produced, adapted or performed for the purpose of enabling or facilitating the circumvention of any effective technological measures".

[44] U.S.-Singapore Free Trade Agreement (hereinafter "Singapore FTA"), concluded on 15 January 2003, available at www.ustr.gov/Trade_Agreements/Bilateral/Singapore_FTA/Final_Texts/ Section_Index.html. U.S.-Chile Free Trade Agreement (hereinafter "Chile

concluded FTAs have wholly integrated the DMCA-type anti-circumvention provisions. In particular, the DMCA-type anti-trafficking ban has also been incorporated into these FTAs[45].

III. Problems and Critiques

At first glance, the recent overhaul of copyright law both at the international and national levels, as shown in the this Chapter, seems to be entirely reasonable since the law must become fully responsive to the right holders' vulnerability to an exponentially increasing number of possible infringing acts. However, a closer look at this overhaul, reveals a host of prickly questions. Amongst these new adaptations of copyright law to technological developments, the legal protection of technological measures, represents the most controversial area of copyright protection and causes a lot of inconsistencies.

First and foremost, copyright holders to a large extent have been accorded a bundle of unprecedented powers in controlling their works. Drawing on the assistance provided by their technology partners, copyright holders have been designing and developing technological measures that prevent users from physically accessing and using protected works. Unlike conventional ways of making available works whose physical access is unconstrained, the new means of distributing works facilitated by technological measures is based upon payment for access. Hence, copyright holders have almost unfettered power to fence off those who are not able to pay for "the key to the technological lock". Moreover, copyright holders are tacitly vested with the difficult situation of controlling the non-copyrighted works whose access can now be constrained with technological measures[46]. On the other hand, compared with the analogue world, the post-access use of works protected by technological measures

FTA"), concluded on 6 June 2003, available at www.ustr.gov/Trade_Agreements/Bilateral/Chile_FTA/Final_Texts/Section_Index.html. U.S. – Australia Free Trade Agreement (hereinafter "Australia FTA"), concluded on 18 May 2004, available at www.ustr.gov/Trade_Agreements/Bilateral/Australia_FTA/Final_Text/Section_Index.html. U.S. – D.R.-Central American FTA (hereinafter "D.R.-Central American FTA"), concluded on 5 August 2004, available at www.ustr.gov/Trade_Agreements/Bilateral/DR-CAFTA/Section_Index.html. U.S. – Morocco Free Trade Agreement (hereinafter "Morocco FTA"), concluded on 15 June 2004, available at www.ustr.gov/Trade_Agreements/Bilateral/Morocco_FTA/FInal_Text/Section_ Index.html. Apart from the above five concluded FTAs, the bilateral negotiations on the proposed U.S. – South African Customs Union Free Trade Agreement, U.S. – Bahrain Free Trade Agreement, U.S.-Andean Free Trade Agreement, and the U.S. – Panama Free Trade Agreement are ongoing.

45 Singapore FTA, Art.16.4.7 (a) (ii); Chile FTA, Art.15.7.5 (b); Australia FTA, Art. 17.4.7 (a)(iii); D.R.-Central American FTA, Art. 15.5. 7 (b); Morocco FTA, Art. 15.5.8 (a)(i).

46 See *Terri Branstetter Cohen*, Anti-Circumvention: Has Technology's Child Turned against its Mother?, 36 Vand. J. Transnat'l L. 961, 978 (2003) ("If a work cannot be copyrighted or its copyright protection has expired, its owner can merely use a digital rights management tool such as encryption to protect the work, and anyone wishing to access the work would be without a practical means to do so, other than by requesting permission from the owner"); *Terese Foged*, U.S. v. E.U. Anti-Circumvention Legislation: Preserving the Public's Privileges in the Digital Age? 24 E.I.P.R. 525, 526 (2002) ("Technological measures may cause material to be protected that would not have been protected by copyright laws").

has been limited such that the users' conventional freedom of exploiting works is restricted. Those CDs protected by technological measures, for example, may be designed to be unplayable in the computer drive so as to prevent copying—and are then similarly unplayable in "permitted" devices such as in-car stereos.

Secondly, *competition* on the level of the *free movement of goods* is adversely affected. There are DVDs that are equipped with a code which enables them to be played only in corresponding machines in designated countries or regions, for example the United States, but not in others, for example Asian or European countries[47]. In other words, using methods such as the Content Scramble System (CSS), suppliers are able to isolate markets from one another, in order to both extend the initial period of exploitation in cinemas and subsequently, once the sale of DVDs commences, to extract significantly higher prices in certain regions[48]. In addition, right holders may require consumers to purchase playback equipment or other related accessories[49]. Therefore, the Court in *Chamberlain Group, Inc. v. Skylink Technologies, Inc.*[50] argued that, notwithstanding the protection afforded by the anti-circumvention law, the copyright holder's monopoly is still subject to antitrust law or the copyright misuse doctrine[51]. A recent report also noted that "there will be nothing to prevent competition law operating if [technological measures] are used in an anti-competitive way"[52].

---

[47] There are currently 6 global region codes that identify specific DVDs that are compatible with the players typically sold in that region. For example, when a person residing in Europe has the intention to buy a copy of DVD of "The Thorn Birds" from Amazon, he will be reminded that "Your order contains at least one Region 1 (Canada and U.S.) encoded DVD. Region 1 DVDs might not play in DVD players sold in the country where this order is being shipped. Please also note that some Region 1 DVDs contain a Regional Coding Enhancement. Some of our international customers have had problems playing these enhanced discs on their 'region-free' DVD players".

[48] In the US, *Universal City Studios, Inc. v. Reimerdes* is a case pertaining to decryption of CSS. See 82 F. Supp. 2d 294 (S.D.N.Y. 2000). In this case, computer hackers devised a computer program called DeCSS allowing unauthorised decryption of DVDs encrypted with a CSS encryption system. In November 1999, Eric Corely posted a copy of DeCSS on his magazine's website coupled with an article describing the genesis and function of DeCSS. Eight motion picture studios brought suit against him, seeking injunctive relief under the DMCA. After a bench trial, the district court entered a permanent injunction to enjoin Corely from posting DeCSS or knowingly providing links to any other website containing DeCSS.

[49] See *Dan L. Burk*, Anti-Circumvention Misuse, 50 UCLA L. Rew. 1095, 1113 (2003); *Peter Moore*, Steal This Disk: Copyright Protection, Consumers' Rights, and the Digital Millennium Copyright Act, 97 Nw. U.L. Rev. 1437, 1448–1452 (2003) (discussing the similar concern).

[50] 381 F.3d 1178 (2004).

[51] See ibid, at 1201 ("The DMCA, as part of the Copyright Act, does not limit the scope of the antitrust laws, either explicitly or implicitly").

[52] *UK Patent Office*, Consultation on UK Implementation of Directive 2001/29/EC on Copyright and Related Rights in the Information Society: Analysis of Responses and Government Conclusions, available at www.patent.gov.uk/about/consultations/responses/copydirect/index.htm.

Thirdly, technical protection measures may lead to *consumer discrimination*. Traditionally, users are free to enjoy, sell, loan, lease, or display copies of works after purchasing them. They thus enjoyed the maximum freedom of works of authorship. This landscape has been drastically changed by copyright holders equipped with technological measures since they now have the discretion to limit the way in which users can use their works. This is particularly true for the use of works in the networked digital environment. It is possible to limit the online enjoyment of works—itself an alternative offered with increasing frequency by the entertainment industry. In direct contrast to conventional data media which allows one purchase to be played any number of times, each online usage, such as listening to a music track, must be paid for individually if the copying of that music track is technically excluded (an example of such a limitation is called "streaming media"). In short, technological measures allow the copyright principle of privileged enjoyment to be overruled at will.

Fourthly, the wide use of technological measures may further exacerbate the imbalance in the trade of copyrighted products. The US economy, at the expense of the non-US users, is the principal beneficiary of the legal protection of technological measures[53]. The following cluster of figures illustrates the problem embodied in the current international flow of copyrighted products. Europe's balance of trade deficit with the United States for audiovisual products in the year 2000 was estimated at 8.2 billion US dollars—a rise of 14 percent over 1999[54]. US films accounted for 70 percent of the European television market[55], against just 1.6 percent for their German and 2.4 percent for their French counterparts[56]. In the field of cinema, the US again accounted for around 70 percent of the EU market (the figure varies according to the latest box office hits)[57], whereas the market share accounted for by European films in the US hovered around 4 percent[58]. In 2000, the US majors alone made a huge windfall in terms of licensing revenues—2.57 billion US$—from EU consumers. In other words, the EU is a net audiovisual importer on a huge scale. Therefore it is hard to understand why European legislators fail to uphold European interests, rather than unquestioningly adopting positions that favour the big entertainment companies which are usually not based in Europe, but namely in the US or in Japan.

Finally and most importantly, copyright holders who apply technological measures may potentially wield the power to abolish two basic *principles of copyright*

---

53 *UK Commission on Intellectual Property Rights*, Integrating Intellectual Property Rights and Development Policy, at 97, available at www.iprcommission.org/graphic/documents/ final_report.htm (demonstrating that U.S. is the largest exporter of the copyright products).

54 See *European Audiovisual Observatory* The Imbalance of Trade in Films and Television Programs between North America and Europe Continues to Deteriorate (April 9, 2002), available at www.obs.coe.int/about/oea/pr/desequilibre.html.

55 Ibid.

56 Ibid.

57 Ibid.

58 Ibid.

law. The first one exists in the dichotomy of the (protected) "form of expression" and the freedom of the "content". The idea/expression dichotomy, albeit somewhat ambiguous in nature, essentially evidences the attempt to ensure that an idea cannot and should not be monopolized by copyright holders. In this way, copyright law is designed to operate as the "engine of free expression"[59] and act as a catalyst for the enrichment of the public domain[60]. However, the legal protection of technological measures runs counter to the values embedded in the idea/expression dichotomy, because non-copyrightable elements of information can now be protected, and access to, and use of, such information, which has been traditionally free, is now technically constrained[61]. On the other hand, the second principle of copyright law that is under grave threat is the very need to maintain the balance of competing interests stemmed from the "social obligation" of copyright holders. The dynamics of this principle, as expounded in paragraph (I.) [62] herein, lie largely in the application of limitations and exceptions to the bundle of exclusive rights accorded to right holders, facilitating privileged use for certain categories of users. One should note that in the analogue world, users' ability to invoke the limitations and exceptions afforded by copyright law is premised on the fact that they can get access to the work concerned[63]. The same is not true in the framework of anti-circumvention regulations. Materials are routinely locked up by the access-control measures, causing works to be inaccessible to users who then have to decide whether they should use works within the boundaries of the fair use exemption.

---

[59] *Harper & Row, Publishers, Inc. v. Nation Enters.*, 471 U.S. 539, 558 (1985) ("[T]he Framers intended copyright itself to be the engine of free expression. By establishing a marketable right to the use of one's expression, copyright supplies the economic incentive to create and disseminate ideas."); *Alfred C. Yen*, A First Amendment Perspective on the Idea/Expression Dichotomy and Copyright in a Work's "Total Concept and Feel", 38 Emory L.J. 393, 398–407 (1989).

[60] *Jessica Litman*, The Public Domain, 39 Emory L.J. 965, 965, 977 (1990) ("Our copyright law is based on the charming notion that authors create something from nothing, that works owe their origin to the authors who produce them.... The concept that portions of works protected by copyright are owned by no one and are available for any member of the public to use is such a fundamental one that it receives attention only when something seems to have gone awry."). See Dan L. Burk & Julie E. Cohen, *Fair Use Infrastructure for Rights Management Systems*, 15 Harv JL Tech 42 (2002) (noting that "emerging technical and legal regimes for digital rights management threaten copyright's traditional balance of rights and limitations and are inconsistent with the preservation and growth of a vibrant public domain").

[61] *Pamela Samuelson*, Mapping the Digital Public Domain: Threats and Opportunities, 66 Law & Contemp. Probs. 147 (2003) (examining the relationship between anti-circumvention law and public domain, and concluding that the DMCA will significantly threaten the public domain and reasonable uses of digital information); Yochai Benkler, *Free as the Air to Common Use: First Amendment Constraints on Enclosure of the Public Domain*, 74 NYU L Rev. 354 (1999).

[62] See supra notes 23–25 and the accompanying text.

[63] See *Jane C. Ginsburg*, Copyright Legislation for the "Digital Millennium", 23 Colum.-VLA J.L. & Arts 137, 140 (1999) (observing that "it may be fair use to make nonprofit research photocopies of pages from a lawfully acquired book; it is not fair use to steal the book in order to make the photocopies").

In general, these two principles may be effectually achieved as long as only a "mere" copyright-based protection exists. On the basis of that type of protection, a tribunal court has to decide whether a creation should be entitled to legal protection or whether a privileged use is justified. Henceforth, such considerations are an impossibility if the protection is extended to the technological measures. If the copyright holder is in the position to take such measures in order to ensure non-infringement of his copyright then any differentiation would be excluded. Even if that legal protection depends on the existence of a copyright protection of the (technically) protected work, the coverage of that "double" protection goes much further than the sole copyright protection. The reason is easily understood: technological measures per se are incapable of distinguishing privilege from non-privilege use, and does not respect the dichotomy of protected expression and free idea. In other words, the ruler over a technological protection measure gets hold of the authority of the contents.

This last problem is probably of greatest severity because it affects the foundation of the information society. The more we use and rely on an information infrastructure like the Internet, the more dependent we are upon access to the relevant information through this new media—and the more vulnerable we become if the providers of that information constrict the gateways to it.

The most likely to be affected is the highly copyright-based sector of the information society viz, the broad field of research[64]. It is worthwhile exploring this example because it points out the possible effects of misguided copyright protection. However, we have to bear in mind that this example is just one representative of many other fields which are similarly affected.

IV. Example: The Negative Outgrowth for Research

1. From the Book to the Online Media

For a relatively long period of time, publishers and authors had developed a symbiotic relationship. In the 1960s, some sectors in the copyright-based industry, including producers of phonograms and videotapes and broadcasting organizations, were, for the first time, exposed to a cold wind of new electronic technologies. By contrast, publishers were still on a safe vessel navigating in the ocean of copyright products. Thanks to the "state-of-the-art" limitation existing in the analogue world[65], photocopied books had never been an adequate substitute for

---

64 See e.g., *Pamela Samuelson*, , 293 Science 2028 (September 14, 2001).

65 In the analogue world, copying an entire work is a relatively onerous task in most circumstances. The photocopied books routinely suffer from the "degraded quality" problem, which means that compared with the original copies of works, the photocopied ones are inferior in terms of quality. According to Professor Hardy, there are four factors limiting copying: (1) entitlement-like protection; (2) contract-like protection; (3) state-of-the-art limitations; and (4) special-purpose technical limitations. See *Trotter Hardy*, Property (and Copyright) in Cyberspace, 1996 Univ. Chicago Legal Forum 217 (1996). With regard to the state-of-the-art limitation, he further observed: "For any medium of expression, making a copy entails costs, yet obviously different media entail very different copying costs. Technological changes affect

their original counterparts which were distributed in the marketplace with the authorization of right owners. Furthermore, no electronic media fitting into the mass distribution of the data published in books existed at that time. Maybe this was the reason why there had been no national and international legislation proposed to vest the so-called "neighbouring right" in publishers, who were not affected by electronic devices facilitating infringing acts (e.g. tape or video recorders that copying phonograms and films). Even if they were somehow affected by copying machines, they would have recourse to collecting societies for remedial compensations.

However, a few years ago that status quo dramatically changed. The first step into the digital arena—from the printed book to *offline* media—was insignificant. Perhaps this was due to the fact that there was never the crucial number of products on the market to replace the printed book. Another reason was probably that the advantages of a CD over a book did not necessarily outweigh its disadvantages. For instance, the price of a CD was not considerably less than the price of a book, whilst, like a book the CD could not updated and therefore became outmoded as quickly as a book. As a result, the penetration of offline media was rather limited. In any case, the CD might not be the medium to replace a printed book.

However, with the second step into the digital area—from the printed book (and, even more, the printed journals) to *online* media—was a different matter. Many of us have probably been part of the series of such changes. In the digital age, all information flowing in different parts of the whole world was—at least theoretically—linked together. Today, we no longer have to rush into a library to find the information we badly need. On the contrary, we find much more information on the Internet with the aid afforded by search engines like Google. For academics, a wide range of databases connected to the Internet significantly facilitate their research. In short, the Internet, equipped with search engines and particularly databases, has immense capability to disseminate information inexpensively and ubiquitously. In the knowledge-based society, the Internet is undoubtedly the lifeblood of our global information exchange system[66].

---

this cost. For example, if a manuscript must be written out by hand to make a copy, the cost of doing so—in time, money, and 'trouble'—imposes a natural limit on how many copies one will make of the manuscript. Similarly, a glossy magazine like the National Geographic can be photocopied on a photocopier, but this fact seems almost irrelevant to the National Geographic's plans for distribution. Readily accessible, inexpensive copy machines only produce black and white copies on poor quality paper. Photographs reproduce especially poorly." See Hardy, Ibid. at 224–225.

[66] *UK Commission on Intellectual Property Rights*, Integrating Intellectual Property Rights and Development Policy, at 107, available at www.iprcommission.org/graphic/documents/final_report.htm ("Digitalization and the potential for instant, low-cost global communication have opened tremendous new opportunities for the dissemination and use of scientific and technical databases...in the world."). See also *The Royal Society*, Keeping science open: the effects of intellectual property policy on the conduct of science, at 17–22, available at www.royalsoc.ac.uk/displaypagedoc.asp?id=11403.

2. Databases as Business Models

Of course, most publishers responded to the aforementioned shift promptly with their excellent business acumen. They created databases, gathered related information together and thereby generated new products for sale in the marketplace. At first glance one might think that everybody would be happy with the change, which on its surface would at least facilitate the search, location, and retrieval of information. The reality, however, seems to be different. So what is the problem? It is a matter of fact that the evolution from the printed book to the electronic database did not—contrary to how it appears at first glance—happen in the blink of an eye, but was much more gradual and subtle. Even if a book still looks more or less the same as it did a hundred years ago, the technique to produce this book has changed fundamentally:

Costly hot type disappeared more than twenty years ago. Desktop publishing became the keyword and made the printing of books and journals much easier. Authors became more and more used to typing their texts on their own computers—with an extremely positive effect for publishers: they were able to abolish their former armies of typesetters as the authors took over their job—free of charge. Today a researcher well accepts the fact that he himself formats the text as far as the fonts, the type size and the design of the paragraphs and titles are concerned. Moreover, he is well aware that—depending on the field of the product (a monograph, a collected edition or an article in a journal)—the subsidy for printing costs will rise if he leaves such sophisticated work to the publisher. On the reverse side of the coin, however, the author discovered what he was able to do by himself—an experience that emerged as a kind of boomerang for the publishers, as we will see in a moment.

Surprisingly, price of journals did not become lower. The table below reveals a contrary reality: journal prices have instead exponentially increased[67]. If we look at the price development of U.S. periodicals since 1985 (periodicals being an important source for scientific research, not so much for lawyers, but for scientists), we can see that they have outstripped the Consumer Price Index and even the Higher Education Price Index.

It is likely that scientists did not try to find out more about it—they simply noted that books remained quite expensive in spite of the abolition of numerous factors that make publishing a costly form of business. Researchers desperately need the information contained in books and they underscore the value therein for pursuing research. Furthermore, the majority of them are paid employees of state-run or private organisations, so it is seldom that they themselves pay for the great number of books they use for research purpose. To put it bluntly, there

---

[67] See report of the *UK House of Commons, Science and Technology Committee, Scientific Publications*: Free for All? (July 2004), www.publications.parliament.uk/pa/cm200304/cmselect/cmsctech/399/399.pdf., at 29; according to this report, the number of journal published annually has increased significantly during the past then years, from 4,000 in 1993–94 to 6,500 in 2001; in the same period the average journal price has spiralled by 58%.

U.S. Periodical Prices

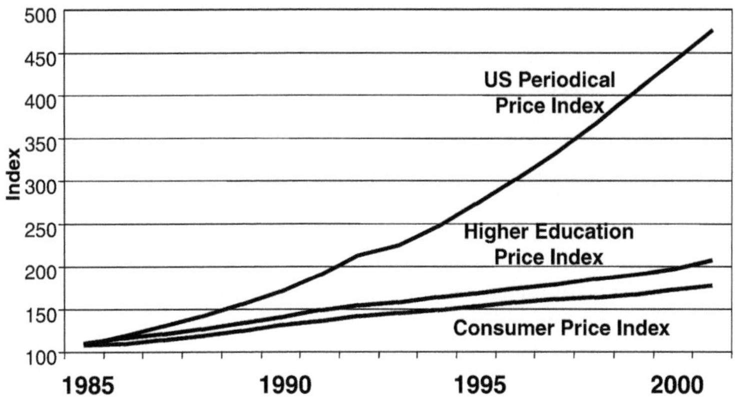

Source: Barbara Albee and Brenda Dingley, "U.S. Periodical Prices— 2002", available at www.ala.org/ALCTSTemplate.cfm?Section=alctssectionscont&template=/ContentManagement/ContentDisplay.cfm&ContentID=40416

were—and still are—not many scientists who are bothered by this situation. The burden of escalating high cost of journals is most felt by scientific organisations and—more indirectly—of public authorities. A confluence of three conflicting developments contributes to said problem: (a) financial problems of the public authorities, (b) the rise of new technological devices to access information, and (c) the greed, at the prospect of easy money, of some less reputable publishing houses. The following section will elaborate on the nature of these three conflicting developments.

3. *Conflicting Developments*

a) Many states, particularly in Western Europe, have *financial problems* today.[68] The economies have worsened, many businesses are not profitable and therefore do not pay taxes, and the treasuries do not have the resources to pay for the public requirements. Some of these states have reacted more intelligently, others less so. The budgets in such states for public research have been noticeably or even dramatically cut. The research establishments, on the other hand, do not have much room for reduction. They can neither reduce the lease costs for their laboratories or their offices, nor—as public employers—release employees or deviate from the required pay scales. The only room to manoeuvre remains the day-to-day expenditure which includes the "purchase" of information[69]. To be

---

[68] See *Fred Bergsten on the world economy*, The Economist (9 September 2004) (discussing various factors that cause financial problems in different categories of countries).

[69] *UK House of Commons, Science and Technology Committee*, Scientific Publications: Free for All? (July 2004), www.publications.parliament.uk/pa/cm200304/cmselect/cmsctech/399/399.pdf, at 23, 50–51.

sure, their idea is not to reduce the volume of information, since they do need the complete information for fundamental research[70]. They would rather obtain the single items of information at a cheaper price.

b) Meanwhile, *new technologies* had provided hope that information could indeed become cheaper. The keyword for that hope was the "Internet". On the Internet, potentially any information is available—often free of charge. This then raises the question: then why should we have to pay? At first glance the situation seems to be truly puzzling: the public authorities are publicly funded in order to conduct research and yet their results are not available free of charge to the researchers.. On the contrary, any research establishment has to pay for the research results of other research establishments which are publicly funded [71]. It is not because they pay each other a certain price for information, but because any researcher has to commit his research results to a third party—the publisher—who sells it to other researchers, mostly for his own profit. This detour was rational as long as a costly added value was apparent: the printed book. If the physical object no longer has to be produced but only the electronic data and if this electronic data is produced and formatted by the researchers themselves—where has the publisher added value? Should researchers pay themselves for doing this type of work? Of course, such a viewpoint is too simplistic and somewhat lop-sided. However, at the root of the matter, the consideration is not completely wrong. Further, we must be fully aware that this consideration was provoked by a third development—the dubious attitude of a few publishers.

c) Some publishers made early investments in scientific databases. They realized that electronic online media would sooner or later replace printed media, at least in essential parts like short-lived articles as opposed to books. Early on, law publishers in the United States had good reasons to believe in an emerging market[72]. With products like LexisNexis and Westlaw, the case law system—based on a nearly unmanageable volume of interrelated decisions—obtained an entirely new face in practice. The gain in efficiency helped to develop a huge market in no time. That market model worked: a lawyer was even happy to pay for data if he could access it in an extremely short time compared with the former research in printed legal practice; time is money, so the lawyer was still the winner. Therefore, publishers got used to the idea that such products could be sold at fancy prices. However, the "transfer" of that business model to scientific fields was not so easy.

---

[70] Committee on Issues in the Transborder, Flow of Scientific Data, U.S. National Committee for CODATA, Commission on Physical Sciences, Mathematics, and Applications, and National Research Council, *Bits of power: Issues in Global Access to Scientific Data* (Washington, D.C.: National Academy Press, 1997) at 115 (proving that systematic scientific research heavily depends on substantial public investment and a large pool information with respect to science and technology) at 114–16.

[71] In the U.S. this problem was addressed by a bill for a "Public Access to Science Act" (HR 2613, available at http://thomas.loc.gov), which was introduced during the 108th Congress, but did not become public law.

[72] For example, "Lexis service", the first commercial, full-text legal information service, began its operation by LexisNexis in 1973. The companion Nexis news and business information service was launched by LexisNexis in 1979. See *LexisNexis*, Company Information, available at www.lexisnexis.com/about.

4. *Perception of the Scientific Society*

In research, time does not have the same value as it does in commerce. A researcher's interest in using electronic databases is spurred on by chance to achieve access to worldwide information worldwide rather than to gain time. They know full well that the real value of databases lies in the fact that useful and time-sensitive information existing elsewhere that cannot be accessed through traditional media can now be traced and used with great ease. In the view of an alliance of scientific associations, "the most profound change associated with the digitization of science is the ability to access scientific data worldwide from the desktop, via the Internet"[73]. For the completeness of that information, researchers are willing to pay something. So the only remaining question is - what the right price for access to the information that enormously bolsters scientific research?

It is the pricing that indeed sets the ball rolling. Some publishing houses consider the benefit of electronic data for researchers to be so high that they are increasingly shifting the business of printing journals to publishing electronic journals[74]. First, they set payment as the precondition for accessing the electronic media as a supplement to printed journals. Later they tried to promote the so-called "e-only" publishing bases, which enable subscribers to receive a print version of a journal—but at an additional price[75]. Research establishments promptly realized that printed versions were a luxury; any researcher could obtain the contents of electronic journals via the Internet or the intranet on screen. Why should research establishments, under such circumstances, pay an extra fee for printed versions of journals just to put them in libraries, which are already crammed full?

Therefore, it was the research establishments who made the most reasonable yet ironic decision: they scrapped their plan to subscribe to the journals operating in the aforementioned fashion. The publishing houses received the bill as a consequence of the "e-only" philosophy: the profits of printed journals crashed. There was a mixed reaction of the publishing houses to that event. At least one of them showed remarkable arrogance and broke the camel's back. It was Elsevier who took the first step. One of Elsevier's major contractual partners is the Max Planck Society. Not surprisingly, they recently plunged themselves into a dispute

---

[73] Committee on Issues in the Transborder, Flow of Scientific Data, U.S. National Committee for CODATA, Commission on Physical Sciences, Mathematics, and Applications, and National Research Council, *Bits of power: Issues in Global Access to Scientific Data* (Washington, D.C.: National Academy Press, 1997) at 126.

[74] The typical example is the recent proliferation of online journals in the intersection of high-tech, law and intellectual property. On the other hand, one can find that a lot of journals in this area, including the *Stanford Technology Law Review* and *Virginia Journal of Law and Technology*, are readily available online for free. Indeed, they only publish academic articles online, rather than in hard-copy form. Even some journals, for instance *Harvard Journal of Law and Technology* and *Berkeley Technology Law Journal* are still circulated in hard-copy form; they also provide articles online with free access.

[75] For example, Cambridge University Press, which publishes a vast number of journals, now provides online full text for over one hundred journals in the sciences, social sciences, and humanities (http://journals.cambridge.org/). At the same time, they set up a pay-per-view system. Access to each article may cost around 10 US dollars or even more in some cases.

which may be taken as representative of the current situation, even if the matter has been settled in the meantime.

5. *The "Elsevier Case"*

The following figures illustrate the business relationship between Elsevier and the Max Planck Society:

- — Elsevier publishes some 2,129 journals, containing some 4,500,000 scientific articles[76].
- — The 80 Max Planck Institutes had subscriptions to about 430–440 of these journals in print at the beginning of the controversy.
- — The total subscription fees for all the institutes added up to 3.3 million euros each year.
- — If the whole Society had subscribed to each journal only once, the fee would have gone down to roughly 1.2 million euros a year (around 35%).
- — Electronic access was at that time possible for an extra fee of 0.33 million euros a year (10% of the subscription fees for all printed journals).

The dispute was caused by Elsevier's proposals to change its distribution policy. Electronic delivery was to be the standard with an extra fee charged for print versions. In figures, Elsevier aimed at a total fee of 3.9 million euros per year.

However, the Max Planck Society reckoned that the aforementioned price was entirely unreasonable because of the following two factors:

- — At that time the total fee for printed journals was 3.3 million euros plus 0.33 million euros for electronic access, all together amounting to about 3.6 million—but not the 3.9 million Elsevier was now requiring.
- — If the whole Max Planck Society had reduced their subscriptions to one printed journal each (instead of the required copies for all the concerned Institutes) plus electronic access, the lump sum would have been around 1.5 million euros—but not the required 3.9 million (corresponding to 260% of the actual price).

The negotiations were extremely tough and did not lead to a satisfying solution for a long time. It seemed that Elsevier had been in a dominant position, for they knew too well that they held the power at that moment: without the leading journals, a research establishment like the Max Planck Society could close down.

That was the initial position. I do not think it is necessary to explain how strongly the Max Planck Society—financed about 98% by taxes—felt inclined to react. One should note, however, that the above-mentioned negotiations were held in 2003, the year in which the German Federation as well as all Federal States decided that the Max Planck Society should receive no increase of its budget instead of 5% as promised (which increase was promised because of the

---

76 See *Elsevier*, Journal Title List, available at www.elsevier.com/wps/find/journal_browse.cws_home.

additional cost of the efforts of the Max Planck Society in Eastern Germany). So in truth the Max Planck Society had to digest a reduction of roughly 5%—and was confronted at the same time with incomprehensible price demands from its major information agent.

6. *Reaction of the Max Planck Society*

The reaction of the Max Planck Society to Elsevier's demand was based upon the considerations mentioned above:

— If research establishments obtain public resources in order to produce new, useful information; and
— if that new information is primarily the basis for further research that sustains and enhances the flow of information; and
— and if this further research is inextricably based on public resources,

then why should the different research entities not exchange the appropriate information without a detour through publishing houses? Of course they all would be well advised to accept this detour as a matter of fact, if an added value with a justified price would lead to advantages. However, at the same it is necessary to clarify that the added value does not exist in the content itself. Rather, the content is usually given to the publishers for free. Nor does the quality control measure ("peer review") significantly contribute to the added value. Even if the argument of the expensive peer review is frequent, it is not convincing. First of all, only limited parts of articles are actually reviewed by experts in the field. Second, quality control may be *organised* by the publisher but the main work is the peer reviewing, which is effectuated by researchers routinely on a free-of-charge basis. In other words, the only things that may be considered as added value on the part of the publisher are the hosting of data, the maintaining of the information infrastructure and the refinement of electronic data.

To come back to the question of the justified price: if the added value for electronic publishing is very limited, but the price very high—higher than it was when the whole information was printed and distributed on paper—then publishers give research establishments a reason to avoid the detour through a publishing house and to take things into their own hands.

That was essentially the proposal of the Max Planck Society. On 20–22 October, 2003, the Max Planck Society organised an international conference on "Open Access to Knowledge in the Sciences and Humanities" in Berlin[77]. This conference was extremely successful. High-profile representatives of various research institutes came from all over the world to attend this conference and it culminated with the "Berlin Declaration on Open Access to Knowledge in the Sciences and Humanities"[78].

---

77 For an introduction to the Conference, see the Program List available at www.zim.mpg.de/openaccess-berlin/program_prelim.html.

78 The Declaration is available at www.zim.mpg.de/openaccess-berlin/berlin_declaration.pdf.

7. The "Berlin Declaration"

First, in the Preface of the Declaration, the importance of the Internet as an instrument for distributing scientific knowledge and cultural heritage is emphasised[79]. Then, under the title "Goals", the Declaration sets out the vision that the web has to be "sustainable, interactive, and transparent. Content and software tools must be openly accessible and compatible"[80]. Moreover, the Declaration defines open access as "a comprehensive source of human knowledge and cultural heritage that has been approved by the scientific community"[81]. In order to tap into the potential of such open access, the Declaration prescribes two conditions for the "Open-Access Contribution" which are as follows:

— that authors and right holders grant to all users a "free, irrevocable, worldwide, right of access to, and a license to copy, use, distribute, transmit and display the work publicly and to make and distribute derivative works, in any digital medium for any responsible purpose, subject to proper attribution of authorship (…), as well as the right to make small numbers of printed copies for their personal use";
— that the complete work itself, as well as a copy of the mentioned permission (the voluntary license), be placed in an open-access online repository, which is, "supported and maintained by an academic institution, scholarly society, government agency, or other well-established organisation that seeks to enable open access, unrestricted distribution, interoperability, and long-term archiving"[82].

It is obvious that these provisions for a (voluntary) license go much further than the limits in our copyright acts. If a right holder accepts it, he rejects many of the capacities deriving from his copyright, capacities that could of course have been turned into money. No explanation is necessary to understand that this target excludes any commercialisation of the included electronic contents.

Finally, the "Open Access Paradigm" is concerned with the pursuit of the interest in "the further promotion of the new open access paradigm to gain the most benefit for science and society"[83]. To this end, the signatories intend, among other things, to make progress by:

— encouraging their researchers and grant recipients to publish their work according to the principles of the open access paradigm;
— developing means and ways to evaluate open access contributions and online journals in order to maintain the standards of quality assurance and good scientific practice;

---

[79] The Preface states that: "The Internet has fundamentally changed the practical and economic realities of distributing scientific knowledge and cultural heritage. For the first time ever, the Internet now offers the chance to constitute a global and interactive representation of human knowledge, including cultural heritage and the guarantee of worldwide access." See ibid.

[80] Ibid.

[81] Ibid.

[82] Ibid.

[83] Ibid.

— advocating that open-access publication be recognised in promotion and tenure evaluation[84].

The list of signatories is excitingly long[85] and is open to new participants to join this open-access initiative aimed at promoting the sustained and healthy economic, social, and cultural development in the digital age.

8. *Some Comments on the "Berlin Declaration"*

Indeed, the Berlin Declaration is a timely response to the ill-effects brought about by the recent trend in commodification of information pursued by the copyright industry. It is difficult to say today how we should consider that evolution. There is no doubt that the model of the "Open Access" has its strong points, at least if we assume that a relevant fraction of the concerned publishing houses have excessive imaginations concerning their profits and if players like Elsevier thereby hinder global scientific research. However, some question s remain, above all in view of the fact that the initiative still seems to be a vision, rather than a fully developed "business model". In particular, we should take account of the fact that "free access" does not at all mean that such an enterprise could be obtained at no cost. If we may believe the experiences of some publishers (and if we notice how many of them failed with similar—but commercial—projects), we can conceive of the consequences of such an engagement. Of course the mind of the "Berlin Declaration" is alluring and conclusive that publicly financed research results should not be "privatised" in line with their publication. On the other hand, we should not forget that "privatisation" does not necessarily lead to profits only; but usually includes the risk of exploitation. Even if it is true that in practice publishers do not really undertake risks, since they often call for a subsidy of the printing costs, we have to follow the idea through: the hosting of the data, the maintenance of the information infrastructure and above all, the refinement of the data to achieve a (technical) added value—all that generates considerable costs that have to be paid. In other words, public authorities may on the one hand—eventually– avoid paying the costs to private content providers for access, but on the other hand they have to pay the costs of doing their job. Considering that prospect, the "Open Access Model" risks amounts to a zero-sum game. Substantial economic advantages will only be able to be gained if the efficiency and the professionalism are outstanding. Admittedly, if that succeeds, tax money is well invested since the result would be the decline in the dependency on unreliable contractual partners like "Elsevier"[86].

---

[84] Ibid.

[85] The complete list of the signatories is available at www.zim.mpg.de/openaccess-berlin/signatories.html.

[86] However, arriving at that point, one might raise the question of principle whether such a substantial investment of public money to provide public research on the basis of an open access doctrine does not already lead to an alternative economic approach, i.e. an alternative incentive model: we might consider the resulting intangible good as a public good and challenge the intervention of the legislator by granting exclusive rights; see also *Kenneth J. Arrow*, Economic Welfare and the Allocation of Resources for Invention, in: The Rate and Direction of Inventive Activity: Economic and Social Factors, A Report of the National Bureau of Economic Research, 1962, 609, 623–625; *Robert Cooter/Thomas Ulen*, Law and Economics, 4th ed. 2004, 120–122; *Niva Elkin-Koren/Eli M. Salzberger*, Law, Economics and Cyberspace, 2004, 50–51; *Hans-Bernd Schäfer/Claus Ott*, The Economic Analysis of Civil Law, 2004, 456–457.

If we therefore conclude that it might be worth our while to invest in the "Open Access Paradigm", we might nevertheless be tempted to scrutinize whether that kind of self-help measure is an adequate response. The fact is obvious that the source of all problems is the broad—and still expanding—scope of copyright protection and its inherent hazard to misuse the resulting dominant marketing position of the copyright holder. That leads to the question: do we—as mentors of the future copyright—merely observe backlashes like the one of the Max Planck Society or should we rethink and redevelop the whole system of copyright?

Two trends of thoughts are worth further reflection. Although one of them - the refinement and improvement of competition law—does not focus on copyright law, it is worth emphasising that it might help in scenarios such as the "Elsevier" scenario. However, a much more appropriate competition law could only intervene subsequently to concretely adjust the emerging imbalances[87]. At present, we should concentrate on the other trend of thought—an initially balanced system of copyright protection—since external instruments like competition law only ensure fine tuning adjustments.

V. Thoughts on an Appropriate Copyright System

In order to consider how to achieve an appropriate, balanced copyright system, there is a need to rethink the lessons distilled from the above discussions.

1. *Three Conflicting Interests*

It is necessary to accept the realities of the legal promotion of creativity in different jurisdictions. First and foremost, the U.S. Constitution of 1787 makes clear that the ostensible purpose of vesting copyright in authors is to provide an economic incentive for their creative activities[88]. Accordingly, the American view of copyright is consistently based on the principle of "work made for hire"[89], under which all rights of use accrue *ex lege* to the party who bears the economic risk. On the other hand, American legislators have never displayed serious concern for the very creators of works. As a result, the real creators, in most circumstances, have to tie their hands with contractual dealings with those who would exploit their work for commercial purposes[90]. With respect to moral rights, one should also note that American copyright law provided scant protection for

---

[87] See e.g., *Radio Telefis Eireann v Commission of the European Communities* (C-241/91P) (Magill Case) [1995] 4 C.M.L.R. 718 (ECJ); *IMS Health GmbH & Co OHG v NDC Health GmbH & Co KG* (C-418/01) [2004] 4 C.M.L.R. 28 (ECJ (5th Chamber)).

[88] See U.S. Const. Art. I, §. 8, cl. 8.

[89] For the definition of "work made for hire", see 17 U.S. Const..§§101, 201(b) (1994). For an introduction to this practice, see *David Nimmer, Peter Menell and Diane McGimsey*, Pre-existing Confusion in Copyright's Work-for-Hire Doctrine, 50 J. Copyright Society of USA 399 (2003).

[90] But see 17 U.S.Const..§ 304(c), which provides for a termination right with regard to transfers on licenses of copyrights other than a copyright in a work made for hire.

creators before 1988[91]. Although the United States acceded to the Berne Convention and WCT, morals rights are still not adequately protected in the United States[92]. As a result, certain groups of creators and artists have long since banded together in "guilds" to assert their interests in contractual dealings with those who would exploit their work. The weak protection of moral rights again demonstrates the utilitarian nature of U.S. copyright law[93]. In such an entrepreneur-oriented legal culture, the American copyright industry, however, has taken off and prospered with an unprecedented success[94].

Nevertheless, from the traditional European "droit d'auteur" perspective, the exclusive rights accorded to exploiters appear to be untenable. The weak legal protection of authors runs contrary to the inclination towards an understanding based on the principles of "natural justice" that focuses on the creative persona. But does the reality in the United States differ much from that in Continental Europe? Moreover, is the granting of new economic rights merely intended to act as the means to ends of bolstering the economic power wielded by the copyright industry, while the interests of the real creators of works have scarcely been taken into account? In considering this question, one should note particularly that the latest rights to be introduced—above all the legal protection of technological measures—obviously do not improve the creator's position. Such remedies further maintain the interests of the exploiter of the rights who, for instance, wish to avoid losses from private copying. Regardless of these facts, the European Directive on copyright in the Information Society proclaims in one consideration: "A rigorous, effective system for the protection of copyright and related rights is one of the main ways of ensuring that European cultural creativity and production receive the necessary

---

[91] In 1988, the U.S. Congress enacted the "Berne Convention Implementation Act" in order to modify U.S. Copyright law with the goal of enabling the U.S. to adhere the Berne Convention (see H.R. 4262, CCH Copyrights, New Developments para. 20,510, at pages 11,372–11,377). One of the aims was to bring U.S. Copyright Act into compliance with the obligations regarding moral rights protection embodied in the Berne Convention. Whether this aim was finally achieved or not is open to doubts; see *Julie E. Cohen* et al., Copyright in a Global Information Economy (New York: Aspen Law & Business, 2002) at 395 (pointing out that the U.S.'s reluctance to accede to the Berne Convention is largely based upon the Berne Convention's requirement to moral rights).

[92] See *Cohen*, ibid. at 13 (concluding that "despite global harmonization efforts, U.S. copyright law with its utilitarian underpinnings does not fully embrace protection for moral rights"). 17 U.S.Const. § 106A that confers the rights of attribution and integrity in certain works of visual art is not considered to be in accordance with the Berne Convention and the WCT; see *Marshall Leaffer*, Understanding Copyright Law (New York: Matthew Bender, 3rd ed. 1999) at § 829.

[93] For an animadversion on American vision of moral rights protection, see *Burton Ong*, Why Moral Rights Matter: Recognizing the Intrinsic Value of Integrity Rights, 26 Colum. J.L. & Arts 297 (2003).

[94] Over the last 24 years (1977–2001), it is estimated that the U.S. core copyright industries' share of the gross domestic product (GDP) grew more than twice as fast as the remainder of the U.S. economy. In 2001, the total copyright industries contributed an estimated $791.2 billion to the U.S. economy. This accounts for approximately 7.75% of US's GDP. The copyright industries also surpass all other major industry sectors in terms of the overseas sales volume, achieving foreign sales and exports of approximately $88.97 billion. See *Stephen E. Siwek*, Copyright Industries in the U.S. Economy: The 2002 Report (2002).

resources and of safeguarding the independence and dignity of artistic creators and performers"[95]. However, these new rights are nothing else but tools in the hands of the industry—above all the US entertainment industry.

Therefore, the *first lesson to be learnt* is that the divide between conflicting interests runs not so much between creators and consumers as greatly emphasized by the traditional perception of copyright. Instead, the discrepancy arises from the fact that the copyright-exploiting industry wants to optimise its profits by all possible means they can deploy, while the end consumer wants to pay as little as possible to have access to and use of the copyrighted works[96]. In other words, there are three categories of conflicting interests. Further, we should be aware that an enhancement of copyright protection scarcely helps the creators of the works, but rather burdens the consumers.

2. *Justified Economic Interests of the Industry*

It should be recognised that few are willing to do a good job for nothing - "people respond to incentives"[97]. Public policymakers "should never forget about incentives since many policies change the costs or benefits that people face and, therefore alter behaviour" [98]. This is also true of policy-making for copyright law. Policymakers should be sufficiently mindful that the copyright industry, therefore, has legitimate reason to demand adequate legal protection for their investments. The only question which needs to be answered is what the "adequate legal protection" means are. In that context, we must give full consideration to the following aspects of copyright law:

— we must realise that the recent discussion on "users' rights" is far from being infallible. Even if it might be true that the balance of copyright protection was disturbed by the recent expansions of copyright, an excessively far-reaching backlash could have a series of negative impacts on the production and dissemination of information, in the long run. Excessive observance of consumer interests might, impede a sustainable development of a broad commercialization of existing protected materials, leading to the underproduction problem about which some commentators have

---

95 Information Society Directive, Recital 11.

96 Jane C. Ginsburg has an interesting account of the relationship between competing interests within copyright law: "I have a theory about how copyright got a bad name for itself, and I can summarize it in one word: Greed. Corporate greed and consumer greed. Copyright owners, generally perceived to be large, impersonal and unlovable corporations...., have eyed enhanced prospects for global earnings in an increasingly international copyright market. Accordingly, they have urged and obtained ever more protective legislation that extends the term of copyright and interferes with the development and dissemination of consumer-friendly copying technologies.... Greed, of course, runs both ways. Consumers, for their part, have exhibited an increasing rapacity in acquiring and "sharing" unauthorized copies of music, and more recently, motion pictures." *Jane C. Ginsburg*, How Copyright Got a Bad Name for Itself, 26 Colum. J.L. & Arts 61, 61–62 (2002).

97 This is recognised as one of the ten fundamental principles for economics. See *N. Gregory Mankiw*, The Principles of Economics (Thomson/South-Western, 2004) at 7.

98 Ibid.

expressed concern[99], and eventually to the detriment of the interests of all members of society.

— we should also be mindful that an author-centred copyright system is likely to result in effects opposite to what has been thought. Disproportionate legal protection actually disadvantages the creator's position as well as that of the copyright industry. If that industry refrains from potential investments because of penalising overprotection, the creator's situation might even worsen: they could have difficulties in finding contracting partners to exploit their works.

Thus, the *second lesson to be learnt* is that it would be better to distinguish between two interests of protection. An adequate legal protection of the copyright industry is not feasible if we define copyright by using as a background the romantic notion of the lonely, nocturnal author, and then transpose thereon a personality-focused right to the commercial exploiter of the created work. The copyright industry does not need all the ballast of copyright but depends on the economic protection of its investments. We should realize that our traditional, author-focused "droit d'auteur"-thinking no longer fully meets the requirements of the industry and answers may be found in a competition-based legal instrument so that future developments should be developed along such lines.

3. *Economic Interests vs. Social Impacts of Copyright*

Having reached that point, the heated discussion of the balance of conflicting interests between right holders and end users may be viewed in another light. Initially, the conflicting parties are not the individual creators and the end users—it is rather the copyright industry and its clients (since the protection of the creator focuses rather on his relationship to the exploiter). Accordingly, the solution to that conflict is no longer overshadowed by a quality rating of more valuable and less valuable interests; rather, simple economic action is required. We realise that the industry, of course, depends on a protected legal position in order to bring certain related products to the market. However, conflicting interests, caused particularly by the social impact of those products, have also to be considered, since we are talking on the level not of a personality-based protection, but of a business transaction.

Thus, the *third lesson to be learnt* is that the quite justified economic interests of the copyright industry end at that point where the justified consumer interests begin. This determination does not immediately lead to an answer. However, it nevertheless provides the leverage for a very important step: it rejects the traditional perception that an allegedly personality-based "property right" is *ipso jure* sublime and would offhand allow the copyright industry an outstanding position.

4. *Advancement of the Information Society*

To design a proper regime for the protection of intellectual property, in general, and copyright, in particular, has become of one of the central issues with respect

---

99 See e.g., *William M. Landes, Richard A. Posner,* The Economic Structure of Intellectual Property Law (Cambridge, MA: Harvard University Press, 2003) at 38–39.

to the advancement of the information society. In December 2003, the World Summit on the Information Society adopted a "Draft Declaration of Principles"[100], part of which deals with intellectual property-related issues[101]. In particular, the Declaration states:

"Intellectual Property protection is important to encourage innovation and creativity in the Information Society; similarly, the wide dissemination, diffusion, and sharing of knowledge is important to encourage innovation and creativity. Facilitating meaningful participation by all in intellectual property issues and knowledge sharing through full awareness and capacity building is a fundamental part of an inclusive Information Society"[102].

However, an overly stringent protection of copyright in the digital environment runs counter to the aforesaid principle regarding intellectual protection proclaimed in the Declaration. Particularly, there is no justification for giving an unbridled legal protection of technological measures. Nevertheless, to take an example, the European Directive on the Copyright in the Information Society[103] tacitly allows an unfettered control of information protected by technological measures. It provides that the "appropriate measures to ensure that right holders make available to the beneficiary of an exception or limitation provided for in national law"[104] shall "not apply to works or other subject-matter made available to the public on agreed contractual terms in such a way that members of the public may access them from a place and at a time individually chosen by them"[105].

If, of all things, online services are exempted from the enforcement of legal limitations and exceptions, the monopolisation of contents therein is highly likely. As a result, such an unconfined protection impedes not only, for example, the feasibility of online quotations. Further more, content providers who utilize technological measures are in the position of being able to block any additional refinement of such contents. If, for instance, a third party wants to act as an information broker—an increasingly indispensable help in the endless ocean of data on the Internet—this may be prevented by the refusal of licensing, even though this third party is willing to pay the right holder. Current examples are journal-based online news services which cannot be developed for copyright

100 *World Summit on the Information Society*, "Draft Declaration of Principles", Document WSIS-03/GENEVA/DOC/4-E (12 December 2003).

101 For example, the Section 7 of the Declaration states that "science has a central role in the development of the Information Society. Many of the building blocks of the Information Society are the result of scientific and technical advances made possible by the sharing of research results".

102 Section 42 of the Declaration.

103 Directive 2001/29/EC of the European Parliament and of the Council of 22 May 2001 on the Harmonization of Certain Aspects of Copyright and Related Rights in the Information Society, 2001 O.J. (L 167) 10.

104 Directive, ibid. Art. 6.4.

105 Ibid. Recital 53 of the Directive explains that "[t]he protection of technological measures should ensure a secure environment for the provision of interactive on-demand services, in such a way that members of the public may access works or other subject-matter from a place and at a time individually chosen by them. Where such services are governed by contractual arrangements, the first and second subparagraphs of Article 6(4) should not apply".

reasons: The journals ban any attempt to build up such independent services despite the serious necessity for various sectors of the economy—not because they would suffer damages (to the contrary, if they were compensated), but because they simply want to maintain their dominant marketing position to the detriment of a diversification of products on the market[106].

The *fourth lesson to be learnt* is that some of the actual regulations are prone to becoming serious hindrances to the fulfilment of the objectives of the information society. If we really desire to have an unrestricted flow of information, we must limit the power of legal protection independently of the applied technique. It is inequitable to privilege right holders particularly in the context of online services. If legislators, feeling constrained to promote the "pay-per-use society", act that blindly, we should not wonder if the concerned users—like the Max Planck Society—try to outsmart copyright law, albeit with a considerable risk of failing. Hence, responsible legislation should be equipped with economic expert knowledge and long-term considerations for social development than notably the European legislature—presumably and unfortunately followed by others (although Art. 11 WCT does not oblige such restrictions)—has shown. Indeed, only a more economic-based, competition-oriented approach may promote the copyright industry in a way that does not ignore the needs of the information society.

5. *Protection of Creators*

Lastly, we return to the roots of the traditional Continental European "droit d'auteur" idea—the protection of the creators. Here we should render an account of the basic desideratum. The end user is hardly the threat to the authors. Even if users claim privileges like private copying, authors may still benefit from such a use if an adequate system of collecting societies is established[107]. The rank and file consumers are not unlawful, but rather willing to pay a justifiable remuneration for the consumption of protected works.

The real hazard to the creators comes from their direct contractual partners: the copyright industry. Even if authors are the source of their business, it is self-evident that the necessity to purchase copyrighted materials is an undesirable expense factor which the copyright industry intends to minimise. It is evident that most creators are, by far, the weaker party in the contractual relationship, although they are constrained to accept even deeply unjustified conditions.[108]

---

[106] In Germany, as a current example, the legitimacy of press reviews is being discussed; the Supreme Court interpreted the legal norm in question (Sec. 49 (1) German CA) relatively broad (11 July 2002, ZR 255/100, published in 151 BGHZ 300, 312 (2002) and 104 GRUR 963, 966 (2002).

[107] See *Jane C. Ginsburg*, Copyright and Control over New Technologies of Dissemination, 101 Colum.L.Rev. 1613, 1645 (2001) (arguing that non-author right holders, rather than the author per se, are the sole direct beneficiaries of the grant of exclusive rights by the U. S. copyright law).

[108] See e.g., *Ryan J. Casamiquela*, Contractual Assent and Enforceability in Cyberspace, 17 Berkeley Tech. L.J. 475 (2002); *Michael J. Madison*, Legal-Ware, *Contract and Copyright in the Digital Age*, 67 Fordham L. Rev. 1025 (1998).

The *fifth lesson to be learnt* is—whilst recalling the first—that we cannot simply enlarge the categories of copyright if we really want to improve the situation of the creators. Rather, we should intervene in the unfettered freedom to contract in similar fashion as European countries' practice in the area of employment law. Creators are in many respects like employees. That does not necessarily mean—coming back to the second lesson—that we should overprotect them. In any event, it is the responsibility of a state authority to ensure a minimum of equal opportunities. In relation to copyright concerns, that means that a minimal standard of protection of authors has to be assured, although the protection should not reach such a level that it abolishes the copyright industry's incentives for investments.

VI. Conclusion

In the digital age, it seems that copyright law is at a crossroad teeming with a variety of outcries from different stakeholder groups. The digital dilemma[109] we are facing teaches us that we need to develop a more reasonable and nuanced approach to adapt copyright law to technological development. This is of paramount importance when it comes to the situation in developing countries. A recent report cautioned:

"The arrival of the digital era provides great opportunities for developing countries in accessing information and knowledge. The development of digital libraries and archives, Internet-based distance learning programs, and the ability of scientists and researchers to access sophisticated online computer databases of technical information in real time are just some examples. But the arrival of the digital era also poses some new and serious threats for access and dissemination of knowledge. In particular, there is a real risk that the potential of the Internet in the developing world will be lost as rights owners use technology to prevent public access through pay-to-view systems"[110].

However, as we have seen in this article, the copyright-related problems catch the developed countries as well. Particularly those special fields which fundamentally depend on specific information, such as science and research, reveal that the fiction of a pay-per-use approach turns out to be the Achilles heel of the whole information society. Indeed, we can harbour the ambition that "law could be designed to shift technological development in a direction that balances the incentive structure of copyright protection with copyright's concern for the public domain and for the legitimate fair use"[111]. However, we should be sufficiently mindful of the fact that only by equipping policymakers and legislators with a better understanding of the ramifications of the five lessons elaborated in this

---

[109] See *Committee on Intellectual Property Rights and the Emerging Information Infrastructure*, The Digital Dilemma: Intellectual Property in the Information Age (Washington, D.C.: National Academy Press, 2000); *Reto* M. *Hilty*, Copyright in a Digital Dilemma, Max Planck Research (3/2003) at 49–53.

[110] UK Commission on Intellectual Property Rights, Integrating Intellectual Property Rights and Development Policy, at 100, available at www.iprcommission.org/graphic/documents/final_report.htm.

[111] *Dan L. Burk & Julie E. Cohen*, Fair Use Infrastructure for Rights Management Systems, 15 Harv JL Tech 42, 54 (2002).

Article can they come up with the right avenues with which copyright law can be engineered to fulfil its long-cherished objectives of promoting "the progress of science and the useful arts"[112].

B: Country Reports

Note: The contributors to the country reports are listed in the introductory preface.

I. China

The current Copyright Act was adopted in September 1990. It is Mainland China's first piece of copyright legislation that is more line with similar IP regimes in the international arena and thus can be considered a "modern" law for the mainland Chinese. As a result, protection is now granted for both:- copyright and neighbouring rights; property rights and moral rights; and traditional works and new ones, e.g., computer programs. Further, the protection period extends to 50 years after the death of the author—China became member to the Berne Convention as of 15 October 1992.

In order to meet the requirements of TRIPS, the Copyright Act was amended in Oct. 2001. Copyright protection afforded thereunder has been strengthened in several aspects:-

a) the categories of rights have been expanded, e.g. right of communication on information networks, right of mechanical performance;
b) the types of statutory licenses have been adjusted. The former one which related to the right of performance has been deleted and a new one created, i.e. favourable provision for the author of official textbooks for schools; and
c) the enforcement of rights has been encouraged. For example, a temporary injunction has been introduced for the first time into civil procedure.

In recent years, debate amongst the academics in this IP regime seems to be centred on the issue of the justification of copyright, particularly in areas such as database protection, and Internet copyrights. However, the voice against over-protection is still quite weak.

II. Hong Kong

1. Introduction

As member of the World Trade Organization in her own right, Hong Kong has a sophisticated set of intellectual property laws which meet the standards set by the WTO Agreement in the Trade-Related Aspects of Intellectual Property Rights (TRIPs) Agreement. The Basic Law of Hong Kong also provides in Arts. 139 and 140 that legal protection should be given to intellectual property rights in Hong Kong.

Hong Kong has legislation dealing independently with each intellectual property regime viz. copyright, trade marks, patents and registered designs. Copyright

---

[112] See U.S. Const. Art. I, § cl. 8.

in Hong Kong is governed by the Copyright Ordinance (Cap 528), which came into effect on 27 June 1997. Unlike the other intellectual property rights such as patents, trademarks and industrial designs, registration is not a pre-requisite for obtaining copyright protection in Hong Kong and neither are there formalities to be complied with to obtain copyright protection for a "work" in Hong Kong. Hong Kong adopts an open qualification system for any original work created or published by anyone anywhere in the world without any need for reciprocity. Therefore, works of authors from any place in the world, or works first published anywhere in the world, also qualify for copyright protection in Hong Kong.

2. *Copyright Ordinance (Cap 528)*

The Copyright Ordinance provides comprehensive protection for recognised literary categories (including computer programs), dramatic, musical and artistic works, sound recordings, films, broadcasts, cable programs, typographical arrangements of published editions, rights in performances, moral rights and designs (not registered or registrable under the Registered Designs Ordinance).

3. *New Rights*

a) Performers' rights and Moral Rights

Performers' protection rights (and rights in fixations of performances) were first introduced in Hong Kong in 1996[113]. The Copyright Ordinance introduced the moral rights of paternity and integrity and they give authors rights to be identified as authors of a work; not to have a work falsely attributed to them; and to object to derogatory treatment of works.

b) Computer Program

The Copyright Ordinance defines each category of "work" that is protected thereunder. "Literary work" is defined as 'any work, other than a dramatic or musical work, which is written, spoken or sung, and accordingly includes:-

(i) a compilation of data or other material, in any form, which is an intellectual creation, including but not limiting to a table[114];
(ii) a computer program; and
(iii) preparatory design material for a computer program.

A computer program falls under the definition of "literary work" in the Copyright Ordinance. Section 25 deals with rental rights and provides that owners of copyright in computer programs and sound recordings (but not films and videos) have the right to preclude others from renting their works. As for computer software, lawful users

113 Performers' protection rights were first introduced to Hong Kong law under the Intellectual Property (World Trade Organisation Amendments) Ordinance (No.11 of 1996).

114 There is no specific legislation dealing with databases in Hong Kong, but databases may be protected as 'literary works'(provided the compilation, by reason of the selection or arrangement of its contents, constitutes an intellectual creation). If the database contains personal data (i.e. data relating to a living individual), then the collection and use of such data will also be governed by the Personal Data (Privacy) Ordinance.

of software, subject to any agreement to the contrary and certain other restrictions, are allowed to make back-up copies or copies or adaptations of software if necessary for their lawful use such as for the purpose of correcting errors.

4. *Balance of Interest*

a) Digital Divide

A gap has always existed between societies who can make effective use of information technology and those who cannot. This gap in turn has precluded many from reaping the fruits of the economic growth that comes with the adoption of new technologies.[115] The term "digital divide" is used to refer to this gap between those who can effectively use new information and communication tools, such as the Internet, and those who cannot. Although there is no consensus on the extent of this divide (and whether it is in fact growing or narrowing), nearly all researchers agree that currently, some sort of divide does exist.[116]

Information and communication technologies alone will never be that single magic pill to cure all economic ills nor does it eliminate the need for sound developmental investments, but neither should their impact be underestimated. Economic development is highly connected to digital divide. Communities that have the tools and skills to compete in the international digital economy posses inherent advantages over communities which do not. However, if communities are to remain competitive in attracting, retaining and developing business in today's economy, they must develop modern telecommunications facilities and cultivate a well-trained workforce to stay viable.

According to a research conducted by Neilsen/NetRatings in August 2003, 61% of the households in Hong Kong have internet access[117]. As of March 2004, there were over 2.5 million at-home internet users in total, i.e. over 35% of the Hong Kong population have internet access at home.[118]

b) Various Amendments to the Law

Hong Kong has resisted the growing trend evident elsewhere—to extend the term of copyright protection for works. This term varies, depending on the type of work protected :-

(i) original literary (including computer programs), dramatic, musical and artistic works—life plus 50 years;

---

[115] Neilsen//NetRatings estimated that, as of the fourth quarter of 2002, a total of 580 million people had internet access via a home PC. However, when this number is considered in context, it is not big at all. 580 million, in fact, represents only 10% of the world's entire population; and of those 580 million, the United States accounts for 29%.

[116] Even among highly developed nations, there exist vast differences in the availability of home Internet access. Germany (35.6 million), the United Kingdom (29 million) and Italy (22.7 million) have the largest number of people outside the US with Internet access via a home PC, together accounting for more than half (54 percent) of the total for all 10 countries outside the US. (Source: Neilsen//NetRatings, Fourth Quarter 2002 Global Internet Trends)

[117] http://www.hkispa.org.hk/spam/20040113-coalition-paper.pdf 0 page 8

[118] http://www.upstreamasia.com/clientnews/nielsennetratings/00000752.html

(ii) sound recordings—50 years from the end of calendar year when it was released or made, whichever is the earlier;
(iii) films - life plus—50 years from the date of death of the last surviving principal director or author of screenplay or author of dialogue or composer of music;
(iv) broadcasts cable programs—50 years from the end of the calendar year when the broadcast was made or the program was included in a cable program service;
(v) industrial designs—15 years;
(vi) typographical arrangement—25 years from the end of the calendar year when the edition was first published;
(vii) moral rights (right to be identified as author or director or right to object to derogatory treatment of the work)—last for as long as copyright in the work subsists;
(viii) moral rights (false attribution)—life plus 20 years;
(ix) rights in performances—50 years from the calendar year when the performance took place or when the performance was released (if the performance was fixed);
(x) computer-generated work—50 years from the end of the calendar year when the work was made.

The Hong Kong stance is that protection should not be extended by broadening the categories protected or extending the protection period, but rather it should come from restricting infringing uses and imposing more severe liabilities on infringers.

In relation to the expansion of the categories of restricted acts, Hong Kong was one of the first jurisdictions to include a provision under which the 'making available of copies of the work' to the public is an infringement—Section 26. Even making available copies of work 'by wire or wireless means, in such a way those members of the public in Hong Kong or elsewhere may access the work from a place and at a time individually chosen by them', i.e. the making available of copies of works by internet is an infringement. The making of transient or incidental copies (such as copies stored in a computer) is also an infringement (Section 23). However, Section 65 expressly permits a copy of a work to be made available to a member of the public if it was technically required for the viewing or listening of the work.

Recent amendments have reflected the government's determination to impose more severe liabilities on copyright infringers. In early 1999, the Intellectual Property Department (IPD) of Hong Kong consulted the public on additional legal tools to combat intellectual property rights infringements. One proposal which had gained widespread public support was a proposal to combat corporate copyright piracy activities through the imposition of criminal liability for the use of infringing products, for example, pirated computer software, during the course of its business.

c) PCPO & OSCO

The Prevention of Copyright Piracy Ordinance (Cap 544) (PCPO) came into force on 29 May 1998. It introduced licensing provisions for optical disc manufacturers and mandatory source identification codes for optical discs. It mandated increased levels of enforcement, particularly through the joint efforts of the Customs and Excise officers. A number of well-publicised actions taken by Customs and Excise in 1999 resulted in record seizures of counterfeit optical and audio discs. The Customs and Excise Department's statistics showed a healthy increase in the number of enforcement actions that had been undertaken from 1999 to 2000.[119] Furthermore, police and Customs officers have since doubled their manpower and conducted a series of aggressive raids against both factories producing illegal optical discs and retail outlets selling them.

The Organised and Serious Crime Ordinance (Amendment of Schedule I) Order 1999 (OSCO) passed in January 2000 elevated piracy and counterfeiting offences under the Trade Description Ordinance and Copyright Ordinance to "serious crimes" under the OSCO.

d) IPMAO

The Intellectual Property (Miscellaneous Amendments) Ordinance 2001 (IPMAO), which took effect on 1 April 2001, introduced criminal liability for end-user piracy in Hong Kong. IPMAO was introduced in an effort to address what was perceived as rampant piracy in Hong Kong at that time[120]. The effect of IPMAO was to make it an offence for end-users to knowingly possess an infringing copy of a copyright work for the purpose of or in the course of, or in connection with, any trade or business.

e) CSAO

The public has viewed the IPMAO provisions imposing criminal liability as being too broad in scope since they applied to all forms of copyright works and to almost all activities carried out in relation to any business. These provisions have also disregarded well-established exceptions to infringement under copyright law. To address the public's concerns that these IPMAO amendments would hamper the dissemination of information in enterprises as well as teaching activities in schools, the Legislative Council then passed the Copyright (Suspension of Amendments) Ordinance 2001 (CSAO) in June 2001 as a temporary measure. The CSAO has partially suspended the effect of the IPMAO amendments—only to the extent that "criminal" provisions continues to apply (with a slightly narrower scope) to only four categories of works, namely—computer software, movies, television dramas and music recordings (the "Four Categories of Works"). The suspension was initially effective only until 31 July 2003.

---

[119] From 347 cases taken under the Copyright Ordinance in 1999 to 625 in 2000.

[120] According to the Seventh Annual Business Software Alliance Global Software Piracy Study (June 2002), the piracy rate in Hong Kong in 1999 was as high as 56% followed by 57% in 2000. Such an excessive degree of violation of intellectual property rights significantly affected the legitimate interests of copyright owners, discouraged innovation and investments, and tarnished the international image of Hong Kong.

f) Why Only Four Categories?

According to the Hong Kong Intellectual Department (HKIPD), the reason for restricting the criminal liabilities to only those four categories is that these types of copyright works are not normally disseminated in enterprises or schools as "information". Moreover, these products generally have substantial commercial value. Piracy of these products, in particular computer software, in Hong Kong, China and elsewhere is rampant and it is therefore necessary for the Copyright Ordinance to provide a higher level of protection to such works.

Due to demand from the public for more time to fully consider the extended criminal provisions under the CSAO, the suspension provisions under the Copyright (Suspension of Amendments) Ordinance 2001 was further extended to 31 July 2004 and recently to 31 July 2006 by virtue of the Copyright (Suspension of Amendments) Ordinance 2001 (Amendment) Notice 2004. The effect of this is that until 31 July 2006, criminal liability for use of pirated copies of copyright works is incurred only in relation to copyright works belonging to those four categories of works, and the criminal act concerned is confined to possession of an infringing copy in the course of business with a view to its being used in that business.

III. Taiwan

The phenomenon of "relentless copyright expansion" can also be observed in the Copyright Act of Taiwan. For the twelfth time, the Copyright Act has been amended, the latest of which became effective on July 9, 2003[121]. One of the amendment's goals is to include some new rights mandated by the WIPO Copyright Treaty (WCT) and the WIPO Performances and Phonograms Treaty (WPPT), despite the fact that Taiwan has yet to ratify and is not allowed to ratify the WCT and WPPT. The impetus for the latest amendment was the fact that:

> *"the current Copyright Act was based on traditional technology, [and] is not properly adjusted to issues caused by the digital Internet technology. [It was necessary in] order to propel the prosperous development of info-communications and e-commerce, to enhance the protection of authors in the digital network environment, and to comply with the development trend of the international copyright law"*[122].

The expansion of copyright has taken place not only vertically and horizontally, but new provisions have imposed higher degrees of criminal liabilities.

1. Vertical expansion

Under the Copyright Act in 1928, copyright in general was given a 30-year term of protection which had remained unchanged despite subsequent amendments to this Act until 1992 when this was extended to 50 years, in compliance with Article 5 of the Agreement for the Protection of Copyright between Taiwan and the US (approved by the Legislative Yuan on April 22, 1993). The 1928 Copyright Act drew a distinction between certain works by granting different terms of protection.

---

[121] The English version of the 2003 Copyright Act can be found at the website of the Taiwanese Intellectual Property Office: www.tipo.gov.tw. Therefore this paper will not cite the exact provisions of the Act, unless necessary during the discussion.

[122] The general legislative reason for the 2003 Copyright Act.

For instance, works such as photographs and films had shorter terms of protection. In 1985 changes included not only an increase of the number of items to this list of differential treatment—editorial works, sound recordings, and computer software works; the term of protection for neighbouring rights was also lengthened from 10 years to 30 years. The 1998 Amendment introduced new categories to the list, namely photographic works, audiovisual works, sound recordings, and performances, and again extended the term of protection for all neighbouring rights from 30 to 50 years after the public release of the work. In compliance with Article 10(1) of TRIPS, the 2001 Amendment took computer software off this list and restored it to the normal term of protection for literary works.

2. *Horizontal expansion*

a) Introduction of new exclusive rights

Motivated by the digitisation of works and proliferation of the Internet as well as the coming into effect of the WCT and WPPT, the 2003 Copyright Act introduces some new exclusive rights: for authors and performers the right of public transmission (Sec. 26-1), the right to distribute (Sec. 28-1), and for performers the right of rental (Sec. 29(2), authors already enjoy such right), thereby following verbatim the WCT and WPPT. However, one major deviation from Article 15(1) of the WPPT needs mentioning.

An analysis of the Taiwanese Copyright Act reveals that it does not follow the international arena's treatment of neighbouring rights. For instance, from 21 January 1998, under Sec. 7-1, a performance by a performer of a pre-existing work or folklore shall be protected as *an independent work* even though most of the international copyright laws do not accord such a high level of protection. The rights of institutions which help in the creation and dissemination of works through their employment of managerial and organisational skills in situations like producers of phonograms, enjoy no protection whatsoever. Another anomaly exists with the new Sec. 26(3) which empowers *the author* to claim remuneration for the public performance of his sound recording from the persons who publicly performed it, and paragraph 4 of the same provision which prescribes that if a publicly performed sound recording is a recording of a live performance, both *the author and the performer* of the recorded work may jointly claim compensation,[123] but the producer of phonograms has been left out of the picture.[124]

b) Firming up the reach of the reproduction right: temporary reproduction is explicitly included

With the arrival of personal computers and computer programs in the 1970s, whether temporary reproduction constitutes "reproduction" became a major issue because for most practical purposes, computer programs "cannot be perceived,

---

123 The Act is silent on the issue of how the remunerations are to be shared between the author and the performer.

124 However, the legislative reason referred specifically to Article 15 of the WPPT, which grants performers and produces of phonograms the right to remuneration for broadcasting and communication to the public.

accessed or run without being copied into computer memory, albeit invisibly to the user."[125] However, it is not clear whether the reproduction right under Article 9(1) of the Berne Convention covers such ephemeral reproduction. The EU takes a positive view early on.[126] Meanwhile, although both the WCT and the WPPT were not able to reach a conclusive decision on this issue and leading Asian copyright laws such as Chinese and Japanese Copyright Act are still silent on this,[127] the Taiwanese 2003 Copyright Act has adopted the EU position by its explicit definition of the term "reproduce" to include temporary reproduction and formulates some exceptions to the exclusive right to reproduce.

3. *Intensifying criminal punishments*

In contrast with the recent "decriminalisation" of infringements in the Patent Act, the 2003 Copyright Act instead intensified its criminal liabilities to such an extent that during the legislation process some university students launched a so-called "Anti anti-piracy" movement. This intensification of its criminal liabilities has been twofold, viz. by (i) expanding the reach of criminal punishment to include not-for-profit private infringement; and (ii) increasing the penalties. Hence, the present Section 91 of the 2003 Copyright Act imposes penal sanctions on illegal reproduction in the following manner:-

(i) (a maximum of 3 years' imprisonment) even without the intent to profit as long as the copying exceeds five reproductions, or where the total value of infringement (based on the market value of lawful copies of the work) at the time of seizure exceeds NT$30,000; and
(ii) a maximum of 5 years' imprisonment (increase from 3 years) for cases where there is an intent to profit; and
(iii) a maximum of 7 years for vocational violation.

The Copyright Act of 2003 penalises with less severity the infringement of the exclusive right of distribution, public recitation, public broadcast, public presentation, public performance, public transmission, public display, adaptation, compilation, and leasing, and also differentiates between those infringements done with the intent to profit and those without such intent as long as a certain threshold number or value has not been exceeded. This Act goes even further - criminalizing so-called "secondary infringement", i.e. dealing in pirated copies, and makes a similar distinction between those infringements done with the intent to profit and those without such intent. Last but not least, this Act has enlarged the scope for public prosecution to include, besides vocational violations, the illegal reproduction and distribution of works, which is undertaken by means of optical discs and with the intent to profit.

---

[125] Copinger and Skone James on Copyright, 14 ed., 1999, 7–58.

[126] Articles 4(a) , 5(1) of the EU "91/250 Directive on the legal protection of computer programs (Software Directive)"; recital (20) of the "2001/29 Directive on the harmonisation of certain aspects of copyright and related rights in the information society (InfoSoc Directive)."

[127] *Haochen Sun*, Re-thinking the Chinese Copyright Law in the Digital Age, 6 The Journal of World Intellectual Property 895, 2003, at 903.

4. Counter-balance to the expansion of copyrights?

To counter-balance authors' and performers' exclusive right of distribution, Sec. 59-1 of the 2003 Copyright Act for the first time addresses the issue of exhaustion:

> "A person who has obtained ownership of the original of a work or a lawful copy thereof within the territory under the jurisdiction of the Republic of China may distribute it by means of transfer of ownership".

The newly established principle of exhaustion only applies domestically, and is therefore detrimental to international trade and to the desires of consumers for great variety of choice. In addition, the exhaustion is based on the transfer of ownership of the original or a copy of a work and is therefore powerless to cover the licensing (to use) practice which is becoming prevalent on the Internet.

The Taiwanese Copyright Act boasts what is likely to be the greatest number of provisions on "fair use" in the world, a total number of twenty-five (25) provisions. Those provisions are composed of twenty-four that list specific restrictions on economic rights and one (Section 65) that enumerates general principles both for the evaluation of the applicability of those specific restrictions and for the judgment of other possible cases of fair use. Despite the fact that these provisions are of little importance in practice, evidenced by the fact that they are seldom used and interpreted by courts, the Copyright Act of 2003 strives to perfect them by making some insignificant literal revisions. What might be worth mentioning are the two paragraphs which have been included into Sec. 65:

> "(3) Where the copyright owners' organisation and the exploiters organisation have formed an agreement on the scope of the fair use of a work, it may be taken as reference in the determination (of fair use) referred to in the preceding Paragraph.
> (4) In the course of forming an agreement referred to in the preceding Paragraph, advice may be sought from the specialised agency in charge of copyright matters (i.e. IPO)."

Thus far, collective bargaining does not exist in Taiwan, let alone any agreement between copyright owners and exploiters of works. Should the practice start or some agreements emerge, the courts will no doubt use them as yardstick for determining the applicability of fair use, whether Sec. 65(3) so prescribes or not. In the same vein, Sec. 65(4) is likewise redundant. Since 1992 the Copyright Examination and Mediation Committee of the IPO has provided (at least theoretically) for consultation services in connection with copyright mediation.[128] The 2003 Copyright Act should have dealt with more important topics of fair use such as: is the principle fair use still applicable once anti-circumvention provisions are introduced; whether it is reconcilable with the "three-step test" principle of the WCT Article 10(1)) and WPPT [Article 16(1)] that only allows

[128] Sec. 82 (1) of the 2003 Copyright Act prescribes: The specialised agency in charge of copyright matters shall establish a Copyright Examination and Mediation Committee to handle the following matters: 1. Examination of rates of compensation for use under the provisions of Sec. 47(4). 2. Mediation of disputes between copyright intermediary organisations and users concerning compensation for use. 3. Mediation of disputes concerning copyright or plate rights. 4. Other consultation in connection with copyright examination and_mediation.

limitations of or exceptions to the copyrights "in certain special cases that do not conflict with a normal exploitation of the work and do not unreasonably prejudice the legitimate interests of the authors."[129]

5. *Overall evaluation—A tilted scale*

The continual expansion of copyright both vertically and horizontally raises various kinds of concerns. Extensive criminalisation is subject to overwhelming criticism and raises important questions regarding social justification of copyright expansion. First and foremost, the criminalisation of illegal reproduction, distribution, public recitation, public broadcast, public presentation, public performance, public transmission, public display, adaptation, compilation, and leasing undertaken without the intent to profit impedes the dissemination of works. It also endangers legal certainty in daily living since we are experiencing unprecedented advances of reproduction, storage and transmission technologies which have made any layman a powerhouse of mass reproduction, storage and distribution. The liability threshold can be easily exceeded. The state will be investigating not only enterprises and organisations, but even the ordinary household. It is untenable that an ordinary citizen should live in fear that he might be persecuted for the innocent personal use of technological advances. Is it the intention of such advancement in technology to result in a slow down of its use?

Secondly, the penalisation of the following secondary infringements by Sec. 93(1) is questionable: the export of copies of sound recordings made under a compulsory license, the import of reproductions made without the authorisation of copyright owners, and the exploitation for business purposes of a copy of a computer program that is known to infringe on economic rights in such computer program. For sound recordings made under a compulsory license, there will be a payment of at least 5% of the wholesale price;[130] the export thereof does not necessarily cause harm to the economic interests of the copyright holder, and so should accordingly not be characterised as a wrongdoing warranting criminal sanctions. No subjective element of "with the knowledge" is required from the importer; however, without such an element no criminal penalties can be rightfully inflicted. The mere use of a computer program within the business context with the knowledge that the program infringes on economic rights of a copyright holder is of course not a noble act, but it does not amount to "copyright piracy on a commercial scale" as demanded by Article 61 of the TRIPS[131] to render criminal sanctions justifiable.

---

[129] China has introduced the three-step test into the 2002 Regulations for the Implementations of Copyright Act, see *Haochen Sun*, id., at 918.

[130] According to Sec. 12 (2) of Regulations Governing Applications for Approval of Compulsory Licensing of Musical Works and Royalties for Use Thereof, royalties = the wholesale price of a sound recording which is scheduled to be published × 5% × the quantity to be published divided by the quantity of the musical work which would be used for the sound recording to be published.

[131] The expression of "copyright piracy on a commercial scale" corresponds to what have been referred to as "professional infringers". See *Daniel Gervais*, The TRIPS Agreement-Drafting History and Analysis, 2nd, ed. 2003, 2.473.

Thirdly, the overly pro-copyright holders regime, by means of criminal sanctions as a response to the challenge of technology, rules out the possibility of a self-engineered balance between right holders, sustainable development of technology and the general public's interest to have access and use of information. This one-sided approach adopted by the Copyright Act has been used to artificially create and protect a new interest, instead of protecting a mature interest commonly accepted in society, and has overstretched the limits of criminal sanctions.

All this has triggered protest and led to a "P2P Action Alliance", which, besides bluntly rebuking the Act as it is, proposes to introduce the so-called "copyright compensation system" for Internet transactions by adding a new article, Sec. 51-1, that would exempt Internet service providers who provide music-casting, and/or uploading, downloading and swapping of music files on the Internet from possible infringement liability, provided that they share with copyright holders a certain percentage of their revenues designated by the Intellectual Property Office. That clearly points out a new alternative of profit-sharing (not one stakeholder takes all the profits by the force of law) through a collective mechanism, on which all stakeholders of copyright law should reflect.

IV. Japan

1. *Introduction*

While the protection of right holders under copyright law has certainly expanded in the last decade, Japan has tried to give the public's interest a proper place as well. Part of the legislative changes mentioned below concern the rights of foreigners that Japan was unwilling to protect prior to 1 January 1995 when TRIPS came into force. One major change concerned legislation on collecting societies, an issue that is dealt with in chapter 3. Where additional rights of rental or lending were introduced, either there are clauses exempting books and printed media therefrom, or the exclusive right of authorising rental and lending was limited to one year from the date of release (phonograms). In addition, the courts have done much to rein in many rights considered excessively broad, e.g. by limiting the (inexhaustible) right of distribution to film works proper, thereby excluding videogames from this provision (see chapter 2). Still, the Japanese legislature and the courts have been fairly generous to right owners in asserting contributory liability (see chapter 6), in neglecting the public-interest angle in copyright contract issues (chapter 5), and in implementing relatively strict rules on the protection of anti-circumvention devices and programs (chapter 4).

2. *Legislative Changes in the last decade*

a) Introduction of 50 years' retroactive protection for performers and phonogram producers and facilitation of damage account on 26 December 1996:[132]

Under the provisions of a U.S.-initiated WTO Dispute Settlement Process, Japan was forced to grant retroactive protection for U.S. "oldies" from 1946.[133]

---

[132] Law No. 117/1996; see *T. Hamaguchi* in 430 Copyright [1997], 26–32.

[133] *K. Okamoto*, 421 Copyright [1996], 17–28; *C. Heath*, All Her Troubles Seemed So Far Away, [1996] EIPR 677–680.

The United States favoured an interpretation of Article 18 (3) Berne Convention that applied the principle of retroactivity.[134] The Japanese side acceded - without losing face - by denying a general obligation to grant retroactive protection on the diplomatic level, while amending the corresponding supplementary provisions (Sec. 2(3); Sec. 15(2)) to the Copyright Act in favour of the U.S. position by a declaration that Japan had to keep pace with the protection level of developed countries.[135] Since this dispute was not the first to question Japanese readiness to meet international copyright obligations, concerns about international reputation may have contributed to the enactment of the amendment.[136] Another amendment enabled judges to request for necessary documentary evidence on the amount of damages for infringement of one party, if requested by the other (Sec. 114-2).[137] Finally, Sec. 55 which had provided a lower level of protection for photographic works in comparison to other works, was abolished to bring Japanese law in conformity with the international tendency towards acknowledgment of full copyright protection for works of photography.[138]

b) First adaptation of the Copyright Act to the World Copyright Treaty (WCT) and Performances and Phonograms Treaty (WPPT)[139] on 18 June 1997:[140]

Authors were provided with the new right of "public transmission" (*kôshû sôshin*), including the right of "making available" their works (Sec. 23). Performers and phonogram producers were granted the isolated right of making their sound recordings available to the public for individual demand (Sec. 92-2 for performers, Sec. 96-2 for phonogram producers). Special consideration was given to computer software, because program works are excluded from the limitation clause according to which the transmission within a Local Area Network (LAN) is not covered by copyright (Sec. 2(1)(vii-2).

c) Restriction of the rights of publication and being named as author in the case of administrative use of works on 7 May 1999. [141]

This was done by special order to enforce the Act on Administrative Publication of Information.[142] If the author offers his yet unpublished work to an administrative

---

134 Article 18 of the Berne Convention, quoted in Article 14 (6) TRIPS, grants retroactive protection in newly acceded countries, this retroactivity being limited by the controversial Section 3. According to the Japanese interpretation, Section 3 grants freedom of choice, whether a member state wants to acknowledge the principle of retroactivity or not. However, the United States and the European Union regard Article 18 (3) as a permission to take only preliminary facilitative measures in favour of the domestic culture industry, which otherwise may be exposed to heavy impairment by sudden retroactivity in case of recent access.

135 "Aktuelle Information" in GRUR Int. 1997, 1036.

136 C. *Heath*, [1996] EIPR 677–680

137 See T. *Hamaguchi* in 430 Copyright [1997], 26–32; "Aktuelle Information" in GRUR Int. 1997, 1036.

138 T. *Hamaguchi* in 430 Copyright [1997], 26–32.

139 Both treaties in 28 IIC 208–223 [1997].

140 Law No. 86/1997; see P. *Ganea* in GRUR Int. 1998, 571–579.

141 Law No. 43/1999.

142 Law No.42/1999.

authority, he is deemed to have given his consent in making it publicly available by this authority (Sec. 18(3)). If considered necessary, the authorities may also abrogate the author's right of being identified as such in the course of administrative publication (Sec. 19 (4)).[143]

d) Second adaptation of the Copyright Act to WCT and WPPT on 23 June 1999:[144]

Authors, performers and phonogram producers were granted the distribution right (literally "right of transfer", Sec. 26-2 for authors, Sec. 95-2 for performers, Sec. 97-2 for phonogram producers). Unlike the existing distribution right (*hanpuken*) of the film producer (Sec. 26), the "right of transfer" is exhausted after first sale domestically or abroad.[145] As a further adaptation to both WIPO treaties, legal measures against circumvention of electronic protection mechanisms and against alteration of rights management information have been introduced (Sec. 2(1)(xx), (xxi)). Whereas the WPPT is limited to the protection of performers and phonogram producers, the Japanese protection against circumvention of technical measures and against manipulation of copyright information is extended to broadcasting enterprises. The offering or making available of circumvention mechanisms and manipulation of copyright information are subject to criminal sanctions (Sec. 120-2).[146] With regard to technical protection measures, not only the Copyright Act but also the Unfair Competition Prevention Act has been amended in 1999 (Sec. 2(1)(x), (xi)).[147] Setting illegal circumvention mechanisms into circulation and providing unauthorised users with legal circumvention mechanisms, originally handed out to a limited circle of users, is seen as unfairly affecting the interests of content providers. A third amendment has been the introduction of the author's right to audio-visually display his work (Sec. 22-2). Finally, Article 14 of the additional provisions to the Copyright Act, which for a term of nearly 30 years "preliminarily" deprived music copyright holders of the right to publicly play their works fixed in phonograms (see Chapter 3), was abolished.

e) New rules on damage calculation and submission of documents, introduction of special fines for infringement by legal persons and adaptation of WCT-provisions related to foreigners:[148]

Courts are not bound by the "normal" licence fees raised by the various collective societies when calculating adequate damages according to a licensing analogy.

---

143 See O. *Kishimoto*, 460 Copyright [1999], 32–35.

144 Law No. 77/1999; comparative table of new and old provisions in English, translated by *T. Doi*, Patents & Licensing 1999, Vol. 29, No. 4, 12–29.

145 O. *Kishimoto*, 461 Copyright [1999], 47–53.

146 *T. Koshida*, 460 Copyright [1999], 24–31.

147 Law No. 33/1999 as of 23 April 1999; see Intellectual Property Office of the Administration for Trade Policy of the Ministry of Industry and Trade, 460 Copyright [1999], 38–40.

148 Law No. 56/2000; comparison of old and new regulation in 469 Copyright [2000], 38–41; see *K. Momii*, 471 Copyright [2000], 19–25.

Instead, the actual circumstances of the case must be taken into consideration, and this may also include damages exceeding the calculated licence fee if the infringement was of severe character (Sec. 114(2), (3)). Courts may also calculate damages at their own discretion if a calculation on grounds of a licensing analogy etc. is not possible (Sec. 114-4). Furthermore, courts are authorised to request the necessary documents containing evidence of infringement. Such a request may only be refused for justified reasons, e.g. if the requested documents contain a business secret (Sec. 114-2). With regard to criminal liability, a fine not exceeding 100 Million Yen has been introduced as a special deterrent in case of infringements that occurred under the supervision of a legal person (Sec. 124(4)(i)). Finally, the principle of reciprocity was adopted with regard to the copyright duration of works from WCT member states.

f) Enactment of the Act on the Business of Administrating Copyrights etc. on 21 November 2000:[149]

The Act on the Business of Administrating Copyrights etc. replaces the Act on Intermediary Business of 1939. The new law aims at deregulation in the field of collective administration. Accordingly, official admission is no longer required for the establishment of a new collecting society and for the remuneration standards, but instead only a formal registration with the director of the cultural agency. Only collective societies that dominate a certain field of rights administration are still under special supervision of the cultural agency to avoid abuse of monopolistic marketing power. With regard to the relationship between collective society and author, the individual right owner has the choice between entrustment to fiduciary right administration, which requires right transfer to the collective society, or "entrustment in a narrower sense", which means that the author designates a certain society to exercise his copyright.

g) Introduction of moral rights for performers, internet transmission right for broadcasting enterprises and other amendments on 19 June 2002:[150]

With the introduction of the special moral rights to performers to be named in connection with their performances (Sec. 90-2) and to preserve the integrity of the performance (Sec. 90-3), Japan has brought its copyright law into full compliance with the requirements of the WPPT as the first international convention which in its Art. 5 provides for performer's moral rights. The right in preserving the integrity of the performance is weaker than the corresponding author's right. It cannot be broadly exercised against distortions "against the will" of the performer, but only against distortions which may cause damage to his reputation. Distortions deemed customary in light of the nature of the work and manner of exploitation would thus be permissible. The moral rights of performers are

---

[149] Law No. 131/2000, see *T. Gôji*, 477 Copyright [2001], 26–41 & 478 Copyright [2001], 22–37.

[150] Law No. 72/2002; see the explanations of the Copyright Department, 496 Copyright [2002], 26–39.

inalienable (Sec. 101-2) With regard to the treatment of moral rights after the performer's death, the principle of *droit moral perpetuel* has been adopted (Sec. 101-3), which also applies to the author's moral rights (Sec. 60). Since the Japanese neighbouring rights provisions now fully comply with the WIPO requirements, the protection of performers and phonogram producers under the Copyright Act has been extended to performances which have taken place or which have been first recorded in a member state to the WPPT (Sec. 7), and to phonograms the rights to which belong to a resident of a member state to the WPPT or which have been first recorded in a member state to the WPPT (Sec. 8). With regard to the so-called secondary right of the neighbouring right holder to receive remuneration for the communication to the public or broadcast of his sound performance or phonogram—Art. 15 (3) WPPT allows member states to make a reservation that they would not grant such rights—Japan has adopted the principle of reciprocity (Secs. 95, 97). As a further amendment, broadcasting enterprises have been granted the right to make their broadcast publicly available for individual access (internet availability—Sec. 99-2 with regard to wireless broadcasting enterprises; Sec. 100-4 with regard to cable broadcasting enterprises). Finally, in Sec. 101 the date from which the protection term for phonograms (50 years) is counted has been changed from the date of first fixation to the date of first publication (i.e. the date at which a sufficient number of reproductions to satisfy the demand has been made commercially available—Sec. 4-2).[151] Only in cases where the phonogram is not published within 50 years from first fixation will the protection term be counted from the date of first fixation.

3. *Jurisprudence*

Japanese court decisions show a relatively balanced pattern in the last couple of years. Even more than the legislature, the courts have tried to balance rights of copyright owners with legitimate interests of users and the public in general.

a) Affirming responsibility of Karaoke bar owners, lessors of Karaoke machines and internet service providers for copyright infringements.

The issue is further explained in chapter 6 and basically involves a string of cases between 1986 and 2003 that has tightened the screws for those assisting others in infringing copyrights. In the first case, owners of karaoke bars were held liable for copyright infringement by the performance of their guests[152]. A subsequent decision extended liability to the lessors of karaoke equipment unless these at the time of concluding the lease agreement had made sure that the karaoke bar owner had obtained proper permission from the collecting society[153]. Finally, the Tokyo District Court affirmed liability for internet service providers providing software

---

[151] Rule 8 of the Supplementary Provisions to the amendment, however, excludes phonogram protection, the term of which has already expired under the old provisions, from revival.

[152] Supreme Court, 15 March 1988, 663 Hanrei Times 95—"Cat's Eye".

[153] Supreme Court, 2 March 2001, 15 L & T 69—"Karaoke Snack Bar III".

for the peer-to-peer exchange of copyrighted works and making a profit from advertisements run on the server platform[154].

b) Balancing exhaustion rules.

Back in 1994, the Tokyo District Court had held that copies lawfully circulated abroad could be imported unless the copyright owner could exercise additional (non-exhaustible) rights such as the distribution right for film works[155]. This was subsequently confirmed by the introduction of Sec. 26bis (2) (iv) Copyright Act. The additional right for film works, however, was denied for video games not intended for public display in cinemas[156]. Attempts to exercise copyright beyond exhaustion have not been viewed favourably by the Japanese Fair Trade Commission[157].

c) Broadening moral rights.

An increasing number of lawsuits seem to be raised in connection with alleged infringements of the author's moral rights. An interesting landmark decision was rendered by the Supreme Court in 2001. The case concerned the sale of memory cards for a video game, the aim of which was for the main male character to win the love of his high school sweetheart and make her propose to him at the graduation ceremony. In the course of the game, the main character had to choose how to dedicate his time in order to achieve this goal: Train in a gym, learn more maths, or improve his social skills. The "turbo" memory card endowed the main character already at the beginning with such an array of talents that achieving the goal of the game became child's play. The Supreme Court held that such alteration via the memory card was an infringement of the right of integrity, as the whole gist of the game was altered[158].

d) Strengthening effective enforcement.

The nadir of unsatisfactory enforcement of copyrights was finally crossed with the landmark decision "Wall Street Journal" that concerned the translation and re-publication of new items from The Wall Street Journal by a new subscription-based service[159]. Prior to this decision, it was widely assumed that interim relief against unauthorised translations could only be obtained for existing works rather than (as in the case of a newspaper) for works that would only be created in the future.

154 Tokyo District Court, interim orders of 9 April 2002, 11 April 2002. Main action, Decision of 29 January 2003, 35 IIC 354 [2004] – "File Rogue".

155 Tokyo District Court, 1 July 1994, 27 IIC 570, 571 [1996]—"Beauty and the Beast".

156 Supreme Court, 25 April 2002, 35 IIC 467 [2004]—"Second-Hand Computer Games".

157 E.g. FTC, 15 December 1983, 389 Kôsei Torihiki 34—"Nihon Record".

158 Supreme Court, 13 February 2001, 1422 Hanrei Jihô 78 = GRUR Int. 2002, 256; also *T. Ueno*, Memory card no shiyô to chosakusha no dôitsusei hojiken shingai tô (Use of a memory card and infringement of the author's right of integrity), 125 Minshōhō Zasshi 6 (2002), 739.

159 Supreme Court, 8 June 1995, 30 IIC 223 [1999]—"The Wall Street Journal II/III".

In the last couple of years, cases of copyright infringement have been decided in first instance within one year, and judicial competence has significantly improved[160].

V. Korea

Korea is the world's leader in broadband penetration, and its citizens are among the most Internet-savvy people in the world. Korea's society and economy continue to embrace the internet at lightning speed. More than 26 million Koreans—some 59% of the total population—regularly access the Internet. Furthermore, broadband access is now enjoyed by over 70% of Korean households, more than 10 million in all.[161]

Unfortunately, Korea is not leading the way as an online marketplace for materials protected by copyright. Despite the 2003 Copyright Amendment, big gaps remain, especially in legal tools for fighting online music piracy, treatment of temporary copies and circumvention of technical protection measures. [162]

For the protection of copyrights in the internet age, WIPO convened a diplomatic conference in Geneva and produced the WIPO Copyright Treaty (WCT) and the WIPO Performances and Phonograms Treaty (WPPT) in 1996. The new major features of the WCT included, Right of Communication to the Public, Obligations concerning Technological Measures, and Obligations concerning Rights Management Information. Korea has been implementing these features of the WCT in its Korean Copyright Act (KCA) and Computer Program Protection Act (CCPA), sometimes voluntarily whilst at other times under pressure from the United States—even before the ratification of the treaty. Last September, the Korean Government decided to ratify the WCT in the near future.

In 2000, the KCA was amended to expand its coverage of the author's right of transmission. The goals of such amendments concern the activities of server and network connections and of transmission. The KCA defines the concept of transmission.[163] Also, Section 18–2 of the KCA provides that "(t)he author shall have the exclusive right to transmit this work". Besides this, and in order to comply with the WIPO Performances and Phonograms Treaty, a right of transmission was also granted to performers and phonogram producers in 2004. Indeed, it seems logical to expand the right of transmission of authors/ performers and phonogram producers already to the stage of transmission.

However, the rights of users of copyrighted works should not be ignored in the digital environment. The interests of copyright holders and users of copyrighted works need to be properly balanced. Recent copyright legislations throughout the

---

[160] *Jizuka/Heath/Komada*, The Enforcement of Copyrights, in: *Ganea/Heath/Saito*, Japanese Copyright Law, Kluwer Law International 2005, 105–129.

[161] See http://www.iipa.com/rbc/2004/2004SPEC301KOREA.pdf.

[162] Considering the current situation of US concerns over Korean protection of copyrights, enactment of temporary copies and access control in Copyright Act and Computer Program Protection Act might be crucial controversies between the two countries. See Park, *Deokyoung*, A Study on Korean Implementation of WIPO Copyright Treaty, Vol. 14 Journal of Industrial Property Law 225–247 (2003).

[163] Copyright Act, Section 2, No. 7–2.

world, in particular, DMCA and European Copyright Directive, tend to strengthen, or expand the exclusive rights of copyright owners. It is understandable that copyright holders should be able to keep their share of the copyright pie in the face of new technologies. Nonetheless, stronger protection of copyright is not always the right answer as it may result in unfairly diminished public access to copyrighted materials. Therefore, the most important issue in the digital economy is to achieve a balance between the interests of copyright holders and users of copyrighted works. At present, the fair use doctrine, in particular, is a hotbed of debates because the Korean copyright system is considering the adoption of the US fair use doctrine into both the KCA and the CPPA. It should be noted that the scope of copyright limitations is wider in the United States than in Korea, and that the United States may apply copyright limitations flexibly on a case by case basis, even to unexpected situations such as internet.[164]

VI. Singapore

1. Introduction

The history of copyright *is* about expansion. The first copyright enactment of the world—the British Statute of Anne 1710—protected only published books and other writings against unauthorised printing and for a period of twenty-one years. By the time the TRIPS Agreement was concluded 285 years later, the international consensus was that copyright protection should be granted to various types of subject-matter including computer programs against a whole range of unauthorised acts such as broadcasting and for a minimum term of 'life+50'. This expansion has been justified on the basis that it is necessary to take into account technological advancements which whittle away the copyright owner's ability to control the distribution and exploitation of his work, and ultimately, the incentive for creation.

Ironically, in the last decade, which experienced an unprecedented explosion in technology, this justification seemed to have lost some lustre. The higher standard of protection set out in the 1996 WIPO Copyright Treaty (WCT) and the WIPO Performances and Phonograms Treaty (WPPT) to address the challenges thrown up by digital technology, including the introduction of provisions on anti-circumvention measures, has not yet become an international norm.[165] This has prompted some countries to lobby for higher levels of protection in bilateral trade agreements. Critics of this move argue that it is a deliberate ploy by the developed nations to shift the discussion out of the international forum in order to deprive

---

[164] *Dae-Hee Lee*, Comparative Analysis of Software Copyright Limitation in the US and Korea, Vol. 2 No.1 Journal of Digital Property Law 200–201 (2002).

[165] As of early 2004, only 46 and 43 states have become member to the WCT and the WPPT respectively. Note, though, *Ficsor and Schlesinger*, WIPO Treaties Implementation Globally: The Key Issues, a paper presented at the Fordham University School of Law's 12th Annual Conference on International IP Law and Policy (15 April 2004), where the authors estimated that, as of April 2004, at least 64 countries/territories (including non-WCT/WPPT members) have enacted legislation which attempts partial or full implementation of the WCT and WPPT.

the developing nations of the benefit of the unity of voice they enjoy; the US, in particular, has been criticised for being 'the principal architect of the global regulatory ratchet for intellectual property',[166] a ratchet which only travels in one direction—upwards. The people who harbour some discomfort about the perceived relentless copyright expansion are not limited to those in the developing countries. In fact, the most severe critics of the US copyright regime are probably her own citizens, some of whom have gone so far as to challenge the constitutionality of their Digital Millennium Copyright Act (DMCA),[167] which implements the 1996 WIPO treaties, and the Sonny Bono Copyright Term Extension Act.[168] Stanford professor Lawrence Lessig is advocating a re-think of the role of copyright in the Information Society when he said in his latest book, *Free Culture: How Big Media Uses Technology and the Law to Lock Down Culture and Control Creativity*:[169]

> "My point is not that we should abolish copyright or go back to the eighteenth century [the Statute of Anne and the early days of copyright]. That would be a total mistake, disastrous for the most important creative enterprises within our culture society. But there is a space between zero and one, Internet culture notwithstanding. And these massive shifts in the effective power of copyright regulation, tied to the increased concentration of the content industry and resting in the hands of technology that will increasingly enable control over the use of the culture, should drive us to consider whether another adjustment is called for. Not an adjustment that increases copyright's power. Not an adjustment that increases its term. Rather, an adjustment to restore the balance that has traditionally defined copyright's regulation—a weakening of that regulation, to strengthen creativity."

Therefore, the question which was raised at this conference was certainly not one which concerns only the developing countries, the 'have-not's in the 'digital divide' between the developing and developed countries.

2. *Singapore's response*

Although Singapore is a developing country and a net importer of copyright works, she has embraced the horizontal and vertical expansion of copyright in the last decade. It should be noted, though, that her economy is that of a 'more advanced developing country'[170] who has been aggressively promoting the use of technology amongst her people and businesses;[171] in particular, her Government has a vision for the ICT industry (comprising the communication, information technology and media sectors) to grow from the 7% it had contributed to the country's GDP

---

166 *Drahos*, Expanding Intellectual Property's Empire: The Role of FTAs, at p 7, available at the website of the Genetics Resources Action International (GRAIN) at http://www.grain.org/publications/tripsplus.cfm.

167 Eg. *University City Studios Inc v Eric Coley* 273 F.3d 429; Felton v RIAA [01-CV-2669 (GEB)].

168 *Eldred v Ashcroft* 239 F.3d 372, affirmed. The failure to overturn the Sonny Bono Copyright Term Extension Act has given rise to efforts to lobby for the Public Domain Enhancement Act at http://eldred.cc/.

169 2004, The Penguin Press, at 169.

170 This is the classification made by the Organization for Economic Co-operation and Development (OECD).

171 In The Economist's 2004 survey on e-readiness ranking by its Economic Intelligence Unit, Singapore was ranked 7th out of 64 countries, and the 1st in Asia.

in 2000 (S$26 billion in terms of revenue) to 10% by 2012.[172] Thus, her favourable response to strong copyright protection should be understood in that light, and it also perhaps explains why she agreed to the TRIPS-plus protection for copyright in her Free Trade Agreement (FTA) concluded with the US in 2003.[173]

Even before 2003, Singapore had taken some steps to ensure that her copyright law kept in pace with technological advancements. In 1999, she amended her Copyright Act, which was passed in 1987, to "address various issues arising from the use of copyright material in the digital environment".[174] The speech made by the Minister of Law when he introduced these amendments in Parliament provides an insight to the thought process of the policy makers:

> "The proposed amendments address the more urgent needs of copyright owners and users of copyright materials in the on-line environment. The amendments will improve copyright protection and enforcement measures for copyright owners in cyberspace, thereby promoting the use of the Internet by businesses. They will also promote greater legal certainty for both copyright owners and users of copyright works, as well as intermediaries such as network service providers, concerning the application of copyright protection in the digital environment.
>
> In formulating these proposals, the Committee considered various international models, including the 1996 World Intellectual Property Organisation Copyright Treaty and the 1996 World Intellectual Property Organisation Performances and Phonograms Treaty."

The following is a summary of the significant changes brought about by the 1999 amendments:

— Copyright protection for databases was clarified. Singapore does not have a *sui generis* database right. Up till the amendments, there was some doubt as to the extent to which databases would be protected in Singapore as original literary works.[175] The amendment refined the definition of 'literary works' in the Copyright Act to specify that it includes a 'compilation in any form' which can be a compilation of data other than copyright materials (authors' works, sound recordings, cinematographic films, published edition of an author's work, television/sound broadcast, cable programme and a recording of a performance) which 'by reason of the selection or arrangement of its contents, constitutes an intellectual creation'.[176] The Minister of Law, when he introduced this amendment in Parliament, specifically said that this amendment was to extend copyright protection to compilations such as multimedia works. The amendment further explained that the nature of the copyright subsisting in the compilation is in addition to, and independent of any right subsisting in the material or data contained in the

---

172 See the 2002 report made by the ICT Working Group in the Economic Review Committee available at the website of the Ministry of Trade and Industry at www.mti.gov.sg.

173 The US-Singapore FTA, signed by the heads of state of the two countries on 6 May 2003, is available at the website of the US Trade Representative Office: http://www.ustr.gov/new/fta/Singapore/final.htm.

174 See the Explanatory Statement to the Bill of the Copyright (Amendment) Act 1999.

175 For a pre-1999 overview of this issue in Singapore, see *Ng-Loy*, Copyright Protection for Traditional Compilations of Facts and Computerized Databases – Is Sweat Copyrightable? [1995] Singapore Journal of Legal Studies 96.

176 See Sec. 7A(1) and (3) of the Copyright Act.

compilation.[177] This amendment implements Art 5 of the WCT, which is really a re-statement of Art 10(2) of the TRIPS Agreement.

— The reproduction right, in relation to authors' works, now expressly includes storage of the work on 'any medium by electronic means' as well as 'the making of a copy which is transient or incidental to some other use of the work'.[178] This clarification, in essence, reflects the WCT's understanding of the ambit of the reproduction right guaranteed by the Berne Convention.[179]

— The introduction of a 'user caching' defence permitting the making of a transient or electronic copy of a copyright material in the user's computer from an electronic copy of the material made available on a network [which falls within the reproduction right (see above)] if the making of first-mentioned copy is required for the viewing, listening or utilisation of the material by a user of this or another network.[180] Browsing through the Internet, therefore, is clearly not an infringing act in Singapore; there is no need to rely on any doctrine of implied consent.

— The introduction of civil remedies to protect Rights Management Information, implementing in part Art 12 of the WCT. This will be discussed further in Part 4 of this report.

— The exemption of network service providers (NSP) from copyright liability in two specific situations: (1) where the NSP acts to enable access;[181] (2) where the NSP acts at the direction of another.[182] This will be discussed further in Part 6 of this report.

The copyright law of Singapore, as it now stands, has already taken into account much of the technology-related essence of the WCT, with the notable exceptions of Art 8 on the right of communication to the public and Art 11 on prohibiting anti-circumvention measures.[183] This will change very shortly. Under the US-Singapore FTA, Singapore has to introduce the right of communication to the public as well as

---

[177] See Sec. 7A(2) of the Copyright Act.

[178] See Secs. 17 and 15(1A) of the Singapore Copyright Act. Similar provisions were inserted for entrepreneurial works and performances: see s 81(2) and s 252(1B) respectively.

[179] See the Agreed Statement to Art 1(4) of the WCT, and generally, *Reinbothe & von Lewinski*, The WIPO Treaties 1996 – Commentary and Legal Analysis (2002) at pp 37–44.

[180] See Sec. 193E of the Copyright Act. This 'user caching' defence, according to the International Intellectual Property Alliance in their 2000 Special 301 Report on Singapore, contravenes Art 9(2) of the TRIPS Agreement as it gives a blanket exemption from copyright liability, including the user who accesses a pirated copy of copyright works knowing that it is a pirated copy. Is this criticism justified? The surfer on the Internet cannot stop caching – i.e. reproduction of the work in his computer – occurring. If he should be made liable for copyright infringement once he knows that the material on the webpage is an infringing copy, it is tantamount to arguing for a case that a person reading a hard copy of a book knowing that it is pirated copy should be liable for copyright infringement.

[181] See Sec. 193B Copyright Act.

[182] See Sec. 193C Copyright Act.

[183] The other technology-related provision in WCT is Art 4 on computer programs. This exists in the TRIPS Agreement in Art. 10.1 and Singapore's Copyright Act already protected computer programs as literary works from its inception in 1987.

anti-circumvention provisions. This will be discussed in greater detail in Parts 2 and 4 of this report respectively.

This FTA has come under fire in some quarters. For example, the Electronic Frontier Foundation has criticised the US Government for using FTAs to 'effect the global entrenchment of overly restrictive copyright law'[184] and has even put up on its website an article giving 7 recommendations to countries (e.g. Singapore) on how to structure anti-circumvention provisions so as to avoid the pitfalls of the DMCA.[185] From Singapore Government's perspective, however, it would seem that its agreement to more expansive copyright protection in the FTA is not inconsistent with its own agenda. This is evident from the concluding remarks made by the Minister for Law during the 1999 copyright amendments:

> "Sir, in closing, let me say that this [1999 Amendment] Bill reinforces Singapore's commitment to provide a strong intellectual property rights regime to encourage the growth of a knowledge-based or information economy and to promote e-commerce and creative innovation. As technologies are ever evolving and as new issues surface as a result of the constantly changing environment, I must say that *this Bill is by no means the last word on the subject. We will continue to monitor international developments and we may have to propose further refinements to our copyright regime to cope with the technological developments as and when the need arises*. We are committed to ensuring that our copyright law will be responsive to the changing needs of industries and we will continue to evolve to take into account new developments. [Emphasis added]"

Nevertheless, some will argue that this does not explain why Singapore has agreed, under the FTA, to obligations which have little to do with technology, such as the obligations to extend the copyright term by an extra 20 years[186] and the use of criminal penalties to enforce copyright, for example, to deal with 'wilful copyright or related rights piracy on a commercial scale' including "(i) significant wilful infringements of copyright or related rights that have no direct or indirect motivation of financial gains, as well as (ii) wilful infringement for purposes of commercial advantage or financial gains".[187] An example of targets falling into this category would be corporate end users of pirated or unlicensed software. Currently, such activity only constitutes a civil infringement.

The substantive changes to the copyright regime to implement the obligations under the FTA—other than the one related to term extension[188]—have been in

---

[184] See http://www.eff.net/IP/FTAA/.

[185] Getting the Balance Right: Seven Lessons from a Comparison of the Technological Protection Measure Provisions of the FTAA, the DMCA, and the US-Singapore and US-Chile Free Trade Agreements, at http://www.eff.org/IP/FTAA/tpm_implementation.php.

[186] This extension applies to authors' works (including photographic works), cinematographic works, phonograms and performances: see Art 16.1.4 of the US-Singapore FTA. For the US position, see the US Sonny Bono Copyright Term Extension Act, above, note 4. For the EU position, see the Council Directive 93/98/EEC (29 October 1993) [where the 20-year copyright term extension is not as expansive; for example; it does not apply to phonograms and performances].

[187] Art 16.9.21.

[188] Deadline for implementation of this particular obligation: 1 July 2004. This will be done via the Intellectual Property (Miscellaneous Amendments) Act. The Bill to this Act, at the time of writing this report in mid-April 2004, has not been put before the Parliament but it is available at www.newiplaws.org.sg.

place since 1 January 2005 in accordance with the dream and hope articulated by the Senior Minister of State for Law in 2002:[189]

> "As a nation, we need to make the transition from a mentality of mere IP users to that of IP owners, to eventually even become net exporters of IP."

VII. Malaysia

The current copyright law in Malaysia is the Copyright Act 1987 (henceforth called 'the Act'). In tabling this law to replace the older Copyright Act 1969, one of the main aims was to 'make better provisions in the law relating to copyright'.[190] This trend of making the copyright laws 'better' follows the increasing demands placed on expanding the role and scope of copyright. When the Act was introduced, one significant change was that computer programs were recognised for the first time in Malaysia as literary works. Indeed, it seems that in the subsequent years the information and communications technology (ICT) industry has had the biggest role in further expanding the scope of copyright. In Malaysia this was most obvious with the launch of the Multimedia Super Corridor (MSC) in 1996.

Apart from the infrastructural and technological demands of the MSC, it also sought an advanced framework of laws to meet modern day needs and attract foreign investors. This resulted in the 'Cyberlaws', a set of legislation that effected changes in the area of computer crimes, digital signatures, communications, telemedicine and copyright. Where copyright was concerned, according to Khaw, the issues and concerns at the time were:

> "As copyright law in the country already existed in the form of the Copyright Act 1987, all that was required was to identify the needs of the information technology and multimedia industries with respect to content and other related issues, and amend the law, wherever necessary. These included issues relating to the status of multimedia works, that is, interactive products or services that combine a variety of works, such as text, photographs, animation, narration, video, music and computer software, into a single work in digital format; the scope of protection in the network and online environment; the legal protection of electronic databases; copyright clearance; and the liability of online and service providers."[191]

The MSC, together with other international developments at the time,[192] brought about the Copyright (Amendment) Act 1997 that introduced, among other things, several new provisions specifically related to the new electronic network environment. The main changes were the introduction of a 'communication to the public' right designed to cover transmissions via the Internet, and the prohibition of anti-circumvention activities and activities to remove electronic

---

189 Speech made at the launch of the IP-CEP (Creation-Exploitation-Protection) Programme for local enterprises on 8 November 2002 available at the website of the Intellectual Property Office of Singapore: www.ipos.gov.sg.

190 From the Explanatory Statement to the Act.

191 *Khaw LT*, Copyright Law in Malaysia 2nd Ed (Kuala Lumpur, Malayan Law Journal, 2001) at pp. 9–10.

192 Most notably the WIPO Copyright Treaty (WCT) and the WIPO Performances and Phonograms Treaty (WPPT).

rights management information (discussed in greater detail below). The protection for electronic databases came later in the year 2000 as a result of amendments made to comply with TRIPS. Electronic databases are protected as derivative works under the category of 'collections of mere data whether in machine readable or other form, eligible for copyright, which by reason of the selection and arrangement of their contents, constitute intellectual creation'.[193] However, the requirements imply that some skill and effort must be expended in selecting and arranging the contents of the database in order to make it an object of 'intellectual creation'.

Of course, not all changes in the Malaysian copyright law were ICT-related. In 1996, the Act was amended to remove copyright protection for works which are registered as industrial designs. This coincided with the promulgation of the Industrial Designs Act 1996, wherein a separate regime was created to protect industrial designs and henceforth there was no need to protect such designs under copyright. In the same year also, a new part[194] was introduced into the Act which enabled matters relating to copyright collective societies and their licensing schemes to be referred to the Copyright Tribunal in the event of a dispute. In 2000, performers were given rights to control their live performances and prevent unauthorised recordings ('bootlegs') of the same and the provisions on border measures were tidied up to comply with the Agreement on Trade-Related Aspects of Intellectual Property Rights (TRIPS Agreement).

In summary, copyright owners enjoy more rights today than when the Act first came into force. The last few rounds of amendments have broadened the rights of copyright owners, created new categories of infringement, and given protection to a new class of persons. However, many of these changes have not been the result of local social pressure or in response to local conditions, but have instead been the influence of foreign policy and instruments such as the TRIPS Agreement, WCT and WPPT. In that sense the development of copyright law in Malaysia has been guided more by external factors than domestic ones.

VIII. Thailand

Internationally, Thailand is featured regularly when discussions of intellectual property protection arise, due to the country's long-perceived image as an IP pirate's haven. Nevertheless, there have been many recent changes to the Thai IP landscape and Thailand is no longer the IP pirate's haven it once was. In the past, the problem had seemed insurmountable. Over the years, Thailand has been subject to constant pressure from those industrialised nations (whose intellectual property rights had been badly infringed) to take pro- active steps to deal with the problem and she has responded positively to this pressure. Since the early 1990s, successions of Thai administrations have incorporated intellectual property protection into their policies and most of them have actually increased the level of enforcement of the related laws. From the legislative point of view, in the past

[193] Copyright Act 1987, s. 8(1)(b).
[194] Part IVA.

decade, Thailand has overhauled many of its IP-related laws to comply with TRIPS, resulting in the imposition of internationally accepted standards by most of her laws—many of the existing laws were revised and several new laws were enacted. As a result, in respect of IP protection, Thailand at least appears to do much better than it once did.

Since Thailand enacted the Copyright Act of 1994, no new copyright concepts have been given legislative credence in Thailand. However, the law is now going through an amendment process.

In my opinion, there is no such thing as over-protection, and there are no imbalances in the framework of copyright law. Anything worth copying is worth protecting.

IX. The Philippines

The Philippines can look back to more than a century of copyright protection. In the early years, copyright protection was justified on the basis of protecting the author's individual property rights. The concept that copyright bears a social function, i.e., an instrument to diffuse knowledge and information for the common good, appears to be of fairly recent origin in the Philippines.

As early as 1914, the Philippine Supreme Court justified copyright protection under a legal doctrine that generally favours authors:

> "Nobody may reproduce another person's work without the owner's consent, even merely to annotate or add anything to it, or improve any edition thereof". [195]

This doctrine is found in Section 7 of the Spanish Law on Intellectual Property of January 10, 1879 that was extended to the Philippines by royal decree on 5 May 1887.[196] In the case titled Laktaw vs, Paglinawan,[197] the plaintiff was the author of a literary work entitled Diccionario Hispano-Tagalog (Spanish-Tagalog Dictionary), published in Manila in 1889. The defendant, without the consent of the plaintiff, reproduced a greater part of plaintiff's literary work and published the same in defendant's literary work entitled Diccionariong Kastila-Tagalog (Spanish-Tagalog Dictionary). In support of its decision, the Court cited Manresa's commentary on the right to intellectual properties:

> "He who writes a book, or carves a statue, or makes an invention, has the absolute right to reproduce or sell it, just as the owner of land has the absolute right to sell it or its fruits. But while the owner of land, by selling it and its fruits, perhaps fully realizes all its economic value, by receiving its benefits and utilities, which are represented, for example, by the price, on the other hand the author of a book, statue or invention, does not reap all the benefits and advantages of this *own property* by disposing of it, for the most important form of realizing the economic advantages of a book, statue or invention, consists in the right to re-produce it in similar or like copies, everyone of which serves to give the person reproducing them all the conditions which the original requires in order to give the author the full enjoyment thereof. If the author of a book, after its publication, cannot prevent its reproduction by any person who may want to reproduce it, then the property right granted him is reduced to a very insignificant thing and the effort made in the production of the book is in no way rewarded."

---

195 *Laktaw v Paglinawan*, 44 Phil 855 (1918).
196 Ibid.
197 Ibid.

The United States copyright law superseded the Spanish Law on Intellectual Property when the sovereignty of Spain over the Philippine Islands was suspended under the Treaty of Paris of 10 December 1898[198]. It was not until 6 March 1924 that a Philippine legislature enacted a copyright law known as "An Act to Protect Intellectual Property"[199] ("Act"). The Act imported substantial portions of the United States law. Under the Act, an author may secure copyright protection only after he registers his copyright claims[200]. The rule was reiterated in an administrative order issued by the then Philippine Patent Office requiring registration of intellectual creations.[201]

In the 1964 case *Santos v. McCullough*[202], a well-known local artist Mauro Malang Santos lost his right to sue for damages when he failed to register and deposit his artistic design for a Christmas card. It is interesting to note that when the Santos case was decided, the Philippines had already acceded to the Berne Convention for the Protection of Literary and Artistic Works[203] on 1 August 1951 ("Berne Convention"). Among the rights granted under the Berne Convention is that the enjoyment and exercise of copyright shall not be subject to any formality.[204] In view of the Philippines' earlier accession to the Berne Convention, the decision in the Santos case has been criticised for disregarding the no-formality rule laid down under the Berne Convention.

The Santos case may have been clarified only in 1972 when the "Decree On Intellectual Property" (PD 49) became the governing law on copyright. PD 49 was an attempt to conform our copyright laws to that of the Berne Convention. PD 49 expressly states that copyright shall subsist from the moment of creation. The statute clarifies that copyright protection is not subject to registration:

> "The rights granted by this Decree shall, from the moment of creation, subsist with respect to any of the following classes of works..."[205].

However, for certain specific classes of work[206], registration and deposit are still required before a party can recover damages in an infringement suit. PD 49 extended copyright protection to works guaranteed under the Berne Convention[207] and new classes of works were introduced that included "computer programs."[208]

The express inclusion of computer programs as a protected class of work is an interesting development. The government, as early as 1972, recognised the need to protect computer programs for the purpose of stimulating "scientific research and invention". While a separate class was designated for computer programs, it is considered a "literary work."

---

198 Ibid.
199 Act No. 3134 (1924).
200 Ibid. Section 11.
201 Philippine Patent Office AO No. 3 (1947) paragraph 33.
202 12 SCRA 321 (1964).
203 Brussels Revision (1848).
204 Berne Convention, Article 4(2).
205 PD 49 Section 2.
206 PD 49 Section 26.
207 Berne Convention Section 2(I).
208 PD 49 Section 2(N).

The explanatory notes of PD 49 introduced the idea that while copyright law is necessary to protect an author's right, it also bears a social function that should not be overlooked:

> "Whereas, tremendous strides in science and technology have made necessary the updating of the Copyright Law to give fuller protection to intellectual property and to encourage arts and letters, *as well as stimulate scientific research and invention, at the same time, safeguard the public's right to cultural information*; . . ."[209] (author's emphasis)

While PD 49 reaffirms the need to protect an author's right, it also took into account the economic and social benefits that should accrue to society: the stimulation of scientific research and innovation and safeguarding of the public's right to cultural information.

The law effectively attempts to strike a balance between the author's right over his work and the benefits that may be derived from the same work by society. This is consistent with the view taken by an authority in Civil Law in the Philippines:

> ". . . The social interest in copyright lies in the adjustment of two objectives: the encouraging of individuals to intellectual labor by assuring them of just rewards, and by securing to society of the largest benefits of their products. The history of the concept reflects our progress in the mechanical communications, our ideas of property and the functions of the state, and our changing social ethics (Copyright Encyclopaedia of Social Studies, Vol. 4, p. 401)."[210]

The government may have had this in mind when Presidential Decree 285 was issued in 1973. When the price of foreign and local textbooks became exhorbitant, PD 285 authorised compulsory licensing for publishing houses to reprint them for classroom use, subject to the payment of royalties. While PD 285 constitutes a limitation on the right of copyright owners to dictate the market price of these textbooks, it served a social purpose to make textbooks affordable and readily available for classroom use.

The social function concept for copyright was again reiterated when the country adopted a new Constitution in 1986. The new Constitution provides:

> "The State shall protect and secure the exclusive rights of scientists, inventors, artists, and other gifted citizens to their intellectual property creations, *particularly when beneficial to the people*, for such period as may be provided by law."[211] (author's emphasis).

Pressure to revisit our Copyright laws came in 1994 when the Philippines acceded to the General Agreement on Tariff and Trade (GATT) and its accompanying Agreement on Trade Related Aspects of Intellectual Property Rights (TRIPS). It led to a revision of the country's intellectual property laws including PD 49. Thus, on 1 January 1998, the Intellectual Property Code[212] (IP Code) took effect superseding the various laws on patents, trademarks and copyright. Part IV of the IP Code pertains to the Law on Copyright.

---

209 PD 49 Explanatory Note paragraph 1.

210 *Arturo Tolentino*, Commentaries and Jurisprudence on the Civil Code of the Philippines (1987), Vol. 2 p. 482

211 1987 Constitution Article XIV Section 13.

212 Republic Act 8293.

The IP Code was even more explicit in stating the policy behind protecting intellectual property in general. The IP Code provides:

"The State recognises that an effective intellectual and industrial property system is vital to the development of domestic and creative activity, facilitates transfer of technology, attracts foreign investments, and secures market access for our products. It shall protect and secure the exclusive rights of scientists, inventors, artists and other gifted citizens to their intellectual property and creations, *particularly when beneficial to the people*, for such periods as provided in this Act…

"*The use of intellectual property bears a social function. To this end, the Sate shall promote the diffusion of knowledge and information for the promotion of national development and progress and the common good. …*"(author's emphasis)

While the IP Code does not define copyright, it enumerates the exclusive rights vested in a copyright holder.[213] It has removed the PD 49 formality pre -requisites to recovery of damages in a copyright infringement suit. The Code still protects the economic interests of authors, giving them the right to exploit their works and to control unauthorised usage.[214] In this regard, "rental rights" includes rental of the original or a copy of an audiovisual or cinematographic work, a work embodied in a sound recording, a computer program, a compilation of data and other materials or a musical work in graphic form, irrespective of the ownership of the original or the copy which is the subject of the rental.[215]

It also protects the so-called "moral rights", which enable authors to be identified with their works and to object to certain kinds of derogatory treatment of their works.[216]

The works that can be the subject of copyright protection could be in the form of original literary, scientific, scholarly or artistic works; sound recordings, films, broadcasts or cable programs, derivative works and typographical arrangements.[217] "Derivative works" includes collections of literary, scholarly or artistic works, and compilations of data and other materials which are original by reason of the selection or coordination or arrangement of their contents.[218]

In addition to the protection of the traditional meaning of "authors", persons associated with the exploitation, dissemination, or productions of work are also protected by "neighbouring rights" under the IP Code. They include publishers, producers, performers and broadcasters.[219]

It should be noted that the granting of exclusive rights to copyright holders does not give them complete and unbridled control over their works. For instance, copyright is not a perpetual right but shall subsist for a limited period of the lifetime of the author and fifty (50) years after his death[220] and the fair use provision in the IP Code provides a limitation on copyright ownership.[221]

---

213 IP Code Section 177.
214 Ibid.
215 Ibid. Section 177.4
216 Ibid. Section 193.
217 Ibid. Sections 172 and 173
218 Ibid. Section 173.
219 Ibid. Chapters XII XIII and XIV.
220 Ibid. Section 213.
221 Ibid. Section 185.

Decompilation of a computer program is considered fair use. Under the fair use doctrine, a copyrighted work may be reproduced or copied without prior permission from the authors or creators when used for the following purposes: (i) research or private study; (ii) criticism or review; and (iii) reporting current events.[222] Further, the IP Code has excluded the following from the ambit of copyright: idea, procedure, method, operation, principle, discovery, or mere data as such; news matters constituting press information;[223] and official texts and writings and other works of the government.[224]

The closest Philippine ruling on this matter is the case of *Joaquin, Jr. vs. Drilon*,[225] a case involving the dating game shows "Rhoda and Me" and "It's a Date." The issue was whether or not the format of a television show, i.e., a dating game, is a proper subject of copyright. The Court ruled that a format of a television show is not included within the enumeration of the classes of work entitled to copyright protection. The list of "protected works" refers to finished works and not to concepts. The Court said that copyright does not extend to an idea, procedure, process, system, method of operation, concept, principle, or discovery, regardless of the form in which it is embodied. Copyright does not extend to the general concept or format of a dating game show.

Significant changes have been made in the course of copyright protection in the Philippines. These changes were spurred on by pressure from the international community to conform with international treaties and conventions. To illustrate, they include the no-formality rule under the Berne Convention and the expansion of the definition of "copyright works" to include computer programs and compilations of data. These changes tend to favour copyright owners, as they facilitated copyright protection and expanded the list of works available for protection. On the other side of the scale, the government believes copyright owners should not have unbridled rights over their works and that a certain degree of regulation of these rights is beneficial to society and for the common good. To illustrate, a previous law had been passed introducing compulsory licensing for the reprinting of foreign textbooks to make them affordable to students. The new IP Code superseded this law. As earlier explained, the IP Code was enacted to make our laws conform to the TRIPS Agreement. Nevertheless, the Courts cannot ignore a principle explicitly stated in the new law: "The use of intellectual property bears a social function.... the State shall promote the diffusion of knowledge and information for the promotion of national development and progress and the common good." It will be interesting to see how the Courts will apply this principle when confronted with a case that requires a justification for resolving an apparent conflict of interest between the author's right over his work and the benefits that may be derived from the lawful use of the same work by society.

---

[222] Ibid. Section 185.
[223] Ibid. Section 175.
[224] Ibid. Section 176. However, prior approval of the concerned government agency is required if any of its official texts is to be used for commercial purposes.
[225] 302 SCRA 225 (1999).

2
Internet Trade, Digital Works and Parallel Imports

CHRISTOPHER HEATH

Issues of exhaustion and parallel importation have become highly politicised in the last decade. A good number of countries have erected barriers against the parallel importation of copyrighted goods, e.g. Taiwan and the US, as has Europe. In addition, more copyrighted works have been endowed with inexhaustible rights of rental and lending, e.g. film works. At the same time, Internet trading has become an important economic factor. How then is Internet trade affected by the above-mentioned mechanisms of rights owners to enforce their rights against parallel importers and distributors of films works (e.g. video tapes) in the digital environment, and, vice versa, can rules limiting parallel importation and distribution of film works still be effectively enforced in a digital environment? To what extent has this issue already been addressed in court cases and legislation?

A. Introduction

I. Starting Point

Intellectual property rights, patents and copyrights in particular, receive protection in order to appropriately reward creative activity, thereby stimulating the ongoing creative process itself. Rights and limits of intellectual rights should thus be balanced in order to reflect the definition of "appropriately". If rights are granted too generously, the public will be unreasonably disadvantaged, as no corresponding creative output can justify such taking from them. On the other hand, giving too little protection might be a disincentive for further production of creative works. Much of this book is related to the appropriate balance of rights and limits. Such limits are first of all those of copyright law proper. Copyright law should protect expressions rather than ideas and raw information. The introductory chapter shows, however, that copyright law has come perilously close to creating monopolies over information. In addition, the appropriate balance also relates to mechanisms of enforcement: examples are collecting societies that do not always work to the advantage of right owners or authors (see chapter 3). Enforcement issues are also related to questions of direct, indirect or contributory infringement (see chapter 6). Here, the recent Grokster case[1] has opened up new forms of liability, and in connection with download activities, private end users for the first time in copyright history have been sued for copyright infringement. Finally, the appropriate limits

---

[1] *Metro-Goldwyn-Mayer Studios, Inc. v. Grokster, Ltd.*, 125 S.Ct. 2764 (2005).

take into account the fact that copyright law is juxtaposed with other fields of law, such as contract law or anti-trust law (see chapter 5).

II. Basic Functions of Copyright

In granting the patentee the right of excluding others from any active use, patent law wants to allow the patentee to obtain a profit by such monopoly. Such a monopoly is not absolute, and in particular does not confer the right of *use*: it only confers the right to exclude others. For patent law, it is largely immaterial whether the infringer copied from the patentee's invention or arrived at the infringing device by himself. Both acts interfere with the patentees' right to exclude others, unless the defendant can rely on prior user rights. In recognition of the literary or artistic quality of a work, similarly copyright law allows the copyright owner to exclude others from certain acts of use. Yet, protection is limited in one material aspect. As the word "copyright" already indicates, the right is confined to protection against acts of copying where one work forms the basis for the other; in cases of concurrent or independent creations, the second author has not taken anything from the first.[2] Under this concept, it is difficult to see how the copyright owner could obtain a right to oppose the use of original copies unless additional post-sale rights have been granted. Imported or not, such copies would certainly be original ones and not reproductions made without consent. The reason for protecting the author against unauthorised copies is the likelihood of diminished earnings due to a substitution of the original by the unauthorised copy. Worded differently, "exhaustion" implies that a copy of the work was made available to the extent that the copyright owner could actually exercise his rights and thereby receive the benefits copyright law wants to confer on him ("remuneration doctrine"). In the international context, this would beg the question of when and to what extent the sale of copyrighted products abroad could amount to sufficient compensation in order to regard import restrictions as an additional remuneration and therefore impermissible.

III. Considerations of free commerce

An alternative justification for the exhaustion rule is that continuing rights over products circulating in the market place would be an impediment to free commerce. While the possession of tangible property normally means a presumption of ownership and thereby a protection of good faith purchasers, no such presumption would exist under copyright law if the owner could control or interrupt the circulation of copyrighted goods on the market. This has led to greater interest in ensuring the free circulation of goods than in continuing rights of the copyright owner, with the English courts applying the doctrine of implied licence at least to patented goods: unless restrictions are imposed, they cannot be invoked against subsequent buyers.[3] This rule would of course only be effective in markets within

[2] This principle was established in England by the decision *Corelli v. Gray*, (1913) 29 T.L.R. 570, and is still good law under the UK Copyright, Designs and Patents Act 1988, which in Sec. 17(1) prohibits "reproducing the work in any material form".

[3] *National Phonograph Company of Australia v. Menck*, Privy Council 1911, 28 R.P.C. 229.

which goods can freely flow, and this usually means the domestic market, or a common market such as the European Community or the European Economic Market.[4]

It appears that modern-day copyright doctrine is increasingly moving towards a reward-based balance between public and private copyrights (as is further elaborated in chapter 7)[5], making it preferable to determine exhaustion rules according to the appropriate remuneration the copyright owner should receive rather than extraneous factors such as the degree of integration of certain markets.[6] The latter consideration would make a compelling case for introducing a rule of international or regional exhaustion in trade agreements, but it is well known that the foremost agreement on intellectual property rights, TRIPS, is silent on this matter.

IV. Copyright Exhaustion in the Analogue Environment

1. *Principles of National Exhaustion*

a) The Remuneration Doctrine

The above remuneration doctrine was applied by a German decision of 1906:[7] "The old law (Act of 7 June 1870) did not recognise an exclusive right of commercial distribution for authors and publishers. Sec. 25 only extended civil and criminal liability to those who intentionally and commercially distributed copies of the protected work printed against the law. The law thereby left a loophole in cases where copies of the work were lawfully made abroad in countries where the author did not receive protection, and such works were subsequently commercially marketed domestically. The same was true for a geographically divided publishing right (Sec. 8(3) Copyright Act), where copies were lawfully made in one region and subsequently commercially distributed in another. For the sake of protection of authors and publishers, these and other cases were meant to be covered by granting the author an exclusive right of commercial distribution similar to the one under Sec. 4 Patent Act for the inventor in order to protect the author and

---

[4] E.g. *P. Ganea*, Ökonomische Aspekte der urheberrechtlichen Erschöpfung, GRUR Int. 2005, 102, 105.

[5] Some support for this view can be found in the decision of the German Federal Supreme Court of 6 July 2000, I ZR 244/97 where contractual limitations over the subsequent use of computer programmes on diskettes were held void due to exhaustion. The view that contractual agreements are superseded by exhaustion is easier to reconcile with a reward-based exhaustion doctrine than one based on considerations of the fre movement of goods.

[6] Of course, one can argue that integrated markets mean a lesser degree of arbitrage between different geographical regions and thereby less economic necessity for price differentiations. But this may be arbitrary in itself, as markets integrated by free trade agreements etc. are not necessarily compatible in terms of economic development, or vice versa. Further, countries with the same language and a similar level of economic development may not necessarily be part of an integrated market. Thus, trade integration does not necessarily go hand in glove with economic parity. This point has been well argued by Ganea, above note 4. Ganea draws the conclusion that internet exhaustion rules would not appropriately reflect economic realities. While this might be so, the consequence should be to draw the limits of international exhaustion along the lines of economic equivalence. This has not been seriously advocated, however.

[7] German Imperial Supreme Court, 16 June 1906, RGZ 63, 394—"Königs Kursbuch".

the publisher against competition with copies that were lawfully made, yet marketed by persons other than the author or publisher. Yet the idea is not to grant the author and publisher an exclusive and absolute right of commercial distribution in the sense that apart from them and their licensees, no one for the duration of the copyright would be entitled to commercially distribute copies of their protected works without their permission. Only on condition of such an absolute, exclusive right could authors and publishers be entitled to prevent the commercial distribution by others, and thereby determine the sales price. Thereby authors and editors would be endowed with a truly exorbitant right, which no other commercial enterprise has. Sec. 11(1) Copyright Act cannot be interpreted in that sense. The exclusive right of copying persists according to its nature during the whole period of copyright protection and repeats itself as often as the copy of a protected work is concerned. The right of commercial distribution is exercised by the work being sold from the factory to the public, and thereby put in commerce. According to the law, no one should be entitled to do so prior to the author or publisher. Yet once author and publisher have sold the work to the public into commerce and thereby exercised their rights, these rights are exhausted. Certainly legislation could have granted the author and publisher an exclusive right of commercial distribution, which would entitle them for the whole period of copyright protection to exercise an exclusive right against third parties, also for copies brought into commerce by the author or publisher. This would equal an exclusive commercial privilege for which, according to Sec. 7(1) Act on Commerce, a clear and unambiguous wording of the law would be necessary which is lacking here. The publishing business would thereby have been granted a monopoly which no other merchant actually has. Especially second-hand bookstores would be almost abolished thereby."

In other words, for traditional objects of copyright protection such as books, there is an exhaustion upon first sale. Subsequent acts of use, even rental or lending, do not interfere with the author's rights against copying, as the object is not multiplied thereby.[8] These principles have also determined the law in the United States. Here, Sec. 106(3) US Copyright Act gives the copyright owner the exclusive right to distribute copies of a work to the public by sale or other transfer of ownership, or by rental, lease or lending. Such a right is limited by the so-called "first sale doctrine" established in Sec. 109(a):

> "The owner of a particular copy or phono record lawfully made under this title, or any person authorized by such owner is entitled without the authority of the copyright owner, to sell or otherwise dispose of the possession of that copy or phono record".

Thus, under US law the copyright is also exhausted by any "lawfully made" copy. The result seems so self-explanatory, at least for works in "traditional" form that no decisions of other countries deserve mention.

[8] E.g., German Federal Supreme Court, GRUR 1986, 736—"Schallplattenvermietung" for records; German Federal Supreme Court, GRUR 1985, 134—"Zeitschriftenauslage in Wartezimmern" for journals being offered as reading materials in doctors' waiting rooms. German Federal Supreme Court, 6 July 2000, I ZR 244/97 regarding diskettes with computer programs.

b) Commercial Use Triggering Exhaustion

The German decision "König's Kursbuch" concerned an act of *sale* that triggered exhaustion. The question is whether the same would apply to other acts of commercial distribution as well. Under the current Sec. 17(2) German Copyright Act, exhaustion is only triggered by a commercial distribution that amounts to a sale. The distribution by way of rental or lending thus would not do, while a sale under retention of title just might. The US Copyright Act 1976 in sec. 106(3) refers to the distribution of copies to the public *by sale or other transfer of ownership, or by rental, lease, or lending*. The provisions as such do not unambiguously indicate whether a first rental or lease would also trigger exhaustion. Yet sec. 109 (a) limits exhaustion not in terms of the copy as such, but grants rights over further acts of sale only to the *owner* of a lawfully made copy. The WIPO Copyright Treaty in Art. 6 (2) seems to permit exhaustion only *after the first sale or other transfer of ownership*. Also Art. 4(2) of the Council Directive 2001/29/EC of 22 May 2001 on the Harmonisation of Certain Aspects of Copyright and Related Rights in the Information Society (InfoSoc Directive) makes exhaustion conditional upon a first sale or other transfer of ownership.

2. Principles of International Exhaustion

The rules for international exhaustion, however, are not as simple as the above concept based on the remuneration doctrine might imply.

a) Distinct from the case law applicable to patents, English common law does not apply the doctrine of implied licence to the sale of copyrighted material abroad:

> "The plaintiffs had neither the implied licence of Time to import the books nor a licence to resell them after importation [, as] it was inappropriate to imply a licence to supply business efficacy to the contract of sale since the warranty of acquired possession was not a warrantee that the owner consented to the importation and sale of the books in Australia. ... The argument directed to the analogy with resale of the patented article was irrelevant. There was no licence implied by law as the term inherent of the nature of the contract. Patent cases in which such licences were implied were irrelevant because they were of a special character and turned upon the unique ability which the law conferred upon patentees of imposing restrictions upon what use may be made after sale of patented articles. The copyright owner has no right in relation to the subsequent use of an article or copy of the work which he has sold and accordingly no need for an implied licence arises."[9]

This approach is consistent with the UK Copyrights Act of 1911, 1956 and 1988 (the current ss. 22, 27 UK Copyright, Designs and Patents Act 1988) whereby "infringing copy" is defined as a copy whose "making in the United Kingdom would have constituted an infringement of the copyright in the work in question, or a breach of an exclusive licence agreement relating to that work". The importation is thus infringing if the manufacturer of the copy abroad would (hypothetically) not have had permission to manufacture such copy in the United Kingdom (or Australia, India or South Africa, for that matter).

---

[9] *Time-Life International (Nederlands) v. Interstate Parcel Express Co.*, Supreme Court of New South Wales, 29 September 1977, [1978] Fleet Street Reports 251. Expressly applied by the English Court of Appeal in *Polydore Ltd. v. Harlequin Record Shop*, 15 May 1980, [1980] Fleet Street Reports 362. Also applied by the Indian High Court of Delhi in *Penguin Books Ltd. v. India Book Distributors*, 1 August 1984, [1985] Fleet Street Reports 120; also applied for South Africa in *Video Parktown North v. Paramount Pictures Corp.*, 1986(2) SA 623(T).

b) Of the common law countries, only Singapore has adopted a different approach. In a 1988 decision, the Singapore Court held that:

"The plaintiffs have not alleged in their pleadings that the video tapes were pirated copies but, instead, have admitted that the video tapes were non-infringing tapes. A purchaser of non-infringing copyright articles obtains full ownership of such articles although he does not obtain the copyright subsisting therein. Any dealings by him with such articles in the way of trade, whether for sale or hire, are not acts of infringement of copyright because the copyright owner has no exclusive right to any such dealing with such articles".10

c) Subsequently, the common law countries of Australia and New Zealand amended their copyright laws to allow for the parallel importation of copyrighted articles legitimately manufactured abroad. While the New Zealand Copyright Act of 1994 extended the definition of "pirated copy" to parallel imported copies, the Copyright Amendment Act of 1998 in Sec. 12(3) clearly states that infringing copies are not those "made by or with the consent of the owner of the copyright, or other equivalent intellectual property right, in the work in question in the country in which the object was made".

For Australia, the Copyright Statute was amended in 1990 to permit the parallel importation of books by changing the definition of "non-infringing book" under Sec. 10(1) and the implementation of a new provision, Sec. 44(A), on the importation of books. Further amendments were made by the Copyright Amendment Acts 104 and 105 of 30 July 1998 in order to allow the parallel importation of sound recordings under Sec. 44D Copyright Act 1968.[11]

d) Despite the different approach taken by the German courts in the above 1906 decision "König's Kursbuch", the arguments concerning the lawfulness of parallel imports come very close to what is argued under English common law. Eugen Ulmer writes as follows:

"Requirement of domestic exhaustion of the distribution right according to Sec. 17(2) German Copyright Act is the fact that the copyrighted articles have been put into commerce with the consent of the copyright owner by way of sale. If the copyright owner has consented, contrary to some decisions and academic writings it is materially unimportant if such sale has been effected domestically or abroad. If, e.g., an Austrian or Swiss publisher obtains the worldwide rights of publication also for Germany, there is no way to prevent the distribution of copies marketed in Austria or Switzerland also in Germany. This reflects a decision of the legislature for reasons of public policy. Yet the wording of the law needs one addition which corresponds to its implied meaning: It is important that the right owner has consented to a domestic distribution. If, e.g., the German publisher has granted a licence to an American publishing house limited to the territory of the United States, this means a consent to a distribution in

---

10 *Television Broadcasts Ltd. v. Golden Line Video and Marketing Ltd.*, High Court of Singapore, 14 November 1988, [1989] 1 Malayan Law Journal 201. See also *T. Wei*, Parallel Imports and the Law of Copyright in Singapore, [1992] European Intellectual Property Rights 139 and O. *Dean*, Infringement of Copyright by Dealing in Parallel Imports,41 Copyright World (June 1994), 19. See also *Ng Loy Wee Loon*, Parallel Imports in Singapore, in: C. Heath (ed.), Parallel Imports in Asia, Kluwer Law London 2004, 137.

11 The exhaustion regime in Australia and New Zealand is described by Kerrin Vautier, Exhaustion and Parallel Imports in Australia and New Zealand, in: C. Heath (ed.), Parallel Imports in Asia, Kluwer Law London 2004, 177.

the United States, yet not a distribution in Germany. In other words, it depends if the person marketing the copies abroad would be entitled to market them domestically, too."[12]

After Sec. 17(2) German Copyright Act was amended in what most academics consider a limitation towards EC-wide exhaustion only,[13] the above doctrine remains valid for Austria[14].

The weakness of the above-mentioned doctrine of divided rights is a doctrinal one. The copyright owner cannot prevent the parallel importation of copies published abroad by himself, as in such case he would have been entitled to market them domestically as well. This is supposed to be different in case of marketing by a licensee, as in such case, the copyright owner contractually cedes the right to distribute copies in certain markets. Such theory evidently means that by licensing, the rights owner could obtain more rights by doing so than by acting personally: licensing out the rights in other countries would entitle the right owner to prevent parallel importation (as the copies are deemed infringing), while such right would not be open to the copyright owner in case of distributing copies abroad himself, as these would not be deemed infringing. A licence, however, by definition, is a right to use. Thereby the rights owner can pass on no more rights than he himself possesses. If the rights owner does not posses the right to prevent the importation of copies marketed abroad himself, how can he obtain such a right once the copies are marketed by a third party with his consent?

e) In the United States Sec. 602(a) Copyright Act prohibits the unauthorised importation into the United States of copies acquired outside the United States. From literal reading, it is not clear if this provision applies to all copies imported without the copyright owner's consent, or only those not lawfully marketed within the meaning of Sec. 109(a) Copyright Act mentioned above. According to a 1994 decision by the US Court of Appeals, Sec. 109(a) Copyright Act only refers to copies lawfully made *in the United States*:[15]

"The owner of a registered copyright has the 'exclusive rights' to authorize or distribute copies of the copyrighted work to the public. 17 U.S.C. 106(3). However under the 'first sale' doctrine, embodied in 109(a) of the Copyright Act, 17 U.S.C. 109(a), a sale of a 'lawfully made' copy terminates the copyright holder's authority to interfere with subsequent sales or distribution of that particular copy. Section 109(a) thus provides a defense to liability under 106(3) for lawful purchasers of copies of copyrighted materially, so long as the copies were 'lawfully made under this title.' Drug Emporium contends on appeal that this section protects it from 602 liability for copyright infringement.

Whether Drug Emporium may rely on the first sale doctrine depends on the relationship between this doctrine and the 'importation right' codified at 17 U.S.C. 602(a). Section 602(a) provides that unauthorized importation of foreign purchased copies of U.S. copyrighted materials is an infringement of the distribution rights provided in 106. There are at least two plausible interpretations of the interaction of the importation right and the first sale doctrine as embodied in 602(a) and 109(a). Drug Emporium contends

---

[12] E. *Ulmer*, Urheber- und Verlagsrecht, 3rd ed., 1980, 237. Ulmer's opinion is shared by the Austrian Supreme Court, decision of 10 June 1979, GRUR Int. 1980, 185. but a different opinion was expressed in Oberlandesgericht Hamburg, GRUR Int. 1970, 377—"Polydor".

[13] E.g., *Loewenheim*, in: Schricker, Urheberrecht, 2nd ed., 1999, Sec. 17, marginal notes 35–58.

[14] Most recently reaffirmed by the Austrian Supreme Court, 23 May 2000, GRUR Int. 2000, 1028—"HWP WIN Programm".

[15] *Parfums Givenchy v. Drug Emporium*, US Court of Appeals, 9th Cir., 21 October 1994, 38 F.3d 477.

that 109(a) supersedes 602(a). In its view, a lawful sale abroad of U.S. copyrighted foreign goods would terminate the exclusive right of the U.S. copyright holder to import and distribute those goods in the United States, in the same way that a lawful domestic sale terminates the exclusive distribution rights of domestically manufactured materials. Thus, Drug Emporium argues, Givenchy USA may not interfere with the U.S. distribution of Amarige, lawfully obtained abroad, even though it owns the U.S. copyright to the Amarige box design, and even though the perfume was imported into the United States in the original box without Givenchy USA's authorization. In contrast, Givenchy USA contends, and we agree, that the importation right survives as to a particular copy unless and until there has been a 'first sale' in the United States".

Prior to the 1976 amendments to the Copyright Act, the unauthorised importation of non-pirated copyrighted articles was not prohibited. See Act of Mar. 4, 1909, ch. 320, 30, 35 Stat. 1075, 1082 (1909). Section 602(a) was enacted in order to provide greater remedies for U.S. copyright owners, and 'makes the mere act of importation—regardless of sale—an infringement of Section 106(3)'s distribution right, and prohibits unauthorized importation, not only of pirated copies, but also of copies that were lawfully made.' See *Parfums Givenchy v. C & C Beauty Sales* which recognized, 602(a) in effect gives 106(3) an extraterritorial scope. Id. This section ensures that a U.S. copyright owner will gain the full value of each copy sold in the United States, by preventing the unauthorized importation of copies sold from abroad from being used as a means of circumventing the copyright owner's distribution rights in the United States. Id. at 1390-91."Already from the court's definition of "copies lawfully made", it is clear that copies lawfully made in the US, subsequently exported and re-imported, cannot qualify as infringing as was confirmed by the Supreme Court's *Quality King* decision.[16] As has been explained above, this is not even a case of parallel importation. This is confirmed by Justice Ginsburg's concurring opinion in the *Quality King* case which states:"This case involves a 'round trip' journey, travel of the copies in question from the United States to places abroad, then back again. I join the court's opinion recognizing that we do not today resolve cases in which the allegedly infringing imports were manufactured abroad".As already stated above, the common law distinction between direct distribution and distribution by a licensee is thin on the ground from a doctrinal point of view. Countries that have explicitly permitted the parallel importation of copyrighted articles (Australia and New Zealand), or prohibited their importation (the United States) have mostly done so for political reasons. Barring any clear political statement one way or the other, the reasoning given by the Singapore High Court (as above) appears to be the one most consistent with the traditional notion of copyright (although the decision apparently had the modern notion of free international trade in mind).

Finally, and for the sake of completeness, it should be noted that Japan allows the importation of copyrighted works, yet does not presume exhaustion for rental or lending rights deemed inexhaustible under Japanese law.[17]

---

[16] *Quality King Distributors v. L'Anza Research International, Inc.*, 9 March 1998, 523 U.S.135 (Supreme Court 1998).

[17] Tokyo District Court, 1 July 1995, 27 IIC 570 [1996]—"Beauty and the Beast".

IV. Rights Over Acts of Secondary Exploitation

Even before the advent of modern technology, acts of secondary exploitation such as recital or performance were forms of exploitation to be reckoned with. Such acts did not fall under the definition of "copying" a work, yet where they brought economic profit, the author or copyright owner should be entitled to participate therein. It was thus deemed appropriate to broaden the scope of rights allocated to the copyright owner beyond the copying of a work towards acts of secondary exploitation that would not be exhausted by the first sale of a copy of a work. In other words, the sale of a copy of the work did not give the purchaser rights over the public recital or performance of the work, and exhaustion rules in this case reflected the economic interests of the author in participating in such forms of secondary exploitation[18]. Technology has added to the distribution of performances by broadcast, or the fixation of such performances and subsequent use thereof. Traditionally, the collection of fees for acts of secondary exploitation has been entrusted to collecting societies (see chapter 3 of this book). The Berne Convention recognises the right of public performance (Art. 11 for dramatic and musical works, Art. 11ter for literary works), and of broadcast (Art. 11bis). The WIPO Copyright Treaty has added the right of communication to the public (Art. 8). There has been some debate as to the extent these rights are subject to exhaustion. An example is a German Supreme Court decision of 1980[19] where a third party without the radio broadcaster's consent had simultaneously re-transmitted a programme to those parts of town where the programme could otherwise not be received due to skyscrapers in between. As the re-transmission did not broaden the range of intended listeners, the Federal Supreme Court regarded the broadcasting right as exhausted.[20] Such an interpretation seems no longer possible in view of Art. 3 (3) InfoSoc Directive that makes inexhaustible "any act of communication to the public or making available to the public."

V. Exhaustion, Technology and Electronic Distribution

1. Additional rights beyond the first commercial distribution

The electronic age has seen two new developments in the field of copyright exhaustion. For one, additional and inexhaustible rights of rental and lending have been added to certain categories of works. The addition of such rights has

[18] It is interesting to note that just as in most cases where IP rights have been broadened, societal acceptance thereof took a slow start. For rights of secondary exploitation, a good example is the cavalier attitude of Japanese performers and broadcasters towards authors' rights in this case. In the 1920's, a good many pieces of modern-day music were performed and broadcast, while the authors or copyright owners did not receive royalties. It took the dogged efforts of Dr. Wilhelm Plage, a representative of European collecting societies, to make the Japanese concert organisers and broadcasters pay up: *P. Ganea*, Copyright History, in: Ganea/Heath/Saito, Japanese Copyright Law, Kluwer Law International 2005, 7–9.

[19] Federal Supreme Court, 7 November 1980, BGHZ 79, 350—"Kabelfernsehen in Abschattungsgebieten".

[20] The decision has been criticised by *E. Ulmer*, Die Entscheidungen zur Kabelübertragung von Rundfunksendungen im Lichte urheberrechtlicher Grundsätze, GRUR Int. 1981, 372, 374.

meant that the first distribution of a copy of the work does not exhaust the rights in further economic exploitation by way of rental or lending. While the Berne Convention is silent in this respect, the TRIPS Agreement requires such additional rights be granted to film works and computer programs (Art. 11), and the WIPO Copyright Treaty does likewise, adding phonograms to the list (Art. 7; the WIPO Phonograms Treaty stipulates the same in Art. 13). Under European law, such additional rights of rental and lending have been stipulated by Council Directive 1992/100/EC of 19 November 1992 on rental rights and lending rights and on certain rights related to copyright. The Directive relates to all kinds of works, yet makes exemptions to public lending where the authors receive an equitable remuneration. Under US law, additional rights of rental and lending relate to computer programs and phonograms, sec. 109(b)(1)(A). Non-profit lending by a non-profit library or non-profit educational institution is generally exempt from the list of exclusive rights.

2. *Exhaustion in the Case of Digitally Transmitted Works*

Finally, the issue arises if digitally distributed works should follow the same rules of exhaustion that apply to works in tangible form. The problem is most pertinent for those types of works whose first distribution exhausts further acts of resale, e.g. books. For instance, would the sale of a book in digital form trigger exhaustion in the same way the sale of a hard copy? In commercial terms, the most relevant scenario would not seem to be the sale of books or software over the net over an individual bases, but the brokerage of software licenses. Dealers of "used" software would purchase spare licences from bankrupt or shrinking business and sell or transfer these licenses to third parties at a price far cheaper than the purchase of a license from the manufacturer. Yet, since software is increasingly sold over the net without the dispatch of physical copies, the question arises if the sale of such licenses can indeed be undertaken without the copyright owner's consent. And even where the original software package comes in tangible form, it would only be sent once in order to be installed on a number of computers. Where only single licenses are sold, the original package would then stay with the original buyer who sells off some of his licenses, or sells all licenses to different buyers, or sells all licenses to a broker who sells them on to different buyers. All this brings the sale close or perhaps closer to a sale of rights rather than a sale of copies of works.

Both US and European law refer to originals of works or copies thereof and thus do not seem to limit exhaustion to hard copies. On the other hand, online services are not subject to exhaustion rules, as is made clear in Recital 29 of the above InfoSoc Directive:

> "The question of exhaustion does not arise in the case of services and on-line services in particular. This also applies with regard to a material copy of a work or other subject matter made by a user of such a service with the consent of the rightholder...Unlike CD-Rom or CD-I, where the intellectual property is incorporated in a material medium, namely an item of goods, every on-line service is in fact an act which should be subject to authorisation where the copyright or related right so provides."

The recitals of several copyright directives contain the assumption that on-line delivery of works equals on-line services with the consequence that there should be no exhaustion[21], yet the directives themselves do not contain unambiguous provisions in this respect. Further, Art. 6 (1) WIPO Copyright Treaty itself is inconclusive, since, as mentioned above, the provision relates to "copies" irrespective whether of their nature is digital or tangible.

In academic literature, exhaustion is sometimes questioned as regards works delivered online with an argument that the purpose of exhaustion is to smoothen the tension between ownership in the tangible object and ownership in the copyright: free commerce demands rules that do not permit a copyright owner to interfere with the circulation of copies[22]. In contrast, those who regard the exhaustion principle as justified by a sufficient remuneration of the rights owner for the sale of a copy of the work, must reach the conclusion that the sale of online copies or hard copies makes no difference[23].

An ancillary line of argument would be that a digital copy which includes authorisation to make a hard copy of the work should automatically include the ability to distribute that copy. This, however, would depend on the question if the supply of a digital copy could be regarded as a form of distribution—if so, the above exhaustion rules would apply. If not, the matter would have to be examined further in terms of an analogous application of exhaustion rules[24]. In this respect, one should bear in mind that at least in those cases where the purchaser had received permission to make a hard copy from an online-delivered work, he has obtained a copy of the work made with the copyright owner's consent. In terms of the above definition of exhaustion under European, US and international law, this should be sufficient to trigger exhaustion for the further distribution of that copy, at least if the assumption holds true that a concept developed for the offline world should be applied to the online world in the first place[25]. This should be affirmed at least as long as there is no clear pay-per-view contract that limits the use of delivered work to a one-off occasion.

Perhaps the first decision on the matter of exhaustion of digitally distributed works was rendered by the Munich District Court on 19 January 2006[26]. Here, the court held the sale of software licences by software brokers as infringing for the following reasons: (1) In order to sell the licence, the software dealer's customer has to undertake an additional act of copying; (2) the software was only licensed rather than sold, thus limiting the rights of the licensee to acts

---

[21] Database Directive 96/9 of 11 March 1996 in recitals 33, 34; InfoSoc Directive recital 28; report on the implementation of the Software Directive of 10 April 2000, COM 2000, 199, s. VII p. 17.

[22] *Bergmann*, Zur Reichweite des Erschöpfungsprinzips bei der Online-Übermittlung urheberrechtlich geschützter Werke, in: Festschrift für Erdmann, Cologne 2002, 17, 26. *Heydn/Schmidl*, Dealing with used software: Ingenious business model or piracy?, World Intellectual Property Report March 2006, 28, 30. Also *Ganea* (above note 2), 106, 107.

[23] *Koehler*, Der Erschöpfungsgrundsatz des Urheberrechts in Online-Bereich, 2000, 177 et seq.

[24] *Knies*, Erschöpfung Online?, GRUR Int. 2002, 314, 317.

[25] E. T. T. *Tai*, Exhaustion and Online Delivery of Digital Works, [2003] E.I.P.R. 207, 211.

[26] Munich District Court, 19 January 2006, case 7 O 23237/05, Kommunikation & Recht 2/2006.

as permitted by the licensor; (3) a uniform license right may not be split, and (4) only the uniform licensee is allowed to have further copies made, not third parties.

On each of the above-mentioned points it would have been possible to decide differently. The most important issue refers to the qualification of the transaction: A sale of software with conditions attached, as was decided by the German Federal Supreme Court in 2000, or the grant of a licence due to the lack of a tangible object, as was decided by the Munich District Court in 2006. Once a court finds for the latter, exhaustion rules will not apply. Once a court likens the transaction to one of sale, there will be exhaustion and the buyer will be entitled to sell part of his rights—the permitted number of copies (i.e. licenses)—to third parties. In other words, the legal consequences depend on the analogy drawn (transfer of a right v. transfer of an object). This author finds it doubtful whether a change in the distribution model (online transmission instead of transfer of tangible copies) should entitle the seller to a disproportionately broader scope of rights. After all, a change in the distribution scheme is unrelated to the amount of investment in the copyrighted works in question.

B. Country Reports

Note: The contributors to the country reports are listed in the introductory preface

I. China

Currently, there are no explicit provisions in any piece of legislation that relate to the issue of the parallel importation of copyrighted works, and neither have there been any reported cases. This could be due to the fact that prices of commodities in Mainland China are still relatively low in comparison with those of other countries in the region.

II. Hong Kong

1. General

As a member of the World Trade Organisation (WTO), Hong Kong is subject to the provisions of the TRIPS Agreement. Article 6 TRIPS Agreement provides that nothing in the Agreement affects the exhaustion of intellectual property rights. Accordingly, Hong Kong is free to adopt its own policy on parallel imports.

a) Principle of Exhaustion

The principle of exhaustion posits that once intellectual property right holders have sold or put onto the market place a product to which their intellectual property rights are attached, they cannot control the resale or further commercial exploitation of that product. In this way the intellectual property rights are said to be 'exhausted' following the first entry of the product on the market. This coincides with one of the distinctive features of internet trade, i.e. territorial or geographical boundaries are of little significance.

b) Parallel Imports Legislation

Prior to 1997, the copyright law in Hong Kong was based on the UK Copyright Act 1956 which was made applicable to Hong Kong in 1972. The first draft of the Hong Kong Copyright Ordinance did not contain any criminal liability provisions for the parallel importation of copyright protected works. The Copyright Ordinance which came into effect on 27 June 1997, provides that parallel importation constitutes an infringement of copyright which attracts both criminal and civil liability. Under Section 35(3), a copy of a copyright work which has been parallel imported and which, if made in Hong Kong would either infringe the copyright in that work or breach an exclusive license agreement relating to that work, is regarded as an infringing copy. In addition, any person dealing in copies of such works is also subject to similar liabilities if that person had any reason to believe that the goods were parallel imported.

c) Duration—18 Months

However, section 35(4) provides that criminal liability does not arise in respect of a copy of a work that is imported into Hong Kong at any time after the expiration of 18 months from the date of first publication of the work in Hong Kong or elsewhere. Thereby Section 35(4) has reduced the harshness of the criminal liability provisions—violators may be subject to a maximum fine of HK$50,000 per infringing copy and four years imprisonment. In general, the parallel importation or subsequent sale of a copy of the work which has been published for more than 18 months will not attract criminal liability but civil remedies such as injunction, delivery up and damages are still available to the right holder.

2. Copyright (Amendment) Bill 2001

a) Liberalisation of Parallel Importation of Computer Software

A survey by the government in May 2001 revealed that there was widespread support from both the users of computer software in the business community and the Legislative Council to remove the current restriction on parallel importation of computer software. The Copyright (Amendment) Bill 2001(2001Bill) was introduced into the Legislative Council on 19 December 2001. Its aim was to remove civil and criminal liabilities under the Copyright Ordinance relating to the parallel importation and any subsequent dealings in articles which have embodied in them computer programs with or without other copyright works.

The Legislative Council had endorsed the proposed liberalisation. This is in line with Hong Kong's free market philosophy; its policy to facilitate the free flow of genuine goods; and to keep in step with the growing popularity of on-line shopping. Recent amendments to the IPMAO have imposed criminal liability for possession of pirated copies of copyright work in the course of business. The government believed in the chain effect that liberalisation increases competition and availability of products in the market, which results in more choices and lower prices for consumers. Then such effects would certainly help ease the financial burden on small and medium enterprises when they undertake replacement of their pirated computer software with legitimate products in order to comply with those amendments.

b) Parallel Imported Computer Software Permitted—Current Law

The 2001 Bill was enacted as the 2003 Ordinance on 28 November 2003. Section 35A of the 2003 Ordinance has removed civil and criminal liability relating to parallel importation and subsequent dealings in parallel imported computer software. Exceptions have been carved out in works whose principal use is to be viewed or played as a movie, a television drama, a musical audio or visual recording as well as an e-book.

There was intense opposition from the local movie and music industries against lifting those parallel import restrictions for movie and music recordings. Technological convergence has led to the appearance of products that contain both computer programs and other copyright works such as audio-visual material. Movies and musical recordings are increasingly packaged and sold as digital multimedia products that can be viewed on a computer. The amendment provides that an article which has embodied in it a computer program and a movie or television drama is excluded from the scope of liberalisation if the viewing duration of the movie and television drama is more than 15 and 10 minutes respectively. In any event, the movie or a television drama cannot be embodied in the article in its entirety. The film and music industry associations in Hong Kong are content with the general approach adopted by the legislature in excluding movies and music recordings from the liberalisation.

Before enactment, the 2003 Ordinance had faced vigorous opposition. The drafting of the 2003 Ordinance is the reason for this Ordinance's receipt of particular criticism for its lack of precision in its language. For instance, a "parallel import" is defined as a work that has been "lawfully made" in the country in which it was made. This language is problematic because it misapplies the principle of international exhaustion. In the given example, the definition has failed to distinguish between the place where a product is manufactured and the place where it is put on the market. A better way of defining parallel imports in relation to the doctrine of exhaustion is to refer to copies that are "lawfully put on the market" anywhere in the world rather than to copies that are "lawfully made".

Another situation where the term "lawfully made" raises problems—the 2003 Ordinance defines it as "not including a copy that was made in a country, territory or area where there is no law protecting copyright in the work or where the copyright in the work has expired". This is an inadequate definition because it merely states what is not included. It does not define what the term actually means and therefore does not assist in the proper construction of the term.

A final illustration relates to the provision dealing with removal of criminal liability for making back-up copies and adapting parallel imported copies of a computer program. The removal of criminal liability is implemented by reference to a "lawful user" rather than to copies that are "lawfully made".

This inconsistency causes ambiguity and will most likely lead to considerable confusion.

Although the Copyright 2003 Ordinance may have failed to satisfactorily fulfil all its expectations, it has nonetheless lifted criminal liability for the parallel importation of computer software. In summary, the current position in Hong Kong is—parallel importation of computer software per se is permitted even though parallel importation of films or musical works continues to be restricted.

III. Taiwan

1. Introduction[27]

Issues of whether and to what extent IP right holders should be given the exclusive right of importation and when such rights are exhausted only came to head in Taiwan in the late 1980s, when the parallel import of genuine goods gathered momentum. It began with soft drinks such as Coca Cola, but at present parallel importation is common place for automobiles, cosmetics and consumer electronic appliances and such industries are now suffering from serious international price discrimination[28] and/or high tariffs.[29]

Given these facts,—Taiwanese do not hold many IP rights in foreign countries and she is an importer of such rights—the introduction of an exclusive right of importation which enables right holders to stop parallel imports of their products is at odds with Taiwan's interests as a whole. More specifically, the right to parallel import IP-covered products affects the competitiveness of Taiwanese industries and the free flow of goods, both of which are vital to its economic well-being. The matter has been succinctly stated by the Taiwanese Supreme Court in decision No. 5380 (1993): "The parallel import of genuine goods...may prevent the market from being monopolised, facilitate intra-brand price competition, allow consumers to enjoy the benefit of reasonable prices, and so far as it is not at odds with the purpose of the Trade Mark Act shall be deemed to have been consented to by trade mark right holders."[30] The leading academics are pro parallel import.[31]

---

[27] For a more comprehensive account of parallel import and exhaustion regimes, please see *Kung-Chung Liu*, Exhaustion and Parallel Imports in Taiwan, in Christopher Heath (ed.), Parallel Imports in Asia, Kluwer Law International, The Hague, 2004.

[28] According to the observation of Professor Mao-Rong Huang, Commissioner of the Fair Trade Commission between 1992–1995, serious international price discrimination exists in Taiwan. See *Mao-Rong Huang*, Parallel Imports, Intellectual Property and the Fair Trade Act (in Chinese), 2 Fair Trade Journal no. 2 (April 1994), 1–14 (14).

[29] After becoming a member of the WTO, high tariffs for certain luxury articles became history in Taiwan.

[30] All court decisions are available at www.judicial.gov.tw.

[31] *Huang*, ibid.; *Ming Yang Shieh*, Importation Right of Patents and Parallel Imports (in Chinese), The Taiwan Law Review, no. 2 (June 1995), 80-86 (84, 86); *Dao-Chung Ci*, The Analysis of Parallel Import Problems—From Judicial Practice (in Chinese), 36 Tai-Wan Ching Chi Chin Jung Yueh K'an (Taiwan Economics and Finance Monthly, 11, November 2000), 98–103 (100, 102).

Foreign right holders and their government do not favour parallel imports into Taiwan and the United States government has taken issue at the bilateral trade talks with Taiwan. This has distorted the paradigm of the Taiwanese IP regime on parallel imports: It is neither been systematically nor strategically conceived and bends towards the interests of right holders, resulting in the gradual closing of doors to parallel imports. It is indeed regrettable for Taiwan, especially in light of the fact that the TRIPS Agreement of the WTO expressly eschewed the issue of exhaustion and gave the contracting parties freedom to make their own decision (Art. 6).[32]

2. Indirect Right of importation

The ubiquitous nature of works protected by copyright law carries tremendous commercial interests, especially in the easy-to-reproduce era beginning in the late 1970s. No wonder trade talks between the U.S. and Taiwan embarked on copyright protection as a first priority. One of the burning issues was parallel imports. The bilateral agreement on the protection of copyright between the U.S. and Taiwan led to a brand new Copyright Act in 1992. Sec. 87(3) provided: Any of the following circumstances, except as otherwise provided under this Act, shall be deemed an infringement of copyright or plate rights:

> "The import into the jurisdiction of the Republic of China of copies, the reproduction of which would violate copyright or plate right,[33] with an intention to distribute them in the jurisdiction of the Republic of China."

The legislative consideration was:

> "In order to intensify the protection of copyright and plate rights, certain circumstances are deemed to infringe copyright or plate rights, although as such they do not... No. 3 is a provision for the import of copies the reproduction of which in this country violates copyright or plate rights, into this country with an intention to distribute them domestically."

The provision was based on Art. 14(1) Draft Agreement for the Protection of Copyright Between the Coordination Council for North American Affairs and the American Institute in Taiwan of 1989 (formally signed in 1993):

> "(1) Infringing copies of a work protected in accordance with this Agreement shall be liable to seizure in either territory where such work enjoys legal protection. An infringing copy shall mean a copy of such work that infringes any of the exclusive rights provided in domestic law and in this Agreement *including a copy which is imported into the territory represented by either Party where, if made in such territory by the importer, would constitute an infringement of the copyright.*"

In spite of the lack of drafting skills, their cross reference to other texts and the underlying principles show indisputably that the import of copies, whether genuine or counterfeit, is subject to the approval of the right holder in the country

---

[32] *Blakeney*, Trade Related Aspects of Intellectual Property Rights: A Concise Guide to the TRIPs Agreement, 1996, 3.07.

[33] According to Sec. 79 Copyright Act, a plate maker who arranges, prints, or photocopies literary and artistic works that have no economic rights or whose economic rights have expired, enjoys a 10-year plate right for the first publication.

of import. Full enforcement of Art. 14 of the Agreement in accordance with its preamble requires defining an "infringing copy", banning parallel imports and thus indirectly granting the right of importation, because seizure was available under the Taiwanese Copyright Act as early as 1964.[34]

The indirect introduction of the right of importation in that Act was flawed in two aspects—ambiguous phrasing and lack of any exhaustion. A revision then quickly followed. In 1993, Sec. 87(3) was divided into two subsections:

"(3): To import any copies produced without the authorisation of the economic right holder or the plate right holder.

(4): To import the original or any copies of a work without the authorisation of the economic right holder."

In order to allow the import of some genuine goods, Sec. 87a was simultaneously added to provide several narrowly defined exceptions, again a masterpiece of trade pressure from the U.S.:[35]

"The provisions of subsection (4) of the preceding Section do not apply to any of the following circumstances:

1. To import the original or copies of a work for the use of central or local government agencies; provided, this does not apply to the importation for use in schools or other educational institutions, or importation of any audiovisual work for purposes other than archival use.
2. To import the original or a specified number of copies of any audiovisual works in order to supply such works to non-profit scholarly, educational or religious organisations for archival purposes, and to import an original or specified number of copies of works other than audiovisual works for library lending or archival purposes where the use of such copies conforms with the provisions of Sec. 48.
3. To import the original or a specified number of copies of a work, where such copy is for the private use of the importer and not for distribution, or, where the import is by a person arriving from outside the territory, the copy forms a part of such person's personal baggage.
4. To import the original or copies of a work incorporated into any legally imported goods, machinery, or equipment; such original or copies of the work cannot be reproduced during the use or operation of the goods, machinery or equipment.
5. To import an instructional or operational manual accompanying any legally imported goods, machinery, or equipment; provided, this does not apply where the instructional or operational manual are the principal objects of the importation.

The 'specified number' set forth in No. 2 and 3 of the proceeding Subsection shall be prescribed by the competent authority."

The decree promulgated by the Copyright Committee in 1993 reflects emphasis on legalism as the solution: for the purposes of Sec. 87a(1) No. 2, one copy of an

---

[34] However, *Zhong -Xi Zhang*, Study on the Parallel Import of Genuine Goods According To Copyright Act (in Chinese),Tzu Hsun Fa Wu T'ou Hsi, July 1998, 58-74 (72), is of the opinion that the original intention of the lawmakers was not to introduce the right of importation. Likewise, the 5th Senate of the Supreme Court held in the decision No. Tai Fe Zi 349 (1997) that the Taiwanese Copyright Act did not prohibit parallel imports of genuine goods until the 1993 revision which led to a new (4) in Sec. 87. The 4th Senate of the Supreme Court in an earlier decision, No. Tai Fe Zi 387 (1995), indicated that Sec. 87(3) of the 1992 Copyright Act is not exactly identical with Sec. 87(4) of the 1993 Copyright Act, and the appellate court should apply the latter provision as the later one.

[35] Sec. 87a(1) Nos. 1–3 Taiwanese Copyright Act clearly resembles Sec. 602(a) US Copyright Law.

audiovisual work and five copies for other works; whilst for the purposes of Sec. 87a(1) No. 3, one copy for any work at any one time is allowed. Literal interpretation easily leads to absurdity. A parent is not legally allowed to from abroad two copies of Harry Potter, one for each child.

Besides civil consequences, the violation of the right of importation is also subject to criminal punishment: two years imprisonment and/or a fine in the maximum amount of NT$ 500,000 (Sec. 93 No. 3 The amount was raised from NT$ 100,000 to NT$ 500,000 in 2003).

3. *Resale and rental of legally imported genuine copies*

In the case of Sec. 87a (1) No. 3, the legally imported copies do not always end up with the importers, but often journey further to other people via resale or rental. The Supreme Court takes the view that resale is not allowed. In a case involving a video shop reselling a laser disc legally imported by a third party, the 5th Criminal Senate reasoned that:

> "The laser disc has been confirmed by the complainant to be genuine; circumstances for the application of Sec. 87a to exclude Sec. 87 No. 4 cannot be found, and it is evident that the disc is an infringing copy. The defendant, knowing that it was an infringing copy, displayed it in his video shop with an intention to sell, and violated Sec. 87 No. 2."[36]

Meanwhile, the 6th Criminal Senate upheld the lawfulness of rental of the legally imported copy, a case concerning the rental of laser discs, which were legally imported by third parties and sold to the lessor:

> "As the final decision has specified, the owner of legal copies of works may rent such copies to others, as stipulated by Sec. 60.[37] The fact that the 10 confiscated laser discs are legal copies of works has been confirmed by the defendant and the complainant as well. The defendant has acquired the ownership of those legal copies, and is legally allowed to display and rent the discs."[38]

Some commentators have criticised the Supreme Court for lack of consistency.[39] However, the seemingly "inconsistency" lies with Sec. 60, which clearly exhausts the rental right of works, except for sound recordings and computer programs, and thus legalises the rental of legal copies of works, whether imported or not. Nonetheless, it is legitimate to point out that the Supreme Court has made two errors in banning the resale of legally imported genuine goods pursuant to Sec. 87a(1) No. 3: firstly, the violation of the right of importation has criminal consequences and thus should only apply where the Copyright Act clearly

---

[36] Supreme Court, decision No. Tai Fe Zi 17 (1999).

[37] Sec. 60: "(1) The owner of a legal copy of a work may rent such a copy, provided this shall not apply to copies of sound recordings and computer programs.

(2) The provision of the preceding Subsection shall not apply to copies of computer programs incorporated in products, machinery or equipment to be legally rented, and where such computer programs do not constitute the essential object of such rental."

[38] Supreme Court, decision No. Tai Fe Zi 397 (1998). The 7th Senate of the Supreme Court came to the same conclusion, Supreme Court, decision Tai Fe Zi 158 (1998).

[39] *Ming-Yang Shieh*, Does the Rental or Sale of Parallel Imported Laser Discs Violate Copyright [in Chinese], Taiwan Law Journal No. 7 (February 2000), 62–71 (62).

prohibits such activity, which is not the case here and secondly, the interests of the importers were entirely neglected.

4. The introduction of the distribution right in 2003- an exhaustible right

Although in 1992 the Copyright Act had already stipulated in Sec. 3(1) No.12 that "Distribution" means, with or without compensation, to provide the original of a work, or a copy thereof, to the public for the purpose of trade or circulation. It did not comprehensively recognise the distribution right until the 2003 amendment[40]. Sec. 28a provides:

> "Except as otherwise provided in this Act, authors of works have the exclusive right to distribute their works through transfer of ownership. Performers have the exclusive right to distribute their performances reproduced in sound recordings through transfer of ownership."

The introduction was based on Article 6 WCT and Article 8 &12 WPPT. The distribution right is limited by the principle of domestic exhaustion which was codified by the 2003 amendment to the Copyright Act as Sec. 59a:

> "A person who has obtained ownership of the original of a work or a lawful copy thereof within the territory under the jurisdiction of the Republic of China may distribute it by means of transfer of ownership."

5. The introduction of the right of public transmission in 2003- a non-exhaustible right

Again following the WCT (Article 8) and WPPT (Article 10) the 2003 Copyright Amendment Act introduced the right of public transmission, in order to capture the interactive feature that is unique to the Internet and cyberspace. Sec. 26bis proclaims:

> "Except as otherwise provided in this Act, authors of works have the exclusive right of public transmission of their works.
> Performers have the exclusive right of public transmission of their performances reproduced in sound recordings."

"Public transmission" is defined as: to make available or communicate to the public the content of a work through sounds or images by wire or wireless network, or through other means of communication, including enabling the public to receive the content of such work by any of the above means at a time or place individually chosen by them (Sect. 3(1) No.10). The right of public transmission will not be exhausted by the transmission itself, as no exhaustion clause was provided for in the Copyright Act.

IV. Japan

1. Introduction

Japan has developed relatively straightforward rules on the issue of domestic and international exhaustion of printed works, see paragraph 2. below. Issues get complicated for the secondary exploitation of certain works such as films and

---

[40] The rental right introduced into the Copyright Act in 1985 is a sort of distribution right.

phonograms due to additional rights of rental, lending or distribution, as is explained under paragraph 3. below. Rules for international exhaustion are dealt with under paragraph 4., and rules for the exhaustion of digital or digitally transmitted works under paragraph 5.

2. *Domestic exhaustion rules for printed works*

As opposed to patents and trade marks, the Copyright Act has a provision which touches upon exhaustion: Sec. 26bis(2) Copyright Act which provides as follows."

(1) The author shall have the exclusive right to offer his work...to the public by transfer of ownership of the original or copies of the work...

(2) The provision of the preceding paragraph shall not apply in the case of transfer of ownership of the original or copies of a work under the following conditions:

(i) The original or copies of a work, the ownership of which has been transferred to the public by a person so authorised under the preceding paragraph, or with his consent;

...

(iv) The original or copies of a work, the ownership of which has been transferred abroad, without prejudice to the right equivalent to that mentioned in the preceding paragraph or by a person who has the right equivalent to that mentioned in that paragraph or with the authorisation of such person."

Despite the imprecise wording of the provision it seems clear that acts of first sale, whether domestically (alternative (i)), or abroad (alternative (iv)) will trigger exhaustion. Exhaustion does not apply to the additional rights mentioned in Sec. 26bis(1), that is, copies of cinematographic works specifically covered by Sec. 26. The above interpretation is also shared by academic writers.[41] The revision was introduced in 1999.

3. *Rules regarding the secondary use for specific types of works*

a) That domestic first sale of ordinary copyrighted items exhausts further rights of distribution has never been questioned. What has been extremely contentious, however, is the extent of Sec. 26(1) Copyright Act which grants additional rights of rental and lending to film works, and which according to the courts has the following function:

"According to the current Copyright Act, Sec. 26(1), the copyright owner holds the exclusive rights of rental and lending. Together with the corresponding provision of the Berne Convention (Brussels revision) on the distribution right for cinematographic works, the following should apply: If the maker/author produces the film with the intention of presentation in a cinema and an indeterminate number of copies are made thereafter, the maker/author in order to secure his rental/lending rights in the film will make his consent to further distribution or assignment subject to payment to those cinemas to

---

[41] M. *Kato*, Chôsakuken chikujô kôgi (Copyright Act Annotated), Tokyo 2000, 117. Ministry of Culture (ed.), Chôsakukenhô, fusei kyôsô boshi hô gaisetsu (Explanation on the Copyright and Unfair Competition Prevention Acts), Tokyo 1999, 194.

whom he has rented out the film for presentation. This shall serve the protection of the maker/author of a cinematographic work. Pursuant to Sec. 2(1)(xx) Copyright Act, this right is independent of 'whether the transfer and lending of copies of a work to the public is made' with or without payment, and in the case of a cinematographic work or a work reproduced therein, it includes the transfer and lending of copies of such work for the purpose of making the cinematographic work available to the public. According to Sec. 26(1) Copyright Act, the presentation in cinemas is only a special, but not the only, expression of the author's exclusive rights. To this extent it is obvious that the sale of videotapes meant for public presentation also falls under the rental/lending right in Sec. 26(1) Copyright Act."[42]

In other words, film works enjoy inexhaustible rights over the subsequent distribution of works. The scope of works with "inexhaustible" rights is thus limited to film works and other works that enjoy particularly rights of lending, e.g. phonograms. Secs. 95ter and 97ter Copyright Act grants exclusive right of rental and lending for the first 12 months, thereafter upon equitable remuneration and paragraph 2 (c) deals in detail with this.

b) A particularly contentious issue concerns the applicability of Sec. 26 (1) to video games. The Supreme Court has held that video games fall within the ambit of "cinematographic works" but that the distribution right for video games would exhaust upon first sale.

"In the course of enacting the present Copyright Act, Sec. 26 (1) on the distribution right was introduced in order to meet the obligations imposed by the Berne Convention for the Protection of Literary and Artistic Works (revised in Brussels on 26 June 1948) which provides for such a distribution right with regard to cinematographic works. That such a distribution right was only provided for cinematographic works is due to the huge investment into a film production and the necessity of an effective capital return by controlling the film circulation; when the Copyright Act was enacted, the above mentioned distribution system was customary, which was mainly based on the rental of a number of copies, and because the act of showing the film without the consent of the copyright owner was hard to control, it was necessary to control the previous act of distribution, including ownership transfer and rental. Taking this situation as a starting point, Sec. 26 Copyright Act is interpreted to mean that the right to transfer or to rent (Copyright Act, Secs. 26 and 2 (1) (xix)) a cinematographic work or its reproductions within the above mentioned distribution system for the purpose of public display does not exhaust upon first sale. Sec. 26, however, provides for no further rule which would give a definite answer to the question whether the distribution right exhausts or not, so that this question must be understood as being left open to interpretation.

Consequently, with regard to the assignment of ownership in reproductions of cinematographic works intended for use on home TV game devices and not for public showing, and from the viewpoint of securing a smooth market circulation of goods as explained under a), b) and c), the right in the public transfer of these works has exhausted. Once legally assigned, it has achieved the purpose of its grant, so that the copyright has no more effect on the act of subsequent public distribution of computer game reproductions.

Pursuant to Sec. 26bis (1) of the 1999 amended Copyright Act (Amendment Law No.77/1999), works other than cinematographic works are provided with a right of ownership transfer; Sec. 26bis (2) of the amended law further provides that this right shall exhaust once a lawful transfer has taken place. The reason for not applying (1) of the same provision to cinematographic works is that the distribution right granted in cinematographic works already comprises the right of ownership transfer. (2) of the same provision affirms the above mentioned exhaustion principle, but it would be inappropriate to deduce from (1) and (2) *a contrario* that these provisions would not allow the exhaustion of the transfer right in copies of the cinematographic work form "computer games".[43]

The above Supreme Court decision gives an interesting account of previous concurring decisions of the District Courts and Higher Courts of Tokyo and Osaka.

---

[42] Tokyo District Court, 1 July 1995, 27 IIC 570, 571 [1996]—Beauty and the Beast.
[43] Supreme Court, 25 April 2002, 35 IIC 467 [2004]—"Videogames".

The first round "Tokyo District Court vs. Osaka District Court" ended in a tie. Both courts concentrated on the question of whether computer games constituted cinematographic works or not. The Osaka court adhered to the prevailing opinion which had classified computer games as cinematographic works, arguing that they corresponded to the legal definition of cinematographic works contained in Sec. 2 (3) as works "expressed by a process producing visual or audio-visual effects analogous to those of cinematography and fixed in material form".[44] Consequently, the copyright owners enjoyed the non-exhaustive distribution right reserved to cinematographic works. In contrast, the Tokyo District Court denied computer games the quality of cinematographic works, arguing that the characteristic feature of such works would be an unalterable sequence of moving images, whereas the sequence of the images of a computer game varied depending on the player's operations.[45] Even though arriving at contrary results, what both decisions have in common is that they did not cast further doubts on the exhaustive character of the distribution right as such.

Appeals were filed against both decisions, so that in the next round the High Courts of Tokyo and Osaka were pitted against each other. The Tokyo High Court[46] largely upheld the decision of the Tokyo District Court, but on different grounds, stating that computer games in fact were cinematographic works, but that in light of the legislative purpose for granting a distribution right to the film copyright owner, reproductions of computer games were different from the "cinematographic work reproductions" mentioned in Sec. 26 Japanese Copyright Act (hereinafter "JCA"). The latter would only cover film copies produced in small numbers, each of them intended for presentation before a large audience, thereby representing a high economic value. Reproductions of computer games instead were produced in high numbers for distribution to many individuals, so that they could not possibly correspond to what the legislature had in mind when formulating the term "cinematographic work reproductions". Consequently, the distribution right exclusively granted for cinematographic works was not applicable to reproductions of computer games, even though the latter were cinematographic works as defined by Sec. 2 (3) JCA. The Supreme Court preferred to follow the reasoning of the Osaka courts.

c) Apart from film works under Sec. 26, other types of works were also endowed with rights of secondary exploitation, namely rental and lending (in Japanese, the expression *taiyoken* covers both). Here, a decision by the Fair Trade Commission confirmed that attempts to introduce rights of rental and lending in the absence of specific provisions to this end were contrary to the Antimonopoly Act[47]. Rights of secondary use of phonograms were introduced in 1983. The amendment was directly prepared and enacted by Parliament due to concerns about heavy losses caused to right owners by the growing phonogram rental

---

[44] Osaka District Court decision of 7 October 1999, Hanrei Jihô 1699, 48.

[45] Tokyo District Court decision of 27 May 1999, Hanrei Jihô 1679, 3; German translation in GRUR Int .2001, 183.

[46] Tokyo High Court decision of 27 March 2001, Hanrei Jihô 1747, 60.

[47] FTC, 15 December 1983, 389 Kôsei Torihiki 34—"Nihon Record".

industry. The final revision of 25 May 1984,[48] regularly presented by the Copyright Council, became effective on 1 January 1985. According to the amendment, authors were granted an exclusive rental right (Sec. 26ter), the introduction of which was deferred for magazines and books (Sec. 4bis Supplementary Provisions). Performers and phonogram producers were also granted an exclusive rental right, the exclusivity of which, however, was limited to a maximum of one year after first publication—for the rest of the protection term, their rental right was reduced to a mere remuneration right (for performers: Sec. 95ter; for phonogram producers: Sec. 97ter). Despite this limitation, the rental right of neighbouring right owners caused the first serious collision of the interests of authors and phonogram producers. Due to a tacit agreement between right owner groups and the Copyright Council, neighbouring right owner organisations promised not to enforce their rental right with regard to phonograms, but to accept remuneration instead. Some phonogram producers, however, disregarded this promise and sued a number of rental shops.[49] Foreign demands for granting rental rights to foreigners were held off by referring to domestic problems that had to be resolved before extending rights to foreigners.[50] On May 1991, the rental right was extended to phonogram producers being residents of member states to the Geneva Phonogram Treaty and to the Rome Convention.[51] The TRIPS Agreement required Japan to broaden protection to include all nationals of WTO Member States. The wording of Art. 14.4 TRIPS Agreement is a tribute to the earlier Japanese solution of remunerating phonogram producers and performers. According to this provision, a member that had already in force a system of equitable remuneration for the rental of phonograms instead of an exclusive right to authorise such rental, could maintain such system. Thus, additional rights of rental and lending *de facto* exist for phonograms, but not for other copyrighted works.

4. *Rules for international exhaustion*

There has been no copyright case directly related to *international* exhaustion of ordinary copyrighted works. The only precedent concerned the importation of video cassettes of a Walt Disney film. The court prohibited further distribution, though not based on international exhaustion rules, but rather on the specific provisions of Sec. 26(1) Copyright Act that would apply equivalently to domestic films:

> "It was established above that Disney owns a rental/lending right in Japan in the cinematographic work and its copy. Through the unauthorised sale of the videotapes, the plaintiff infringed the copyright (rental/lending right) of the copyright owner in the film, Disney. As stated above, the copies were produced and distributed in the U.S. with the consent of the copyright owner, the U.S. Walt Disney company. The plaintiff purchased the copies from a U.S. company and imported them. Therefore, the videotapes are parallel imported goods. According to the opinion of the plaintiff, Disney received

---

48 Law No. 46/1984.

49 See Zadankai (chat round) of JASRAC representatives in *JASRAC*, Vol.II (1990), 307–312.

50 *S. Matsuoka* in Copyright 1989, 152-159; *T. Kudô* in 365 Copyright [1991], 2–15.

51 Law No. 63/1991; Japan acceded to the Rome Treaty in 1989 (see below).

reasonable compensation already through the sale of the videotapes so that the further distribution of the videotapes purchased in the U.S. within the country cannot constitute an impairment of the copyright owner in any way and thereby no infringement of the rental/lending right can be construed. If, within the country, consent of the copyright owner to the distribution of copies of a cinematographic work in the form of videotapes (as is the case with regard to parallel imported goods) does not exist, the lack of an infringement of the distribution right cannot be based on law or on relevant court decisions. As far as the Copyright Act gives the copyright owner certain exclusive rights under the provisions of Secs. 21–28, only the author or the party to whom he has assigned the rights or the exercise thereof is entitled to exercise such rights. This contains an unambiguous presumption in favour of protection of the author's rights. To this extent, the copyright owner currently decides for each country when a cinematographic presentation shall take place and when he, or third parties with his consent, put videotapes on the market to secure an adequate return in investment on the production of the film. If, e.g. in a country after the launch of the film, videotapes of that film are sold and these are parallel imported in great amounts into another country while the film is still being shown in cinemas, this means a substantial loss of interest in the presentation in cinemas, and in the end may lead to enormous damage incurred by the person who, without authorisation, undertakes the sale of the videotapes of the film financed by the copyright owner. Allowing the copyright owner in a film, i.e. a motion picture company, to decide on the time of the presentation, as well as on the sale of videotapes separately for each country, for Japan is an obligation under the Berne Convention with regard to cinematographic works. This obligation was met by the enactment of Sec. 26 Copyright Act that regulates the exercise of the rental/lending right, and to that extent is also determined to serve the purpose of copyright as such, namely protection of the author. The videotapes in question were produced and distributed in the U.S. with the consent of the copyright owner. There, Art. 109a Copyright Act and the first sale doctrine are applicable according to U.S. copyright law. This means that after the first international release, a limitation of distribution or dissemination is not permissible. There is no sufficient evidence to assume that this consent also includes the distribution in Japan, however. For this reason, infringement of the domestic distribution right by the parallel importation of the videotapes cannot be ruled out just because of the consent to distribution on the U.S. market. The above understanding leads to a limitation of the market for parallel imports and thereby to a limitation of price competition for videotapes of the film. The possibility of deciding on the time of distribution of videotapes in Japan regardless of other countries may also limit the conditions for a direct distribution of videotapes for the film here. That this right, which serves the protection of the author, disregards public use of cultural property or does not contribute to cultural development is an opinion that cannot be agreed to..."[52]

In other words, the court has based its reasoning on the specific provision of Sec. 26 and the domestic (inexhaustible) right of further distribution for film works, not the importation as such. The decision was rendered prior to the 1999 revision of the Copyright Act that, as mentioned above, explicitly allows international exhaustion on the conditions mentioned there. Thus, video cassettes of films may be imported, but not distributed without the copyright owner's consent.

5. *Exhaustion Rules in the Digital Environment*

A specific right of public transmission has been included in the Japanese Copyright Act to cover the digital distribution of works:

Definitions in the Copyright Act:

Sec. 2(1)(vii^bis^): "public transmission" means the transmission of radio communication or wire-telecommunication intended for direct reception by the public, excluding the transmission (other than that of program works) by wire-telecommunication installations one part of which is located on the same premises where the other part is located or, if the premises are occupied by two or more persons, both parts of which are located within the area therein occupied by one person."

---

[52] Tokyo District Court, 1 July 1995, 27 IIC 570-572 [1996]—"Beauty and the Beast".

Sec. 2(1)(ix^{quater}): "interactive transmission" means the public transmission made automatically in response to a request from the public, excluding the public transmission falling within the term "broadcasting" or "wire-diffusion."

Sec. 2(1)(ix^{quinquies}): "making transmittable" means the putting in such a state that the interactive transmission can be made by either of the following acts: (a)to record information on public transmission memory of an interactive transmission server already connected with telecommunication networks for the use by the public ("interactive transmission server" means a device which, when connected with telecommunication networks for the use by the public, has a function of making the interactive transmission of information which is either recorded on such a part of its memory as used for the interactive transmission (hereinafter in this item referred to as "public transmission memory" or inputted to such device; the same shall apply hereinafter), to add a memory recording information as a public transmission memory of such an interactive transmission server, to convert such a memory recording information into a public transmission memory of such an interactive transmission server, or to input information to such an interactive transmission server;

(b) to connect with telecommunication networks for the use by the public an interactive transmission server which records information on its public transmission memory or which inputs information to itself. In this case, where a connection is made through a series of acts such as wiring, starting of an interactive transmission server or putting into operation of programs for transmission or reception, the last occurring one of these acts shall be considered to constitute the connection."

Rights conferred:

Section 23. (1)The author shall have the exclusive right to make the public transmission of his work (including the making transmittable of his work in the case of the interactive transmission).

(2)The author shall have the exclusive right to communicate publicly, by means of a receiving apparatus, his work of which the public transmission has been made.

The above provision under Sec. 23 does not indicate the extent to which rights of distribution are exhausted by public transmission. Although this provision seems to confer a similar inexhaustible right as the one in Sec. 26 (distribution right for film works), the courts may well distinguish between different types of exhaustible transactions, e.g. the purchase of a digital copy of a work, and inexhaustible ones, e.g. schemes of music on demand. There are no court decisions or academic writings on this subject yet.

V. Korea

Nowadays, a high volume of musical works are available in digital format. Development of the transmission technology, Streaming and P2P has allowed digital music works to be easily distributed and duplicated. Further, with the development of portable communication devices, musical works are now available for many mobile service users by means of downloading onto mobile phones, for example ring back tones, or ring tones. While this means that right holders have increased avenues of profit-making, the possibility of infringement has also been greatly increased .[53]

Cyberspace may be likened to the locust of the music industry in Korea which is plagued by piracy. The most successful online music site, Bugs Music, with about 14 million subscribers has streamed record music without authorisation of

[53] *Yun, Sunhee/Cho, Yongsoon*, A Legal Study on Use of Digital Music Works—Focus on Streaming services and Mobile services, Vol. 13 Journal of Industrial Property Law 289–322 (2003).

the neighbouring copyright owner. Unlike P2P services, streaming music services has a characteristic feature—it does not leave behind any files at the user's computer. This feature has been the cause of many debates over the illegal copying of streaming music in Korea. While this new medium offers record companies an unprecedented opportunity to reach more consumers around the globe, it also threatens the very control that the industry exercises over its sound recordings and may undercut traditional record sales.[54] In the US, copyright law copes with this kind of problem through the imposition of liability. An effective response to the changing internet environment in Korea will require both new legal tools and substantial improvements in enforcement practices.

The technical issue is the "exhaustion" of an intellectual property right.[55] The exhaustion of rights doctrine is one of the most fundamental limitations on intellectual property rights.[56] Under the theory of the "exhaustion of rights," when an intellectual property right holder sells an article embodying those rights, they are exhausted with respect to that article. Thus, a purchaser can resell the article without being liable for infringement. The owner of intellectual property cannot control the resale of a legally purchased good, and parallel imports are legal. Unless otherwise specified by law, subsequent acts of resale, rental, lending or other forms of commercial use by third parties can no longer be controlled or opposed by the owner of the intellectual property or its licensee. There is a fairly broad consensus that this applies at least within the context of the domestic market. The exhaustion of rights doctrine takes on its greatest significance when goods embodying intellectual property rights are traded internationally. When rights are held in multiple nations for the same piece of intellectual property, the question arises whether, when and which of these rights are exhausted by sale of the goods.[57]

Although parallel imports are increasing in Korea, Korean law is, basically, silent on these issues. Primarily, intellectual property laws govern the legal classification of parallel imports into Korea,[58] although other types of laws may also be relevant.[59] Complications arise since Korean law does not expressly provide for

---

[54] U.S. music sales declined 4 percent to $13.7 billion in 2001 from $14.3 billion in 2000, according to the Recording Industry Association of America, which represents U.S. record labels. Recording Industry Announces 2001 Year-End Shipments, at http://www.riaa.com/News(uscore)Story.cfm?id=491 (last visited 3 February 2003).

[55] It is also sometimes referred to as the "first sale doctrine."

[56] *Darren E. Donnelly*, Parallel Trade and International Harmonization of the Exhaustion of Rights Doctrine, 13 Computer & High Tech. L.J. 448 (1997).

[57] Inherent in patent, trademark, and copyright protection is the right to prevent infringing imports. Typically, right holders use this protection against "pirated" copies, but the protection may also be effective to prevent the importation of genuine goods. See, *Id.*

[58] The Patent Act (*Teugheobeob*), Act No. 4207 on 13 January 1990; The Utility Model Act (*Silyongsinanbeob*), Act No. 4209 on 13 January 1990; The Design Act (*Euijangbeob*), Act No. 4208, on 13 January 1990; The Trade Mark Act (*Sangpyobeob*), Act No. 4210 of 13 January 1990; The Copyright Act (*Cheojakkweonbeob*), Act No. 3916 of 31 December 1986.

[59] The Antimonopoly Act (Monopoly Regulation and Fair Trade Act ("MRFTA"), Act. No.4198, on April 1, 1991; The Custom Act (*Kwansebeob*), Act No. 6305 of 29 December 2000.

international exhaustion and this is further compounded by the lack of uniform treatment of parallel imports across her intellectual property regime. The Korean Copyright Act does not contain explicit prohibition of parallel imports of copyrighted products. The parallel importation of copyrighted goods seems to be lawful. Under Sec. 20, an exclusive rights is the right to distribute the original or reproduction of the work to the public. Sec. 43(1) of the Act provides the basis for exhaustion of rights—"The original or reproduction of a work offered for transaction by means of selling with the authorisation of the owner of the right of distribution may be distributed continuously". [60] The Act also provides that the importation into Korea, for the purpose of distribution, of objects made by an act which would be an infringement of copyright or other rights protected under this Act, if they were made in Korea at the time of such importation.[61] At present, Korea permits parallel imports of copyright products, but there is no decision on the parallel importation of copyrighted goods. [62]

Because of the undesirable consequences of rental of phonograms and computer programs, which are almost always copied for private use after rental, many countries stipulate exclusive right to authorise rental of them or a levy system on copying machines and media. To respond to the challenges of the new digital era, in 1994, the Korean Copyright Act adopted a phonograms rental right,[63] and the Computer Program Protection Act granted a computer program rental right.[64] There has been a few legal decisions on authorisation to rent phonograms and programs, especially multi-media titles. The provisions of rental rights operate as a prohibition provision but there are no provisions about a rental right for books and home video tapes—these are everyday occurences. The phonograms rental right amendment to *the Copyright Act* does not apply retroactively. As regards computer programs, the rental right is restricted to cases where the program itself is not the essential object of the rental. Only legislation can effectively solve those issues relating to the legality of parallel importation of genuine goods and the rights of the copyright holder.

VI. Singapore

Internet trade or e-commerce as a means of delivering copyright works is fast becoming a way of life in Singapore. According to a 2002 survey on infocomm

---

[60] The owner of the right of distribution shall have the right, notwithstanding the provision of the Sec. 43(1) of the Copyright Act, to authorise the rental of commercial phonograms for profit-making purposes, Sec. 43(2) Copyright Act.

[61] Sec. 92(1)(i) Copyright Act.

[62] *Byung-il Kim*, Parallel Imports in Korea, in: Christopher Heath (ed.), Parallel Imports in Asia, 81 (Kluwer Law International, 2004). The Korean Fair Trade Commission (FTC) has announced guidelines on parallel imports in 1995 (FTC Notification No. 10/1995), and changed the *Guidelines on Types of Unfair Trade* Conducts regarding Parallel Import in 1997 (FTC Notification No. 27/1997) and 1998 (FTC Notification No. 18/1998) to raise legal transparency regarding parallel imports by specifically illustrating major examples of unfair parallel imports

[63] Sec. 43 of the Copyright Act.

[64] Sec. 19 of the CCPA.

usage in households and individuals in Singapore,[65] the total number of Internet users in Singapore grew from 1.6 million in 2001 to 2.1 million in 2002, representing an increase of 27.4% in just one year. Since the total population of Singapore then was about 4.16 million, this means that about 50% of the total population were Internet users in 2002.

This 2002 survey also measured the levels of various types of Internet applications and services, including e-entertainment. The table below is an extract of some results of this survey:

E-Entertainment	**Level of Usage**	**Level of Awareness**
Download software applications	48.8%	92.0%
Download and/or upload music (eg. MP3)	41.9%	93.7%
Download and/or upload digital photos	37.6%	85.5%
Download games	37.4%	92.9%
Download and/or upload video (eg. Mpg)	28.9%	88.6%
Music streaming	25.3%	78.1%
Video streaming (watch movies, live webcasts)	25.2%	80.7%

Base: 1,374,000 Internet users aged 15 and above

A comparison between the actual levels of usage and the levels of awareness indicates that there is still much potential for growth for on-line distribution of copyright works in the e-entertainment industry.

Currently, Singapore grants a broadcasting right and an inclusion in a cable programme service right to owners of copyright in authors works, cinematographic films, broadcasts and cable programmes. It may be argued that these two rights adequately protect on-line transmission of these copyright works, in particular, that the Singapore definition of 'cable programme service' allows for services involving asynchronous transmission of sounds and/or images[66] and are

[65] This survey is an annual survey conducted by the Infocomm Development of Singapore (IDA), the statutory board set up to foster a competitive world-class infocomm industry in Singapore, prepare residents for living and working in the 'New Economy', spearhead the delivery of citizen-centric e-government services, and build and operate the Government's IT infrastructure. The survey is available at IDA's website at www.ida.gov.sg.

[66] See Sec. 7(1) of the Copyright Act defining 'cable programme service' as "a service which consists wholly or mainly in the sending by any person, by means of a telecommunication system (whether run by him or by any other person), of sounds or visual images or both either —

(a) for reception, otherwise than by wireless telegraphy, at 2 or more places in Singapore, whether they are so sent for simultaneous reception or at different times in response to requests made by different users of the service; or

(b) for reception, by whatever means, at a place in Singapore for the purpose of their being presented there either to members of the public or to any group of persons" [emphasis added].

The argument that Internet webpages fall within this definition finds some support in the controversial decision in *Shetland Times v Will* (1996) 37 IPR 71, which interpreted a similar (but not identical) definition of 'cable programme service' in the UK Copyright Designs and Patents Act 1988. Note that the UK has repealed the cable casting right, replacing it with a right to communicate to the public: see the UK Copyright and Related Rights Regulation 2003.

interactive,[67] such as web services. However, an alternative view is that Internet transmissions cannot technically be described as broadcasts or cablecasts, and that the right set out in Art. 8 of the WCT serves as a "model for devising a 'transmission-neutral' right which is in line with the spirit of digital convergence and platform convergence".[68] Therefore, Singapore's agreement under the US-Singapore FTA to comply with Art. 8 of the WCT is not entirely a surprising move. The Singapore authorities have already intimated that they are reviewing the copyright law to introduce 'a right of making available on an interactive mode' and a 'right of dissemination through digital means—separate from wireless broadcast right and cable program right'.[69]

There is another right in the WCT which should be examined in the context of Internet trade of copyright works. This is the right to 'make available to the public of the original and copies of works through sale or other transfer of ownership'—often referred to as the distribution right—in Art. 6. It is clear from the Agreed Statement to this article that only fixed copies that can be put into circulation as tangible objects are subject to the distribution right. In other words, distribution of tangible objects embodying the copyright works (e.g. video tapes) is governed by Art. 6, while online distribution of copyright works (e.g. video streaming) is governed by Art. 8.[70] A material difference in this distinction is the fact that the right in Art. 6, but not the right in Art. 8, can be exhausted. This is expressly provided for in Art. 6(2) of the WCT,[71] thereby preserving the *status quo* in Art. 6 of the TRIPS Agreement. Therefore, if a person orders via Internet a legitimate copy of a music CD from the US, Singapore copyright law can provide that resale of this copy in Singapore does not infringe the copyright owner's right, as it has been exhausted.

Currently, Singapore does in fact provide for an international exhaustion of right in her copyright law:[72] the importation and sale of parallel imports is

---

[67] Note that the Singapore definition of 'cable programme service', *ibid*, is not subject to an exception for interactive services, as was the case in the UK (see s 7(2)(a) of the Copyright, Designs and Patents Act 1988, repealed by the UK Copyright and Related Rights Regulation 2003, *ibid*).

[68] See, for example, *Seng*, Copyright Norms and the Internet: The Problems of Works Convergence (1998) 2 SJICL 76, at 104–108.

[69] This announcement was made by the Intellectual Property Office of Singapore on 15 August 2003 at a seminar on copyright for the media industry organised by the Media Authority of Singapore. The Copyright (Amendment) Act 2004 introduced, with effect from 1 January 2005, a new right of 'communication to the public' for authors' works, cinematographic films, broadcasts and cable programmes. The former broadcast right and the cable program right are now subsumed under this new right of 'communication to the public'. In the case of sound recordings, the Amendment Act 2004 introduced a new right to 'make available to the public a sound recording by means of, or as part of, a digital audio transmission'.]

[70] See *Reinbothe & von Lewinski*, The WIPO Treaties 1996—Commentary and Legal Analysis (2002) at p 87 and p 108.

[71] This provides that: "Nothing in this Treaty shall affect the freedom of Contracting Parties to determine the conditions, if any, under which the exhaustion of the right in paragraph (1) applies after the first sale of other transfer of ownership of the original or a copy of the work with the authorisation of the author."

[72] For an overview, see *Ng-Loy*, Exhaustion and Parallel Imports in Singapore, in Christopher Heath (ed.), Parallel Imports in Asia (Kluwer Law International 2004).

allowed where the imported article is made with the consent of the owner of the copyright in the country of manufacture, and in determining whether there is such consent, any condition restricting sale, distribution or other dealings in the article (other than a compulsory license) shall be disregarded.[73]

Within this framework, the only exceptions are those which are mandated by TRIPS, in particular the commercial rental right for computer programs and sound recordings.[74] Singapore has not introduced this right for cinematographic works; presumably, her position is that commercial rental of cinematographic works in the Singapore scene falls into the exception permitted by TRIPS, namely, such rental has not led to widespread copying of the works which is materially impairing the exclusive right of reproduction.[75] This position has not been challenged, not even by the International Intellectual Property Alliance (IIPA), which has always scrutinised closely the developments in Singapore's copyright law for the purpose of making its annual Special 301 reports to the USTR. This is probably due to IIPA's own finding that, even though the VCD piracy rate in Singapore has climbed from 2% in 1995 to 15% in 2003, pirated VCDs do not originate in Singapore; rather, most of them enter Singapore from Malaysia.[76] In other words, the reproduction is taking place outside of Singapore. This is support for Singapore's stance that commercial rental of films here does not materially affect the reproduction right of the film copyright owners.

VII. Malaysia

Copyrighted goods have a wide audience base in Malaysia, and at the consumer level the most popular items are books, music, movies and software (not necessarily in that order). Much of the trade in these occurs in the real world, that is,

---

[73] See Sec. 25(3)–(4), read with the secondary infringement provisions (ss 32–33 and ss 104-105) in the Copyright Act. Note that if there is no copyright owner in the country of manufacture, then the relevant person to give the consent would be the copyright owner in Singapore: s 25(3)(b). Commercial exploitation of infringing copies of copyright works with the relevant knowledge constitutes a criminal offence which attracts an imposition of a fine of up to S$100,000 and/or imprisonment of up to a term of 5 years: see Sec. 136 of the Copyright Act. In some cases, the defendants charged under Sec. 136 raised the defence that the articles they were selling were genuine parallel imports. It has been held that the prosecution bears the burden of proving beyond reasonable doubt that the articles were manufactured without the consent of the owner of copyright in the country of making, that is, they are not legitimate parallel imports: *Highway Video Pte Ltd v PP* [2002] 1 SLR 129 at 143. In one case where such a defence was raised but the prosecution succeeded in discharging the onerous burden of proof that the articles were not legitimate parallel imports, the prosecution urged the sentencing judge to impose a higher fine on the defendant because he had raised a sham defence. This argument was dismissed by the court who held that the defendant "was entirely justified in raising the issue of parallel imports as the burden lies on the prosecution, in making out the offence under s 136": *PP v Poh Kim Video Pte Ltd* [2003] SGHC 304.

[74] See Art 11 of TRIPS and s 26(1)(c) [for computer programs] of the Copyright Act; Art 14(4) of TRIPS and s 82(1)(b) of the Copyright Act [for sound recordings].

[75] Art 11 TRIPS.

[76] See, generally, the website of IIPA (www.iipa.com) for their annual Special 301 reports/recommendations on Singapore.

through the purchase of hardcopies. The Internet has not had substantial impact on the trade of copyrighted goods (especially digital works) in Malaysia due to the profile of the local Internet users.

According to the 2002 Internet Subscriber Study published by the National Information Technology Council (NITC), there are 7.8 million Internet users in Malaysia.[77] This places Malaysia 19th in world ranking by number of Internet users.[78] While the numbers may seem high, they might not accurately reflect the number of persons who are actually downloading digital works from the Internet because a majority of the 7.8 million users gain Internet access from their workplace where there are policies against such activities. Instead, any downloading activity is more likely to happen at home and in this sense there are only 2.9 million Internet subscribers in Malaysia, a vast majority of whom are on dial-up connections.[79] Dial-up users are no serious down loaders due to the speed limitations of a 56K modem and the per-minute dial-up charges. That leaves only the broadband subscribers, of which there are only about 110,000 in Malaysia (or a 0.44% penetration rate).[80] While this minority group represents the most active and prolific downloaders and consumers of digital works, their small numbers mean that their impact on the overall trade in digital copyright works is negligible.

Nevertheless, it is arguable whether in the very first place the distribution of a work in the digital environment is even considered as a parallel import. Distribution via the Internet is quite separate and distinct from the conventional distribution channels; not only is the channel different ('cyber space' versus 'real space') but the format of the work is also different (electronic compared to physical, or 'softcopy' against 'hardcopy'). Parallel importation normally concerns itself with one particular mode of distribution. Typically, the trader who complains about parallel imports is a person who has been given exclusive territorial rights to distribute a product (in a particular channel and format) and whose rights are violated by the importation of equivalent products (in the same channel and format) by another. The scope of the trader's rights is crucial because a digital work distributed via the Internet might not be within the trader's territorial scope in the first place and hence, there is no cause for a complaint of parallel importation.

In this Internet age, it is common for the copyright owner to reserve the online distribution for himself or another (segregating the market by delivery channel), and specify that the trader only distributes the hardcopy version (segregating the market by format of the goods). This already happens in the film industry where the primary release is through cinemas followed later by a domestic release on videocassette or DVD—the release rights holders may be two different entities, and neither can complain about the other since their rights and markets have been delineated. Similarly, so long as the copyright owner defines the Internet

---

[77] Also reported in *The Star* newspaper, 20 June 2003.
[78] Source: http://www.internetworldstats.com/top25.htm
[79] As at Q4 2003. Source: Malaysian Communications and Multimedia Commission website, http://www.mcmc.gov.my/mcmc/facts_figures/stats/index.asp
[80] Ibid.

market as separate from the conventional one, any legitimate online distribution of the digital version would not be considered a parallel import of the hardcopy.

In any event, parallel importation of copyrighted goods is now no longer an issue. While Malaysia adopts the international exhaustion rule when it comes to patents and trade marks, the position for copyright was less clear earlier. The Act clearly allows a person to import into Malaysia lawfully made copies of a work,[81] but whether such a person could then distribute the imported works is another consideration altogether. This stems from the argument that the Act allows the copyright owner to control the distribution of copies of the work within Malaysia. In one case touching on this issue, the judge supported the view that under copyright law the distribution right was not exhausted even after a sale, thus entitling the right holder to control the resale or rental of copies of his work.[82] However, he was only speaking in the context of copyrighted works within the local market and did not deal with the case where imports came into the picture. Still, the non-exhaustion of rights, albeit in a local sense, led one writer to conclude that 'copyright owners are vested with full control over the first and subsequent distributions of their works, which entitle them to also effectively prevent parallel importation of their works into Malaysia.'[83] The position regarding this has been clarified by the Copyright (Amendment) Act 2000. The distribution right is now confined only to controlling the 'circulation of copies not previously put into circulation in Malaysia'; once the work has been circulated in Malaysia, the right to control distribution is exhausted together with any right to control subsequent importation of the work into Malaysia.[84]

Lastly, insofar as digital works that are meant to be distributed via the Internet are concerned, for example streaming media, these are protected in Malaysia under the 'communication to the public' right[85] which is defined as 'the transmission of a work or live performance through wire or wireless means to the public, including the making available of a work or live performance to the public in such a way that members of the public may access the work or live performance from a place and at a time individually chosen by them'.[86] This right replaced the previous 'broadcasting' and 'communication by cable' rights and came into effect in 1999 to cater for internet transmissions or 'netcasts'.

VIII. Thailand

Before I go into the details, I need to give a brief explanation about the Thai legal system. Thailand is a civil law country. Hence, when deciding what is the

---

[81] Copyright Act 1987, s. 36(2).

[82] *Class One Video Distributors Sdn Bhd & Anor v. Chanan Singh Sher Singh & Anor* [1997] 3 CLJ 694.

[83] *Wang L*, Class One Video Distributors Sdn Bhd & Anor v. Chanan Singh Sher Singh & Anor—A Commentary, [1997] 3 CLJ xix.

[84] See the proviso to Sec. 13(1) Copyright Act 1987.

[85] Copyright Act 1987, Sec. 13(1)(aa).

[86] Copyright Act 1987, Sec. 3.

applicable law in any given situation, Thai lawyers resort first to the Thai statutes whilst decisions of the Supreme Court would be their last resort. Such decisions are what we consider our precedents. It should be noted that although they are not regarded as having equal standing with the codified law, they are persuasive authority and in many instances are followed by lower courts and the Supreme Court itself (of course, they can be reversed or ignored). Supreme Court decisions are the *only* type of court decisions which are published, and not even all of them are published regularly. Decisions of other courts are never published on a regular basis and one must have either worked on the case or been told about them to know of their existence.

Issues of Internet trade, digital works and parallel imports involving copyright have not been widely discussed in Thailand. Neither have there been any Supreme Court decisions. The Copyright Act does not cover issues of copyright in the digital environment. Nevertheless, it should be noted that, under the present Copyright Act, the copyright owner has a right to bar others from distributing his work (or authorised copies of his work). This is because Section 15 provides that the copyright owner has the exclusive right of communication of his work to the public (among other rights), and Section 4 provides that communication to the public means "making a work available to the public by performing, lecturing, praying, playing, causing it to be heard and/or seen, construction, **distribution** or by any other means." And when these two sections are applied to parallel importation, it means that the copyright owner can bar other parties from selling his work or authorised copies of his work which may have been imported into Thailand without his consent.

In my opinion, theoretically such rules limiting unauthorised distribution of works can be enforced in a digital environment because the Copyright Act does not limit the manner in which the distribution is done. (There is no definition of the term "distribution" in the Act.) However, in practice, whether the copyright owner can really bar others from distributing copies of his work through the Internet is a big question.

In any event, these two points in the draft amendment bill (which is not yet final) should be noted:-

(i) the word "distribution" has been removed from the definition of "communication to the public." This indicates that the authors of the bill intend to incorporate the doctrine of exhaustion of rights into the copyright law; and

(ii) the term "communication to the public" has been given a new definition—"making a work available to the public by performing, lecturing, praying, playing, causing it to be heard and/or seen, construction, including the making available to the public of the work in such a way that members of the public may access the work from a place and at a time individually chosen by them, or by other means. Moreover, in respect of program computers, it shall mean making available to the public a computer program in such a way that member of the public may access the work from a place and at a time individually chosen by them." Apparently, this new definition of the term is designed for the digital environment.

IX. The Philippines

The IP Code is silent on the subject of exhaustion of rights and regulating parallel imports. While there are border control measures found in the IP Code, it is directed against the entry of counterfeit products within Philippine territory.[87]

Nevertheless, the IP Code reaffirms the exclusive right of a copyright holder to cause the first public distribution of the work[88]. This provision effectively covers the right to prohibit importation of a copyrighted work in the event such importation and sale would constitute a violation of the copyright owner's right to first public distribution.

However, the IP Code expressly allows a person to import a work without the authorisation of the copyright owner, provided such importation is solely for his personal use [89]. The copies imported under the exceptions may not be used in any way to violate the rights of the copyright owner otherwise, "such unlawful use shall be deemed an infringement and shall be punishable as such without prejudice to the proprietor's right of action". [90]

Notwithstanding the absence of a specific provision under the IP Code prohibiting parallel imports, the Courts have technically enjoined parallel imports based on the provisions of the Civil Code governing contractual breach, abuse of rights, malicious interference and unfair competition.[91]

In Yu vs. Court of Appeals[92], the Supreme Court effectively enjoined the parallel importation of wall-covering products when it recognised the right of the petitioner to an exclusive distributorship agreement. The Court found that the private respondent had misled the House of Mayfair in England into thinking that the goods FNF Trading (in concert with private respondent) was purchasing were intended for Nigeria. The goods were eventually shipped to and sold in the Philippines. The private respondent had thereby induced the House of Mayfair to violate its distributorship agreement with petitioner, which then gave rise to an action for damages under the Civil Code.

The Yu case was cited by the Court of Appeals in the case of *U-Bix Corporation v. Ariancorp International Inc.*[93] in support of its decision enjoining the sale of parallel import products. In its decision, the CA said that the Yu case recognises exclusive distributorship agreement as an exemption to our laws against restraint of trade. Hence, sales in violation of the exclusive distributorship agreement (e.g., as a result of parallel importation) likewise give rise to an action for damages under the Civil Code.

While the Courts have effectively enjoined parallel importation, the government, on the other hand, took a different view when it authorised the parallel

---

[87] Copyright owners may request the court issue an injunction preventing the entry of counterfeit goods under IP Code Sec. 216(a).

[88] IP Code Sec. 177.3.

[89] IP Code Sec. 190.1.

[90] IP Code Sec. 190.2.

[91] As defined in New Civil Code Artic 28 and to be distinguished from Unfair Competition or "passing-off" found in IP Code Sec. 168.

[92] 217 SCRA 328–333 (1993).

[93] CA-G.R. No. 41620 (1995).

importation of pharmaceutical products. After the aforesaid decisions, the Department of Health authorised the parallel importation of pharmaceutical products into the Philippines, regardless of the existence of exclusive distributorship agreements.[94] The government action was intended to lower drug prices and make the same more affordable for the less privileged people in society.[95]

The government's action is not surprising since there are no specific provisions of law prohibiting such importation, and public policy considerations had warranted the parallel importation of pharmaceutical products. In addition, the above cases in disallowing parallel imports were decided based on peculiar facts. The cases reveal parallel importation had been enjoined on the basis of deception and existence of proprietary rights arising from an exclusive arrangement. In the Yu case, the Supreme Court said that a third party inducement of such arrangement is an actionable wrong that became the basis for enjoining a parallel import. In the U-Bix case, the Court of Appeal held that an exclusive distributorship agreement is exempted from laws prohibiting restraint of trade, and enjoined further sales of parallel import products. In these cases, there was no mention of possible violation of intellectual property rights.[96]

The absence of specific law prohibiting parallel importation and the ease with which internet trading can take place certainly facilitated this practice. Hence, it would be difficult to sustain an action against the entry of parallel import goods, including films works (e.g. video tapes) in the digital environment. Moreover, the government had in the past allowed parallel importation of certain products based on public policy considerations.

Nevertheless, it has been said that intellectual property protection could not be simply overlooked, as they are hallmarks of a free trade system. In a parallel import situation arising from internet trading, the government will have to find other ways of giving protection and incentives to the owners of copyrights.[97]

---

[94] Department of Health Administrative Order No. 85 (2000).

[95] Ibid. See Explanatory Note.

[96] *Alex Ferdinand S. Fider*, Exhaustion and Parallel Imports in the Philippines,in C. Heath (ed.), Parallel Imports in Asia, Kluwer Law International 2004, 120–121.

[97] Ibid.

3
The Collective Exercise of Copyrights

KUNG CHUNG LIU

More than ever, the collective exercise of copyrights has become a crucial instrument of copyright management and enforcement, even a possible alternative for extensive criminalization of copyright infringements that is now taking place on a worldwide scale. And yet, the concerted actions by the collecting societies may evoke market power and antitrust concerns.

The country reports indicate how collecting societies have developed in their home countries in terms of members, market shares, and revenues, and how domestic legislation is dealing with the collective exercise of rights, e.g. by way of a control of royalty fees, compulsory management of copyrights, and exemption from cartel prohibitions.

A. Introduction

I. Modes of Exercising Copyright

1. From the Individual to the Collective

Copyright as an exclusive right by definition should be exercised by the individual copyright owners. Whenever possible, copyright owners would prefer to enforce their rights of their own volition. However, technological advancements have greatly enhanced the possibilities of exploiting copyrighted works. Thereby, it became neither feasible nor economical for most right holders and the users in the area of musical works (with the exception of dramatic works, or so-called 'grand rights' musical works[1]) to come to terms with respect to the exploitation of works on the basis of individual contracts. As early as 1851, an intermediary mechanism between right holders and users at large was established in France: The "Société des Auteurs, Copositeurs et Editeurs de Musique (SACEM).[2]" As the first collecting society, SACEM is still functioning with success. Many countries followed suit and witnessed the emergence and proliferation of collecting societies for all kinds of works.

The practical needs of cooperation between collecting societies in different countries led to the formation of international non-governmental organizations, the first being the International Confederation of Societies of Authors and Composers (CISAC) established in 1926.[3] As of 2004, CISAC numbers

---

1 Because the use of such works is confined to a small number of localities. See *Mihály Ficsor*, Collective Management of Copyright and Related Rights, WIPO, 2002, paragraph 73.

2 *Kung-Chung Liu*, Das Recht der Urheberrechtsverwertungsgesellschaften, VVF 1991, 5.

3 Ficsor, above note 1, paragraph 29.

210 authors' societies from 109 countries and indirectly represents more than 2 million creators covering the whole artistic repertoire: music, drama, literature, audio-visual works, graphic and visual arts. The total amount of domestic royalties collected by CISAC's member societies in 2003 amounted to more than €6.2 billion. Despite the challenging environment caused by digital piracy and decline in CD sales, this figure represents an increase over the previous years.[4]

2. *From the Collective to Rights-Clearance and the Individual*

Much later than the emergence of collecting societies which operate as communities with members behind them, rights-clearance agencies came to the fore, as corporate right holders (producers and publishers, etc) chose—in parallel to or independent of the collective exercise of their rights—to commission an agency to clear their rights on their behalf with few or no collectivised elements. The agency has the sole task of collecting and transferring royalties in accordance with individual rates and conditions as quickly and precisely as possible, and in proportion with the value and actual use of the productions involved (therefore in the following discussion, if not otherwise specified, collecting societies do not include rights-clearance agencies). Rights-clearance agencies function as a platform of licensing and of acquiring licenses.[5] In an inter-connected digital world of networks, agency-type rights management becomes more appealing to individual creators, because it is easy to use such an agency: individual creators, rather than becoming a member of any collecting society, just need to sign an authorization agreement at no cost. Of course, a handling fee is paid to the agency but no subsidies are paid to their peers, whether domestic or foreign.

A case in point would be the Copyright Clearance Center (CCC) based in the U.S. CCC manages the rights to over 1.75 million works and represents more than 9,600 publishers and hundreds of thousands of authors and other creators. The right holders maintain control by choosing what works to pre-authorise and what royalties to charge content users. All the agreements are non-exclusive and can be cancelled at any time.[6]

Especially in recording industry, the assumption that no individual member of a collecting society can negotiate licences no longer holds true for big sound reproduction companies which can and do enter into individual negotiations when the size and importance of the licensee makes it worthwhile to do so.[7] In other words, large right holders will choose where and when it is advantageous to license individually.

---

[4] What is CISAC? More information is available at http://www.cisac.org (last visited 30 July 2005).

[5] *Ficsor*, above note 1, paragraph 37.

[6] According to information available at the website of CCC http://www.copyright.com (last visit July 31, 2005).

[7] *John Temple Lang*, Media, Multimedia, and European Community Antitrust Law, (1998) 21 Fordham International Law Journal, at 1343.

II. Functions of Collecting Societies

1. *Effective Tools to Exercise Authors' Rights*

By pooling their individual copyrights in a collecting society and mandating it to administer them via a centralized mechanism, authors gain significant bargaining power to counter-balance the market power of large-scale users and secure better deals with them. In addition, collecting societies also function as units and solidarity organizations of authors[8] and aim "to ensure the safeguarding, respect and protection of the moral rights and professional interests attached to every kind of literary or artistic production.[9]" Collecting societies have proven to be the most effective and indispensable tool for the exercise of copyrights.

2. *Reducing Transaction Costs*

On a collectivized basis (such as standardized tariffs, licensing conditions and distribution rules), collecting societies reduce the "transaction costs" that would otherwise exist in searching, ascertaining and negotiating individual licenses, monitoring the uses, policing infringements and collecting royalties.[10] Collecting societies can further reduce transaction costs by concluding licensing agreements with organizations of users. Pursuing this rationale, the Gesetz über die Wahrnehmung von Urheberrechten und verwandten Schutzrechten (the Act on the Exercise of Copyrights and Related Rights enacted in 1965, hereinafter "WahrnG of Germany") even prescribes that collecting societies are obliged to conclude "Gesamtverträge" (common contracts) with users' organizations, provided that the number of their members is not too small (Sec.12).[11]

However, with the concentration of the music industry that led to five media companies (Universal, Warner, Bertelsmann, EMI and Sony) accounting for 80% of royalties collected and distributed, the economic advantage of using collecting societies could turn to the contrary at least in the area of mechanical rights. For example, Polygram reported in 1996 that it had identified potential savings of $2.5 million per annum if royalties payable from Polygram Records to Publishing were processed directly.[12]

---

[8] *Lang*, above note 7, at 1342.

[9] Article 4 of the 2004 Statutes of CISAC.

[10] *Bently/Sherman*, Intellectual Property Law, Oxford University Press, 2001, at 270.

[11] Martin Kretschmer's critique that "The transaction cost argument does indeed support some form of collective administration but not remotely in the shape of a traditional, membership-based collecting society.." is rather directed at questioning the economic rationale of including both authors (composers and lyricists) and publishers in collecting societies for music works, since the publishing companies offer enough commercial values to authors to command a full transfer of their copyrights to freely administer these rights as they see fit, without the intervention of authors. See *Martin Kretschmer*, The Failure of Property Rules in Collective Administration: Rethinking Copyright Societies as Regulatory Instruments,[2002]E.I.P.R. at 127–128

[12] *Kretschmer*, above note 11, at 132.

3. Facilitating the Expansion of Copyrights

The continuous creation of new copyrights is a motor for the development of copyright law. Increasingly, the speed of copyright expansion depends on the functions that collecting societies are able to offer to right holders and users. The more functions and trustworthiness collecting societies exhibit, the more willing the legislature would be to recognise new copyrights, such as the *droit de suite* and the right to levies on reproduction machines, that are manageable and enforceable only by virtue of a collective mechanism. In Germany, the well-developed collecting societies did lay the groundwork for a series of so-called "rights exercisable by collecting societies only" (verwertungsgesellschaftenpflichtige Rechte), such as rights of remuneration for the rental of records and video tapes (Sec.27(1)), for reproducing radio comments and newspaper articles (Sec.49(1)), and for reproduction apparatus (Sec. 54h(1)).[13]

4. Cultural and/or Social Functions of collecting societies

It is common practice the world over that collecting societies reach beyond collective management and pursue cultural and social objectives. They do this either voluntarily—under the Guidelines of CISAC, up to 10% of the collected license fees may be channelled into a socio-cultural fund (the so-called socio-cultural deduction)[14]—or as a legal obligation. In Germany for example, the WahrnG requires a distribution formula whereby "culturally important works and contributions shall be fostered" (Sec.7) and pension and social funds be set up (Sec.8).

The cultural and social functions of collective management organisations are particularly important in developing countries which incur huge trade deficits by extracting fees from local users and paying them to foreign collecting societies. With socio-cultural deductions in place, collecting societies in developing countries can keep a portion of fees collected on behalf of foreign collecting societies so as to achieve cultural and social objectives. It is understandable that right holders in the developed countries may be enraged by this practice. However, it has been convincingly argued by Dr. Ficsor that such practice is more than just a matter of generosity or solidarity for right holders in the developed world. Rather, it "may be a matter of foresight or even that of a mere cool-headed calculation in recognising that, through this, they may better and more efficiently achieve their overall objectives in a globalized world."[15]

III. Copyright Law and Collecting Societies

1. Constituting Procedural Copyright Law

Copyright law as we know it today comprises of at least two natures, viz. substantive and the other procedural. The former deals with the substantive rights of

---

[13] Schricker/Schricker 2. A. (1998) Einl. 25.

[14] *Kretschmer,* above note 11, at 134. The International Federation of Reproduction Rights Organizations (IFRRO) also recognises such deduction in its 1992 Principles for Bilateral Agreements, Type A, available at http://www.ifrro.org/papers/mod-prin.html (last visited 30 July 2005).

[15] *Ficsor,* above note 1, paragraph 36.

authors, performers and producers of works; the latter concerns the ways and means of enforcing and managing copyrights and related rights via collecting societies. The development of the procedural copyright law would surely have an immediate and significant impact on the future of substantive copyright law. The procedural and substantive copyright laws have become inseparable parts of copyright regimes.

2. Transforming Copyright from Property Rights to Liability Rights

If the regime choice between property rules and liability rules is to be made with economic considerations, then the former would be preferred where transaction costs are low, parties involved are few and the value of the assets is difficult to assess, while the latter would be chosen where there are many parties and high transaction costs.[16] Although it is commonly perceived that copyright is a property right, the compulsory representation, compulsory licensing, the collective remuneration scheme based on tariffs, the socio-cultural deductions and the distribution formula of collecting societies level the character of property, and to a certain extent transform copyright to a liability right to receive remuneration and transform users' license fees into a tax upon their use of protected works.[17]

3. The Organisational Structure and Management of Collecting Societies

Basically, collecting societies are organisations of right owners. Right owners who acquire their rights by creating new works are authors, and they again can assign their rights or grant the right to use to commercial users such as publishers and producers, who then become commercial right holders. As a consequence, collecting societies may either be exclusively composed of authors (authors' societies) or commercial right holders or be a combination of both groups. In a collecting society that accords membership to authors and commercial right holders, it is critically important that these two groups of members can reconcile with each other. In SACEM, for example, changes to membership and distribution rules could only be implemented by the mutual consent of both groups.[18]

Historically, collecting societies have confined their activities to their own countries and have given collecting societies in other countries the right to grant licenses and collect payment there on their behalf and vice versa. Through these reciprocal representation contracts, national collecting societies avoid wastefully duplicating collecting mechanisms in foreign countries and secure for each of them an exclusive turf without competition. In addition, reciprocal representation contracts also tend to make all protected works, whatever their origin, subject to the same conditions for all users in the same country.

---

[16] *Anselm Kamperman Sanders*, Unfair Competition Law—Some Economic Considerations in Adrian Sterling (ed.), Intellectual Property and Market Freedom, London, 1997, at 141.

[17] *T. Streeter*, Broadcast Copyright and the Bureaucratization of Property, (1992) 10 Cardozo Art & Entertainment Law Journal, at 576.

[18] *Kretschmer*, above note 11, at 127.

IV. The Laws and Regulations governing Collecting Societies

The importance of collecting societies, both economic and cultural, has motivated many countries to take legislative measures for their regulation. However, in spite of control of varying degrees, in particular for well-established collecting societies in the West, "there has been a tendency towards empire-building and inefficient bureaucracy," as is notoriously exemplified by excessively high administration costs (up to 25% of the collected fees) of certain collecting societies, the one-man rule of the German GEMA by Erich Schulze between 1947–1995, and the Tournier dynasty over SACEM in France for most of the twentieth century.[19]

1. *Ex ante Regulation by Copyright or Related Laws*

Along the lines of regulation, nations around the world either add provisions into the Copyright Law (Korea and Thailand) or enact special laws,[20] e.g. the WahrnG of Germany and the Copyrights Intermediary Organizations Act of Taiwan (enacted in 1997).[21] In some parts of the world, the regulation takes the form of granting collecting societies a legal monopoly (SIAE, Italy)[22] in the hope of reducing uncertainty caused by competition between different collecting societies and of improving the enforcement of copyrights claims.

2. *Ex post Regulation by Competition Law*

Roughly speaking, there is a contrast between Asian (with the exception of Japan) and Western countries in terms of curbing the misuse of market power by collecting societies. While the latter are regularly applying their antitrust and/or competition laws to collecting societies, the former have rarely done so, as is further elaborated in the following country reports. This can be attributed to the short history of both collecting societies and antitrust and/or competition law in Asia.

a) Control of Cartels

By way of analogy, collecting societies resemble patent pool arrangements, in which all the rights are gathered together and managed in a uniform manner. By pooling copyrights, collecting societies are able to rival the bargaining power of big corporate users, and reach economies of scale. However, the consolidated and concentrated exercise of copyrights by collecting societies could amount to concerted anti-competitive activities, such as price-fixing and tie-ins that are prohibited by competition laws. Basically, there are two approaches in determining the lawfulness of collecting societies' collective activities.

---

[19] *Kretschmer*, above note 11, at 134.

[20] However, in the common law countries, such as Hong Kong, Malaysia, Singapore, there is little regulation on collecting societies, besides copyright tribunals to solve disputes concerning licensing issues.

[21] This is especially the case in continental civil law countries. There is a similar piece of law in Japan as well, see *Naoki Koizumi*, Die Treuhandverwaltung von Urheberrechten durch Verwertungssellschaften in Japan, GRUR Int. 1998 Heft 7, at 580.

[22] See *Irini Stamatoudi*, The European Court's Love-Hate Relationship with Collecting Societies,[1997]6 EIPR at 289.

aa) Rule of Reason The practice of blanket licensing was of special concern in the U.S. Both the largest and second largest collecting societies, the American Society of Composers, Authors and Publishers (ASCAP) and Broadcast Music, Inc. (BMI) have adopted a blanket licensing practice that excludes licensing on per-piece basis, the lawfulness of which was questioned. Blanket licenses give the licencees the right to perform any or all of the compositions owned by the members or affiliates for a determined period of time as often as the licensees desire. Fees for blanket licences are ordinarily a percentage of the total revenues or a flat dollar amount, and do not directly depend on the amount or type of music used. In 1948, a federal district court interpreted the ASCAP's blanket licensing scheme as a (prohibited) tie-in.[23] In the aftermath of the ASCAP case, the Department of Justice, ASCAP and BMI reached a consent decree whereby ASCAP and BMI agreed to allow their members to issue individual licenses to users and act as a second source of licensing.[24] In 1979, the US Supreme Court confirmed that this kind of blanket licensing coupled with individual licenses by members should be scrutinised under the rule of reason, and was not illegal per se.[25]

In Europe, both the European Commission and the European Court of Justice (ECJ) are very mindful of the competition-restrictive effects of practices adopted by collecting societies. In the GEMA decision,[26] the Commission ruled that members should be free to assign only particular categories (and not all) of rights, or to withdraw rights already assigned if they so wished. In particular, individual right holders should be able to join foreign collecting societies to manage their rights in countries where individual right holders' national society merely acts through a reciprocal representation contract with those foreign collecting societies. The practice of European collecting societies of refusing to grant a licence or to entrust their repertoire abroad to a society other than the one established in the territory in question, first via exclusive-rights clauses in the reciprocal representation contracts, and when such clauses were removed at the request of the Commission, then by means of a concerted practice, caught the attention of the ECJ in the 1989

---

[23] Alden-Rochelle, Inc. v ASCAP, 80 F. Supp. 888 (S.D.N.Y. 1948), 894–895.

[24] *Kenochan*, Music Performing Rights Organizations in the USA, Copyright, Nov. 1985, at 396–397.

[25] The US Supreme Court held that the blanket license is not a "naked restraint of trade with no purpose except stifling of competition, but rather accompanies the integration of sales, monitoring, and enforcement against unauthorized copyright use, which would be difficult and expensive problems if left to individual users and copyright owners. Although the blanket license fee is set by ASCAP and BMI rather than by competition among individual copyright owners, and although it is a fee for the use of any of the compositions covered by the license, the license cannot be wholly equated with a simple horizontal arrangement among competitors. In light of the background, which plainly indicates that over the years, and in the face of available alternatives including direct negotiation with individual copyright owners, the blanket license has provided an acceptable mechanism for at least a large part of the market for the performing rights to copyrighted musical compositions, it cannot automatically be declared illegal in all of its many manifestations. Rather, it should be subjected to a more discriminating examination under the rule of reason." *BMI v. Columbia Broadcasting System, Inc.* 441 U.S. 1, 20, 24 (1979)

[26] [1971]O.J. L134, June 20, 1971.

SACEM case. In that case, the ECJ unambiguously stated: "Concerted action by national copyright-management societies with the effect of systematically refusing to grant direct access to their repertoires to foreign users must be regarded as amounting to a concerted practice restrictive of competition and capable of affecting trade between the Member States."[27] In the same vein, the ECJ reasoned that "the refusal by a national society for the management of copyright in music works to grant the users of recorded music access only to the foreign repertoire represented by it does not have the object or effect of restricting competition in the common market, unless access to a part of the protected repertoire could entirely safeguard the interests of the authors, composers and publishers of music without thereby increasing the costs of managing contracts and monitoring the use of protected music works."[28]

bb) Statutory Exemption Collecting societies find a different fate in Germany. During the period of enacting the Act on the Exercise of Copyrights and Related Rights in 1965, it was hotly debated whether collecting societies would constitute cartels, and whether they should in principle be exempted from the cartel prohibition under Sec.1 German Act Against the Constraint of Competition (GWB). No court decisions were available. So the legislature decided to clarify the issue by adding a new provision to the GWB.[29] Pursuant to Sec.30 of the current GWB, the prohibitions on cartels and vertical agreements that restrict prices or trading conditions apply neither to the establishment of collecting societies who are subject to the supervision of the WahrnG, nor to their contracts and decisions which are necessary for the effective exercise of rights and have been reported to the supervisory authority, the German Patent and Trademark Office. The German Patent and Trademark Office shall transmit the reports to the Federal Cartel Office. In turn, the Federal Cartel Office will exert supervision on whether collecting societies abuse their positions derived from the exemption. This provision of partial exemption from the reach of the GWB has little significance in practice. So far, only two cases were brought under this provision, and none of them has led to a court decision.[30]

b) Abuse of Dominant Market Power

In many countries, collecting societies enjoy a legal or factual monopoly for a particular kind of work.[31] Their *de facto* monopoly can reach beyond borders by securing the entire world repertoire of works through reciprocal representation contracts with other national copyright management societies. Often complaints are heard and lawsuits filed regarding arbitrary and excessive royalties, and refusal to grant access to only a part of the works administered by rights management

---

[27] Case 395/87, Ministére Public v. Tournier,[1989]E.C.R. 2521 (paragraph 23).
[28] Case 395/87, Ministére Public v. Tournier,[1989]E.C.R. 2521 (paragraph 33).
[29] Möschel in Immenga-Mestmäcker (3. Aufl., 2001), Sec. 30 Rdnr. 4.
[30] *Möschel* in Immenga-Mestmäcker, Sec. 30 Rdnr 9.
[31] De facto monopolies exist in China, Belgium, France, Germany, Hong Kong, Indonesia, Japan, the Netherlands, the Philippines and Singapore.

societies (tie-ins). That the counts are aware of such abuse of their dominant position has been confirmed by the ECJ in the SACEM case which stated that "for a copyright-management society occupying a dominant position… to fix a scale and rate of royalty which is several times greater than that applied by all copyright-management societies in the member countries of the EEC without any objectively justifiable ground and is unrelated to the sums redistributed to the authors, so that the royalty is disproportionate to the economic value of the service provided".[32]

V. Challenges to Collecting Societies—Competition Between National Collecting Societies

From its inception, the French collecting society SACEM has tried to extend its activities to neighbouring countries such as Belgium, Germany, Switzerland and the United Kingdom.[33] This aroused suspicion of cultural imperialism and soon led to the establishment of national collecting societies. Entrenched within respective borders, national collecting societies have a *de facto* monopoly on issuing licenses for exploitations of works taking place within their territories, and conclude bilateral agreements with foreign collecting societies to empower the latter to exercise the rights entrusted to them in the relevant foreign countries, and vice versa.

However, collective rights management is in essence a service that would be achieved best through competition among market players, both domestic and foreign. As evidenced by the experience in Europe, copyright management on a national basis has precluded the economies of scale.[34]

In fact, there has already been competition among collecting societies from Germany, France, the Netherlands and the United Kingdom for the so-called Central European Licensing deals, which allow any record company to acquire a license from one central point (namely one collecting society) for all the European shipments of international products.[35] While in some countries, competition from abroad is permitted, such as the Belgian Copyright Act that allows other European collecting societies to operate in Belgium so long as they satisfy the admission criteria applicable to their Belgian counterparts, in some other countries foreign collecting societies are barred from entering the domestic markets, e.g. the Austrian Act on the Exercise of Copyrights and Related Rights.[36] It is expected that competition between national collecting societies will increase, most prominently in the European Union where the "right of establishment" (Article 43 EC Treaty) also for foreign collecting societies would mandate abolishing borders for collecting societies.

---

[32] Case 395/87, Ministére Public v. Tournier,[1989]E.C.R. 2521(paragraph 38).

[33] *Kung-Chung Liu*, above note 2, at 18.

[34] *Tilman Lueder*, Legislative and Policy Developments in the European Union, paper presented at the 13th Annual Fordham Conference on International Intellectual Property Law & Policy (31 March–1 April 2005).

[35] *Walter Dillenz*, Harmonisierung des Rechts der Verwertungsgesellschaften in Europa, GRUR Int. 1997 Heft 4, at 321; Kretschmer, above note 11, at 133.

[36] *Dillenz*, above note 35, at 328.

VI. The Internet

The increasing use of the Internet has the potential to revolutionize the landscape for collecting societies. First, micro-payments directly from consumers to right holders enables the individual right holders once again to take full control over the exploitation of their works. Right owners may not feel the same need for a collective rights management as they used to. Second, the rights-clearance agency is likely to engage in head-on competition with the traditional collective rights management once more and more individual creators become subscribers. That in turn may trigger national legislature to grant protection to creators' societies "in order that they may maintain and strengthen their position and may continue fulfilling all of their complex economic, social and cultural functions,"[37] most probably by making the collective management of certain rights mandatory.

More importantly, according to a survey made by the European Commission in April 2004, the current way of collective management of copyrights within national borders is a source of considerable inefficiency, as content destined for consumption by the entirety of Europe may be subjected to clearance 25 times through 25 different national authorities.[38] That on-line content providers increasingly see the national management of copyright as an impediment to the rollout of trans-border online services may eventually lead to a whole array of initiatives ranging from drafting of codes of conduct in order to harmonise the collective rights management, to binding legislation.

VII. Future Prospects for Collecting Societies

1. *Collecting Societies as Regulatory Instruments?*

In the information society, the collective exercise of copyrights through collecting societies has more than ever become a crucial instrument of copyright management and enforcement, even a possible alternative to the extensive policing and penalising of copyright infringements that are now taking place on a worldwide scale. In consequence, it is worthwhile to take seriously the suggestion that collecting societies themselves become regulatory instruments so as to reward creative activity wherever commerce is generated through the use of creative content. In essence, such a suggestion advocates changing copyright law itself into a non-exclusive reward right, deprived of property altogether and akin to a tax system on the users of cultural works.[39]

2. *Streamlining Management*

The collective management of rights requires a uniform remuneration for different works, which is a form of unionisation and a subsidy made either by larger players to smaller right holders or by certain works to other works.[40] These are disincentives that will drive right holders away from the collective management

[37] *Ficsor*, above note 1, paragraph 40.
[38] *Tilman Lueder*, above note 34.
[39] *Kretschmer*, above note 11, at 135.
[40] *Kretschmer*, above note 11, at 134.

of copyrights. With the help of information technology, collecting societies should be better equipped to monitor the actual use of every work. It is therefore suggested that the distribution of revenues should reflect the actual use of copyrighted works and the costs of administration be more directly allocated to the costs incurred in collecting revenues for particular works. Members should be free to administer particular categories of rights themselves.[41]

B. Country Reports

Note: The contributors to the country reports are listed in the introductory preface

I. China

According to Sec. 8 (1) Copyright Act (2001), copyright owners may authorise a collective society to exercise their rights. Pursuant to Sec. 8 (2) Copyright Act (2001), the State Council is currently preparing a draft of the Regulations of the Collective Administration of Copyright. Currently, these are the main issues which are subject to intensive discussions:

(i) whether the collective administration of some rights should be compulsory;
(ii) whether collective societies should be granted a monopoly position; and
(iii) how the interests of the right owners who are not members of the societies should be safeguarded.

It is expected that after the promulgation of these Regulations, new collective societies will come into being.

2. The Music Copyright Society of China (MCSC) which was established in December 1992 as the first collective society and at present it is still the only such society. At the end of 2003, its membership was at least 3500, and it was managing more than 14 million musical works. Its revenue in 2003 amounted to RMB 27 million. In the past 12 years, it has brought action before the People's Courts against a series of infringers. Its activities have brought about some firsthand experiences in this field.

Despite its extensive efforts, the collecting society continues to face challenges. For example, its negotiations with the China Central Television Station and Beijing Radio and Television Group have not made substantial progress.[42]

II. Hong Kong

1. General

a) Necessity for Collective Management of Copyright

The World Intellectual Property Organisation (WIPO) had defined collective management[43] simply as 'the exercise of copyright and related rights by organisations

[41] Suggestions by the British Monopolies and Mergers Commission in Performing Rights (1996), H.M.S.O. Cm 3147.
[42] See the inside front cover of the China Copyright, 2004 No. 1 and the 2002 Annual Report of the MCSC.
[43] http://www.wipo.int/about-ip/en/about_collective_mngt.html#P67_8306

acting in the interest and on behalf of the owners of rights'. The justification for the emergence of collection management are obvious, as summarised by WIPO "An author is not materially capable of monitoring all uses of his works; he cannot for instance contact every single radio or television station to negotiate licenses and remuneration for the use of his works. Conversely, it is not practical for a broadcasting organisation to seek specific permission from every author for the use of every copyrighted work. An average of 60,000 musical works is broadcast on television every year, so thousands of owners of rights would have to be approached for authorisation. It is the magnitude of such impracticability, for both the owner of rights and the user, that creates a need for collective management organisations, whose role is to bridge the gap between them in these key areas, among others."

b) Collecting Societies in Hong Kong

In Hong Kong, the main collecting societies are: the Composers and Authors Society of Hong Kong Limited (CASH), International Federation of the Phonographic Industry (Hong Kong Group) Limited (IFPI(HK)), Phonographic Performance (South East Asia) Limited (PPL)[44], Copyright Licensing Association Limited and the Hong Kong Reprographic Rights Licensing Society Limited.[45]

2. CASH

The Performing Rights Society of the United Kingdom set up an agency in Hong Kong in 1946 to protect in musical works. This agency formed the basis for CASH which was set up in 1977 by a group of local composers. As of 20 February 2004, CASH had a total of 2570 members, including over 2300 writers and over 220 publishers. CASH at present controls the copyright of musical works of over 1 million local members and members from over 60 overseas affiliated societies. CASH's main objective is to administer and enforce collectively the rights of composers and authors of musical works which are protected under the copyright law of Hong Kong SAR.

On behalf of its members, CASH licenses the use of such works to music users and collects royalties from them. Statistics show that in 2002, 66.8% (HK$53.6 million) of the Hong Kong performing royalties were distributed to CASH's members. The remaining 33.2% (HK$26.6 million) were distributed among CASH's 61 corresponding overseas societies. Furthermore, royalties amounting to HK$6.5 million were received during 2002-2003 from 39 Overseas Affiliated Societies for the performance and broadcast of CASH members' works in the territories administered by these societies.

---

[44] A subsidiary of IFPI(HK)

[45] Recently, there have been proposals from the Hong Kong Performing Artists Guild relating to collective management of copyright within the industry in both local and international markets. It remains to be seen whether a similar collecting society will be adopted, which if adopted, will cater to the needs of the copyright owners better in an information era with the obvious advantages of collecting societies in general.

3. PPL

PPL was established in August 1984 and represents the vast majority of recording companies in Hong Kong, including all the major local and international recording companies. PPL is authorised by the recording companies to grant licenses with respect to the broadcasting and public performance of all sound recordings, music videos and karaoke videos owned or controlled by them.

PPL is a subsidiary of International Federation of the Phonographic Industry (IFPI)—IFPI (Hong Kong Group) Limited, which has a membership of over 55 recording companies. The individual members of IFPI (Hong Kong Group) Limited have given authorisation to PPL to issue licenses for the public performance of their owned and licensed sound recordings, music videos and karaoke videos in Hong Kong. After deduction of the administrative costs, all royalties collected by PPL are distributed among the record companies themselves.

4. Copyright Licensing and Copyright Tribunal

Collecting societies in Hong Kong are self regulated and may apply their own policies and adopt different tariffs in respect of license fees. Under Division IX of the Copyright Ordinance, a special Copyright Tribunal has been established[46] to hear and determine questions arising under collective licensing schemes[47] and employee's compensation,[48] etc. The Copyright Tribunal's jurisdiction extends to copyright licensing[49], under which parties may bring proceedings before the Tribunal when a dispute in relation to copyright licensing arises.

The Copyright Tribunal consists of nine[50]members with a diverse background:-

- — Ms. Teresa CHENG Yeuk-wah, S.C., J.P. (Chairman)—Senior Counsel of Temple Chambers;
- — Mr. KWONG Chi-keung (Deputy Chairman)—Senior partner of Sit, Fung, Kwong & Shum;
- — Ms. Vivien CHAN, J.P.—Partner of Vivien Chan & Co.;
- — Mr. Martin LIAO Cheung-kong—Barrister;
- — The Honourable Howard YOUNG How-wah, S.B.S., J.P.- Member of the Hong Kong Legislative Council;
- — Professor CHING Pak-chung—Professor of Electronic Engineering of City University of Hong Kong;
- — Mr. YU Pang-chun, J.P.—Chairman of Hong Kong Retail Management Association;
- — Mr. Danny YUNG Nine-tsun—Artistic director;
- — Mr. Marcellus WONG Yui-keung—Council member of the Taxation Institute of Hong Kong;

---

[46] Sec. 169 of Copyright Ordinance
[47] Division VIII of Copyright Ordinance
[48] Sec. 14 of Copyright Ordinance
[49] Sec. 173 of Copyright Ordinance
[50] See http://www.info.gov.hk/cm/eng/cbc/a63.htm

Up to 13 June 2001, the Copyright Tribunal had handled 6 cases, all of which related to disputes over copyright royalty charges. Among these 6 cases, 1 case was subsequently withdrawn by the applicant and the other 5 were settled before a formal hearing was held.

5. *Challenges*

Collecting societies in Hong Kong face similar challenges as those which confront others elsewhere in the world—these challenges have been brought on by the fact that copyrighted works will be increasingly delivered in digital form via global networks such as the internet. As a result, the collective management of copyright and related rights by public, semi-public and market sector entities will have to be re-engineered to take advantage of the efficiency gains offered by information technology. The ever-increasing opportunities offered to the holders of rights by the internet and the advent of "multimedia" productions are affecting the conditions of protection, the exercise and management of copyright and related rights, and also the enforcement of rights.

III. Taiwan

1. *Regulatory Setting*

a) The Enactment of the Copyright Intermediary Organisations Act in 1997

In Taiwan, it was not until the first half of the 1980s that collective management of copyrights started to emerge from pure academic theory to reality[51] to enable right holders to enjoy more convenient and effective enforcement of copyrights; and out of a regulatory concerns about the copyright law regime, roughly 130 years after the establishment of the SACEM in France.

In the sweeping 1985 revision of the Copyright Act, for the first time in copyright history it was prevised that "in order to protect and balance their interests, authors and exploiters of music works can jointly establish collecting societies, which are responsible for the recording, reproduction, exploitation of music works, for collecting and distributing royalties from the exploitation, and shall be subject to the scrutiny and assistance from the competent authority. The Rules for Supervision and Assistance are to be promulgated by the competent authority" (Sec. 21). The motive for pointing out to authors and exploiters of musical works the possibility of establishing some organisation to take care of their interests was not to remind them of their constitutional right to form organisations, but rather to "implement the statutory licensing provision introduced by Sec. 21 for reproducing records." It was perceived by legislature that "authors and exploiters of musical works should follow the international practices to jointly establish collecting societies, which are responsible for the recording, reproduction, exploitation of music works, for collecting and distributing royalties from

[51] The first documented introduction in Taiwan of the idea of collective management of copyright and the relevant practices in the U.S. and Japan was probably made by *Chung-Sen Yang*, The Protection of Copyright (in Chinese), 1976, Taipei, at 141–167.

the exploitation. In order to avoid irregularity, the competent authority is hereby empowered to promulgate Rules for Supervision and Assistance."

It was obvious that the afore-mentioned provision was ill thought-out and not feasible; the competent authority was aware of this and refrained from promulgating the Rules for Supervision and Assistance. The 1992 revision of the Copyright Act transformed the said provision into a declaratory clause for further legislative initiative: "(1) Economic copyrights holders may, with the approval of the competent authority in charge of copyright matters, establish copyright intermediary organisations for the purpose of exercising rights or for collecting and distributing compensation for use. (2) The approval for establishment, the organisation and capacities of the organisations referred to in paragraph 1, as well as the supervision and guidance thereof, shall be otherwise provided for by act." (Sec. 81) After five years of deliberation, the Copyright Intermediary Organisations Act (CIO Act) was promulgated into law by the President on November 5, 1997. The Act followed the trend of most of the Western countries which passed special legislation to regulate collecting societies.

b) Heavy-handed Regulation by the CIO Act

The CIO Act clearly takes the German Gesetz über die Wahrnehmung von Urheberrechten und verwandten Schutzrechten (the Act on the Exercise of Copyrights and Related Rights enacted in 1965, hereinafter as WahrnG) as a model and has comprises a total of 46 provisions.[52]

aa) Prescribed Membership, Form of Association and Licensing The CIO Act prescribes that only owners of the economic copyrights to works of the same category[53] may establish *an association* that has the capacity of managing said rights in its own name (Sec. 3(1)). Due to the fact that an exclusive copyright licence excludes the owners of copyrights from exercising their rights themselves, and the CIO Act had from the outset foreseen an exclusive licensing relationship between a CIO and its members (Sec. 13(2)), in 2001 the Copyright Act extended CIO's membership to exclusive licensees of copyrights (Sec. 81(2)). Members of a CIO may not at the same time join another CIO managing the same category of work (Sec. 10(2)).

This overly restrictive mandate is not only incompatible with the constitutionally guaranteed freedom of association, but also ignores the needs of owners of the economic copyrights to choose the form of organisation that best facilitates effective management of copyrights and use of copyrighted works.[54]

[52] The English version of the CIO Act is available on the Website of the Taiwanese Intellectual Property Office (TIPO): www.tipo.gov.tw/eng/laws/laws.asp (last visited 4 August 2005).

[53] According to Sec. 5(1) Copyright Act, there are at least 10 categories of works: literary works, musical works, dramatic and choreographic works, artistic works, photographic works, pictorial and graphical works, audiovisual works, sound recording works, architectural works, and computer programs.

[54] *Kung-Chung Liu*, The German Legal Regime on Collective Management of Copyrights and Its Implications for Taiwan (in Chinese), 113 Economic and Trade Policy of Major Countries Monthly (in Chinese), November 2000 at 5.

bb) Prior Approval and Possible Withdrawal of Approval for a CIO The establishment of CIO is subject to prior approval by TIPO, which may only reject an application for the following four reasons:

(i) The title of the organisation is the same as that of an approved CIO,
(ii) the information supporting the application reveals that it is unable to effectively manage intermediary affairs,
(iii) matters applied for are violating any laws or regulations or are found untrue and the statutory procedures are not met; and
(iv) no correction is made within a period given by the competent authority (Sec. 7(1)).

The TIPO may later rescind the approval (Sec. 40). In practice, thus far ten applications have been filed with the TIPO, one of which was rejected, and one of which has been pending since December 4, 2002. One CIO, after two years of operations, was ordered by the TIPO to dissolve on the grounds that it was unable to effectively manage the rights entrusted to it.[55]

cc) Compulsory Management and Licensing of Copyrights Fearing that CIOs may achieve dominant or even monopolistic market power and discriminate amongst copyright holders and/or exploiters, compulsory management and licensing of copyrights is therefore mandated by the CIO Act:

(i) A CIO may neither reject anyone applying for membership who is qualified as a member in accordance with the statute of organisation (Sec. 11(1)), nor refuse a request for management of the economic copyrights to works from a non-member owner of such rights (Sec. 28).
(ii) In the event that a request for execution of a generalised or individual license agreement with a CIO based on the standard sample of the individual or generalised agreements, the table of royalty and conditions other licensed exploiters have obtained is refused by the CIO or led to no agreement, the person making the request shall be deemed to have obtained authorisation if payment has been made before utilisation according to the table of royalty. If the refusal or non-agreement is due to disagreement in respect of the royalty rate between the requester and the CIO, the person making the request may raise opposition to the CIO after payment is made, provided that the payment has been made according to the rate of royalty maintained by the CIO and a reservation has been declared thereof (Sec. 30).

dd) Controlled Royalty Rates While both royalty rates and the rate/or amount of management fees are to be reported to TIPO, only the former is subject to review and approval from TIPO during the examination of the application to establish a CIO (Sec. 4 (1) No.4, (2)). There is no control at all over management fees. The adjustment of royalty rates shall be reported to TIPO for review and approval if the approved rate is exceeded (Sec. 15 (7)). The review and approval is to be carried

---

[55] *Ming-Jin Lee*, Study on the Mechanism to Decide Rates of Royalties (in Chinese), 2005, Taipei, at 101.

out by the Copyright Review and Mediation Board, which is composed of a Chair held ex officio by the Director General of TIPO, and twenty-one to twenty-nine members selected by the Director General from among the relevant government authorities, scholars, experts and TIPO officials, for concurrent assignments of two years. All Board members act on a pro bono basis. However, non-TIPO Board Members may receive reimbursement of transportation fees or research fees in accordance with relevant regulations (Secs. 3 and 8, Organisation Regulation for the Copyright Review and Mediation Board of TIPO).

2. *Collective Management of Copyrights in Practice*

The practice of collective management of copyrights makes a rather gloomy picture. In blunt contrast to the legislature's fear of monopolies, collecting societies in Taiwan are weak in terms of members, revenues and repertoire. As of now, there are seven (7) collecting societies in existence, three (3) of them in the category of musical works, and two (2) in audiovisual works and sound recording works, respectively. In other words, the other seven categories of works remain uncharted land for collective management of copyrights—although there has been an application for establishing a collecting society for literary works pending since 4 December 2002.

a) Musical Works

aa) The Music Copyright Association of Taiwan (MCAT) MCAT was approval as an association on 20 January 1999. As of 10 August 2005, it had 23 corporate members (mainly record companies) and 179 individual members (creators and their heirs), a decline from 25 and 185 respectively by the end of 2004. MCAT manages a repertoire of about 42,750 works and collected a royalty of ca. New Taiwan Dollars (NT$)[56] 50 million in 2004.[57] There are two kinds of management fees: for members, it is 25% to 30% of the collected royalties (for satellite musical networks), 10% of which for the social and cultural fund and for non-members, it is 25% plus 10% (for data processing).

bb) The Music Copyright Intermediary Society of Chinese Taipei (MUST) MUST was approved as an association on 20 January 1999 and became a full member of the CISAC on 1 December 1999. By the end of 2004, it had 69 corporate members (mainly record companies) and 601 individual members (creators and their heirs). MUST manages a repertoire of about 60,000 works and collected a royalty of ca. NT$ 90 million in 2004.[58] MUST charges 20% of the collected royalties as management fee and appropriates 10% of it for the social and cultural fund.

cc) The Music Copyright Intermediary Society of Taiwan (TMCS) TMCS was approved as an association on 27 February 2002. As of 10 August 2005, it had 2

---

[56] The exchange rate between NT$ and US$ is roughly 32:1.

[57] *Ming-Jin Lee*, above note 6, at 102. The website of the MCAT: www.mcat.org.tw (last visit August 10, 2005)

[58] *Ming-Jin Lee*, above note 6, at 107. The website of the MUST: www.must.org.tw (last visit August 10, 2005)

corporate members (record companies) and 50 individual members (creators). TMCS's area of activities focuses on licensing karaoke manufacturers. In 2004, the TMCS had collected a royalty of NT$1,5 million, which fell short of its costs by 20%.[59] The amount of its management fees is unclear; however, there is a 10% surcharge for non-members.

b) Audiovisual Works

aa) The Audiovisual Music Copyright Owner Association (AMCO) AMCO was approved as an association on 20 January 1999. As of 10 August 2005, it had 16 corporate members (record companies) and 10 individual members (creators). In 2004, the AMCO had collected royalties of NT$10 million.[60]

bb) Audi-video Copyright Disseminated Society of Chinese Taipei (VAST) VAST was approved as an association on 31 October 2001. Although its statute does allow individual members, the VAST has only 35 corporate members (mainly media companies).[61]

c) Sound Recording Works

aa) The Association of Recording Copyright Owners of ROC (ARCO) ARCO was approved as an association on 20 January 1999. As of 10 August 2005, it had 28 corporate members (record companies) and 12 individual members (creators). ARCO administers the broadcasting right and public performance right of sound recording works. In 2004, the ARCO collected royalties of NT$25 million.[62]

bb) Recording Copyright & Publications Administrative Society of Chinese Taipei (RPAT) RPAT was approved to operate on 22 October 2001. It manages the reproduction (for archival use of TV- and radio stations), broadcasting and public performance rights of sound recording works. As of 10 August 2005, RPAT had 43 corporate members (mainly record companies) and 10 individual members (creators). The collected royalties for 2004 were a nominal amount: NT$0.85 million.[63]

IV. Japan

1. Introduction

In order to understand the current state of affairs for collecting societies in Japan, it is necessary to delve into a bit of copyright history and an episode in the 1930s that has become know as "Whirlwind Plage". Current legislation on the matter is relatively recent and dates from 2000.

---

[59] *Ming-Jin Lee*, above note 6, at 114. The website of the TMCS: www.tmcs.org.tw (last visit August 10, 2005)

[60] *Ming-Jin Lee*, above note 6, at 124. The website of the AMCO:www.amco.org.tw (last visit August 10, 2005)

[61] *Ming-Jin Lee*, above note 6, at 127. The website of the VAST: www.vast.org.tw (last visit August 10, 2005)

[62] *Ming-Jin Lee*, above note 6, at 118. The website of the ARCO: www.arco.org.tw (last visit August 10, 2005)

[63] *Ming-Jin Lee*, above note 6, at 121. The website of the RPAT: www.rpat.org.tw (last visit August 10, 2005).

2. *Whirlwind Plage*

After foreign right owners in 1928 were given the rights over public performances of musical works, and in 1931 performance rights over broadcasting, European collecting societies started to claim remuneration for stage performances and phonogram broadcasts of operas and operettas of contemporary European composers such as Giaccomo Puccini, Franz Léhar, and Gustav Mahler. Two umbrella organisations of European collecting societies for stage works, the Bureau Internationale de l'Edition Musique Mechanique (BIEM) and the Cartel des Societés d'Auteurs de Perception non-Theatrale appointed the German Wilhelm Plage as their representative in Japan.[64] Plage, as representative of the Cartel soon stood alone against a hostile alliance of Japan's cultural industry and the press. Despite having spent many years in Japan and being fluent in Japanese, he obviously understood little of the Japanese way of conflict management, which is to find mutual consent and to enable the opponent to save face, no matter how justified one's own claim is. Plage instead annoyed the Japanese cultural circles by threatening concert organisers who refused to pay the claimed remuneration and even by instituting police raids against unauthorised stage performances.[65] Critical journalists and commentators translated his name (German for "menace" or "plague") into Japanese, while more friendly critics characterised him as the reincarnated Michael Kohlhaas, a famous literary character developed by Heinrich von Kleist, who was unwavering in his quest for justice irrespective of the damage it would cause to the achievements attained.

While being attacked for his rigid attitude towards low-brow stage performers, Plage also fought on a second front, namely against the Japanese Broadcasting Union (*Nihon Hôsô Kyôkai*—NHK) which had held that any of his claim for remuneration for the broadcast of European musical works was unreasonably high, especially in comparison with the remuneration paid to Japanese authors.[66] Undeterred, Plage, kept up with his remuneration claims and prohibited the broadcast of European musical works for about one year.

Soon Japan's legislature joined the Anti-Plage alliance of domestic performers, concert organisers and broadcasting enterprises. An amendment to the old JCA of 1 April 1934 provided that not only if the immediate work creator was untraceable, but also if he as a non-resident of Japan had no legal representative in Japan, remuneration for the exploitation of his work had to be paid in form of a legal licence as specified by cabinet order (Sec. 27 old JCA). This amendment allowed performers and concert organisers to deny Plage's qualification as a legal representative of European music authors and to pay less remuneration according to official standards.[67] The other amendment provided that performances fixed in sound could be

[64] Plage became a representative of BIEM on 6 August 1931 and of the "Cartel" on 1 August 1932. Japanese translations of both authorisations in History of Japanese Music Copyright I (above note 21), 294 et seq.

[65] One Japanese tenor is reported to have fluffed his (unauthorised) performance due to a warning letter sent to him by Plage: see S. *Shinbo*, Purâge hakushi towa donna otoko ka? (What Sort of a Man is Dr. Plage?), in: History of Japanese Music Copyright I (above note 21), 321 et seq.

[66] Who, however, proved quite reluctant to enforce their rights: see S. *Ôie*, Nippon chosakuken monogatari (Japan Copyright Story), Tokyo 1981, 31 et seq.

[67] S. *Ôie* (above note 29), 116 et seq.

broadcast and mechanically performed without asking the right owners for permission and even without remunerating them.

These amendments could not really slow down the "Whirlwind Plage". Therefore, the Ministry of the Interior began to conceive an even further-reaching measure which would once and for all deprive the German of the basis for doing collecting business in Japan. In 1937, the high-ranking official Kunijio Kôichirô had the bright idea of enacting a law that regulated the business of collecting societies in Japan, providing that only officially approved organisations would be permitted to conduct such activity. Kunijio's proposal is said to have been based on the German Act on the Intermediation of Music Performance Rights of 4 July 1933 which required collecting societies for musical works to be approved by the Ministry for Propaganda and which is said to have been enacted for the purpose of expelling representatives of foreign collecting societies.[68] On 5 April 1939, the Japanese Act on Intermediary Business Concerning Copyrights was enacted. Based thereupon, the Ministry of Interior appointed the newly established Great Japan Music Copyright Society (which after the war was renamed into Japan Society for Rights of Authors and Composers)—"JASRAC") as the only organisation authorised to conduct nationwide collective management. Plage also applied for official approval, but since the sole motive behind the new law was to get rid of him, it was only natural that he failed.[69] After being fined for continuing illegal copyright administration via an office in Manchuria, Plage finally gave up and returned to Germany in December 1941.

3. *Current Legislation*

Collective administration of copyright is now regulated by the "Act on Management Business of Copyright and Neighbouring Rights" (hereinafter "Copyright Management Act") of 29 November 2000, replacing the "Act on the Intermediary Business Concerning Copyright" of 1939 which was introduced as a means to expel Wilhelm Plage, a single representative of European collective societies.

Even though not explicitly prescribed by the old law, the approval practice of the Cultural Agency under the Ministry of Education admitted only one collecting society in each field of copyright exploitation. Especially in the field of music copyright management, the monopoly of the Japan Society for Rights of Authors and Composers (JASRAC) turned out to be detrimental to the interests not only of users, but also of text authors and composers. Owners of musical copyright who wanted to profit from collective administration of their rights were forced to transfer all their present and future exploitation rights to the JASRAC.[70] JASRAC has the following income and membership structure:

The replacement of the old system by the Copyright Management Act also aims at breaking up such monopolistic structures. The new act explicitly promotes the

---

[68] *N. Koizumi*, Die Treuhandverwaltung von Urheberrechten in Japan, GRUR Int. 1998, 579.

[69] After having failed, Plage published an emotional article titled "The Whirlwind Plage does not slow down!" in the magazine 12-4 Ongaku Sekai (Music World) [1940], reprinted in History of Japanese Music Copyright I (above note 21), 339 et seq.

[70] *N. Koizumi*, Die Treuhandverwaltung von Urheberrechten durch Verwertungsgesellschaften in Japan, GRUR Int. 1998, 579.

Statistics - JASRAC

Annual Collection

2003 (April 1,2003-March 31,2004)

- Domestic Collection -	
General Performances	¥20,967,146,970
Broadcasting	19,729,433,505
Wire Diffusion	1,828,466,417
Films	90,671,992
BGM	326,227,725
Sub Total (Performing rights)	42,941,946,609
Audio Discs	28,276,252,931
Audio Tapes	2,297,142,826
Music Boxes	21,704,936
Recording for Broadcast	130,935
Recording for Broadcast of Commercials	1,507,441,713
Synchronisation	33,756,666
Videograms	13,715,867,633
Sub Total (Mechanical rights)	45,852,297,640
Publications	1,743,114,516
Lending	3,732,691,889
Composite Usage	13,802,884,224
Remuneration for Private Recording	844,243,135
- Foreign Collection -	
Income from Abroad	554,835,635
Grand Total	¥109,472,013,648

Annual Distribution

2003(April 1,2003-March 31,2004)

- Distribution of Domestic Collection -	
General Performances	¥20,798,834,863
Broadcasting	19,792,998,134
Wire Diffusion	1,739,048,116
Films	79,853,288
BGM	281,947,229
Sub Total (Performing rights)	42,692,681,630
Audio Discs	27,577,480,169
Audio Tapes	2,243,393,400
Music Boxes	21,898,330
Recording for Broadcast	7,527,756
Recording for Broadcast of Commercials	1,403,871,367
Synchronisation	26,833,254
Videograms	12,116,590,484
Sub Total (Mechanical rights)	43,397,594,760
Publications	1,676,065,128
Lending	4,029,489,135
Composite Usage	13,472,376,614
Remuneration for Private Recording	840,163,086
- Distribution of Foreign Collection -	
Income from Abroad	558,530,128
Grand Total	¥106,666,900,481

establishment of several competing collecting societies in one field of copyright exploitation by abolishing the approval requirement. Only a registration with the Cultural Agency is required (Sec. 3). Those cases where registration can be refused are explicitly stipulated, for example if the applicant is not a legal person (Sec. 6). Moreover, Sec. 2 (2) Copyright Management Act

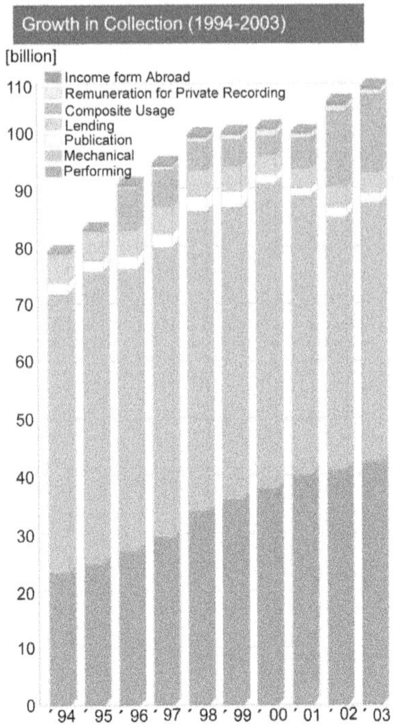

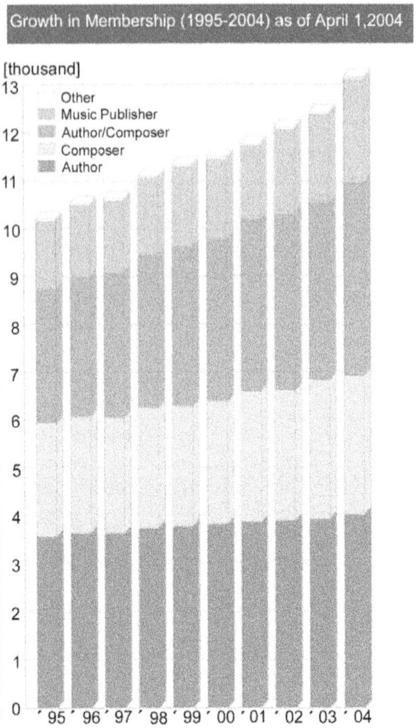

Source: http://www.jasrac.or.jp/ejhp/about/statistics.html

ensures equal treatment of all trustees of a certain society. This does not apply where societies have or manage personal relationships, capital etc. with a certain trustee.

The amount of remuneration for a certain form of exploitation may be freely determined by each society. Also here, a mere registration of the remuneration standards with the Cultural Agency is sufficient (Sec. 13). However, Sec. 23 Copyright Management Act takes into account that some powerful societies may not be driven by competition alone. It obliges so-called "designated management undertakings", i.e. undertakings which dominate a certain field of exploitation by considerable market share or via remuneration standards that are authoritative for the other undertakings in the same field, to enter into consultations with user representatives. If the parties fail to agree, the Director of the Cultural Agency may determine an adequate remuneration at the request of one of the parties (Sec. 24 (1)).

Less powerful societies enjoy a greater freedom, because Sec. 13 (2) only obliges them to hear the opinion of the user circles, but does not require the societies to have users participate in determining the remuneration standards. However, the Director of the Cultural Agency may intervene if he deems the standards set by a certain collecting society to be detrimental to the smooth exploitation of works, by extending the 30-day-period after which a newly announced remuneration standard becomes effective, to three months from notification (Sec. 14 (2)). In case of a biased remuneration regulation by a "designated undertaking", the period may be extended to six months, thereby giving the parties the opportunity to arrive at a more balanced solution (Sec. 14 (3)).

Regarding the relationship between authors and colleting societies, the new law distinguishes between two forms of contract, namely the "entrustment of fiduciary right administration" which requires copyright transfer to the collecting society and "entrustment in a narrower sense" which means that the copyright remains with the author and that the collecting society is merely authorised to exercise the right in the author's name. In both cases, however, the remuneration standards are not individually negotiable, so as to avoid preferential treatment of certain trustees to the disadvantage of the others.

It should be noted that the Copyright Management Act does not prohibit the establishment of organisations which do not meet its requirements. A collective business which, for example, manages the rights of a determined circle of right owners and therefore contravenes Sec.2 (2) will simply be regarded as an organisation outside the application of the Copyright Management Act, but no provision will prevent it from commencing business.

For the collection of neighbouring rights, the situation is as follows:

According to Sec. 95 (5)—(14) Copyright Act, the right of performers to claim remuneration from *broadcasting* or wire diffusion organisations can only be exercised through an association which is composed of a considerable number of professional performers practising in Japan and designated by the Commissioner of the Agency for Cultural Affairs. Founded in 1965, the Japan Council of Performers' Organisations (*Nihon Geino Jitsuenka Dantai Kyogikai*—GEIDANKYO) has been the only collective management society collecting remuneration for broadcasting. Since 1985, this also has included the remuneration for the rental of *phonograms on behalf of performing artists*. The rights of *phonogram producers* over the secondary use of phonograms are administered by the Recording Industry Association of Japan (RIAJ), which is a member of IFPI. GEIDANKYO has a membership of 6,000 and in its history has collected fees amounting to 15 Billion Yen or 120 Million Euro.[71]

Levies imposed on digital audio recording machines and blank data carriers since 1992 have been collected by the Society for the Administration of Remuneration for Sound Recording (SARAH), for digital video recording machines and video tapes since 1999 by the Society for the Administration of Remuneration for Video Recording (SARVH). The latter two organisations are exempt from the Copyright Management Act.

It remains to be seen whether the expected variety of possible undertakings and business forms will enhance efficiency in the field of collective exploitation, or

[71] Figures given in GEIDANKYO's homepage http://www.geidankyo.or.jp/03hit/04nen.htm as of 20 August 2005.

whether the Copyright Management Act will have the opposite effect, namely increased search costs due to an enhanced complexity of the market.

V. Korea

The recent experience has confirmed that Collective management is an essential tool for the efficient exercise of rights. Collective management societies therefore play an important and very useful role, both for authors/creators and for users. The importance and usefulness of collective management is such that many national legislators have taken that aspect into account in the drafting of laws.[72]

Although not clearly set down in the Copyright Act, there is a general consensus that individuals cannot collect remuneration from the users of their performances or phonograms. Rather, individual performers or phonogram producers collect remuneration indirectly through collecting societies. The Act regulates the activities of these societies in the field of administration and exploitation of copyright, as well as neighbouring rights. The basic idea set forth in the Act is that collecting activities are only permitted when special authorisation has been granted under certain conditions by the Ministry of Culture and Tourism (MOCT). Under the Act, a person who desires to operate the copyright agency business only as agent or mediator should report to the MOCT. [73] There are hundreds of agents or mediators operating agencies in Korea. However, they do not play an important role in administering the copyright business, because the domestic market is not large enough and because big publishing companies would directly negotiate with copyright owners.

A person who desires to act as trustee in addition to acting as agent or mediator must obtain permission of the Ministry, Sec. 78. In the field of rights of performers or phonogram producers, only the organisations representing them may collect remuneration and the organisations must be designated by the Ministry, Secs. 65(2), $65^{bis}(2)$, $67^{bis}(2)$. In Korea, there are five collecting societies permitted or designated by the Ministry which represent authors, composers, performers, phonogram producers, and playwrights.[74]

There is no general standard to determine whether an abuse of copyrights is a violation of the MRFT, but the standard applied to unfair trade practices in international contracts can be applied *mutatis mutandis* to the abuse of copyrights between domestic business persons. Section 32 MRFT prohibits unfair trade practices in international contracts, and the Fair Trade Commission has announced the "Types and Standards of Unfair Trade actions in International Contracts" pursuant to section 32.[75] Under the MRFT, if a record company or collecting society license an affiliated entity to broadcast or distribute music over the

---

[72] See http://www.wipo.int/documents/en/document/pcipd/doc/1_7.doc.

[73] Sec. 78 Copyright Act.

[74] *Ki-Su Lee*, Intellectual Property Law, in Korea, 148-149 (Heath ed. Kluwer Law International, 2003)

[75] Monopoly Regulation and Fair Trade Act (1997) Sec. 32.

Internet via an interactive service, third parties have an equal right to obtain such license on non-discriminatory terms.

VI. Singapore

1. *Collecting Societies in Singapore*

The following are the copyright collecting societies which have been established in Singapore:

a) COMPASS

Composers and Authors Society of Singapore Ltd (COMPASS)—It administers the public performance, broadcast, diffusion and reproduction rights in music and musical associated literary works on behalf of its members, as well as members of affiliated societies such ASCAP, BMI and PRS. COMPASS is the oldest collecting society here, having been formed in 1987 when the Singapore Copyright was enacted. As of 31st December 2002, its membership stood at 712 and its total revenue amounted to S$7.8 million, out of which about S$4.88 million were distributed as royalties to its members. The license fees it levies depend on various factors such as the nature of the business of the user—it has classifications ranging from aerobics/dance studios to telephone on-hold-music[76]—floor area of the premises, number and size of video monitors, etc.

b) CLASS

Copyright Licensing and Administration Society of Singapore Ltd (CLASS)—it administers the reprographic reproduction right of its members, as well as members of affiliated societies such as ALCS. It was incorporated in 1999, but the first collection of license fees was made only in May 2002. The total domestic fees it collected in its last financial year amounted to S$169,000.

c) RIPS

Recordin g Industry Performance Singapore Pte Ltd (RIPS)—it administers the communication to the public (e.g. broadcasting, public performance) rights in karaoke and/or music videos owned by recording companies.

2. *Abuse Control*

(a) Some control over collecting societies comes in the form of scrutiny by the Copyright Tribunal which has been established under Part VII of the Copyright Act. Two types of situations that fall within the jurisdiction of the Copyright Tribunal are particularly relevant here.

(i) Complaints that the licensor's proposal to grant the license for public performance, broadcast and cablecasting rights in a literary, dramatic or musical work, is subject to the payment of unreasonable charges and/or conditions.[77] Two cases have been brought before this Tribunal. In the first, the national broadcaster had challenged PRS' method of charging

---

[76] For details, see http://www.compass.org.sg/website/.

[77] See Sec. 163(3)(a) of the Copyright Act.

royalties—based on a percentage of the broadcaster's revenue; this Tribunal found in favour of PRS.[78] In the other, a concert promoter had challenged an existing license scheme introduced by COMPASS where the royalty rate was fixed at 3% of the gross ticket receipts, following a decision of the UK Tribunal's decision to increase the tariff to 3% in the UK. This Tribunal held that it was not reasonable for the royalty fee rate in Singapore to be automatically pegged to the rates in the UK, and therefore exercised its power to vary the scheme by lowering the rate to 2.5%.[79]

(ii) The intervention of this Tribunal in the operation of a statutory licensing scheme which allows educational institutions to make multiple copies of copyright works for educational purposes subject to them paying an equitable remuneration to the copyright owners.[80] Where the parties cannot agree on the amount of license fees, it shall be determined by this Tribunal. Having it as the final arbiter ensures that CLASS will not abuse its dominant position in Singapore. CLASS has concluded reprographic licenses with various polytechnics and two universities here. In its' license with the Nanyang Technological University, it was agreed that CLASS would receive S$5 per student per academic year.

b) Singapore's Competition Act[81] provides another source of control over collecting societies.

The Act embodies concepts of European competition law such as prohibition of conduct, which amounts to 'the abuse of a dominant position'[82] and of agreements which have as their object the 'restriction or distortion of competition'.[83] The Singapore Competition Commission has indicated that they "will regard IPRs as being essentially comparable to any other form of property... [and] as with other forms of private property, certain types of agreements or conduct with respect to IP may have anti-competitive effects which come under the purview of competition law.".[84]

Whether there will be more complaints against collecting societies before the Competition Tribunal remains to be seen; if not, it might be tempting to conclude that the establishment of the Copyright Tribunal is sufficient to curb any anti-competitive conduct in copyright collective management here. On the other hand, it may be because collecting societies here will tread even more cautiously in the presence of the competition law. At the very least, they would be following

[78] *Singapore Broadcasting Corporation v Performing Right Society Ltd* (1991) 21 IPR 595.

[79] *Sunvic Production Pte Ltd v* COMPASS CRT No. 1 of 1992.

[80] See Sec. 52 of the Copyright Act.

[81] Singapore's Competition Act 2004 came into force on 1 January 2005. This legislation is available at the website of the Singapore Competition Commission at http://www.ccs.gov.sg/

[82] See Sec. 47 of the Competition Bill [modelled on Art. 82 of the EC Treaty (ex Art 86)], to come into force on 1 January 2006.

[83] See Sec 34 of the Competition Bill [modelled on Art. 81 of the EC Treaty (ex Art 85)], to come into force on 1 January 2006.

[84] See the Competition Commission's Draft Guideline on the Treatment of Intellectual Property Rights (October 2005).

closely the response of their counterparts to the recent warning issued by the European Commission to collecting societies in 16 EU countries (e.g. PRS) that they were behaving like a cartel in signing the Santiago Agreement, which limits traders to purchasing a licence from the collecting society in their country.[85]

VII. Malaysia

Copyright collecting societies came into existence in Malaysia in the late 1980s after the Malaysian Copyright Act came into force on 1 December 1987. The first was Public Performance Malaysia Sdn Bhd (PPM)[86], founded in 1988, which was then followed closely by Music Authors' Copyright Protection Bhd (MACP)[87] in 1989. For many years PPM and MACP were the only two collecting societies in Malaysia, but this changed in 2001 when a third agency, called Performers' and Artists' Rights (M) Sdn Bhd (PRISM) was incorporated. The scope of these collecting societies is discussed briefly below.

a) PPM

It is a wholly owned, non-profit subsidiary of the Recording Industry Association of Malaysia (RIM), which in turn is affiliated with the International Federation of the Phonographic Industry (IFPI). PPM represents the rights of those Malaysian recording companies which are members of RIM, plus those overseas recording companies (also typically members of IFPI) which had given exclusive licenses to RIM members to control their rights in Malaysia. At present, 37 companies have given the mandate to PPM to collect royalties on their behalf. Users who play sound recordings and music videos (as contained in cassettes, CDs, VCDs, DVDs, LDs, etc.) in their business require a license from PPM.

b) MACP

It safeguards the rights of songwriters, composers and publishers of music. Thus their members are typically individual persons or smaller companies. Today, over 1,400 members and 25,000 local musical works are represented by MACP, and through reciprocal agreements with other foreign performing rights societies, MACP also represents more than 2 million composers, lyricists and publishers from around the world, and is able to license over 12 million foreign musical works. Any user who publicly uses or performs a musical work controlled by MACP needs a license.

c) PRISM

The third and most recent agency, PRISM, deals with the licensing of video/sound recordings that embody a public performance, for example a recording of a live concert. In this regard, PRISM's activities and scope are very similar to PPM, although limited as to the type of subject matter. PRISM is still in its infancy and currently out sources its collection work to PPM.

---

85 The Guardian, 4 May 2004.
86 Formerly known as Phonographic Performance Malaysia. Website: www.ppm.org.my
87 Website: www.macp.com.my

The recognition of copyright and collecting societies in Malaysia has grown tremendously since the late 1980s. In the early years the notion of copyright was not well understood and the public did not appreciate the fact that royalties needed to be paid for the commercial use of copyright material. As a result collections were difficult and minimal, and the collecting societies ran at a loss. Today the scenario is far happier; with greater awareness of copyright and more enforcement activities supported by the government, many more businesses are obtaining licenses to use copyrighted music and sound recordings. PPM's annual revenue now stands at around US$4 million, with a trend showing an increase from year to year, and they have offices or representatives in all the states of Malaysia. The story is similar to MACP, since the collections of both societies go quite hand-in-hand; a business that licenses a sound recording f a business that licenses a sound recording for use also or representatives in all the states of Malaysia and maintain a sizeabrom PPM typically also has to pay royalties to MACP to account for the portion of the songwriters and composers.

Collecting societies in Malaysia are very much self-regulated. There is little supervision over their activities and they set their own policies and licensing rates (guided by international norms). In the event of a dispute, say over unreasonable terms or a license being unfairly declined, the parties have recourse to the Copyright Tribunal that was established under the new Part IVA of the Act, which deals with copyright licensing.[88] Thus far, no cases involving the collective administration of copyright have been determined by the Copyright Tribunal. That is not to say that there have been no complaints from the licensees; rather these complaints have been resolved without reference to the Copyright Tribunal.

VIII. Thailand

The idea of paying for the use of copyrights became reality in 1994, when the International Confederation of Societies of Authors and Composers (CISAC) set up the first collective copyright society in Thailand. Music Copyright (Thailand) Limited (MCT) was set up to represent Thai and foreign music authors and composers in collecting royalties from users of their music in Thailand. MCT bases its claims on the right of communication to the public of music written by its members. At the time of its establishment, it was an uphill battle for MCT to collect royalties because then it was unacceptable to the Thais to pay since it had all along been thought to be public domain. There was much angst and resentment .A few years later , some foreign record companies joined forces to form "Phonoright" for the collection of royalties from the commercial users of their phonograms.

Both MCT and Phonoright relied heavily on the help of the Department of Intellectual Property (DIP) of Thailand to educate the Thai public about paying for using music. It was many years before MCT could start collecting royalties. Although support came from foreign authors and composers (through their countries' collective societies), the local authors and composers lent little support to MCT as they were not confident that it would succeed. Their lack of confidence

---

[88] Inserted by the Copyright (Amendment) Act 1996, Sec. 5.

was compounded by the fact that many new Thai authors and composers were contractually obliged to write for influential local record companies under draconian terms so that many had relinquished all their rights to their employers or hirers. Such authors and composers had nothing left for MCT to collect. The record companies, meanwhile, set up their own royalty collection operations to collect directly from users. Rivalries within the record companies meant that they could not set up their own collection societies. This threw the development of collective society into disarray.

At present, this is still a problem in Thailand. Users are confused because they have to pay royalties to many parties, and it does not help that they are unwilling to pay in the first place. Heated debates between collectors and users are frequent occurrences. The DIP appears to be caught in the middle, with collecting societies often pressuring them for help them from their end whilst users pressure the DIP to step in to help them fend off collectors. DIP themselves has very little resources to do so. Recently, the DIP has chosen to solve the problem through the enactment of provisions in the copyright amendment bill dealing with collective societies

The present Copyright Act does not have any provisions on collective societies. Under the current draft of the bill (which is not final), collective societies are required to sunbmit to the Copyright Board (which consists of copyright experts from the public and private sectors appointed by the Cabinet of Ministers and is chaired by the Director-General of the DIP) data and other documents revealing their operational methods to enable the Board insight into the running of such collective societies. Moreover, should collective societies and the users reach an impasse over the royalty rate, either may petition the Director-General for his decision and appeal against his decision to the Copyright Board. The Copyright Board will be duty bound to produce model copyright licensing contracts and to encourage its use to minimise confusion and disputes. It remains to be seen whether these proposed provisions will be accepted by the National Legislative Assembly.

IX. The Philippines

While the IP Code grants a wide range of copyrights to creators or authors plus a bundle of neighbouring rights to those associated in the exploitation, dissemination, or production of works, the Code possessed inherent limitations when it comes to managing and enforcing these rights. To illustrate, a musical composer would not be in a position to monitor by himself the number of times his composition is played in the radio, television, hotels and restaurants, in the local scene and abroad and thereafter collect royalties, as it is simply humanly impossible to do so. A collecting society must be designated to monitor and enforce his rights. The IP Code expressly recognises the right to designate a collecting society:

> "The copyright owners or heirs may designate a society of artists, writers or composers to enforce their economic rights and moral rights on their behalf."[89]

---

[89] IP Code Sec.183.

The aforesaid right was a reiteration of the right previously recognised in Section 32 of PD 49. [90] In the Philippines, the Filipino Society of Composers, Authors and Publishers, Inc. (FILSCAP) represents the rights of both local and foreign composers, lyric-writers and music publishers.

This paper will limit its discussion to FILSCAP, the first collective management society in the Philippines and in Southeast Asia.[91] It is a non-stock, non-profit association of composers, lyric-writers and music publishers established in 1965.[92] It was established seven (7) years prior to the issuance of PD 49, the first statute expressly allowing the designation of collecting societies in the country.

Its role is that of a "unified body of music copyright owners to which application for a permission/license may be made by a person or organisation intending to perform, authorise the performance of, mechanically reproduce and/or synchronise copyrighted music in any manner or by any method, for profit or otherwise."[93] It owns or controls, in the Philippines, an extensive worldwide repertoire of copyrighted local and foreign musical works.[94]

During a national seminar organised by the World Intellectual Property Organisation in Manila in 1998, entitled "Collective Management of Copyright and Neighboring Rights and the WIPO 'Internet' Treaties (WIPO/ CNR/ MNL 98)",[95] a presentation was made on FILSCAP's experience as a collecting society in the Philippines. It was reported that the initial years of FILSCAP were "difficult." FILSCAP has long failed to be a self-sustaining organisation. They have explained that the difficult years were attributable to its perception that "copyright laws were not widely enforced at that time and as such, the general public was virtually unaware that such rights or laws existed."[96]. Some of the problems which FILSCAP encountered in 1998, and which may still be applicable today, include:

(i) lack of awareness of the owners of establishments playing musical compositions of the copyright issue;
(ii) slow legal process;

---

[90] "...The creator or his heirs may designate a society of artists, writers or composers as agent to claim the right in his or their behalf. In such case, the society shall forward the proceeds to the creator or his heirs upon demand or at the end of every quarter of each calendar year." (Sec. 32, PD 49)

[91] Cf. *Ang Kwee Tiang*, Collective Management Societies—A Survey of the Asia Pacific Region, WIPO National Seminar On Collective Management of Copyright, et al. , WIPO/ CNR/ MNL/ 98/5 (October 1998), pp. 4–5

[92] *FILSCAP*, A Handbook on FILSCAP and Music Copyright (June 2000) p.12.

[93] Ibid.

[94] Ibid.

[95] The seminar was organised by WIPO in cooperation with the Intellectual Property Office of the Philippines and the University of the Philippines. It was held in Manila on 22–24 October 1998.

[96] Ms. *Dorothy Tadeo*, The Experience in Collective Management of Copyrights and Related Rights in the Philippines, WIPO National Seminar on Collective Management of Copyright, et al., WIPO/ CNR/ MNL/ 98/4 (October 1998), p. 4.

(iii) lack of awareness on the part of copyright owners of their rights; and
(iv) lack of financial resources in operating the society.[97]

FILSCAP enjoyed limited success in its licensing efforts in 1971 but the amount of fees collected were insufficient to cover its administrative expenses. Hence, it could not initiate copyright infringement cases due to lack of funds.[98]

It was reported that FILSCAP became a viable concern only in 1992 when the International Confederation of Societies of Authors and Composers (CISAC), together with a group of dedicated Filipino composers, contributed to the society the necessary "financial, technical, legal and management assistance".[99] To date, FILSCAP has 818[100] members, a notable increase from a membership level of 230 in 1992 and 770 in 1998.[101] It is affiliated with 45 foreign collecting societies.[102] The revenues collected for 2003 reached PhP20.0M.[103]

There has been no Supreme Court case dealing directly with the issue as to whether the activities of collecting societies are anti-competitive in nature. At the very least, the existence of FILSCAP finds support in the IP Code provision which expressly allows copyright owners or their heirs to designate a society of artists, writers or composers to enforce economic and moral rights on their behalf.[104]

In the 1987 Supreme Court case of *FILSCAP v. Tan*[105], the definition of public performance was raised. It was a case on appeal by FILSCAP after an adverse decision by the lower court. The defendant was an operator of a restaurant at which professional singers were hired to play and sing various musical compositions to entertain their patrons.. FILSCAP took the view that while the patrons of the restaurant pay only for the food and drinks and apparently not for listening to the music, the acts of the professional singers constitute "public performance for profit under the then Copyright Law." The Supreme Court agreed with the contention of FILSCAP. However, FILSCAP failed in its bid to reverse the lower court's decision, as the musical compositions sought to be protected have long become part of the public domain and no longer entitled to copyright protection.

While the ruling was adverse to FILSCAP, it nevertheless clarified the definition of "public performance for profit". The decision has enhanced their legal basis to demand royalty payment from restaurants and other establishments playing musical composition notwithstanding the absence of fees collected from their patrons for the musical performance.

---

[97] Ibid. p.9.
[98] Ibid, p.5.
[99] *Ang Kwee Tiang*, above fn 50.
[100] The figure was provided by FILSCAP Licensing Manager Ms. Marie Jane Suarez based on records.
[101] Ms. *Dorothy Tadeo*, above fn 55.
[102] *FILSCAP*, above fn 51 .
[103] Ms. *Dorothy Tadeo*, above fn 55.
[104] IP Code Sec. 183; see also PD 49 Sec. 32.
[105] *Filipino Society of Composers, Authors and Publishers, Inc. v. Tan*, 148 SCRA 461 (1987).

4
The Law on Anti-Circumvention and Digital Rights Management

ANDY Y. SUN

Measures against the manufacture and distribution of programmes or devices meant to overcome or circumvent copyright management systems (or, less euphemistically, systems to prevent the copying of works) are required by the WIPO Copyright Treaties and in this respect represent clear elements of TRIPS plus protection. While such programmes or devices may well have unlawful purposes in allowing users the copying of works beyond what copyright law actually allows, this is not necessarily so: After all, copyright limits allow the copying for purposes of fair use. Such limitation could be successfully overridden by right owners in installing technical means, while users would not be able to purchase programmes or devices that would allow them to exercise their lawful rights. The country reports should address how this friction has been solved by national law, if at all.

A. Introduction

Part 1—The U.S. Perspective on Anti-Circumvention

I. Introduction

Hand in hand with the explosive growth in the use of the internet, the U.S. copyright industry in 1994, also witnessed widespread availability of devices and/or measures for circumventing the technical measures they had employed for the protection of their copyrighted work online. Thus, the industry began lobbying the U.S. Congress to pass legislation banning the circumvention of these technical measures and the sale of "circumvention devices." When Congress failed to act, the industries succeeded, instead, in convincing the Executive Branch, especially the Office of the U.S. Trade Representative, to move forward with an international treaty mandating such protection. On 20 December 1996, the World Intellectual Property Organization (WIPO) successfully concluded two international "Internet Treaties," *i.e.*, the WIPO Copyright Treaty (WCT) and the WIPO Performances and Phonograms Treaty (WPPT).[1] As a result, pressure

[1] World Intellectual Property Organization (WIPO) Copyright Treaty, adopted in Geneva on 20 December 1996, 36 I.L.M. 65 (1997); WIPO Performances and Phonograms Treaty (WPPT), adopted in Geneva on 20 December 1996, 36 I.L.M. 76 (1997). Note that WCT entered into force on 6 March 2002, see WIPO Copyright Treaty Notification No. 32 (6 December 2001); whereas WPPT entered into force on 20 May 2002, see WIPO Performances and Phonograms Treaty Notification No. 32 (20 February 2002).

began to mount on the U.S. Congress to act quickly so that hopefully a "bandwagon effect" could be created for other nations to respond quickly, accelerating national adoption of both treaties.[2]

On 28 October 1998, the Digital Millennium Copyright Act (DMCA) in the United States was enacted.[3] Title I of the DMCA was designed to implement the WCT and WPPT. Article 11 WCT and Article 18 WPPT both specifically require all Contracting Parties to "provide adequate legal protection and effective legal remedies *against the circumvention of effective technological measures* that are used" by authors, performers, or producers of phonograms "*in connection with the exercise of their rights*" under either treaties or the Berne Convention and that "restrict acts, in respect of their works, which are not authorised by the authors concerned or permitted by law."[4] [Emphasis added.] As a result, Section 103 of the DMCA creates a new Chapter 12 to the existing Copyright Act, with Section 1201 being added to Title 17 of the United States Code, designed specifically to regulate protective technical measures in connection with the protection of copyrighted works.

Since its inception, these anti-circumvention provisions have proven to be highly controversial. At the international level, just what exactly does the phrase "effective technical measures" mean? Does it impose an objective or a subjective standard? What may be considered as "ineffective technical measures," and what are their consequences? For instance, should an obsolete software still be considered an "effective technical measure," since the program may still function in the manner in which it was designed? Is the claim against circumvention supposed to be a separate right from the copyright it is intended to cover? These issues naturally spill over to any and all of the domestic legislative regimes which need to comply with their treaty obligations.

In the United States, with the introduction of anti-circumvention statutes, its copyright law for the first time touches on the regulation of technology itself, instead of focusing on the protection of expression of creative ideas. It follows that the anti-circumvention provisions inevitably reignite the debate on what exactly should be the scope of copyright? Should protection afforded by a technical measure be treated separately from the copyrighted work it intends to cover? What may be the socio-economic impact if indeed that is the case? Should there

---

[2] Both treaties required ratification by 30 Contracting States before entering into force. The actual effective date was three months after the deposit of the 30th instrument with the WIPO. See WCT, Art. 20; WPPT, Art. 30.

[3] Pub.L. No. 105–304, 112 Stat. 2860 (1998). This legislation marks the most sweeping reform of the U.S. copyright regime since the enactment of the Copyright Act of 1976. See Pub.L. No. 94–553, 90 Stat. 2541 (1976). The DMCA is the result of prolonged negotiations among various interested groups and individuals. While most of the issues were ironed out by mid-1997, an unexpected issue, the liability of Internet service providers, which is not addressed at all in the WCT and WPPT, popped up and turned out to be the most difficult sticky point. It took another year before all sides eventually agreed on the so-called "notice and take-down" principle. Once a compromise was finally reached on 1 April 1998, however, the bill moved smoothly through the legislative process.

[4] The theory behind the WCT and WPPT is that technological protections encouraged copyright owners to make digital content widely available, and circumvention of technological measures reduced that benefit. See also House Rep. 105–551, Part 2, at 63 (22 July 1998).

be a separate "right" for public access or fair use "right" (which has traditionally been considered a mere affirmative defence in litigation) as opposed to the enumerated exclusive rights of the copyright holders? Courts in the United States have been confronted with these challenges and are still in the process of crafting out rules and reshaping the future of electronic commerce.

This article intends to survey the current landscape of copyright regime in relation to anti-circumvention. This article will also discuss critical cases to showcase the controversies and challenges confronting the courts.

II The Legislative Structure

1. *Types of prohibitions*

Section 1201 of the Copyright Act prohibits three types of circumvention:

1) Gaining unauthorised access to a copyrighted work by circumventing a technological protection measure put in place by the copyright owner, i.e., the act of circumvention itself, such as decryption and descrambling technologies;[5]
2) Manufacturing and/or making available devices, technologies, or services used to defeat technological protection measures put in place by the copyright owner to prevent unauthorised access to a copyrighted work, i.e., providing means for access; and
3) Manufacturing and distributing means or devices for circumventing technological measures put in place by the copyright owner to prevent unauthorised copying, i.e., providing means for copying. In other words, the statute distinguishes between access control (anti-trafficking) and copy technologies and treats them differently, with direct prohibition on the act of circumvention being imposed with respect to access control technologies only.[6]

Note that with regard to the prohibition against circumvention devices, it is applicable only to devices or services that are primarily designed or produced for circumvention (primary purpose test); that have only limited commercially significant purposes or uses other than circumvention (significant purpose test); or that are marketed for use in circumvention. With a few exceptions, Section 1201 does not require consumer electronics, telecommunications or computing equipment manufacturers to design their products to respond to any particular technological measure taken by a copyright owner.[7] As a result, normal household devices such as videocassette recorders or personal computers do not qualify, since they are not primarily designed to circumvent technological protections granting access to copyrighted works.[8]

---

[5] This portion of the statute became effective as of 28 October 2000, whereas the other forms of prohibition became effective immediately since DMCA entered into force.

[6] 17 U.S.C. § 1201 (a)(2)(2000 Supp. II).

[7] These exceptions are: For consumer (not professional) analogue VCRs and camcorders, they must comply with "automatic gain control technology" (which causes distortion in the images upon playback), or (2) "colour stripe copy control technology" (which causes distracting visible colour stripes to appear through portions of the viewable picture in normal viewing mode) within *18 months* since the enactment of DMCA. See 17 U.S.C. §. 1201 (k) (2000 Supp. II).

[8] See House Rep. 105–551, Part 1, at 10 (22 May 1998).

2. Liabilities

Violations of this section may result in civil and/or criminal liabilities. Section 1203 gives federal courts power to grant civil damages, an injunction, costs, attorney fees, and even the impounding, modification or destruction of the devices or products involved in the violation. The court also has the discretion to award *treble damages against repeat offenders*, and to *limit damages for innocent violations* (where the defendant proves he/she was not aware and had no reason to believe his/her acts constituted a violation).

In addition, criminal penalties may be available if the violation of section 1201 is done *wilfully* and for purposes of commercial advantage or private financial gain. Section 1204 provides for fines up to US$500,000 or up to five years imprisonment for the first offence, and fines up to $1,000,000 or up to ten years imprisonment for subsequent offences. Note, however, that these penalties are *not* applicable to non-profit libraries, archives and educational institutions.

To reduce the potential of overlap of liabilities, Section 1201 has expressly provided three "savings clauses," stipulating that no direct copyright infringement, secondary infringement (vicarious and contributory), rights of free speech or the press using consumer electronics, telecommunications or computer products will be affected. In other words, circumvention is treated as an independent cause of action separated from all other existing infringement actions.[9]

3. Exemptions

Legislative exemptions. During the legislative process of DMCA, many concerns were raised between the addition of this new cause of action and fair use. As a result, Congress was mindful about this issue and the statute itself eventually incorporated seven categories of exemptions to potential circumvention liabilities. They are:

1) Security exemption—A general exception for law enforcement, intelligence, and other governmental activities;
2) Educational exemption—For non-profit library, archive and educational institutions, circumvention is permitted for the sole purpose of making a good faith determination as to whether they wish to obtain authorised access to the copyrighted work;
3) "Reverse engineering" exemption—Circumvention is permitted for software developers of a lawfully obtained computer program to identify the elements necessary to achieve interoperability of an independently created computer program with other programs;
4) "Encryption research" exemption—Circumvention is permitted for access control measures, and the development of the technological means to identify flaws and vulnerabilities of encryption technologies;
5) "Minors protection" exemption—This allows a court to consider the necessity for the incorporation of circumvention in technology that prevents access of minors to material on the Internet (i.e., parental control);

9 17 U.S.C. § 1201 (c)(2)–(4)(2000 Supp. II).

6) "Personal privacy" exemption—Circumvention is permitted when the technological measure, or the work it protects, is capable of collecting or disseminating personality identifying information about the online activities of a natural person (e.g., "cookies"). It is available only if the user is not provided with adequate notice that his online activities is being collected, and the circumvention has no other effect on the ability of the user to gain access to the work; and
7) "Security testing" exemption—This is the permission to circumvention over access control measures, and the development of technological means for such circumvention, for the purpose of testing the security of a computer, computer system or computer network, with the authorisation of its owner or operator.[10]

Administrative exemptions. Recognising that the statute may not be able to catch up with and reflect on the ever changing technological developments, in addition to the above-listed legislative exemptions, DMCA authorises the Librarian of Congress (but in fact with recommendations from the Register of Copyrights and the Assistant Secretary for Communications and Information at the U.S. Department of Commerce) to periodically review and grant exemptions to certain classes of works so that the anti-trafficking provision shall not apply to persons who engage in non-infringing uses of those particular classes of works.[11]

The Librarian of Congress has determined that, between 28 October 2003 and 27 October 2006, persons who engage in non-infringing use of the following four classes of copyrighted works are not liable for circumvention:[12]

1) "Censorware" applications, *i.e.*, lists of Internet locations or websites blocked by commercial filtering software applications intended to prevent children and other users from viewing objectionable materials while online. Note that the rule tries to emphasise its focus on "blocking" rather than "accuracy." In order to clam critics over excessive blocking, this exemption specifically excludes software designed to protect against damage to computers or networks, such as firewalls, anti-virus and anti-spam software programs.
2) "Dongles" or hardware locks. However, this is only limited to the computer program being used, *i.e.*, the exempted class includes *only* the software that actually cannot be accessed due to a damaged or malfunctioning dongle, and only when the dongle cannot be replaced or repaired;
3) Computer programs and video games in obsolete format or medium; and
4) "Special format" for the blind and visually-impaired to gain meaningful access to literary works distributed as e-books.[13]

---

[10] 17 U.S.C. § 1201 () (d)–(j)(2000 Supp. II).

[11] 17 U.S.C. §. 1201 (a)(B) and (C)(2000 Supp. II). Since the effective date of this provision (28 October 2000), the reviews and recommendations take place each succeeding three (3) year period.

[12] 17 C.F.R. § 201.40 (2004), which codifies Exemption to Prohibition on Circumvention of Copyright Protection Systems for Access Control Technologies, 68 Federal Register at 62011 (31 October 2003) and 65 Federal Register at 64555 (30 October 2000).

[13] 17 U.S.C. §. 121 (2000 Supp. II).

As can be seen, the second and third class of exemptions deal primarily with obsolete software. "Obsolete" means the machine or system necessary to render perceptible a work stored in that format is no longer manufactured or reasonably available in the commercial marketplace.[14] Note that in order to make a *prima facie* case of exemption, proponents must bear the burden to prove, by a preponderance of the evidence, that there has been or is likely to be a substantial adverse effect on non-infringing uses by users of copyrighted works.[15] *De minimis* problems, isolated harm or mere inconveniences are insufficient.[16]

During the latest round of review, at least 25 proposed classes of exemptions were turned down by the Register of Copyrights. Examples include, among other things, "legitimate research projects" that need to be carried out over musical recordings and audiovisual works protected by access control mechanisms; malfunction, damage or obsoleteness to media that render inaccessible audiovisual works embodied in that media (*e.g.*, digital video/versatile disks (DVDs) backup); as well as literary works (especially e-books), sound recordings and audiovisual works protected by access controls that prevent post-sale uses of works, or "tethered" works (*i.e.*, works that cannot be copied to and used on other devices). With regard to the proposed DVD backup exemption, the evidence was found to be insufficient to prove the fragility of DVDs; with regard to "legitimate research projects," the proposal was denied since the proposed class is defined largely in terms of the purpose of the circumvention, and the scope is too broad by virtually covering the entire spectrum of audiovisual works. With regard to proposed "tethered" works or e-book exemption, it was denied on the ground that the consumer often has choices between various e-book formats. Alternative formats are also available. Thus "tethered" works result in a user's inconvenience at best, as long as such alternatives are available.

III The Judicial Interpretations

Since the enactment of DMCA , several federal circuit courts have had the opportunity to interpret and define the ambit of Section 1201, particularly its anti-trafficking provision. Those decisions inevitably touched on or reopened debates over some of the most fundamental copyright principles. Nonetheless, the U.S. Supreme Court, has yet to have the opportunity to express its opinion on such debates.

1.*Universal City Studios, Inc. v. Corley*[17]

This is the first case concerning the constitutionality of anti-circumvention statutes. The Content Scramble System (CSS) is a technology created to control

---

[14] 17 U.S.C. § 108 (c)(2000 Supp. II).

[15] See above note 12, also 68 Federal Register at 62102.

[16] Ibid.

[17] 273 F.3d 429 (2ndCir. 2001).

[18] First introduced in 1996, CSS was jointly developed by Matsushita and Toshiba, later adopted by the movie studios as the standard to divide the world into eight respective "zones" or regions for better control of DVD's market distribution. CSS is not a copy protection system *per se*; rather it is an access control system in the hope to achieve copyright protection: it prevents the playback of discs on unauthorised devices. Therefore, a DVD from one zone may not be played by a device from another zone, even though both are legitimate products.

access to the contents of DVDs or video compact discs (VCDs).[18] In 1999, a then sixteen-year-old Norwegian by the name Jon Johansen managed to reverse engineer and circumvent the CSS lock key. He then released his code-cracking software on the Internet and dubbed it "DeCSS." As a result, users can play a very large video computer file on a non-CSS-compliant player as well as copy, manipulate, and transfer that file just like any other computer file.[19] Eric Corley, the defendant in this case, picked this development up and published the entire source code of DeCSS on his website and magazine geared primarily for the so-called hacker community. This was but one of the many other websites that published DeCSS then. Eight major Hollywood movie studios brought suit and sought injunction against Corley under the DMCA anti-trafficking provision after he refused to comply with the movie studios' cease-and-desist letter by removing DeCSS.

The U.S. Court of Appeals for the Second Circuit affirmed the district court's decision to grant an injunction. The court declared that the DMCA "targets the *circumvention* of digital walls guarding copyrighted material (and trafficking in circumvention tools), but does not concern itself with the *use* of those materials after circumvention has occurred. Subsection 1201(c)(1) ensures that the DMCA is not read to prohibit the 'fair use' of information just because that information was obtained in a manner made illegal by the DMCA."[20]

On the constitutionality of anti-circumvention and anti-trafficking statutes, having concluded that computer code conveying information is "speech" within the meaning of the First Amendment, the court nevertheless found premature and speculative the defendant's constitutional challenge that the lower court's DMCA injunction over posting and linking hindered freedom of expression. The court held that intermediate scrutiny, with the showing of a legitimate government interest, was the appropriate review standard. Being content-neutral in nature, both the anti-circumvention and anti-trafficking provisions under the DMCA were held to meet that standard.[21]

In summary, the Section 1201(c)(1) prohibition (no encroachment on fair use) applies to the manufacturing, trafficking in and making of devices that would circumvent encryption technology, not to the users of such technology. It is the technology itself, rather than the users of the copyrighted material, that is at issue.

2. *The Chamberlain Group, Inc. v. Skylink Technologies, Inc.*[22]

While *Corley* was concerned only with the constitutionality issues, the *Chamberlain* case provided the first opportunity for the court to construe the full

---

[19] See above note 17, at 437,438.

[20] Ibid. at 443.

[21] The court noted that while the initial use of DeCSS to gain access to a DVD movie created no loss to the movie producers because the initial user must purchase that DVD, once the DVD was purchased, however, DeCSS enabled the initial user to copy the movie in digital (and technically "perfect") form and transmit it instantly in virtually limitless quantity, thereby depriving the movie producer of sales. "The advent of the Internet creates the potential for instantaneous worldwide distribution of the copied material." Ibid. at 453.

[22] 381 F.3d 1178 (Fed. Cir. 2004).

boundaries of the anti-circumvention and anti-trafficking provisions under the DMCA.

This case concerned alleged circumvention of copyrighted computer software embedded in a garage door opener (GDO) system. The plaintiff, The Chamberlain Group, adopted the so-called "rolling code" software program that constantly changes the hand-held transmitter signals needed to synchronise with the codes in the GDO motor to open the garage door. The defendant, Skylink, was the plaintiff 's competitor. Skylink had made a model (called a "universal transmitter") to interoperate with general GDOs, including the plaintiff's models, even though it did not use rolling codes.

Chamberlain initially sued Skylink for both patent infringement and anti-circumvention. After the patent claim was dismissed and the motion for summary judgment under DMCA was declined, only the latter issue was brought before the Federal Circuit.

From the outset, the Federal Circuit court acknowledged that this was a case of first impression and there was no binding precedent governing the substantive issue of this case. The court then construed the statute by first making a distinction between property and liability. The court declared that Sections 1201(a) and (b) establish causes of action for liability only; they do not establish a new property right.[23] Such a distinction was critical because it went straight to the *authorisation* issue upon which the district court's summary judgment was based. In copyright infringement, a plaintiff only needs to show that the defendant has used the copyrighted work; the burden of proving that the use was authorised falls squarely on the defendant.[24] However, since Section 1201(a)(3)(A) defines circumvention as an activity undertaken "without the authority of the copyright owner," it naturally follows that the plaintiff who is alleging circumvention or trafficking must bear the burden of proof that the defendant's access was unauthorised. Therefore, with the basic assumption that access is permissible unless prohibited, the defendant must prove authorised copying and the plaintiff must prove authorised access.

The *Chamberlain* court completely rejected the plaintiff's arguments on statutory construction. Recognising that its ruling could create uncertainties down the road, the court nevertheless concluded that the anti-circumvention provisions prohibit only forms of access that bear a reasonable relationship to the protection that the Copyright Act otherwise affords copyright owners.

---

23 "The circumvention provisions convey no additional property rights in and of themselves; they simply provide property owners with new ways to secure their property ... Contrary to Chamberlain's assertion, the DMCA emphatically did not 'fundamentally alter' the legal landscape governing the reasonable expectations of consumers or competitors; did not 'fundamentally alter' the ways that courts analyze industry practices; and did not render the pre-DMCA history of the GDO industry irrelevant." Ibid. at 1192–94.

24 "The premise underlying this initial assignment of burden is that the copyright laws authorise members of the public to access a work, but not to copy it. The law therefore places the burden of proof on the party attempting to establish that the circumstances of its case deviate from these normal expectations; defendants must prove authorised copying and plaintiffs must prove unauthorised access." Ibid. at 1193.

To summarize, the court held that a plaintiff alleging a violation of Section 1201(a)(2) must prove the existence of several conditions and they are: (1) ownership of a valid *copyright* on a work; (2) that has been circumvented despite effective control by a *technological measure*; (3) that third parties can now *access* (4) *without authorisation*, in a manner that (5) infringes or facilitates infringing a right *protected* by the Copyright Act, because of a product that (6) the defendant either (i) *designed or produced* primarily for circumvention; (ii) made available despite only *limited commercial significance* other than circumvention; or (iii) *marketed* for use in circumvention of the controlling technological measure. Failure to prove any of one of elements (1) through (5) would mean that a *prima facie* case of circumvention has not been established. A plaintiff capable of proving those five elements need prove the existence of only one limb of (6)(i), (ii) or (iii) to shift the burden back to the defendant. At that point, the various affirmative defences under Section 1201 become relevant.[25]

The district court's earlier decision to focus primarily on whether Skylink's behaviour, intent and product was within the context of industry expectations was re-affirmed. The Federal Circuit court also emphasized that in addition to failing to prove the fourth element (lack of authority), plaintiff had neither alleged copyright infringement nor explained how the access provided by defendant's product facilitated the infringement of any right that the Copyright Act sought to protect. Therefore, the plaintiff failed to demonstrate the nexus between access and protection and the district court was correct in denying its motion for summary judgment.[26]

3. *Lexmark International, Inc. v. Static Control Components, Inc.*[27]

Just a couple of months after the Chamberlain decision, the U.S. Court of Appeals for the Sixth Circuit passed judgement on the anti-trafficking provision of the DMCA. The plaintiff, Lexmark International, a world renowned manufacturer of computer printers and related accessories, sued its competitor for selling compatible, remanufactured products, thereby circumventing the built-in control measure that was placed within the plaintiff's own toner cartridges. The software program and the microchip in each Lexmark printer were designed to authenticate the source of the refill or replacement toner and only the plaintiff's own toner cartridges would be accepted. To compete with the plaintiff, the defendant copied the plaintiff's code in its own microchips so that its refill toner cartridges are interoperable with the plaintiff's but sold at a substantially lower price.

Lexmark sued on the ground that the unauthorised reproduction of the microchip code constituted copyright infringement, and that the interoperable product violated the anti-circumvention provisions under the DMCA. The district court granted the motion for preliminary injunction. The defendant appealed.

---

[25] Ibid. at 1203.

[26] Ibid. at 1203–04.

[27] 387 F.3d 522 (6th Cir. 2004).

The Sixth Circuit vacated and remanded the case to the district court on the ground that the plaintiff failed to demonstrate likelihood of success on merit. The court first examined whether the computer program in question was copyrightable (the "Toner Loading Program," or TLP). Drawing from the idea-expression dichotomy, the court held that the TLP, designed primarily to achieve the function of blocking out other name brand products, was not copyrightable—"lock-out" codes, in general, fell on the function-idea rather than the original-expression side of the copyright line.[28] Furthermore, the court held that when external factors constrained the choice of expressive vehicle, the doctrine of "scènes à faire," *i.e.*, scenes that must be done, precluded copyright protection. In the computer software context, the doctrine meant that the elements of a program dictated by practical realities (such as hardware standards, mechanical specifications, and compatibility requirements) may not obtain copyright protection.[29] To the extent that compatibility required that a particular code sequence be included in the component device to permit its use, the merger and scènes à faire doctrines generally preclude the code sequence from obtaining copyright protection.[30]

Having concluded that the computer program in question was not copyrightable, the fair use issue was naturally moot. The *Lexmark* court, for the sake of further proceedings, however, nevertheless chose to comment on the district court's fair use interpretation under Section 107 of the U.S. Copyright Act.[31] With regard to the first factor listed under Section 107 (purpose and character of the use), the court distinguished between mere profit-making and profiting from the exploitation of the copyrighted material without paying the customary price charged by the copyright owner. The court found the defendant copied the computer program for the purpose of achieving interoperability (a particular function),

---

[28] "Lock-out codes" are described as a "security system [employed by manufacturers] to bar the use of unauthorized components." Ibid. at 536.

[29] Ibid. at 535.

[30] Merger doctrine in the copyright context means if an idea and the way to express it are so intricately tied that the ways of expression of that idea have little possible variation, there is no copyright infringement. Citing *Sega Entertainments, Ltd. v. Accolade, Inc.*, 977 F.2d 1510 (9th Cir. 1992), the court, in turn quoted the CONTU Final Report: "When specific instructions, even though previously copyrighted, are the only and essential means of accomplishing a given task, their use by another will not amount to infringement." Id, 536; see also Final Report of the National Commission on New Technological Uses of Copyrighted Works, at 20 (31 July 1978).

[31] "Notwithstanding the provisions of sections 106 and 106A, the fair use of a copyrighted work, including such use by reproduction in copies or phonorecords or by any other means specified by that section, for purposes such as criticism, comment, news reporting, teaching (including multiple copies for classroom use), scholarship, or research, is not an infringement of copyright. In determining whether the use made of a work in any particular case is a fair use the factors to be considered shall include—(1) the purpose and character of the use, including whether it is of a commercial nature or is for non-profit educational purposes; (2) the nature of the copyrighted work; (3) the amount and substantiality of the portion used in relation to the copyrighted work as a whole; and (4) the effect of the use upon the potential market for or value of the copyrighted work. The fact that a work is unpublished shall not itself bar a finding of fair use if such finding is made upon consideration of all the above factors. " 17 U.S.C. §.107 (2000 Supp. II).

not for the exploitation of plaintiff's expressions. Thus, this factor did not necessarily tilt in the plaintiff's favour. On the fourth factor (effect on the potential market), the court put its emphasis not on the toner cartridge market, but on the market of the computer loading program itself. Given that neither party provided any evidence on the adverse effect to the market of the toner loading software program, the court was reluctant to hold this factor in plaintiff's favour, either.[32] As a result, even if the computer program were copyrighted work, fair use may be in store for a defendant to claim.

On the plaintiff's DMCA claims, Plaintiff Lexmark argued that the defendant's microchips that contained the TLP "lock-out" code was a "device" used to circumvent the "technical measures" that "effectively controls access" to plaintiff's "Printer Engine Program," or PEP (which is copyright-protected and embedded inside each printer itself). The Sixth Circuit disagreed.[33] The court pointed out that it was not Lexmark's authentication sequence that "controls access" to the PEP; rather it was the purchase of a Lexmark's printer that allows "access" to the program. Since there was actually no security device to protect access to the PEP, there was nothing to be circumvented. In other words, anyone who purchased a Lexmark printer might read the literal code of PEP directly from the printer memory, with or without the benefit of the authentication sequence, and the data from the program might be translated into readable source code. Then copies can be freely distributed. Thus, DMCA is inapplicable to readily-accessible copyrighted works.[34]

IV. Analysis and Comments

Copyright law is designed to maintain a delicate balance between the private and exclusive rights of an individual over a creative work with the public's interest in accessing that work. As a result, a number of exceptions to the exclusive rights are created, such as fair use, in the hope to achieve that balance. Whether infringement has actually taken place thus requires a nuanced analysis in light of the specific facts of each case.

By their very nature, technical protection measures, especially access control (sometimes interchangeably referred to as digital right management (DRM) measures) are incapable of such a nuanced analysis, as they lay down layers of invisible walls between the copyrighted work in its entirety and the outside world. Therefore, there have been concerns that the prevalent usage of control access or DRM measures would seriously jeopardise the copyright exceptions, and eventually encroach upon the fundamental value upon which online knowledge dissemination is based.[35]

---

32 See above note 27, at 544.

33 Ibid. at 546.

34 For an excellent analysis of these recent anti-circumvention cases, see *Zohar Efroni*, A Momentary Lapse of Reason: Digital Copyright, the DMCA and A Dose of Common Sense, 28 COLUMBIA J. L. & ARTS 249 (2005).

35 See *Bruce G. Joseph*, Copyright Issues on the Internet, the DMCA and Technological Protection, 830 PLI/PAT. 483 (2005)(Advanced Seminar on Copyright Law, 2005).

These concerns, together with *Chamberlain*, inevitably raise a fundamental issue. Is there is or should there be a public "right" of fair use, (at least some sort of "public right"), to access copyrighted works that derives from the Copyright Clause of the Constitution? Traditionally, fair use has been treated as an affirmative defence to the exercise of a copyright holder's exclusive rights.[36] In *Chamberlain*, though, the court strongly hinted, if not admitted outright, that such a public right of access did exist and should be used to balance against the copyright holder's enumerated exclusive rights.[37] Such a reading of the copyright statute, however, is still a minority view in the U.S. at the present stage.[38]

On the other hand, there are scholars who propose that as an integral part of the copyright system, there should be an exclusive "access right" for the copyright holder in today's digital environment.[39] This is because in the digital environment, physical copies play a secondary role as exploitation quickly shifts to the "experiencing" of works online. When access equals experiencing, copyright law must be relevant and integrated with this newly developed exclusive right, otherwise it will be unrealistic. This proposition, if adopted, naturally leads to the issue of what impact it may have on the traditional "first sale" or exhaustion doctrine, now that the copyright holder may virtually obtain full access control. Does it mean the copyright holder will be granted full control over the "tethered" works? No one seems to know the answer at the present time.[40]

While *Lexmark* made it clear that accessing a set of codes for the purpose of interoperability did not in itself render the act a violation under the DMCA, the court did not provide clear guidelines on what computer programs should be copyrightable. The idea/expression dichotomy certainly does not help those who intend to develop a certain software program without knowing whether that program will indeed be protected by copyright. Nor will others who intend to access the information know for sure whether that access will result in DMCA violation. In other words, both *Chamberlain* and *Lexmark* may have created more confusion and uncertainty than answers to the control access and anti-circumvention issues (especially in the anti-trafficking area). This can, in turn, have a significant impact on market competition as well.

---

[36] See *Campbell v. Acuff-Rose Music, Inc.*, 510 U.S. 569, 590 note 20 (1994). The Second Circuit further elaborated: "[W]e note that the Supreme Court has never held that fair use is constitutionally required, although some isolated statements in its opinions might arguably be enlisted for such a requirement." See *Corley*, above note 17, at 458.

[37] For example, the Chamberlain court stated specifically: "The DMCA does not create a new property right for copyright owners. Nor, for that matter, does it divest the public of the property rights that the Copyright Act has long granted to the public." See above note 22, at 1204.

[38] See *Bateman v. Mnemonics, Inc.*, 79 F.3d 1532, 1542 note 22 (11th Cir. 1996).

[39] See *Jane C. Ginsburg*, Essay: From Having Copies to Experiencing Works: The Development of an Access Right in U.S. Copyright Law, 50 J. COPYRIGHT SOC'Y U.S.A. 113, at 116 (2003).

[40] For another excellent article on the subject, see *Hsien-chen Li*, A Case Analysis of the DMCA Anti-circumvention Provisions from Aspects of Fair Use and Competition, 2 NCCU INTELLECTUAL PROPERTY REV. 134 (2004)(Taiwan).

Scholars have suggested that if there should be any lacking in the anti-circumvention and anti-trafficking provisions, the problem rests not with the courts but squarely with the statute, hence Congress itself.[41] Courts are forced to interpret the statutes with the most reasonable and perhaps best possible outcome while their hands are bound by the statutory language. But one thing is clear from the line of judicial decisions thus far: American courts will not tolerate the use DMCA as a tool to restrict competition by any potential plaintiff.

V. Conclusion

The passage of anti-circumvention provisions in DMCA has pushed the entire copyright system into unchartered territory. Instead of the nuanced, unfettered yet cautiously balanced manoeuvring between copyright holders and the public in the past, courts now must still do the same under DMCA. The courts are still walking on a tightrope, but with both hands tied. The right of "access control" may have indeed changed the copyright fundamentals for the first time in many years, and we, whilst enjoying the advent of the digital era, do not seem ready for all its potential problems, some of which may seriously hinder the progress of e-commerce. Perhaps only time will tell. Meanwhile, whether the U.S. DMCA model offers the best possible solution remains to be seen. The jury is still out but the initial verdict is already in: given that both the WCT and WPPT do require each member state to comply with their respective rules, the practical effect is that all nations must sooner or later adopt the anti-circumvention standards and balance them against fair use. One would only hope that anti-circumvention provisions will lead to a more pro-competitive global society and provide effective ways for knowledge and information dissemination, particularly to the poor. Given the complexity of this area, it will take global input to craft a better and more effective, balanced and harmonised copyright system for tomorrow.

Part 2—The 1996 WIPO Treaties

HAOCHEN SUN

I. Introduction

At the heart of this report lies the question of whether the Chinese anti-circumvention law is in line with the minimum standards set forth in the WIPO Copyright Treaty (WCT)[42] and the WIPO Performances and Phonograms Treaty (WPPT).[43] Given that China has set up the initiative to join the WIPO Treaties of 1996[44], it is therefore theoretically and practically useful to examine the status of legal protection of technological measures in China. This report will examine

---

[41] See above note 34.

[42] WIPO Copyright Treaty, 20 December 1996, 36 I.L.M. 65.

[43] WIPO Performances and Phonograms Treaty, 20 December 1996, 36 I.L.M. 76.

[44] International Intellectual Property Alliance, China Commit to Significantly Reduce the Copyright Piracy Level, News Release (21 April, 2004), (available at http://www.iipa.com/rbi/2004_April21_PRC.pdf, reporting that "China agreed to join the all important WIPO 'Internet' Treaties as soon as possible").

the anti-circumvention provisions set out in the WCT and WPPT, and evaluate the Chinese anti-circumvention law against the canvas of these two Treaties.

II. The 1996 WIPO Treaties

In response to the increasing ease of reproducing and disseminating protected works, copyright owners and their technology partners have designed an entirely new and more effective method—technological measures, to constrain physical access to and use of their copyrighted works. Early in 1991, the E.U. Directive on the Legal Protection of Computer Programs[45] took the lead by providing legal protection against circumvention of technological measures applied to protect computer programs.[46] In the wake of this Directive, the North American Free Trade Agreement (NAFTA)[47] provides criminal and civil remedies against decoding the encrypted program carrying satellite signals and related acts.[48]

The advent of the Internet facilitates the manufacture and trafficking of circumvention devices, and the subsequent dissemination of copies of works whose technological protection measures have been circumvented on a global scale, posing formidable challenges for the effective protection of technological measures. Therefore, an ambitious agenda to provide effective and adequate protection for the potentially increasing use of technological measures was initiated at the WIPO Diplomatic Conference of 1996. Article 11 of the WCT provides that:

"Contracting Parties shall provide adequate legal protection and effective legal remedies against the circumvention of effective technological measures that are used by authors in connection with the exercise of their rights under this Treaty or the Berne Convention and that restrict acts, in respect of their works, which are not authorized by the authors concerned or permitted by law."

Likewise, the WPPT contains a parallel provision for the protection of technological measures employed by performers or phonogram producers.[49]

---

[45] Council Directive 91/250/EEC of 14 May 1991 on the Legal Protection of Computer Programs (OJ L 122, 17.5.1991).

[46] Article 7 (1) (c) of the Directive provides:

"Any act of putting into circulation, or the possession for commercial purposes of, any means the sole intended purpose of which is to facilitate the unauthorized removal or circumvention of any technical device which may have been applied to protect a computer program."

[47] North American Free Trade Agreement, Dec. 17, 1992, Can.-Mex.-U.S., 32 I.L.M. 296 and 32 I.L.M. 605.

[48] Article 1707 of the North American Free Trade Agreement provides:

"Within one year from the date of entry into force of this Agreement, each Party shall make it:

(a) a criminal offence to manufacture, import, sell, lease or otherwise make available a device or system that is primarily of assistance in decoding an encrypted program carrying satellite signal without the authorization of the lawful distributor of such signal; and

(b) a civil offence to receive, in connection with commercial activities, or further distribute, an encrypted program carrying satellite signal that has been decoded without the authorization of the lawful distributor of the signal or to engage in any activity prohibited under subparagraph (a).

Each Party shall provide that any civil offence established under subparagraph (b) shall be actionable by any person that holds an interest in the content of such signal."

[49] See WPPT, Art. 18.

1. Unlawful Acts

Under the 1996 WIPO Treaties, "Contracting Parties" are obligated to provide "adequate and effective" legal protection against the "circumvention" of effective technological measures. Therefore, it is patently clear that "Contracting Parties" are obligated to provide legal protection against the direct circumvention of effective technological measures. At the same time, "Contracting Parties" are still obligated to prohibit a circumventor's initial act of manufacturing devices primarily for the purpose of circumventing technological measures, given that such an act is arguably an integral part of the illicit act of direct circumvention.

However, it remains disputable whether the third party's manufacture and distribution of protecting-defeating devices will be subject to the anti-circumvention provisions. Some commentators posit that WIPO Internet Treaties mandate that "Contracting Parties" should prohibit both the direct circumvention of technological measures and the manufacture and distribution of circumvention-targeted devices.[50] Yet others opine that the 1996 WIPO Treaties only target the direct circumvention of technological measures.[51]

Article 13 of the *Basic Proposal* of the draft WCT provided affirmative and unequivocal answers to the above controversy.[52] Obviously, the *Basic Proposal* focused on prohibition of the preparatory activities rather than on direct

---

[50] *Jörg Reinbothe and Silke von Lewinski*, The WIPO Treaties 1996: The WIPO Copyright Treaty and The WIPO Performances and Phonograms Treaty: Commentary and Legal Analysis (London : Butterworths, 2002) at 144–145 (contending that preparatory act are prohibited under the WCT and WPPT); *Jane Ginsburg*, Achieving Balance in International Copyright Law (reviewing The WIPO Treaties 1996: The WIPO Copyright Treaty and The WIPO Performances and Phonograms Treaty: Commentary and Legal Analysis (London: Butterworths, 2002) (2003) 26 *Colum. J.L. & Arts 201* at 212 (arguing that the final version of the WCT and WPPT contain the anti-device measures).

[51] See *Julie E. Cohen*, Some Reflections on Copyright Management Systems and Laws Designed to Protect Them, 12 Berkeley Tech. L.J. 161, 167(1997) (noting that the final version of the WIPO Treaties focuses on the need for protection against the act of circumventing copyright management system, rather than the nature of the device used to accomplish circumvention). *Terese Foged, U.S. v. E.U.* Anti-Circumvention Legislation: Preserving the Public's Privileges in the Digital Age? (2002) 24 E.I.P.R. 525, 526 (arguing that "the WIPO Treaties appear to concern only the direct act of circumvention of the technological protection measure itself").

[52] *WIPO*, Basic Proposal for the Substantive Provisions of the Treaty on Certain Questions Concerning the Protection of Literary and Artistic Works to Be Considered by the Diplomatic Conference, (WIPO Doc. CRNR/DC/4, August 1996). The proposed Article 13 provided:

"(1) Contracting Parties shall make unlawful the importation, manufacture or distribution of protection-defeating devices, or the offer or performance of any service having the same effect, by any person knowing or having reasonable grounds to know that the device or service will be used for, or in the course of, the exercise of rights provided under this Treaty that is not authorized by the right holder or the law.

(2) Contracting Parties shall provide for appropriate and effective remedies against the unlawful acts referred to in paragraph (1).

(3) As used in this Article, "protection-defeating device" means any device, product or component incorporated into a device or product, the primary purpose or primary effect of which is to circumvent any process, treatment, mechanism or system that prevents or inhibits any of the acts covered by the rights under this Treaty."

circumvention. This proposed provision stemmed from the premise that the primary solution to the multitude of tricky problems brought about by the Internet lay in the eradication of circumvention-targeted devices and services. Although the final texts of the 1996 WIPO Treaties fundamentally differed from what was originally proposed , the spirit of providing "adequate and effective" protection against all forms of circumventions remains intact and has been embedded into the adopted anti-circumvention provisions. Given that acts of circumvention are not amenable to detection and control in the digital environment,[53] the legal protection of technological measures "can hardly be enforced in an effective manner if it focuses exclusively on the act of circumvention".[54] Absent an effective oversight of the downstream supply of circumvention devices in the marketplace, it would become increasingly more difficult to deter acts of circumvention, and right owners' interests would be seriously prejudiced. Due to the fact that the circumvention can be accomplished relatively easily with the aid of readily available devices, protection against circumvention will soon be inadequate and ineffective, if the law only targets the direct circumventor. As rightly proclaimed in the Preambles of both the WCT and WPPT, the absence of the dual protections against direct circumvention and preparatory activities will disturb the balance of copyright protection as. Therefore, "Contracting Parties" are obligated to outlaw preparatory activities in the national anti-circumvention regulation.[55]

Yet one may argue that the fundamental change of language in the final version of the anti-circumvention provisions entails the exclusion of anti-trafficking regulatory measures from the 1996 WIPO Treaties. The treaty negotiation history proffers the best source from which the nature of such a change can be clarified. Despite the support from the U.S. and E.U., the anti- trafficking provisions proposed by the *Basic Proposal* were met with vehement opposition from many delegations. The delegate from the Republic of Korea, for example, expressed his concern that the then proposed anti-circumvention provisions might cause possible abuses of technological measures by right owners.[56] Furthermore, a delegate from Canada stated that the then proposed anti-circumvention provisions were not acceptable to the Canadian Government for two reasons: firstly, they would threaten the development of devices which might have significant non-infringing uses but which could also be used to defeat technological measures; secondly, the draft provisions would have the potential to impede access to works in the public

---

[53] See *Dean S. Marks and Bruce H. Turnbull*, Technical Protection Measures: The Intersection of Technology, Law and Commercial Licences (2000) 22 E.I.P.R 198 at 201.

[54] *Jörg Reinbothe and Silke von Lewinski*, The WIPO Treaties 1996: The WIPO Copyright Treaty and The WIPO Performances and Phonograms Treaty: Commentary and Legal Analysis (London: Butterworths, 2002) at 144.

[55] *Jane Ginsburg*, Achieving Balance in International Copyright Law (reviewing The WIPO Treaties 1996: The WIPO Copyright Treaty and The WIPO Performances and Phonograms Treaty: Commentary and Legal Analysis (London: Butterworths, 2002) (2003) 26 Colum. J.L. & Arts 201 at 212 ("If member states are instructed to provide adequate legal protection and effective remedies against 'the circumvention,' then they should endeavour to forestall that activity from occurring.").

[56] *WIPO*, Records of the Diplomatic Conference on Certain Copyright and Neighbouring Rights Questions, Geneva 1996, at 710 (1999).

domain and to restrict the fair use or fair dealing privileges or other users' privileges under the Berne Convention and the proposed Treaties.[57] Similar views were expressed by delegates from Singapore,[58] Australia,[59] and Norway.[60] The opposition leading to the final revision of the draft anti-circumvention provisions, however, only indicates that the protection afforded by the draft provisions were overly broad and stringent.[61] Obviously, the opposing delegations did not object to the prohibition of manufacture and supply of devices solely for the circumvention of technological measures. What they had objected to was that part of the draft provisions which might unduly jeopardize public interest, and would bring about certain undesirable effects of hampering the economical, social, cultural, and technological development in the information society. Hence, the negotiating history of the anti-circumvention provisions does not indicate that the anti-trafficking protection has been excluded from the 1996 WIPO Treaties.

Based upon the above analysis, it can be concluded that, under the 1996 WIPO Treaties, "Contracting Parties" are obligated to take a dualist approach to provide legal protection against direct circumvention as well preparatory activities. However, considerable latitude has been left to "Contracting Parties" to decide on the extent to which the preparatory activities leading to circumvention of technological protection measures should be penalised at the national level, provided that the anti-circumvention regulation is adequate and effective enough to protect copyright owners' interests. [62]

2. *Eligible Technological Measures for Protection*

The 1996 WIPO Treaties mandate that the eligible technological measure for protection should be "effective" in nature, and differentiate the types of such

---

[57] Ibid. at 711.

[58] Ibid. at 712 (cautioning against the danger of the overprotection of technological measures in the proposed Treaties).

[59] Ibid. at 714 (stating that "the current language might unwittingly restrict access to material in circumstances where it was not subject to copyright").

[60] Ibid. at 715 (observing that anti-circumvention "should not prevent legitimate use of works, for example, private and educational uses, and use of works which had fallen into public domain").

[61] During the diplomatic conference, several delegates expressed concern that the provision as worded in the drafts of the proposed Treaties would cover a variety of devices capable of substantial and valuable non-infringing uses. See *Julie E. Cohen*, Some Reflections on Copyright Management Systems and Laws Designed to Protect Them, (1997) 12 Berkeley Tech. L.J. 161, 167 (citing that "Japan and other Asian nations were up in arms about proposals that would effectively have turned the consumer electronics industry into a branch of publishing."). See also *Pamela Samuelson*, The U.S. Digital Agenda at WIPO (1997) 37 Va. J. Int'l L. 369, 414 (explaining that many delegates expressed concern that the provision might restrict access to public domain materials and frustrate lawful uses of copyrighted works, such as fair use).

[62] *Jane Ginsburg*, Achieving Balance in International Copyright Law (reviewing The WIPO Treaties 1996: The WIPO Copyright Treaty and The WIPO Performances and Phonograms Treaty: Commentary and Legal Analysis (London: Butterworths, 2002) (2003) 26 Colum. J.L. & Arts 201 at 213 ("The WCT thus may imply some upper and lower limits on the purpose and effect of proscribed devices, but it leaves to member states the determination of where, within the tolerable spectrum of characterizations, to draw the line between devices to condemn and devices to allow.")

technological measures employed by the right owners. Article 11 of the WCT states that the technological measures protected should be effective and used by authors in connection with the exercise of their rights under the WCT or Berne Convention. Article 18 of the WPPT contains a similar requirement. Moreover, the 1996 WIPO Treaties divide protectable technological measures into two categories: access-control measures (effective technological measures "that restrict acts, in respect of their works, which are not authorized by the authors concerned or permitted by law") and rights-control measures (effective technological measures "that are used by authors in connection with the exercise of their rights under this Treaty or the Berne Convention").[63]

3. *Knowledge Requirement*

Under the 1996 WIPO Treaties, there are no explicit knowledge requirements in the anti-circumvention provisions. By contrast, the *Basic Proposal* made it clear that a person would be penalized if he or she knew or had the reasonable grounds to know that the device in question would be used for or in the course of the unauthorized exercise of any of the rights provided for thereunder.[64] This knowledge requirement therefore focused on the purpose for which the device or service would be used.[65] However, it was not incorporated into the final texts of the 1996 WIPO Treaties.[66]

4. *Effective Remedies*

Finally, "Contracting Parties" are required to provide effective remedies against circumvention. The 1996 WIPO Treaties are silent on concrete criteria to evaluate the effectiveness of remedies. According to the *Basic Proposal*, "Contracting Parties" are free to choose appropriate remedies according to their own legal traditions.[67] National enforcement system, under the WCT and WPPT, should be

---

[63] See *Dean S. Marks and Bruce H. Turnbull*, Technical Protection Measures: The Intersection of Technology, Law and Commercial Licences (2000) 22 E.I.P.R 198, at 201; see also, *R. Anthony Reese*, Will Merging Access Controls and Rights Controls Undermine the Structure of Anti-circumvention Law?, 18 Berkeley Tech. L. J. 619 (2003).

[64] *WIPO*, Basic Proposal for the Substantive Provisions of the Treaty on Certain Questions Concerning the Protection of Literary and Artistic Works to Be Considered by the Diplomatic Conference, (WIPO Doc. CRNR/DC/4, August 1996) at para.13.02.

[65] See Basic Proposal, ibid.

[66] The knowledge requirement was contentious issue in the negotiations. Recognizing that a provision on circumvention technologies would be a new feature for copyright laws of many countries, Chairman Liedes tried to alleviate potential concerns about the breadth of his proposal by indicating that there would be substantial latitude for national implementations of this norm. States would, for example, be "free to choose appropriate remedies according to their own legal traditions," and they could "design the exact field of application of the provision . . . taking into consideration the need to avoid legislation that would impede lawful practices and the lawful use of subject matter that is in the public domain." See *Pamela Samuelson*, The U.S. Digital Agenda at WIPO (1997) 37 Va. J. Int'l L. 369 at 413.

[67] *WIPO*, Basic Proposal for the Substantive Provisions of the Treaty on Certain Questions Concerning the Protection of Literary and Artistic Works to Be Considered by the Diplomatic Conference, (WIPO Doc. CRNR/DC/4 , August 1996) at para.13.04.

effective and should at least include expeditious remedies to prevent infringements and remedies which constitute a deterrence to further infringements.[68] Therefore, remedies against circumvention should be effective enough to "constitute a deterrent and a sufficient sanction" against illegal acts of circumvention.[69]

B. Country Reports

Note: The contributors to the country reports are listed in the introductory preface.

I. China

1. Anti-Circumvention Regulations in China

Under the Chinese Copyright Act of 1990[70] and Software Regulations of 1991,[71] there were no explicit provisions concerning the protection of technological measures. Though the Chinese software industry has began to use technological measures, they are faced with the dilemma that the technological measures they had applied are vulnerable to circumvention, whereas the law did not provide any legal protection against such activities.[72] Given the importance of both protecting the copyright owners' interests and promoting the development of information industry,[73] the 2001 amendments[74] to the Copyright Act of 1990 set forth

---

[68] WCT, Art. 14; WPPT, Art. 23.

[69] *WIPO*, Basic Proposal for the Substantive Provisions of the Treaty on Certain Questions Concerning the Protection of Literary and Artistic Works to Be Considered by the Diplomatic Conference, (WIPO Doc. CRNR/DC/4 , August 1996) at para. 13.04.

[70] The Copyright Act of People's Republic of China, adopted at the Fifteenth Meeting of the Standing Committee of the National People's Congress of China on 7 September 1990.

[71] Regulations for the Protection of Computer Software, adopted by the State Council of the People's Republic of China on 4 June 1991.

[72] The first reported circumvention of technological measures occurred in 1997. CASC, copyright owner of the software "PKPM", used encryption measure to prevent the software from being pirated. Zhang Lisun developed a computer program that can decrypt the above technological measure. Afterwards, Zhang Lisun put an advertisement in the Chongqing City's local newspaper "Computer" for the sale of the decryption program. CASC then sued Zhang Lisun for infringing their copyright. In another case, the program which allowed users to circumvent the technological measures applied by Jiang Ming Software Company to their anti-virus software was posted on the China Duniao BBS. Unlike CASC, Jiang Ming Software Company, took self-help measures against circumvention rather than suing the hacker. In order to crack down on the circumvention of technological measures applied to their anti-virus software, Jiang Ming developed a "logical lock" that had the ability to cause the locking of a computer a user attempted to the use the pirated version of Jiang Ming's software. However, this self-help action generated vehement opposition and their "logical lock" was denounced as a "logical bomb" on the Internet. Finally, Jiang Ming was penalised by the local administrative agency on the grounds that their anti-circumvention self-help measure had jeopardised the safety of the Internet.

[73] See Ying Ming, Impact of Digital Technology on Copyright System and Revision of Chinese Copyright Law (2000) China Patents and Trademarks 59 at pp.66.

[74] The Decision of the Standing Committee of the National People's Congress Regarding the Revision of the Copyright Act of the People's Republic of China (adopted at the Twenty-Fourth Session of the Standing Committee of the Ninth National People's Congress, 27 October 2001) (hereinafter Copyright Act of 2001).

an anti-circumvention provision, which represents "a significant upgrade of copyright protection"[75] in China. Sec. 47(6) of the Copyright Act of 2001 provides that the following shall be sanctioned:

> "to knowingly circumvent or impair the technological measures employed by the right owner to protect the copyright or related rights in the work, sound recording or video recording, without the authorization of the copyright owner or the owner of related-rights."

Akin to the Copyright Act of 2001, the amended Software Regulations of 1991[76] also outlaws the act of knowingly circumventing or impairing the technological measures employed by right owners.[77] Moreover, the newly revised Interpretation Regarding Various Issues on the Applicable Law for Adjudicating Disputes Relating to Computer Network Copyright[78] issued by the Supreme People's Court of China further states:

> "In the case of the ISP who knowingly uploads, disseminates or makes available any means, device or material designed or manufactured intentionally to circumvent or impair the technological measures that protect copyrighted work, the People's Court shall, based upon the party's claims and the specific case situation, impose liability for civil infringement thereon pursuant to Sec. 47(6) Copyright Act."[79]

a) Unlawful Acts

The plain reading of the above two articles denotes that the law only prohibits the act of direct circumvention, though the impairment of the technological measures and ISP's dissemination of protection-defeating devices are outlawed. One the one hand, subjecting the impairment of technological measures to penalization does not necessarily mean that the law has made the preparatory activities illegal. To impair the technological measures is to a large extent tantamount to the act of circumvention, for both of them have the effect of directly defeating the technological measures. Therefore, the prohibition of impairing the technological measures, by nature, is a measure to outlaw the act of direct circumvention. On the other hand, notwithstanding the prohibition of distribution of the circumvention-enabling devices by the ISP, the aforementioned Interpretation issued by the Supreme Court does not categorically prohibit all preparatory activities. Neither does the ban apply to those other than the ISP, who disseminate devices over the Internet, nor does it forbid the manufacture of circumvention-enabling devices. More importantly, one should note that the Supreme Court, in such an important legal interpretation, merely bars the ISP from distributing circumvention devices or the like. The manufacture of circumvention

---

[75] See Xiaoqing Feng and Frank Xianfeng Huang, International Standards and Local Elements: New Developments of Copyright in China (2002) 49 J. Copyright Soc'y U.S.A. 917 at 922.

[76] Decree N0.399 of the State Council of the People's Republic of China (20 December 2001) (hereinafter Software Regulations of 2002).

[77] See Software Regulations 2002, Art. 24 (3).

[78] Interpretation Regarding Various Issues on the Applicable Law for Adjudicating Disputes relating to Computer Network Copyrights, passed on 23 December 2003 in the One Thousand Three Hundred and Second Meeting of the Adjudication Committee of the Supreme Court, Judicial Interpretation (2004) No.1.

[79] Ibid., Art.6.

devices by an ISP is not prohibited by the interpretation. If its intention was to make it clear that any preparatory activities should be outlawed, the Supreme Court would have explicitly extended the ban to all the above activities that the current Interpretation has not covered.

b) Eligible Technological Measures for Protection

With regard to the protectable technological measures, it has merely been prescribed that technological measures applied in relation to the exercise of copyright or related rights should be protected against circumvention. The Copyright Act 2001, however, does not further specify whether the eligible technological measures for protection should be effective in nature.[80] Moreover, the Act does not draw the line between the access-control and rights-control measures, and further provides varied protections in accordance with their different nature in safeguarding copyright owners' interests. This implies that China may have adopted the merged protection of two disparate control measures.[81]

c) Knowledge Requirement

In respect of the knowledge requirement, under the current anti-circumvention provisions, only the person who *knowingly* circumvents shall be sanctioned. This may imply that those who have just and reasonable grounds to believe their acts are infringing would be able to escape penalisation.

d) Remedies

The remedies afforded by the Copyright Act 2001 include civil, administrative and criminal liabilities. The civil remedies concern the order to cease the infringing act, the elimination of adverse effects caused by the infringing acts, making an apology, and/or paying damages.[82] In addition to the civil remedies, under some circumstances, the person who illegally circumvents may be subject to administrative penalties, including the order to cease the infringing act, confiscation and destruction of infringing copies, and/or imposition of a fine.[83] If a serious infringement occurs, the copyright administrative agency may seize the materials, tools, and devices primarily used for making infringing copies.[84] However, the law is silent on whether the competent administrative agency can forfeit the devices used to circumvent technological measures. The forfeit of protection-defeating devices is critically important in that it helps to deter the potential circumvention of technological measures by preventing them from being circulated to other would-be circumventors. Finally, if the act of circumvention is

---

80 Both the WCT and WPPT explicitly require that technological measures should be effective enough to be protected by law.

81 The author's view in this respect differs from some commentators who opine that only access-control measures are protected under the Copyright Law. See Wang Qian, Dui Jishu Lifa Cuoshi De Bijiao Yanjiu[A Comparative Analysis of Anti-circumvention Rule], Zhishi Chuanquan [Intellectual Property] 2003, No.3, at pp.8.

82 See Copyright Act of 2001, Sec. 47.

83 Ibid.

84 Ibid.

serious enough to constitute a crime, the circumventor shall be prosecuted for his criminal liability.[85]

2. Conclusions

The foregoing juxtaposition suggests that the Chinese copyright law is not fully in line with minimum standards set out in the 1996 WIPO Treaties, largely due to the loophole in the anti-trafficking regulation. Moreover, the lack of the mandate that empowers the competent administrative agencies to confiscate circumvention-enabling devices, as indicated above, may make the law not sufficiently effective to deter illicit circumvention acts. At the same time, the juxtaposition also indicates the following deficiencies in the Chinese anti-circumvention law. Firstly, the law does not make it patently clear that the protected technological measures should be effective in nature and neither does it differentiate between the access-control and rights-control measures. Secondly, there are no limitations on the anti-circumvention rules, which are permissible to be carved out nationally under the 1996 WIPO Treaties. Given that China will join the these two Treaties in the near future,[86] the task of complying with the standards set out in the WCT and WPPT should be regarded as the top priority for the revision of the current Chinese anti-circumvention law.

II. Hong Kong

1. General

Hong Kong was one of the first jurisdictions in the world to implement the anti-circumvention provisions based on the WIPO Copyright Treaty[87] and WIPO Phonograms and Performances Treaty[88].

The relevant anti-circumvention provision in the Copyright Ordinance is Section 273. However, Section 273 does not impose criminal liability but only civil liability for making and dealing in devices designed to circumvent copy protection for commercial use. Section 273 provides that a copyright owner may bring civil action against a person who, knowing or having reason to believe that any devices/means will be used to make infringing copies:-

(i) makes, imports, exports, sells or lets for hire, offers or exposes for sale or hire, advertises for sale or hire, or possesses for the purpose of, in the course of, or in connection with, any trade or business *any device or means specifically designed or adapted to circumvent the form of copy protection employed*; or
(ii) publishes information intended to enable or assist persons to circumvent that form of copy protection.

Copy protection is defined by Section 273(4) to include 'any device or means specifically intended to prevent or restrict copying of a work.

[85] Ibid.
[86] See above note 3.
[87] The WIPO Copyright Treaty entered into force on 6 March 2002 when 30 states ratified or acceded to it.
[88] The WIPO Phonograms and Performances Treaty entered into force on 20 May 2002.

Section 23(2) of the Copyright Ordinance provides that copying of a work means reproducing the work in any material form, and this includes storing the work in any medium by electronic means. Section 23(6) provides that copying in relation to any description of work includes the making of copies which are 'transient or incidental' to some other use of the work.

2. Case Law

Two recent high profile cases can best illustrate the position taken by the Hong Kong courts regarding the anti-circumvention provisions in the Copyright Ordinance, namely, *Nintendo Co. Limited v Lik Sang International Limited* [89] and *Sony Computer Entertainment Inc. v Lik Sang International Limited.*[90] The defendants operated a very successful website selling a variety of legitimate and infringing game products to customers on a world wide basis. In the Nintendo case the products in question were Flash Linker/Cards which enabled the copying of games contained in Nintendo's Game Boy onto a computer and then onto a Flash card. In the case of Sony, the products were modification chips which could be used to modify Sony's PlayStation consoles, thereby enabling the consoles to play unauthorised copies of PlayStation discs.

In both cases, in order to succeed in an action under Section 273, the plaintiffs needed to prove (i) the games were copyrighted works; (ii) the games were issued in a form which was copy protected; (iii) the mod chips (Sony) or Flash Linker/Card (Nintendo) were specifically designed or adapted to circumvent the form of copy protection that the plaintiffs had employed in their games; and (iv) the defendants knew or had reason to believe that the mod chips (Sony) or Flash Linker/Card (Nintendo) would be used to make infringing copies of the plaintiffs' games.

In both cases, the plaintiffs succeeded in proving the above requirements. There were no doubts that both Sony and Nintendo's games were copy protected in the sense that they were specifically designed and intended by the plaintiffs to prevent or restrict copying. In fact, Justice Waung in the *Nintendo* case offered the analogy of a burglar alarm to illustrate this point. He said:-

> "The question is not whether the burglar alarm is 100% efficient, namely it is guaranteed to exclude all burglars no matter how sophisticated or professional the skills of the burglar. Some burglars are extremely inventive and creative and, notwithstanding good burglar alarms, can manage to get in and steal— just as in this case the defendants as clever copyright burglars— managed to steal the copyright from the plaintiffs. The fact that they have high level skills and succeeded in stealing does not, in any way, detract from the product being specifically intended to restrict copying, or to use the expression of the burglar alarm, to prevent the entry by burglars."

Apart from this, the defences raised by the defendant and the rulings by the court in response also merit some comment. It is a popular defence by a defendant in such cases that the devices have other innocent functions, for example, as playing protection, or some legitimate uses that take the devices outside the definition in Section 273(2)(a) of being specifically designed or adapted for circumvention purposes. It was held in both cases that it was no defence that the devices may also have other innocent functions or uses and that this was not a matter of degree and

[89] 58 IPR 187 High Court of Hong Kong, pp 186–192
[90] [2003] HKEC 521

that the devices came within Section 273 of the Copyright Ordinance, so long as at least one of their uses was an infringing use.

Justice Waung held in the *Nintendo* case that the question that should be asked was:-

> "what is the substantial purpose of these Flash products of the defendants and what made them such successful products which sell like hotcakes?... There may be sometimes innocent usage that the product can be put to, but the predominant usage of the Flash product of the defendants is to enable protected software of the plaintiffs to be stolen... What is fatal to the innocent user argument is the upstream ability of the Flash product, namely the specifically designed Flash Linker which is tailor made to enable the Game Boy cartridge to be inserted into it so as to enable the software inside the Game Boy cartridge to be extracted/copied onto a computer. That upstream design has no other legitimate objective except to circumvent the copy protection and to steal the copyright."

3. *Digital Rights Management*

Digital Rights Management is often divided into two functional areas:

(i) the identification and description of intellectual property rights pertaining to works and to parties involved in their creation of administration (digital rights management); and
(ii) the (technical) enforcement of usage restrictions (digital management of rights).[91]

Section 274 of the Copyright Ordinance deals with digital rights management directly by providing rights and remedies in respect of unlawful acts that interfere with rights management information. It provides that a person providing rights management information is entitled to have the same rights and remedies against a person who-

(a) removes or alters any electronic rights management information provided by him without his authority; or
(b) issues or makes available to the public, sells or lets for hire, imports into or exports from Hong Kong, broadcasts or includes in a cable programme service, without his authority, works or copies of works, performances, fixations of performances to which the electronic rights management information is attached knowing that the electronic rights management information has been removed or altered without his authority, as a copyright owner has in respect or an infringement of copyright.

Persons providing rights management information in Hong Kong have been given the same extent of protection as a copyright owner.

III. Taiwan

1. *Introducing protection for electronic rights management information*

The 2003 Copyright Act follows the WCT (Art. 12) and WPPT (Art. 19) in introducing the protection for electronic rights management information. It deviates

---

91 "Current Developments in the Field of Digital Rights Management" -WIPO Standing Committee on Copyright and Related Rights 10th Session Geneva, 3–5 November 2003 at page 4.

from the WCT and WPPT on two points. Firstly, the removal or alteration of electronic rights management information is strictly prohibited, and the subjective element of "knowing...that it will induce, enable, facilitate or conceal an infringement of any right" demanded by the WCT and WPPT is not required of the person who undertook the removal or alteration. Secondly, the 2003 Copyright Act provides two exceptions to such protection:

(i) Where removal or alteration of electronic rights management information of the work is unavoidable in the lawful exploitation of the work given technological limitations at the time of the act.
(ii) Where the removal or alteration is technically necessary in order to convert to a certain recording or transmission system.

The violation of provisions protecting electronic rights management information is subject not only to civil liability, but also to criminal punishment.

2. Introducing anti-circumvention protection

The Taiwanese Government was pressured by the U.S. to introduce remedies against the circumvention of effective technological measures into their 2003 Copyright Act and tabled a draft to that legislature which clearly followed the U.S. Digital Millennium Copyright Act (DMCA). The draft was rejected by the Legislative Yuan, mainly on the ground that "such protection would have too great an impact on the use of works by the general public and on the development of technology, and that the newly revised Sec. 358 Criminal Code already deals with intrusions into computers and therefore there is no need to introduce such protection for the time being."[92] The stalling of the passage of the anti-circumvention protection in 2003 was of great dismay to the U.S. New momentum was soon gathered to mobilise legislators to put forward a new amendment draft on that issue. To everyone's surprise, that effort brought fruits on the typhoon morning of 24 August 2004, when the Legislative Yuan was convening for an extended session. Anti-circumvention protection was enacted, among other things. By and large, this piece of legislature is a work of haste and therefore frowned upon by academics for the following reasons:[93]

a) Discrepancy with regard to the term of technological protection measures

While Sec. 3 (18) defines the term as including technological means employed by copyright owners to effectively prohibit or restrict others from *accessing or exploiting* works without authorisation, Sec. 80-2 (1) prohibits only the act of accessing works via circumvention of technological protection measures without legal authorisation, thereby leaving the legality of the act of by-passing the so-called copy controls to be judged by the general principle of fair use.

---

[92] Sec. 358 of the Criminal Code prescribes: "Breaking into encrypted account numbers, deactivating protective measures for the use of computers, and utilizing the loopholes of computers shall be punished with imprisonment up to three years, detention, and in addition thereto or in lieu thereof a fine up to NT100,000."

[93] Kung-Chung Liu, Study on the Copyright Act Provisions on Technological Protection Measures (in Chinese), 119 The Taiwan Law Review (April 2005), 70–90 (86–90).

b) Wording too wide

As a precaution against restricting the deployment and use of technical devices and information, it is commonly required in the legislation elsewhere (e.g. U.S. DMCA, EU InfoSoc Directive and the German Copyright Act) that only devices which have limited commercial purposes or usages other than circumventing effective technological measures are disallowed to be manufactured, imported, or offered to the public for use. However, the wording of Sec. 80-2 (2) would put a general ban on any and all equipment, device, component, technology or information for disarming, destroying, or circumventing technological protection measures to be manufactured, imported, offered to the public for use, or offered in services to the public, if without legal authorisation.

c) Exemptions highly uncertain

Sec. 80 (3) broadly exempts eight acts of circumvention, namely for the preservation of national security, done by governments, archive institutions, educational institutions, or public libraries, for the protection of minors, for the protection personal data, for testing computers or networks security, and for encryption research and reverse engineering. However, the exact contents of those exemptions are to be prescribed and periodically reviewed by the TIPO via regulations, "which shall be binding upon the people, industries, police officers, prosecutors' offices and courts."[94] Sec. 80 (4) also delegates to the TIPO the identification and determination of further exemptions. What the TIPO has at hand as guidelines to exert this empowerment is the rather succinct legislative reason for Sec. 80 (3) Copyright Act: The disarming, destroying, or circumventing technological protection measures for *legitimate purposes* shall be allowed; a reference to Section 1202 of the US Copyright Act, Paragraph 3 was added to prescribe exempted cases in order to balance the relationship between social public interest and copyright holders.

In a continental-European legal system such as Taiwan, blanket power delegation of this nature is open to challenges from the viewpoint of the principle of certainty of legislative empowerment on the administrative branch, which requires "the purpose, contents and scope of empowerment be specific and clear.[95]"

d) Laxity of requirement for civil and criminal liability

With regard to civil liability, no subjective requirement such as constructive knowledge is required. In other words, once circumvention has taken place, circumvention equipment circulated, and circumvention service provided, circumventors, circulators and service providers will be liable for damages, even if they had no knowledge or reasonable ground to know that their action amounted to

---

94 The legislative reason for Sec. 80–2 (4) Copyright Act.

95 See for example Interpretation No. 570 (December 26, 2003) of the Judicial Yuan. The Interpretation of the Judicial Yuan enjoys the legal status of Constitution in Taiwan.

or facilitated circumvention (Sec. 90-3 (1)). With respect to criminal punishment (up to one year imprisonment) which concerns only circumvention equipment circulators and circumvention service providers (circumventors not included), no inquiry into whether their actions were "for profit" or "for purposes of commercial advantages or private financial gains" is required (Sec. 96-1). This broad-based liability hardly looks justified. In contrast, the US Copyright Act imposes criminal punishment only when the violation is "wilfully and for purposes of commercial advantage or private financial gain" (Sec. 1204(2)), while the German 2003 Copyright Act makes immune from criminal sanctions any circumvention that is exclusively for personal private use (Sec. 102b(1)). The U.S. and German legislatures illustrate the necessity to tighten the criteria for criminal sanctions, and at least to exclude circumvention that is exclusively for personal private use.

e) No obligations imposed on copyright holders to inform the public

The transparency of the digital market place can best be served by imposing obligations on right holders to inform the general public of whether any technological measure has been deployed and the nature of such measures (whether they limit reproduction) before they make their purchase. The German Copyright Act of 2003 adopted this even-handed approach by making it an obligation for copyright holders to indicate whether and what kind of technological measures were applied to the works (Sec. 95d(1)), and who the persons applying technological measures are, as well as their addresses. However, the Taiwanese Copyright Act demands that the general public respect technological measures taken by copyright holders and does not ask of copyright holders anything in return for the consumers.

f) No obligations imposed on copyright holders to ensure exemption clauses

Exemption clauses embody public interest consideration and should be upheld as much as possible. However, looking from the viewpoint of a non-technology-savvy person, technological protection measures would grant copyright owners more control, even absolute control over their works, which would in practice challenge many copyright limitation clauses. The Taiwanese Copyright Act does not address this issue. It is advisable to follow the German Copyright Act, which requires that the copyright holders provide the beneficiaries of copyright limitation clauses with the necessary means to enjoy these exemptions, and grants the beneficiaries the right to ask copyright holders to provide the necessary means (Sec. 95b(1)(2)).

IV. Japan

1. Introduction

The Japanese legislature in 1999 introduced protection against the circumvention of anti-copying devices either by hard- or software, and protection against the removal of or tampering with digital rights management systems, as well as finally limiting the copying for private use by using anti-circumvention devices, or by removing digital rights management signals.

2. *Protection against anti-circumvention devices*

a) Legislative Provisions

Secs. 2(1)(x) and (xi) Unfair Competition Prevention Act read as follows:

(x) the act of assigning, delivering, displaying for the purpose of assignment or delivery, exporting or importing a device with the sole function of enabling the audio or video perception of images or sounds encrypted by anti-copying devices in the course of business, the operation of encrypted programs, or the storage of such encrypted images, sounds or programs, by way of circumventing such anti-copying devices or any equipment where such device is installed, or storage media containing programs having this sole function as such or in combination with other programs, or devices containing such abilities, or of providing a program with this sole function by way of electronic means. This does not apply to devices used by third parties for the purpose of enabling only a limited number of people to access audio or video signals or programs;

(xi) the act of assigning two other parties outside those authorised, delivering, displaying for the purpose of assignment or delivery, exporting or importing a device with the sole function of enabling the reception of audio or video signals restricted by anti-copying devices used for the purpose of business by a certain party for the purpose of preventing others than those particularly authorised from receiving such signals or programs, or the storage of such audio or video signals or programs, through circumventing such anti-copying devices including apparatus where such device may be installed, or storage media comprising of such program having this sole function as such or in combination with other programs, or such storage equipment, or of providing a program with such function only by way of electronic means;

A definition of the terms "anti-copying devices" and "programs" is given in Sec. 2 (5) and (6) UCA:

(5) "Anti-copying devices" are devices that electronically, magnetically, or in any other way not susceptible to the human sense, restrict the perception of sounds or images, the operation of programs, or the storage of audio or video signals or programs by means of storage in a medium or transmission, in connection with audio or video signals or programs whose signals are perceptible by audio-visual equipment (as used for the audio or visual perception of signals, the operation of a program, the storage of audio or video signals or programs. Hereinafter the same), or by employing methods of storage in a storage medium for audio or video signals or programs that convert these in order to make them perceptible by audio-visual equipment in a certain way only.

(6) "Programs" shall mean instructions to a computer that are combined in order to achieve a certain result.

Sec. 120bis Copyright Act reads as follows:

Section 120bis. The following shall be punishable by imprisonment for a term not exceeding three years or a fine not exceeding three million Yen, or both:

(i) any person who transfers to the public the ownership of, or rents to the public, manufactures, imports or possesses for transfer of ownership or rental to the public, or offers for the use by the public, a device having a principal function of the circumvention of technological protection measures (such a device includes such a set of parts of a device as can be easily assembled) or copies of a program having a principal function of circumvention of technological protection measures, or transmits publicly or makes transmittable such program;

(ii) any person who, as a business, circumvents technological protection measures in response to a request from the public;

(iii) any person who, for profit-making purposes, does an act considered to constitute an infringement on moral rights of authors, copyright, moral rights of performers or neighbouring rights under the provisions of Section 113, paragraph (3);

(iv) any person who, for profit-making purposes, does an act considered to constitute an infringement on copyright or neighbouring rights under the provisions of Section 113, paragraph (5).

b) Analysis

aa) The 1999 amendments to both the Unfair Competition Prevention Act (UCA)[96] and Copyright Act prohibit the distribution of devices that are able to circumvent anti-copying mechanisms or mechanisms aimed at restricting access to certain authorised persons (e.g., subscribers). Liability under the UCA is only civil, while that under the Copyright Act is both civil and criminal.

bb) Secs. 2(1)(x) and (xi) UCA basically cover two acts of circumventing anti-copying devices. Subsection (x) covers cases where encryption is absolute; in other words, no one is entitled to circumvent the device. Subsection (xi) concerns cases where the encryption is meant to limit the number of authorised users, e.g., cable television. The prohibition covers both the circumvention via hardware (device) and software (program). Protection is limited to anti-copying devices that are commercially used, and prohibited acts do not apply to acts done for the purposes of experiment or research. Yet as in other cases of prohibited acts under the UCA, it is not necessary that the circumvention is done for commercial purposes, on a commercial scale or for profit. Despite the fact that no competitive relationship exists between the owner of the transmitted material and the person producing or selling anti-copying devices, the person aggrieved by such latter act may claim injunctive relief and damages according to Secs. 4 and 5 UCA, while the presumption of damages is stipulated under Sec. 5. If the jurisdiction on preventing acts of slavish imitation is anything to go by, standing to sue will only be given to the developers of anti-copying devices and encryption software, rather than the licensees or importers.[97] Acts of circumventing anti-copying devices do not entail criminal sanctions.

cc) The Copyright Act contains a very similar provision for preventing the manufacture and sale of circumvention devices in Sec. 120bis Copyright Act. The difference is basically this: while the Unfair Competition Prevention Act provides only for civil sanctions, the Copyright act provides for criminal ones for the respective offence. As is typical for criminal offences, the act has to be conducted on a professional or commercial scale. Strangely enough, neither of the two statutes provides for a prohibition of the *manufacture* of circumvention devices. While the provisions under the UCA can be explained as a protection of investment (which may well be one of the purposes of the UCA), the provisions under the Copyright Act are somewhat atypical in that the Japanese Copyright Act protects creative achievements rather than mere investment. As such, it would have been preferable to include Sec. 120bis Copyright Act into Sec. 13 UCA.

---

[96] Law No. 33/1999 of 23 April 1999, in force since 1 October 1999.

[97] See the decision, Tokyo District Court, 28 January 1999, 1677 Hanrei Jihô 127 [1999]—Caddy Bag. Here the sole import distributor of US-developed caddy bags was denied a standing to sue, as he himself had not invested in the development of such products.

dd) Both the provisions of the Unfair Competition Act and of the Copyright Act only cover cases of circumventing devices with the "sole" function of circumventing anti-copying protection mechanisms: the Copyright Act uses the word "*moppara*", while the UCA uses "*nomi*". Both provisions provide for an exception in cases where the device with such exclusive function can be easily combined with another, neutral device. While the combined device may also have other functions, the provision would apply nonetheless.

It stands to reason that proof can be extremely difficult if the device can also be used for other purposes. Some English translations of the relevant provisions under copyright law have thus interpreted the term "sole function" as "principal function".[98] While such an interpretation may be desirable, the Japanese word *moppara* hardly leaves room in this respect: it simply means "entirely", "solely", or "exclusively". To interpret this as "mainly" or "principally" would at least be problematic[99] and is an interpretation not open to the UCA, where "*nomi*" is even less unambiguous as meaning "only".

ee) There are no cases where the above provisions were applied by the courts.

3. *Digital Rights Management Information*

a) Legislative Provisions

The two relevant provisions of the Copyright Act read as follows:

(Reproduction for private use)

Section 30. (1) It shall be permissible for a user to reproduce by himself a work forming the subject matter of copyright (hereinafter in this Subchapter referred to as a "work") for the purpose of his personal use, family use or other similar uses within a limited circle (hereinafter referred to as "private use"), except in the case:

(i) where such reproduction is made by means of automatic reproducing machines ("automatic reproducing machine" means a machine having reproducing functions and in which all or main parts of reproducing devices are automatic) placed for the use by the public;

(ii) where such reproduction is made by a person who knows that such reproduction becomes possible by the circumvention of technological protection measures or it ceases to cause obstruction, by such circumvention, to the results of acts deterred by such measures ("circumvention" means to enable to do acts prevented by technological protection measures or to stop causing obstruction to the results of acts deterred by such measures, by removal or alteration of signals used for such measures; the same shall apply in Section 120bis, items (i) and (ii)) ("removal" or "alteration" does not include such removal or alteration as is conditional upon technology involved in the conversion of recording or transmission systems).

Sec. 113

(3) The following acts shall be considered to constitute an infringement of the economic or moral rights of authors, or the moral rights or neighbouring rights of performers relating to rights management information:

(i) the intentional addition of false information as rights management information;

---

98 E.g., the Japanese/English work on "Copyright Law of Japan", edited by the Copyright Research and Information Center, Tokyo, November 1999; T. Doi, 1999 Amendment to Japan Copyright Act, 30/1 Patents & Licensing 24.

99 A. Koshida, 1999/7 Copyright 28: "In other words, a normal personal computer that can also be used to circumvent anti-copying devices would in itself be a device with other functions, too, and thus does not come under this provision."

(ii) the intentional removal or alteration of rights management information excluding the case where such act is conditional upon technology involved in the conversion of recording or transmission systems or other cases where it is deemed unavoidable in the light of the purpose and the manner of exploiting works or performances, etc.;

(iii) the distribution, importation for distribution or possession for distribution of copies of works or performances, etc. by a person who knows that any act mentioned in the preceding two items has been done concerning such works or performances, etc. or the public transmission or making transmittable of such works or performances, etc. by such person.

b) Analysis

The above two provisions relate to very different constellations. Sec. 113 imposes a civil law liability for tampering with digital rights management information, either by adding, removing or altering it. Also further acts of distribution are covered once the person undertaking such acts has positive knowledge of the previous tampering—a fact that can rarely be proven. It is unclear to what extent the provision can be applied even in cases where no copyrighted work is at stake. This is doubtful not only in the context of the provision, but also in the light of subsection (3) that requires "works" or "performances". The latter indicates that the provision should only apply where (protected) works or performances are at stake. It is thus irrelevant if by the acts described above also a copyright infringement has been committed, but what is required is a tampering with information in respect of a protected work or performance.

Sec. 30 (2) introduces a limitation to private copying, itself a limitation of the rights of commercial exploitation. The provision is rather problematic, as it does not allow private copying in cases where the copyright owner has used hard- or software in order to prevent copying. In other words, digital prevention becomes legal prohibition. Due to the requirement of positive knowledge, the provision can most likely only be applied to the direct user of a circumvention device rather than the subsequent users. Still, the provision adds a further layer of complexity to the already difficult relationship between technical prevention and contractual prohibition of acts of private use that are further elaborated in chapter 6.

V. Korea

Both Art. 11 WCT and Art. 18 WPPT oblige the contracting parties to provide adequate legal protection and effective legal remedies against the circumvention of effective technological measures that are used by authors, performers or producers of phonograms in connection with the exercise of the rights under the WCT, WPPT and the Berne Convention and that restrict acts, in respect of their works, which are not authorised by the right holders concerned or permitted by law. At the Diplomatic Conference, countries have not agreed upon the exact definition of "effective" technological measures, "adequate" legal protection or "effective" legal remedies, for copy/access control technology was still premature in 1996[100] and most of the participants had no concrete idea about it.[101]

---

[100] Pamela Samuelson, The U.S. Digital Agenda at WIPO, 37 Va. Int'l L.J. 369 (1997).

[101] Naoki Koizumi, Protection of Technological Measures under Japanese Law, Vol.2 No.1 Journal of Digital Property Law 96–98 (2002).

With regard to technical protection measures against the manufacture and distribution of programmes or devices meant to overcome or circumvent copyright management systems, the Copyright Act was amended in 2003 to implement anti-circumvention measures.[102] Unlike Japanese Copyright Act,[103] the 2003 Copyright Amendment did not make certain reproduction for private use by use of circumvention measures subject to liability. It should be noted that the 2003 Copyright Amendment does not include access control but only provides copy control. The legislature (MOCT) thought that the term "in connection with the exercise of their rights under this Treaty or the Berne Convention" in the Art. of WCT does not require implementation on access control.

VI. Singapore

1. Anti-circumvention Measures

Art. 11 of the WCT[104] is of a general nature, leaving contracting parties with some discretion to decide what constitutes 'adequate legal protection and effective legal remedies' against anti-circumvention measures. In 2004, WIPO released a new 'Guide to the Copyright and Related Rights Treaties Administered by WIPO'[105] which describes in greater detail what is required to properly implement Art. 11 of the WCT. Its key recommendations are very similar to the US standard (DMCA); in particular, the protection must extend to both 'access control' and controls on the exercise of exclusive rights, and the business of trafficking of circumvention devices and providing circumvention services, and the exceptions and limitations must not be based on the broad 'fair use' or 'fair dealing' concept but should be focused narrowly. This is to be contrasted with the advice given by the Electronic Frontier Foundation which, for example, encourages countries to provide a general exception for circumvention for legitimate and non-infringing purposes.[106]

This matter is so important to the US that it was not content to leave it to chance where Singapore is concerned: the US-Singapore FTA spelt out the specifics of the anti-circumvention law that Singapore must introduce, and this law is fashioned very closely after the DMCA model. Some examples below illustrate this point.

On the matter of remedies, the range of civil remedies which Singapore must provide include the opportunity for the right holder to elect between actual

---

[102] Act No. 6881, 2003. Sec. 92 (Acts Considered as to be Infringements)
(2) An act of transferring to the public the ownership of, or lending to the public, manufacturing, importing or possessing for transfer of ownership or lending to the public, or offering for the use by the public, a device having a principal function for the circumvention of technological protection measures shall be considered to be an infringement of copyright or other rights protected under this Act. See also CCPA Sec. 30.

[103] Act No. 77, 1999 (Sec. 30: Reproduction for private use).

[104] The discussion that follows on Art 11 WCT should be read to include Art 18 of the WPPT.

[105] WIPO Publication No 891(E) (2004).

[106] above, note 21.

Nature of the prohibition in US-Singapore FTA (Art. 16.4.7)[107]	Equivalent provision in 17 USC
The infringing acts are: (1) Circumvention (with knowledge or reasonable grounds to know) of any effective technical measure that controls access to a protected copyright work/performance.	§1201(a)(1)(A)
(2) Manufacture, import, distribution, offer to the public, provision or otherwise trafficking in devices, products or components, or offer to the public or provision of services, which:are promoted, advertised or marketed for the purpose of circumvention of any effective technological measure; or	§1201(a)(2)(C)
have only a limited commercially significant purpose or use other than to circumvent any effective technological measure, or	§1201(a)(2)(B)
are primarily designed, produced or performed for the purpose of enabling or facilitating the circumvention of any effective technological measure.	§1201(a)(2)(A)
There are very specific limitations to each of the infringing acts. For example, in the case of circumvention of 'access control' measure [see (1) above], there are only 8 limitations permitted, some of which are the following activities (providing that they do not impair the adequacy of legal protection or the effectiveness of legal remedies against the circumvention of effective technological measures):	§1201(f)(1)
(i) Non-infringing reverse engineering activities with regard to a lawfully obtained copy of a computer program, carried out in good faith with respect to particular elements of that computer program that have not been readily available to the person engaged in such activity, for the sole purpose of achieving interoperability of an independently created computer program with other program.	§1201(g)(2)
(ii) Non-infringing good faith activities, carried out by an appropriately qualified researcher who has lawfully obtained a copy, performance or a display of a work, and who has made a good faith effort to obtain authorization for such activities, to the extent necessary for the sole purpose of identifying and analyzing flaws and vulnerabilities of technologies for scrambling and descrambling of information.	§1201(h)

[107] These prohibitions are now found in the new Secs. 261B—261G inserted by the Copyright (Amendment) Act 2004. These new sections came into force on 1 January 2005.

(iii) The inclusion of a component or part for the sole purpose of preventing the access of minors to inappropriate online content in a technology, product, service or device provided that such technology, product, service or device itself is not prohibited hereunder.	§1201(h)
(iv) Non-infringing uses of a particular class of works when an actual or likely adverse impact on such non-infringing uses with respect to such particular class of works is credibly demonstrated in a legislative or administrative proceeding, provided that any exception adopted in reliance on this clause shall have effect for a period of not more than 4 years from the date of the conclusion of such proceeding.	§1201(a)(1)(B) [108]

damages it suffered (plus any profit attributable to the prohibited activity not taken into account in computing the actual damages) or pre-established damages,[109] and criminal penalties must be imposed on a defendant found to have "engaged wilfully and for purposes of commercial advantage or private financial gain in such activities".[110]

2. Digital Rights Management

Since 1999, Singapore has protected rights management information (RMI) by providing civil remedies against unauthorized removal or alteration of electronic RMI with the knowledge or intent to mislead or induce or facilitate an infringement of copyright/performance right.[111] It is worth noting that Singapore takes the precaution of ensuring the limitations to copyright and defences to infringement actions available in the Copyright Act are not affected by the protection of RMI, by making express provision to this effect.[112] Further, 'rights management information' is defined to specifically exclude any information relating

108 See the 2003–2006 list of exemptions made by the Librarian of Congress (Federal Register Vol 68 No 211).

109 Art 16.9.5 of the US-Singapore FTA. See the new Sec. 261F inserted by the Copyright (Amendment) Act 2004 that came into force on 1 January 2005.

110 Art 16.4.8(a) of the US-Singapore FTA. See the new Sec. 261C(4)—(5) inserted by the Copyright (Amendment) Act 2004 that came into force on 1 January 2005.

111 See Sec. 260(2) of the Copyright Act. The beneficiary of this protection is 'the person who provides the rights management information'. The civil remedies available are: an injunction, and/or damages and/or an order that any article by means of which the infringing act was carried out be delivered up to the plaintiff or destroyed: Sec. 261 of the Copyright Act.

112 See Sec. 259(2)(c)–(d) of the Copyright Act. In the US, see Gordon v Nextel Comm. and Mullen Advertising, Inc 345 F 3d 922, where the defendants, who was sued for copyright infringement (for unauthorised use of the plaintiff's photo in a TV commercial) and for infringement of the copyright management information provision in 17 USC §1202 (the photo used by the defendants in the TV commercial did not include the right management information), succeeded in resisting the plaintiff's application for summary judgment by raising, inter alia, the fair use defence.

to the user (e.g. name, account, address) of the copyright work/recording of the performance.[113]

The protection that Singapore currently provides, however, differs from that guaranteed by Art. 12 of the WCT in the following material ways. Firstly, Singapore does not prohibit the other type of unauthorized act mandated in Art. 12(1)(ii), namely, distribution, importation for distribution, broadcast or communication to the public of works or copies of works with knowledge that the RMI has been removed or altered without authority. Secondly, the *mens rea* associated with *intent* in the current Singapore model is more difficult to prove than that associated with *having reasonable grounds to know* in Art. 12.

These differences[114] will have to be addressed as Singapore works towards ratification of the WCT, as agreed under the US-Singapore FTA. Further, while the obligation in Art. 12 of the WCT speaks generally about providing adequate and effective legal remedies,[115] the FTA is more specific in this regard; in particular, civil remedies must include the opportunity for the right holder to elect between actual damages it suffered (plus any profit attributable to the prohibited activity not taken into account in computing the actual damages) or pre-established damages,[116] and criminal penalties must be imposed on a defendant found to have "engaged wilfully and for purposes of commercial advantage or private financial gain in such activities".[117]

VII. Malaysia

In the Information Age, digital works are one of the most important types of copyright, and the Internet one of the most significant distribution channels for

---

[113] See Sec. 260(4) of the Copyright Act. This protection applies only where the electronic RMI is attached to a copy of the copyright work or a recording of the performance, or appears in connection with the making available of such copy or recording, on a network: Sec. 260(1). See also Art. 12(2) of the WCT. In Art. 16.4.8(b) of the US-Singapore FTA, it is expressly provided that "Nothing in this paragraph [relating to protection of rights management information] obligates a Party to require the owner of any right in the work, performance, or phonogram to attach rights management information to copies of it or to cause rights management information to appear in connection with a communication of the work, performance, or phonogram to the public". This provision, it seems, is to ensure that parties do not mandate the use of RMI by a right holder. This has the same effect as the second agreed statement concerning Art. 12 of the WCT which clarifies that Contracting Parties shall not rely on Art. 12 to devise or implement RMI systems that would have the effect of imposing formalities which are not permitted under the Berne Convention.

[114] Another difference, but one which is not particularly material, is the exception which exonerates any act done for the service of the Government [Sec.259(1) of the Copyright Act]. A similar exception for Government activities (law enforcement, intelligence etc) is found in the US Copyright Act [17 USC §1202(d)]. The Copyright (Amendment) Act 2004 has introduced new Secs 258, 260—261A on the protection of rights management information. These new sections came into force on 1 January 2005.

[115] See also Art. 14 of the WCT on the undertaking of Contracting Parties to ensure that their enforcement procedures permit effective action against any act of infringement of rights covered by the WCT, including remedies which constitute a deterrent to further infringements.

[116] Art. 16.9.5 of the US-Singapore FTA.

[117] Art. 16.4.8(a) of the US-Singapore FTA. This obligation to criminalise the prohibited activity only extends to cases where the person is other than a non-profit library, archive, educational institution or public non-commercial broadcasting entity.

such digital works. Digital works may be reproduced perfectly and, with the Internet, also reproduced and disseminated quickly and cheaply. This vulnerability to copyright infringement has led the industry to adopt technological means to control access to and usage of their works in order to deter infringement. For example, some shareware programs have reminder screens to encourage people to pay ('nag-ware'), while others have some functions disabled until the user enters a registration code ('cripple-ware'). Despite this, the user community has always found ways to circumvent these protective measures by making available 'serialz', 'cracks' and 'keygens', which are easily found on the Internet.

Until recently, such activities did not constitute copyright infringement since they did not involve reproduction of the software or otherwise fall into the traditional acts of infringement. In 1997, amendments to the Malaysian Copyright Act were passed to make anti-circumvention activities a form of copyright infringement. The relevant provision is section 36(3) which reads:

> Copyright is infringed by any person who circumvents or causes any other person to circumvent any effective technological measures that are used by authors in connection with the exercise of their rights under this Act and that restrict acts, in respect of their works, which are not authorized by the authors concerned or permitted by law.

This provision was inspired by Art. 11 of the WIPO Copyright Treaty (WCT) and was adopted via the Copyright (Amendment Act) Act 1997. However, it should be noted that Malaysia is not a party to the WCT.

The way section 36(3) is worded suggests that the infringing activity is the act of circumvention itself or the act of causing another to circumvent. No examples are given nor has there been any case law in Malaysia on the issue. In particular, the scope of what amounts to 'causing' another to circumvent is very vague. Moreover, the section does not explicitly deal with the situation where a person makes, supplies or sells the tools or technology to enable or assist in the act of circumvention.[118] Similarly, the section does not elaborate on what is meant by 'effective technological measures' nor does it give allowance or exceptions for 'fair use'.

Related to the section on anti-circumvention is section 36(4), which deals with rights management information. Inspired by Art. 12 of the WCT, section 36(4) was introduced at the same time as section 36(3) and it reads as follows:

> Copyright is infringed by any person who knowingly performs any of the following acts knowing or having reasonable grounds to know that it will induce, enable, facilitate or conceal an infringement of any right under this Act:
>
> (a) the removal or alteration of any electronic rights management information without authority;
> (b) the distribution, importation for distribution or communication to the public, without authority, of works or copies of works knowing that electronic rights management information has been removed or altered without authority.

This section deals only with electronic rights management information, such as digital watermarks or document properties that may be embedded into, say, an Adobe PDF file. There have been no reported cases on copyright infringement involving electronic rights management information.

---

118 Contrast with Secs. 1201(a)(2) and 1201(b) of the American Digital Millennium Copyright Act.

VIII. Thailand

The present Copyright Act does not have any provisions on anti-circumvention measures and digital rights management information and there are no precedents on either of them. It is therefore fair to say there are no legal protections or remedies against circumvention and digital rights management information tampering under the Act. In any event, the DIP has included provisions on such issues in the copyright amendment bill.

In terms of anti-circumvention measures, the current draft of the bill states that the manufacture, importation for sale or rental of equipment designed or specially modified to tamper with the operation equipment used for protection against unauthorized reproduction of copyrighted works is a criminal offence subject to imprisonment of not exceeding one year or a fine of not exceeding THB100,000 (about € 2,500) or both.

In terms of digital rights management information tampering, the bill states that *knowingly* deleting or modifying digital rights management information or selling, importing for sale, broadcasting, or communicating to the public the work of which digital rights management information has been tampered with by an unauthorized party is a criminal offence subject to imprisonment of not exceeding one year or a fine of not exceeding THB50,000 (about € 1,250) or both.

It remains to be seen whether these proposed provisions will be accepted by the National Legislative Assembly.

IX. The Philippines

The WIPO Copyright Treaty (WCT, for brevity) requires member-countries to "provide adequate legal protection and effective legal remedies against the circumvention of effective technological measures that are used by the authors in connection with the exercise of their rights under this Treaty [WCT] or the Berne Convention and that restrict acts, in respect of their works, which are not authorized by the authors concerned or permitted by law."[119] The treaty further provides that protection must be extended to electronic rights management information.[120]

While the Philippines is signatory to the WCT, the government has yet to enact legislation extending greater protection against technologies being adopted to circumvent copyright limits. The IP Code and the Electronic Commerce Act[121] (ECA, for brevity), which provide penal sanctions for infringement of copyrights subsisting in digital works, is silent on regulating the use of digital rights management (DRM) technologies on digital copyrighted works.

The use of DRM technologies by copyright owners will allow them to regulate, control and monitor the use of their digital works, including optical media. To a certain extent, copyright owners will have control over how their works will be utilised by end-users. It is feared that the adoption of DRM technologies will

119 WCT Art. 11.
120 WCT Art. 12.
121 Republic Act 8792 (2000).

constitute undue restrictions on legitimate users of such works. To illustrate, DRM technology can restrict the playback of DVD to two occasions only. The limitation on the number of playback constitutes undue restriction on the use by the end-user since the latter is unable to view his DVD more than twice even if such additional viewing is considered fair use. The user in this case must first seek permission from the copyright owner, probably by paying an additional amount, in order to view the DVD movie more than twice.

While DRM technology may have been developed to address the problem of digital piracy, the same technology may be utilised to avoid copyright limitations. Copyright owners may adopt the technology to circumvent copyright limitations by regulating or controlling instances of fair use as shown above.

The IP Code enumerates the instances of fair use of copyrighted works[122] which can be generally classified into four (4) types, namely:

(i) research or private study;
(ii) criticism or review;
(iii) reporting current events; and
(iv) charitable or non-profit religious undertakings.

Further, the IP Code provides that in determining whether the use made of a work in any particular case is fair use, the factors to be considered shall include:

(i) The purpose and character of the use, including whether such use is of a commercial nature or is for non-profit education purposes;
(ii) The nature of the copyrighted work;
(iii) The amount and substantiality of the portion used in relation to the copyrighted work as a whole; and
(iv) The effect of the use upon the potential market for or value of the copyrighted work.[123]

The detailed provision on copyright law regarding fair use exception must be read in conjunction with the declared policy of the State recognizing intellectual property's social function. It can be said that copyright owners may exceed their rights should they stipulate further limitation on the fair use exception. A further limitation on the fair use doctrine may be construed as inconsistent with the policy. Again, in the absence of local jurisprudence, it would be interesting to see how the Courts will reconcile the social function policy of intellectual property and the adoption of DRM technology on digital works.

122 IP Code Sec. 184.
123 IP Code Art. 185.1.

5
Copyright Contracts, Public Policy and Antitrust

ESTELLE DERCLAYE*

This topic is complementary to the previous one. While in case of anti-copying devices, the means to prevent copying (lawfully or unlawfully) are technological, the same result may be achieved contractually through means such as shrink-wrap and click-wrap licences. Such licences raise two main areas of concern: are such contracts valid and enforceable under contract law and if so, are they also viewed in the same light under copyright law? The bid to find the answers has lead to a number of public policy considerations—should consumers be legally bound by such licences which attempt to override the limits placed by copyright law on exploitation by the right-owner under all circumstances or should public policy and economic considerations dictate that nonetheless some boundaries must be defined on the extent to which such licences may contractually override the protection given by copyright law.

A. Introduction—Can adhesion contracts override copyright limits?

I. Introduction

Traditionally, to exploit their copyrights, right-owners have commonly relied on contracts to determine how and to what extent their works may be used; for example, there may be a condition prohibiting rental[1]. Such contracts were typically entered into after arm's length negotiations between the right-owner and his licencee whilst the end-user of the work was prevented by the principle of privity of contract from having a direct legal relationship with the right-owner.

The use of standard form[2] contracts in order to bind users of copyright works is a relatively recent phenomena. The use of adhesion contracts in copyright transactions really began in 1980's with shrink-wrap licences for software products and thereafter for databases; and then spread dramatically with the advent of the Internet in 1990's. Digitisation and the availability of worldwide networks resulted in easy cheap and perfect reproduction and dissemination of every kind of work

1 * The author would like to thank Professor P. Maggs for his comments on US law.
Spoor, General aspects of exceptions and limitations: general report, in L. Baulch, M. Green and M. Wyburn (eds.) ALAI Study Days—The Boundaries of Copyright: its proper limitations and exceptions, Sydney, Australian Copyright Council, p.27–41 (1999), at point 6: Circumventing the exceptions. This example relates to the time when authors had not been given the right of rentals; *Hugenholtz*, Code as code or the end of intellectual property as we know it, Maastricht J. of Eur. and Comparative law, vol. 6, n. 3, 308 (1999).

[2] The words "standard form" and "adhesion" are used interchangeably.

(books, music, software, newspapers, databases...)[3]. This development and the frequent use of adhesive contracts have made it possible for the right-owner to establish a direct contractual relationship with each and every end-user, binding them in a very speedy and cost-effective manner. Such contracts regulate the delivery of content to users and determine the conditions of use of a work with such ease and at such low cost that many right-owners have jumped on the band wagon. Their use have become such a ready and easy means for right-owners in search of greater rights, so much so that it has added to and even supplanted the current copyright protection[4]. Not only can users rely on copyright to control the use of works but, even better, they can craft their own conditions to do the same. The fundamental problems with these standard form contracts are: they are drafted exclusively by the right-owners and are thus extremely one-sided and contain restrictions which go far beyond the boundaries of protection given to right-owners by copyright law; they prevent users from certain uses, for example from quoting the work or making a parody of it. This situation is rather ironic the term 'licence' means the "formal authority to do something that would otherwise be unlawful[5]".

While the factual landscape has changed, the legal one has remained quasi identical. This due largely to the fact that the use of standard form copyright contracts is relatively recent. Hence, their impact on the limits that copyright law has placed on the right-owner right of exploitation is still unclear. The underlying purpose of copyright law is to strike a balance between conflicting interests; of authors to receive remuneration for their effort; and of society to be entitled to a free flow of ideas, information and commerce. As has been correctly pointed out in other contributions to this book,, this delicate balance has been tipped by recent developments in the widening of ambit of copyright law. For instance, the form of protected works has been extended to include computer programs and databases; the exclusive rights have been expanded; and the term has been lengthened. This leads one to the inevitable conclusion that the rights owner is well protected. Hence, it seems unconscionable that he should be given greater liberties to protect himself contractually. Should s/he be allowed to contract out of the limits under copyright law? For instance, should the right-owner be able to prevent redistribution of the work in opposition to the doctrine of first sale? Should s/he be allowed to forbid reproductions for research purposes or quotations altogether? Should copyright limits be mandatory so that public policy can then dictate that there shall not be any derogation of grant, or are such limits only to be applicable by default only?

This paper attempts to answer the question whether restrictive standard form copyright contracts are valid. By restrictive copyright contract, we mean a contract which overrides copyright limits. Limitations on copyright are the idea/expression dichotomy; the originality requirement; the term; the exhaustion principle and the

---

[3] *Spoor*, above fn. 1, point 6.

[4] *Trotter Hardy*, Contracts, copyright and preemption in a digital world, 1 Rich. J. L. and Tech. 2, at 17 (1995).

[5] A Concise Dictionary of Law, 2nd ed., OUP, 1990, cited by *Rowland & Campbell*, Supply of software: copyright and contract issues, International J. of L.& IT, vol. 10, n.1, 23–40 (2002).

several exceptions or limitations to the author's exclusive rights. Even if individually negotiated contracts still remain used, the discussion will be limited to the validity of adhesion contracts for at least two reasons. They are by far the most wide-spread for the delivery of works[6] and for this reason, they are potentially the most problematic. In order to determine whether restrictive copyright adhesion contracts are valid, two interrelated questions must be answered. The first is whether adhesion contracts restricting copyright limits are valid in U.S. and European contract law (section I.1) and copyright law (section I.2). This will be an analysis of the positive law (*de lege lata*). If they so are, then the second question is whether such contracts should be allowed to override copyright limits (section II). This will be a discussion of normative law (*de lege ferenda*). N. Elkin-Koren once said: "Today, more than ever before, we need a theory that defines the boundaries of the freedom of contract in the context of copyright law."[7] This article argues that there might not be a need for a theory but that the answer lies at the very heart of copyright law itself.

II. Are Restrictive Copyright Contracts valid?

1. *Validity of contracts under contract law*

The adhesion contracts used in copyright transactions are known as shrink-wrap and click-wrap licences.

a) Preliminary Notions

aa) Shrink-wrap licences Four types of shrink-wrap licences can be identified. Some licences have restrictive terms which are readable before opening the package and thus can be read prior to purchase.[8] The second type of shrink-wrap licence has its terms contained within the box and cannot be read unless the seal

---

[6] Adhesion contracts tended, already before the advent of digital technology, to be the exception rather than the rule. A commentator estimated however that 98% of all written contracts in the United States are adhesion contracts. See *Slawson*, Standard form contracts and democratic control of law making power, 84 Harv. L.R. 529 (1971), cited by *Burgess*, Consumer adhesion contracts and unfair terms: a critique of current theory and a suggestion, Anglo-American L.R. 255 (1986). Burgess (see his fn. 3) believes that since marketing methods are highly used nowadays, this figure is approximately as high in other countries. It makes sense therefore to concentrate in this paper on the effects of the use of standard form contracts since they are by far the most spread nowadays. For an overview of the situation regarding classic contracts, the reader is referred to L. *Guibault*, Copyright limitations and contracts, An analysis of the contractual overridability of limitations on copyright (The Hague, 2002).

[7] Copyright policy and the limits of freedom of contract, 12 Berk. Tech LJ 93, at 113 (1997).

[8] For example, adhesives on which the terms of the licence are written are stuck on the back of the box containing the work and invite the purchaser to break the seal if he agrees with the terms. Another example is placing the licence under a clear plastic inside the box containing the copyrighted product so that it can be read in full. An example of such licence is given by *Jerrard*, Contractual protection of software. A guide to the relevant terms, CL&P, 169, at 171 (1985) (licence for the Multimate program): "You should carefully read the following terms and conditions before opening this diskette package. Opening this diskette package indicates your acceptance of these terms and conditions. If you do not agree with them you should promptly return the package unopened; and your money will be refunded."

is broken. A variant of of both these types of licences displays some terms outside of the package and the rest inside.[9] Finally, some licences only appear on the screen once the software is installed on the computer.[10]

The typical shrink-wrap licence includes the following restrictive terms[11]:

— the licence is granted only for personal use
— the software is to be used only on one microcomputer at any given time

such uses are not allowed: making of copies of the diskettes and associated documentation, except for security purposes; altering the software; granting sublicences; and disassembling or decompiling the object code, translating or modifying the software for use with non-compatible hardware.

Of the 4 types of shrink-wrap licences, the licence whose terms the user cannot read before purchase is most popularly used.[12] Unfortunately, questions of contractual validity are fundamental with such types of licences.

bb) Click-wrap licences The click-wrap (otherwise called "click-through" or "click-on") licence differs from the typical shrink-wrap licence in the manner that the restrictive terms are made known to the purchaser before he purchases the product.[13] Generally, the terms appear on the user's screen before the purchaser can download the product in question. A button or icon with the words "I agree" or "I accept" or simply "Yes" are distinctly displayed on the web page. The purchaser clicks and in so doing signifies acceptance of the terms.[14] This difference has drastically affects the enforceability of such licences.

The term "click-wrap" is also sometimes used to describe those situations when the restrictive terms of contract only appears on the screen after the user has bought the product. This is actually what happened on the *ProCD* case (see below). These involve many of the same issues as shrink-wrap contracts.

b) The U.S. Position

aa) Shrink-wrap licences Standard contract terms are enforceable under contract law if the purchaser can review the terms of the licence before he purchases the goods or services. The customer's assent to the licence may be express or implied from the party's conduct.[15]

---

[9] *Trompenaars*, Formation and Validity of On-Line Contracts, in Hugenholtz (ed.), Copyright and Electronic Commerce (The Hague 2000), 269.

[10] *Germanowski*, Is the shrinkwrap licence worth the paper envelope it's printed on ?, Int.J. L. & IT, Vol. 6, No. 3, 312, at 315; *Trompenaars*, above fn. 9, 269.

[11] *Jerrard*, above fn. 8, 171.

[12] For some, the determinative characteristic of all shrink-wrap licences is that the purchaser cannot read the terms of the licence before he purchases the product. See *Johnson*, p. 98.

[13] *Germanowski*, above fn. 10, 315: with the click wrap licence, "the terms of the licence are agreed prior to, or at the same time that the contract is agreed to, rather than being introduced to the customer after the contract is formed".

[14] *Lai*, Recent developments in copyright, database protection and (online) licensing, Int. J. L. & IT 73, Vol. 7 n. 1, 73, at 90–91 (1999).

[15] Restatement (Second) of Contracts, § 18.

Consent can be implied if the party who assents knows or has reason to know the other party may infer assent from her conduct. However, the law does not require that the other party reads or understands the terms. What is required is only that he had the opportunity to review them before assenting.[16] Relying purely on the other party's lack of opportunity to review the term prior to assent alone shrink-wrap licences should be held invalid.

In fact, the U.S. courts for many years had held shrink-wrap licences unenforceable because a party cannot be bound by terms s/he only has knowledge of after contracting.[17] In 1996, in the seminal *ProCD v Zeidenberg* decision, the Court of Appeals for the 7th Circuit held otherwise.[18] Matthew Zeidenberg, a professional, had bought a CD-ROM containing a database of around 3000 telephone directories. The database was held unoriginal. The CD-ROM's software, when run on the computer, displayed a notice on the user's screen stating that the use of the database is restricted to non-commercial purposes. There were no licence terms outside the package, only this notice. Zeidenberg ignored the licence and put the database on the Internet. The court found that such shrink-wrap licences are ordinary contracts and are governed by the common law of contracts and the Uniform Commercial Code ("UCC"). In the court's opinion, such practice of disclosure of terms to the purchaser only after payment has been made is common place. Reference was made to insurance policies, airline tickets, theatre tickets all of which include terms appearing on the policy or ticket after contract. The court referred to § 2-204(1) of the Uniform Commercial Code: "A contract for sale of goods may be made in any manner sufficient to show agreement, including conduct by both parties which recognizes the existence of such a contract." Consequently, "a vendor, as master of the offer, may invite acceptance by conduct, and may propose limitations on the kind of conduct that constitutes acceptance. A buyer may accept by performing the acts the vendor proposes to treat as acceptance". That is precisely what happened in the ProCD case. ProCD had proposed a contract which Zeidenberg accepted by using the software after having an opportunity to read the license at leisure. However, he had no choice since the software had splashed the license on the screen and would not let him proceed without indicating acceptance. So although the district judge was right to say that a contract can be, and often is, formed simply by paying the price and walking out of the store, the UCC does permit contracts to be formed in other ways. ProCD did propose such an alternative way and without protest Zeidenberg agreed."[19] The court found reinforcement for his findings in § 2-606 UCC which states that a buyer is deemed to have accepted the goods if after having had an opportunity to inspect, he fails to make an "effective rejection" as provided under

---

[16] *Guibault*, Copyright limitations and contracts: are click-wrap licences valid?, Journal of Digital Property Law, Vol. 2, n. 1, 148 (2002).

[17] Court of Appeals of the 3rd Circuit, 29 July 1991, 939 F.2d 91 (*Step-Saver Data Systems, Inc. v. Wyse Technology*); Court of Appeals of the 5th Circuit, 20 June 1988, 847 F.2d 255 (*Vault Corp. v. Quaid Software Ltd.*); District Court of Arizona, 27 July 1993, 831 F.Supp. 759 (*Arizona Retail Systems, Inc. v. Software Link, Inc.*).

[18] Court of Appeals of the 7th Circuit, 20 June 1996, 86 F.3d 1447.

[19] *ProCD*, above fn.18, at 1452.

§ 2-602(1) UCC. Zeidenberg could have returned the CD-ROM but he did not. This judicial decision does not touch on the question of whether a contract whose terms are unconscionable or which violate a rule of positive law may be declared invalid[20]

Although heavily criticised[21], the *ProCD* decision influenced the drafting of a new section of the UCC, Art. 2B, which then became the Uniform Computer Information Transactions Act ("UCITA"). In view of the specific nature of contracts relating to information, the National Conference of Commissioners on Uniform State Laws decided to prepare a set of specific rules for states to enact. In short, under the draft law, such as in *ProCD*-type contracts (pay-now-terms-later) are valid if the party who finds the terms unacceptable can return the product and get a refund. Only two states (Virginia and Maryland) have adopted UCITA. In August 2003, the uniform draft law was abandoned completely, thereby removing the possibility of clarifying the law (at least in that direction) all over the United States.[22] The American Law Institute has drafted a new Sec. 2 of the UCC with a new definition of "goods". This new definition excludes "information", but it is not clear how many states will adopt this new provision which is a compromise designed to obfuscate the issue.[23] The ambiguity still remains unresolved. *ProCD* validates shrink-wrap licences, at least for professionals. A number of decisions have applied its ruling.[24] However the previous case law embodied mainly in the *Vault* case which rejects the validity of shrink-wrap contracts remains unchanged. Hence, U.S. Courts are split in their opinion on the validity of shrink-wrap licences. Pending the adoption of a new

---

[20] See *Trompenaars*, above fn. 9, 271 citing *ProCD*, at 1449.

[21] Some commentators have criticised the *ProCD* decision because it does not address the issue of privity of contract. See *Goodger*, Beta plus for effort, beta minus for clarity, EIPR, 636, at 639 (1996); *Lea*, The impossible intangible: shrinkwrap software revisited, Comms. L., vol 1, n.6, 238, at 240 (1996). The manufacturer's licence was just deemed to be a contract *per se*. Another criticism is that the court held it was sale of goods under UCC but failed to address the question whether software can be regarded as goods (in *ProCD*, the CD-ROM included not only the database but also some software). See *Lea*, above, 240.

[22] See http://www.nccusl.org/nccusl/DesktopModules/NewsDisplay.aspx?ItemID=56

[23] For an explanation, see *P. Maggs* 2002, "The Effect of Proposed Amendments to Uniform Commercial Code Article 2" 2002 U. Ill. J.L. Tech. & Pol'y 311.

[24] In *Hill v Gateway 2000 Inc.*, Court of Appeals of the 7th Circuit, 6 January 1997, 105 F. 3d 1147, the court accepted the validity of a software transaction "pay-now-terms-later". See also Court of Appeals of New York, 13 August 1998, 246 A.D.2d 246, 676 N.Y.S.2d 569 (*Brower v. Gateway 2000, Inc.*) (in suit for breach of warranty, enforcing shrink-wrap license agreement identical to that in Hill). In *Mortenson Co., Inc. v Timberline Software Corp.*, Washington Court of Appeals, 4 May 2000, 140 Wash.2d 568, 998 P.2d 305, the court held that "Mortenson's conduct in installing and using the Timberline software was enough to manifest assent to the software licensing terms, binding him to the terms to the extent that they were legal and conscionable". *Trompenaars*, above, fn. 9, 271. The license agreement, like the agreement at issue in *ProCD*, was presented on the user's computer screen each time the software was used, and also was located on the outside of each diskette pouch and on the inside cover of the instruction manuals. There are however some other lower courts who do not follow *ProCD*, see e.g. District Court of Kansas, 15 June 2000, 104 F.Supp.2d 1332 (*Klocek v. Gateway, Inc.*).

uniform law clarifying the issue by a majority of states, the position in the United States on whether shrink-wrap licences are contractually valid is still open-ended.

bb) Click-wrap licences The earlier discussion has highlighted that these are different from shrink-wrap licences since they allow the other contracting party to assent to the contract only *after* he has been able to review the terms of the licence, generally by clicking an icon. The terms are presented to the purchaser before he can download the product or before the product can be shipped to him or her.[25] Therefore the thorny question occurring for shrink-wrap licences does not arise.[26] Commentators generally agree that online licences should be valid.[27] Some courts have held online licences valid.[28] In *Specht v Netscape*[29], the court, while considering the validity of so called browse-wrap licences[30], stated that if a user clicks "I agree" before downloading software, it is sufficient to bind him or her by the terms of the licence.[31] The remaining problem lies in ensuring that the user is legally capable of assenting.[32]

It is worth noting that UCITA had envisaged the problem of validity of online licences and made the requisite provisions.[33] If the online licence presented the terms after the contract was made, the situation was the same as under a shrink-wrap licence, the customer could return the goods and be reimbursed.[34] However, if the terms were presented to the purchaser before the purchase took place, he

---

[25] *Trompenaars*, above fn. 9, 274.

[26] *Germanovski*, above fn. 10.

[27] *Trompenaars*, above, fn. 9, 275; Lai, above fn. 14, 91: online licences are enforceable under s. 208 UCC.

[28] See District Court of the Northern District of Illinois, 8 May 2000, No. 00C1366, 2000 WL 631341 (In re RealNetworks, Inc. Privacy Litigation); District Court of the Northern District of California, 16 April 1998, No. C 98-20064, 1998 WL 388389 (*Hotmail Corp. v. Van$ Money Pie, Inc.*). In the Hotmail case, "the court held that users were bound by Terms of Service posted on a web site as a result of their act of clicking on a button saying 'I agree'." See *Miller*, International News—United Kingdom Click-Wrap contracts, CW (1998).

[29] District Court of the Southern District of New York, 5 July 2001, 150 F.Supp.2d 585.

[30] The court held that when a user does not click "I agree" to the licence before downloading the software, s/he could not be bound by an agreement to arbitration which was on another web page, even where s/he were asked: "Please review and agree to the terms of the … licence agreement before downloading and using the software". *Johnson*, All wrapped up? A review of the enforceability of "shrink-wrap" and "click-wrap" licences in the United Kingdom and the United States, EIPR, 100 (2003). Thus so-called "referral licences" may not bind the user. But also Court of Eastern District of California, 17 October 2000, No. CIV-F-00-5671, 2000 WL 33266437 (*Pollstar v. Gigmania Ltd.*) enforcing such browse-wrap licences.

[31] *Johnson*, above fn. 30, 102.

[32] *Trompenaars*, above fn. 9, 274.

[33] Online licences fell within former art. 2B-208 which dealt with standard forms prepared for and used in a mass-market transaction. *Trompenaars*, above fn. 9, 279.

[34] See also *Rowland & Campbell*, above fn. 5, 32. It also provided that the consumer could be compensated for any costs involved. "This included any costs involved in returning the product and any reasonable and foreseeable costs of restoring the acquirer's computer should this prove to be necessary". Ibid.

had no such right of return. In both cases the validity of the licence was not in question. One possible positive outcome of this section of UCITA is the inducement to right-owners to present their licence terms before payment since otherwise the purchaser may call on his right of return and refund.[35]

c) The EU Position

In Europe, there is virtually no case law on the validity of shrink-wrap and click-wrap licences. Nonetheless some conclusions can be drawn regarding their validity on the basis of decisions dealing with similar situations.

aa) Shrink-wrap licences Since there have been no judicial decisions in France on the validity of shrink-wrap licences[36] very few commentators have discussed this issue. Commentators seem to favour validity of licences so long as the prerequisite that the customer is aware that s/he assents to the terms of the licence when opening the wrapping has been met.[37]

What is the position in Germany? Although there are no reported decisions on the issue, using an analogy of the invalidity of purchases by standard form contract concluded over a videotext system[38], shrink-wrap licences should be invalid. In those contracts, their validity was upheld only when the terms were made known to the purchaser before he buys the product. In addition, courts have ruled that consultation on several pages of videotext of extensive clauses does not fulfil the condition of making the customer aware of the terms of the contract.[39] The condition is that the terms must be short and be legible on the screen by an average person. On the basis of this case law it is clear that shrink-wrap licences would not be held valid under German law.

There is no reported case law in England and Wales on the validity of shrink-wrap licences but there is one Scottish case.[40] This case has little relevance because the Scottish contract law is different from the English contract law.[41] Moreover, the court's ruling only relates to the validity of the licence between the retailer and the end-user and not between the end-user and the manufacturer. The judgement does not examine the value of the acceptance by tearing a wrapping open.[42] Finally, the case is limited to its facts which were quite odd since it is the disadvantaged party who wanted the shrink-wrap to be enforced. Normally, the user would try to escape the restrictive terms of such licence.[43]

---

35 *Trompenaars*, above fn. 9, 281.

36 *Girot*, La validité des licences de logiciel sous plastique en droit français: les renseignements du droit comparé, 1 DIT 7 (1998).

37 *Girot*, above fn. 36, 7; Miller, Shrink wraps are enforceable—an opinion, CL&P, 52 (1992) mentions that apparently shrink-wrap contracts are binding in France.

38 *Guibault*, above fn. 16, 154; Guibault, above fn. 6, 205–206.

39 Landgericht Freiburg, 7 April 1992, 1993 Computer und Recht, 433.

40 Court of Session of Edinburgh, Outer House, 14 December 1995, 1996 SLT 604 (*Beta Computer Systems v Adobe*).

41 The doctrine applied in the case (*ius quaesitium tertio*) is exclusively applicable in Scotland.

42 *Girot*, above fn. 36, 11.

43 *Goodger*, above fn. 21, 639.

In England and Wales, it is difficult establish the argument that shrink-wrap licences are valid because of the principle of privity of contract.[44] This principle requires a direct contractual relationship between the parties. Further conditions to be fulfilled for the existence of a contract between two parties are: there must be an intent to create legal relations; an offer; an acceptance; and consideration.[45] Under English law,, the acceptance of the offer must also be communicated to the offeror.[46] The 3 parties involved in this matter are the manufacturer, the retailer and the end-user/purchaser. A shrink-wrap licence is granted by the manufacturer. The end-user/purchaser buys software at a retail store and in so doing establishes a contractual relationship with the retailer as opposed to the manufacturer[47]. To establish a contract between the manufacturer and the end-user/purchaser one has to overcome the hurdle of the principle of privity of contract. Does the mere opening the package by the end-user/purchaser create that nexus? Have the other pre-requisites to contract been met?

The simple opening of the package, under English and Welsh contract law, cannot create a valid contract between the manufacturer and the end-user for several reasons. The acceptance of the terms must be communicated by the end—user to the manufacturer.[48] Secondly, the condition of consideration must be met. When the licencee pays the distributor (retailer), there is no consideration flowing between the licencee and the licensor. Payment has gone to the distributor not to the manufacturer. It is doubtful that tearing the wrapping open constitutes consideration (between licensor and licensee).[49]

A third problem with shrink-wraps concerns the incorporation of new contractual terms.[50] It is well-settled law that the terms of a contract will not be binding if they were not incorporated at the time of purchase. In other words, "new terms cannot be included in a contract after it has been entered into unless all parties consent".[51] In many instances when a purchaser buys at a retail store, he only

---

44 *Lea*, above fn. 21, 240; *Rowland & Campbell*, above fn. 5, 27; *Trompenaars*, above fn. 9, 271.

45 *Gallagher*, E-commerce contracts, CLSR, 103 (2000); *Millard*, Shrink-wrap licensing, 3 CLSR 8, at 9 (1987); *Rowland & Campbell*, above fn. 5, 29; Smith, Tear-open licences, are they enforceable in England ?, CL &P, 128 (1986).

46 *Gallagher*, above fn. 45, 104.

47 See e.g. *Miller*, above fn. 37. In the situation where the customer buys software in a shop, the offer is made by the customer when he presents the goods at the cashier. The acceptance takes place when the cashier accepts the money. In such a situation there is an intention to create legal relations and consideration.

48 See also *Macqueen* et al., Muddling through ? legal responses to e-commerce from the perspective of a mixed system, in Grosheide & Boele-Woelki (eds.), Europees privaatrecht, Molengrafica 1998 (Lelystad 1998), 195, at 202–203 (1998) who believes that the tearing open a package cannot mean assent to the terms contained in the package.

49 *Goodger*, above fn. 21, 636; *Trompenaars*, above fn. 9, 272; *Lea*, above fn. 21, 240. It is difficult to find some other 'act or forbearance' even if the more generous view of the Court of Appeal of England and Wales in *Williams v Roffey* is taken (Court of Appeal, 23 November 1989, [1990] 1 All ER 512).

50 *Lea*, above fn. 21, 240.

51 *Rowland & Campbell*, above fn. 5, 29.

becomes aware of the terms after payment. This is equally true when the product is purchased by mail order because the terms of the licence arrive with the product whilst payment had already been made and contract concluded.[52] However, it should be noted that it is unnecessary that the user reads those terms, he merely has to know of their existence.[53] In this situation they form part of the contract.[54] "On the other hand, if these terms are not brought to the end-user's notice, or he breaks open a software package not having read the terms of a licence, then these terms have not been incorporated."[55] For instance, imagine the sale of software takes place over the phone and there is no mention at that time of a contractual licence. When the software is received upon delivery e.g. by post, there is however a licence inside the box. Under English law there will be no contract. And there is quite a lot of case law in support of this position.[56] Indeed, even if many English courts have upheld licences where terms are brought to the attention of the customer after the sale (e.g. railway or airline tickets), more recent case law has held that if terms are brought to the attention of the customer after the contract is concluded, they do not bind him. Thus it is not clear whether the result attained in the *ProCD* decision could be equally tenable in England.[57] It seems more likely that shrink-wrap licences would not be enforceable.

The penultimate problem with shrink-wrap licences is that of adequate warning. "Where a term of the licence imposes a particular burden on the purchaser, this has to be adequately brought to the purchaser's attention at or before the time the product was bought."[58]

Finally, similar to other European countries and the U.S., the contract must in substance be reasonable and fair[59]. The provisions of the Unfair Contract Terms Act 1977 and the Directive on Unfair Terms in Consumer Contracts govern the situation where the purchaser is a "consumer".

There are two arguments against the proposition that such licences should be invalidated by privity of contract or by incorporation of new terms. The first is to create an agency relationship between the distributor and the producer.[60] In this case, the retailer acts as agent of the manufacturer and it would be sufficient to establish a binding contract between the producer that the end-user if the

---

[52] *Goodger*, above fn. 21, 636.

[53] See also *Macqueen*, above fn. 48, 202–203: reference to terms should be made at the time of contracting. So a notice made after contracting is ineffective as to the incorporation of those terms in the contract

[54] *Rowland & Campbell*, p. 29, referring to the Court of Appeal's decision, 14 May 1929, [1930] 1 KB 41 (*Thompson v LM & S Railway*). See also *Lai*, above fn. 14, 90: "If the terms and conditions of the licence governing software use are sufficiently brought to the notice of the buyer, he will be taken to have accepted them on the breaking of the seal, and/or undertaking whatever steps necessary to show the manifestation of assent."

[55] *Lai*, above fn. 14, 90.

[56] *Rowland & Campbell*, above fn. 5, 30.

[57] *Johnson*, above fn. 30, 101.

[58] *Goodger*, above fn. 21, 637. See also *McKendrick*, Contract law (Basingstoke 2003), 194.

[59]

[60] *Millard*, above fn. 45, 9; *Smith*, above fn. 45, 129.

end-user communicates his acceptance to the retailer in this capacity as an agent. How can is be said that the end user has communicated his acceptance since it is usual that he opens the package at home or in mail-order situations, he receives the product by post? This is clearly not a case of a bilateral contract with the producer but rather a unilateral contract if it can be argued that the opening of the package constitutes acceptance and consideration. It is uncertain however whether English courts would allow a producer to unilaterally impose the terms of his licence agreement especially if they include sweeping exclusions of warranties and disclaimers of liability.[61] "It is not possible for an offeror to impose contractual liability upon the other party by unilaterally declaring that silence will be deemed to be consent."[62] English courts have in the past not allowed a manufacturer to impose a contract by ultimatum.[63] It seems likely that English courts would not allow such terms to be imposed on the customer.[64] The solution of the agency is therefore not a panacea.

The second solution is to insert a registration card into the box which the purchaser needs to return signed to the manufacturer, stating he has read and accepted the terms of the licence.[65] If this is done, the contract is complete between the producer and the end-user.[66] However, failure to return the tear off slip means that no contract has been formed.[67] It would thus appear, in this case, that there is no contractual relationship between producer and user. Thus this solution is not infallible either since it requires further action from the end-user/purchaser.

Recently, the law has changed. Sec. 1 of the Contracts (Rights of Third Parties) Act 1999 allows a third party to a contract to "enforce a term of the contract if (a) the contract expressly provides that he may; or (b) subject to subsection (2), the term purports to confer a benefit on him". Subsection (2) provides that "subsection (1)(b) does not apply if on a proper construction of the contract it appears that the parties did not intend the term to be enforceable by the third party."[68] Section 1(b) of the Act is most important for software licences, since the software producer will have a benefit conferred on him.[69] Thus "the acquirer of the software, in addition to receiving a licence to use the software, will be subject to restrictions on use contained in the terms and conditions drafted by the third party".[70] It seems therefore that this new Act has answered several of the

---

[61] *Millard*, above fn. 45, 9.

[62] *Smith*, above fn. 45, 129.

[63] Chancery Division, High Court, 11 December 1903, [1904] 1Ch. 354 (*Taddy v Sterious & Co*) and Court of Appeal, 8 July 1904, [1904] 2 Ch. 306 (*McGruther v Pitcher*). See *Millard and Smith*, above fn. 45, 129.

[64] *Millard*, above fn. 45, 9.

[65] *Goodger*, above fn. 21, 637; *Smith*, above fn. 45, 128; *Miller*, above fn. 37, 52.

[66] *Millard*, above fn. 45, 9.

[67] *Smith*, above fn. 45, 128; Lea, above fn. 21, 240; *Millard*, above fn. 45, 9. In absence of the return of the registration card by the user, it is difficult to see there is an acceptance *communicated* by the user to the producer.

[68] See also *Johnson*, above fn. 30, 101; *Rowland & Campbell*, above fn. 5, 28.

[69] *Johnson*, above fn. 30, 101.

[70] *Rowland & Campbell*, above fn. 5, 28.

earlier arguments against eh enforceability of shrink-wrap licences provided the contract was in writing. Nonetheless, the new Act does not deal with the argument relating to incorporation of new terms.

There have been a number of cases dealing with railway and shipping tickets on which standard terms have been printed.[71] The courts have generally given force to them because the purchaser had the opportunity to consider them beforehand (e.g. on timetables) or alternatively could return the ticket and refuse to be bound.[72] On the other hand, there have been other more recent and similar cases, to shrink-wrap contracts where courts had refused to incorporate the new terms because they could not be read prior to contracting and instead were added only after the conclusion of the contract.,[73] This leads to the conclusion that in England and Wales the most likely legal position for shrink-wrap licences are that they are unenforceable. In which event,, only copyright law is applicable so that copyright limitations cannot be overridden by contractually.

In summary, shrink-wrap licences are invalid or at best their enforceability is unclear. Arguably, their enforceability in Europe will be determined by the following factors:

- "the awareness of the user of the existence of a shrink-wrap licence: is a user aware that the product he ordered is subject to a shrink-wrap licence and if so, is he aware that by opening the product's packaging he is taken to have agreed to the licence terms?"[74] (requirement of adequate warning);

— "the user's familiarity with the contents of the licence terms;
— the point in time at which the user informed about the terms".[75]

bb) Click-wrap licences Two Directives have been adopted on electronic contracts (the Distance Contracts Directive[76] and the E-commerce Directive[77]) but neither provides any rules regarding the "assent" that is necessary for validating shrink-wrap or click-wrap licences.[78] Online click-through licences should fall within the definition of "distance contract" under Art. 2(1) of the Distance Contracts Directive.[79] Under that Directive, the consumer has certain rights

---

71 See e.g. *Parker v S.E. Railway Co* (1877) 2 C.P.D. 416, *Thompson v London, Midland and Scottish Railway Co Ltd* [1930] 1 KB 41 and *Hood v Anchor Line* [1918] A.C. 837.

72 See *Johnson*, above fn. 30, 101.

73 *Chapleton v Barry UDC* [1940] 1 KB 532, *Olley v Marlborough Court* [1949] 1 K.B. 532 and *Thornton v Shoe Lane Parking* [1971] 2 Q.B. 163.

74 *Trompenaars*, above fn. 9, 273.

75 Ibid.

76 Directive 97/7/EC of the European parliament and the council of 20 May 1997 on the protection of consumers in respect of distance contracts, O.J. L 144/19, 2 June 1997.

77 Directive 2000/31/EC of the European parliament and the council of 8 June 2000 on certain legal aspects of information society services in particular electronic commerce in the internal market, OJ L178/1, 17 July 2000.

78 *Guibault*, above fn. 16, 152; *Guibault*, above, fn. 6, p. 206–207.

79 *Trompenaars*, above fn. 9, 299; *Johnson*, above fn. 30, 102. This article defines a distance contract as "any contract concerning goods or services concluded between a supplier and a consumer under an organised distance sales or service provision scheme run by the supplier, who, for the purpose of the contract, makes exclusive use of one or more means of

such as receipt of information about the content of the contract which includes identity of the supplier, main characteristics and price of goods or services, arrangement for payment, delivery and performance and the period for which the offer or the price remains valid. This information must be provided in a "clear and comprehensible manner" (art. 4(2)). He also has a right to withdraw from the contract without any penalty and without giving a reason. The supplier has to give total refund without deduction.[80] Some categories of contracts though are not subject to a right of withdrawal (art. 6(3)). One such category is "contracts for the supply of audio or video recordings or computer software which were unsealed by the consumer". This refers to those works as embodied in tangible media such as diskettes or CD-ROMs. However, it should also apply to the online supply of such works.[81] Thus once a consumer has downloaded software on his computer he has no right of withdrawal anymore.[82] In conclusion, any click-wrap licence intended for consumers must comply with the Directive.

On the basis of earlier arguments on shrink-wraps, click-wraps should be valid in France: the purchaser is always aware that s/he assents to the terms of the licence since he has to actively assent by clicking after having reviewed the terms.

On the basis of the case law relating to contracts formed over a videotext system (see above), provided click-wrap licences fulfil the condition of legibility and succinctness they would be held valid in Germany.

There is no case yet in the UK as regards the validity of online licences.[83] Particular note of the difference between shrink-wrap and click-wrap licences which lies in the fact that with click-wrap licences the user must read and agree to the licence before downloading the product, should be taken. Thus, it is highly probable that click-wrap licences would be enforceable.[84] The purchaser knows the terms before contracting[85] and the problem of privity of contract does not arise since the the end-user contracts direct with the right-owner. The offer is made when the licence appears on the user's computer screen and it would be accepted when s/he clicks "I agree".[86] Such licences of course would be valid only if their terms are conspicuous and reasonable.[87]

---

distance communication up to and including the moment at which the contact is concluded". A "consumer" is defined as any natural person acting for purposes which are outside of his trade, business or profession. "Means of distance communication" are any means which without the simultaneous presence of the supplier and the consumer may be used for the conclusion of a contract between those parties.

80 *Trompenaars*, above fn. 9, 300–301.

81 *Trompenaars*, above fn. 9, 302.

82 *Trompenaars*, above fn. 9, 302.

83 *Johnson*, above fn. 30, 102; *Miller* fn. 37.

84 *Johnson*, above fn. 30, 102; *Gallagher*, above fn. 45, 103. This latter author also notes that the English courts could construe e-commerce contracts like contracts made through the exchange of telexes (a court had upheld the validity of such contacts). A contract would be "deemed to be concluded when and where the e-mail accepting the offer is received". Ibid. p. 104.

85 *Rowland & Campbell*, above fn. 5, 31.

86 *Johnson*, above fn. 30, 102.

87 *Johnson*, above fn. 30, 102.

d. Conclusion

In conclusion, while the validity of shrink-wrap licences remain rather uncertain if not completely ruled out in Europe (except perhaps France), those licences are enforceable in the U.S. Click-wrap licences on the other hand appear enforceable both in the U.S. and Europe.

2 Validity of contracts under copyright law

The discussion in this section centres around the question of whether a contract which attempts tp override copyright limitations is valid under the principles of copyright law.

a) The U.S. Position

The U.S. Copyright Act is silent on the mandatory character of exceptions. The view is that the exceptions are overridable.[88] The U.S. legal system is structured differently and complicated by the fact that it is a federation. Under their doctrine of pre-emption, when state law runs contrary to federal law, federal law must prevail. Since contract law is state law, whilst copyright law is a federal matter, a decision on the enforceability of a contract has to take into account the overriding federal copyright laws. There are two ways in which a contractual clause can run afoul of the pre-emption doctrine. In other words, the clause can either be pre-empted by Sec. 301 of the Copyright Act or by the Supremacy Clause of the U.S. Constitution (Art. VI § 2). However, as shall be demonstrated, the pre-emption doctrine does not give clear guidelines as regards the enforcement of restrictive copyright contracts.

Sec. 301 of the Copyright Act, which is federal law, pre-empts all state "legal or equitable rights that are equivalent to any of the exclusive rights within the general scope of copyright as specified by section 106 in works of authorship that are fixed in a tangible medium of expression and come within the subject matter of copyright as specified by sections 102 and 103". Therefore there are two pre-conditions for a state-created right to be pre-empted: the right must relate to a work which is fixed; and the right must be equivalent to the copyright exclusive rights. Since the first condition is generally met, the courts have had to determine when rights are equivalent to the copyright rights. They have ruled that they are not equivalent when there is an "extra element" beyond those necessary to prove copyright infringement. This means that a right is equivalent and therefore pre-empted if it is infringed simply by the mere act of reproduction, performance, display or distribution of the work.[89] However simple this test may appear, in practice, courts have had difficulties applying it because the legislative history of Sec. 301 is confusing. A draft of Sec. 301 originally listed a number of causes of action such as misappropriation, breach of confidentiality and breach of contract, which should not be pre-empted. Then

---

[88] NII Task Force, White Paper, September 1995, p. 49–50 cited by *Guibault*, above fn. 6, 230.

[89] *Guibault*, above fn. 16, 157; *Guibault*, above fn. 6, 234–235.

this list was deleted from the section because there were concerns over the inclusion of the misappropriation cause of action in the list. Thereafter when the act was adopted, the House Report stated that "nothing in the act is meant to derogate from the rights of parties to contract with each other and to sue for breaches of contract".[90] This latter statement seems to suggest that contract causes of action should not be pre-empted while the erasure of breach of contract of the list would seem to suggest on the other hand that contracts can be pre-empted.

Even if a contract right survives the Sec. 301 pre-emption, it must still pass the Supremacy clause test. The clause states: "This Constitution, and the laws of the United States which shall be made in pursuance thereof; and all treaties made, or which shall be made, under the authority of the United States, shall be the supreme law of the land; and the judges in every state shall be bound thereby, anything in the Constitution or laws of any State to the contrary notwithstanding." Under the clause, "a particular cause of action may be pre-empted if its enforcement would stand as an obstacle to the accomplishment of the full purposes and objectives of Congress."[91]

How have the courts applied these two concepts in cases concerning restrictive copyright contracts? In *ProCD*, the court of appeals found the first condition of section 301 was met: the database of telephone listings was within the subject-matter of copyright even if it was not protected by copyright because it was not original. As regards the other condition, the court simply said that rights created by contract are different from rights granted in the Copyright Act.[92] Breach of contract is the extra element which makes the contract escape pre-emption. The court explains why contract and copyright rights are not equivalent: "A copyright is a right against the world. Contracts, by contrast, generally affect only their parties; strangers may do as they please, so contracts do not create "exclusive rights.""[93] However, the court emphasized that it thought "it prudent to refrain from adopting a rule that anything with the label 'contract' is necessarily outside the pre-emption clause".[94] The *ProCD* ruling was confirmed in a recent case.[95] In *Bowers*, the defendant Baystate contended that the Copyright Act pre-empted the prohibition of reverse engineering embodied in

---

90 *Guibault*, above fn. 16, 158; *Guibault*, above fn. 6, 234–235.

91 *Guibault*, above fn. 16, 161 citing Founds, Shrink-wrap and click-wrap agreements: 2B or not 2B, 52 Federal Communications Law Journal 99 (2000), at 114. This is known as the implied conflict pre-emption.

92 The court refers to three cases in which the courts held that contract rights are not equivalent to copyright exclusive rights. See *ProCD*, above fn. 18, at 1454: Court of Appeals of the 8th Circuit, 6 April 1993, 991 F.2d 426, 433, 26 USPQ2d 1370, 1376 (*Nat'l Car Rental Sys., Inc. v. Computer Assocs. Int'l, Inc.*); Court of Appeals of the 5th Circuit, 12 February 1990, 893 F.2d 1488, 1501 (*Taquino v. Teledyne Monarch Rubber*); Court of Appeals of the 4th Circuit, 11 March 1988, 846 F.2d 923, 926, 6 USPQ2d 1810, 1812 (*Acorn Structures v. Swantz*).

93 *ProCD*, above fn. 18, at 1454.

94 Ibid., at 1455.

95 Federal Court of Appeal (Mass.), 29 January 2003, 320 F.3d 1317 (*Bowers v. Baystate Technologies, Inc.*).

Mr. Bowers' shrink-wrap license. The court mentions that most courts have upheld the validity of contracts restraining copying under Sec. 301.[96] The court restates that in *ProCD*, "the court found that the mutual assent and consideration required by a contract claim render that claim qualitatively different from copyright infringement."[97] The court upheld the validity of Bowers shrink-wrap licence.

In *Bowers*, one judge nonetheless dissented. Ryk J. mentioned that only when the contract is freely negotiated is the extra element fulfilled and pre-emption barred.[98] But shrink-wrap licences are contracts of adhesion and are similar to a state law preventing reverse engineering. Ryk J. finds that the facts of this case are different from *ProCD's*. As mentioned, in *ProCD* all the elements comprised in the database remained publicly available. The licence did not withdraw them from the public domain. Here, the judge implied that it is necessary to reproduce part of the expression in the program to be able to exercise the fair use defence. This expression is not available elsewhere. The judge believes that "*Vault*[99]states the correct rule" and that "state law authorizing shrink-wrap licenses that prohibit reverse engineering is pre-empted".[100] Thus he also implied that the licence in this case should have been pre-empted because it was a non-negotiated contract. This reasoning meets the criticisms made against the *ProCD* decision. In *ProCD* the court said that contract rights are not equivalent to copyright exclusive rights because they do not create rights against third parties. Many authors are of the view that since the use of standard form contracts has become so widespread that it can be said to constitute private legislation introducing new, absolute rights.[101] Not only have their use become so widespread, these standard form contracts very often look so similar that a consumer unsuspectingly allows his freedom of choice to be eradicated.[102] At the very least, standard form contracts should be seen as equivalent to copyright's exclusive rights and thus be pre-empted.

---

96 The court refers to *ProCD*, the three other cases to which the ProCD court also referred and Court of Appeals of the 6th Circuit, 6 July 2001, 256 F.3d 446, 457, 59 USPQ2d 1434, 1441-42 (*Wrench LLC v. Taco Bell Corp.*).

97 At 1325, citing *ProCD*, above fn. 18, at 1454.

98 *Bowers*, above fn. 95,at 1337.

99 Above, fn. 17.

100 Id. At 1338.

101 *Lemley*, Shrinkwrap in cyberspace, 35 Jurimetrics journal 311, at 320 (1995). *Elkin-Koren*, above fn. 7, 103-104: "In fact, a contract may be formed whenever the potential licensee acts in a way defined as an acceptance by the offeror (the master of the offer). If that method of acceptance is defined by ProCD to be the use of the software, then any stranger who finds the CD-ROM in the street and uses it would become a party to the license agreement. In other words, if the standard of assent necessary to form contractual relationships is minimal, then no unlicensed access to works will be possible. The outcome will be very similar to the effect of a right in rem."

102 *Lemley*, above fn. 101, 319. "Experience in the computer industry has demonstrated that they unfairly disadvantage users and the general public by allowing one party, the vendor who drafts the license, to set unalterable policy rules. This is particularly problematic because, for a variety of institutional reasons, different software vendors tend to use similar terms in their licenses, destroying even the illusion of user choice."

The *ProCD* and *Bowers* decisions are flawed to the extent that the courts did not analyse the application of Sec. 301 of the Copyright Act and failed to consider whether the contract was pre-empted under the Supremacy Clause.[103] For this reason, it is uncertain whether such contracts can be enforced as a matter of copyright law. Interestingly, in *Vault*[104], a shrink-wrap case preceding *ProCD*, the court skipped the analysis under Sec. 301 of the Copyright Act and even without mentioning the Supremacy Clause, pre-empted an act which gave effect to restrictions on use included in shrink-wrap agreements and consequently held the restrictions on decompilation in Vault's licence unenforceable. To pre-empt the Act, the court referred to patent-related cases in which the Supreme Court held that "when state law touches upon the area of these federal statutes, it is 'familiar doctrine' that the federal policy may not be set at naught or its benefits defined by the state law."[105] Therefore if the analysis in *Vault* were applied to *ProCD's* facts, it would appear that the licence would also pre-empted. This is because ProCD was restricting the use of information as such (in contrast to a copyrightable work) that both the Supreme Court (in the *Feist* case[106]) and Congress (in the Copyright Act) decided to leave unprotected.

Since the *ProCD* and *Bowers* cases are the most recent judicial decisions it would seem that they have laid down the law in the United States. As such, similar licences would be held enforceable even though the judgements in those cases did not take into account the Supremacy Clause or the Supreme Court patent-related cases. In my opinion, the *Vault* decision and the decision of Ryk J., the dissenting judge, in the *Bowers* case are the correct decisions and such adhesion contracts should have been pre-empted. Whether the direction taken in these two earlier cases will be applied in future decisions is left to be seen.

b) The EU Position

Contrary to the position in the United States it is not uncommon to have specific legislation on an area of law in Europe. Two Directives have expressly rendered some provisions imperative. Art. 9, second sentence of the Software Directive[107]

---

[103] *Bowers* has been criticised on this point. See *Gardiner*, Using the shrinkwrap license to circumvent the Copyright Act and escape federal preemption (*Bowers v. Baystate Technologies*, 320 F.3d 1317, Fed. Cir. 2003), 11 U. Miami Bus. L. Rev. 105, at 108 (2003). For the same type of criticism on *ProCD*, see e.g. *Nimmer, Brown & Frischling, Nimmer, Brown & Frischling*, The metamorphosis of contract into expand, 87 Cal.L.R. 1, 17 at 50-51 (1999).

[104] *Vault*, above fn. 17.

[105] Supreme Court, 9 March 1964, 376 U.S. 225 (*Sears, Roebuck & Co. v Stiffel Co.*); Supreme Court, 9 March 1964, 376 U.S. 234 (*Compco Corp. v Day-Brite Lighting Inc.*) and Supreme Court, 21 February 1989, 489 U.S. 141 (*Bonito Boats, Inc. v Thunder Craft Boasts Inc.*), cited by *Guibault*, above fn. 16, 162.

[106] Supreme Court, 27 March 1991, 499 U.S. 340; 111 S Ct 1282 (*Feist Publications v Rural Telephone Service Co.*).

[107] Council Directive 91/250/EEC of 14 May 1991 on the legal protection of computer programs, OJ, L122/42, 17th May 1991.

states that "any contractual provisions contrary to Art. 6 or to the exceptions provided for in Art. 5 (2) and (3) shall be null and void" while Art. 15 of the Database Directive[108] states that "any contractual provision contrary to Arts. 6 (1) and 8 shall be null and void".

Art. 5(2) of the Software Directive allows the lawful user of a computer program to make a back-up copy of the software insofar as it is necessary for that use. Art. 5(3) grants the lawful user of a program the right to observe, study or test the functioning of the program in order to determine the ideas and principles which underlie any element of the program, as long as the user does so when loading, displaying, running, transmitting or storing the program. Finally, Art.6 allows decompilation subject to compliance with certain narrowly drafted conditions, one of them being that only that part of the program necessary for interoperability may be decompiled but not the entire program.

Although Art. 6 is intended to be mandatory in its application, it fact does not have any practical effect. Let us take the situation of when an object code cannot be understood in its entirety. Then, the entire program and not only part of it must be decompiled in order to discover which part of the source code is necessary for interoperability. How then can Art. 6 apply? In such cases it would then appear that decompilation of the whole object code can be overridden by contract.

Art. 6(1) of the Database Directive provides that "the performance by the lawful user of a database or of a copy thereof of any of the acts listed in Art. 5 which is necessary for the purposes of access to the contents of the databases and normal use of the contents by the lawful user shall not require the authorization of the author of the database (...)." Art. 8 (1) of the Database Directive provides that "the maker of a database which is made available to the public in whatever manner may not prevent a lawful user of the database from extracting and/or re-utilizing insubstantial parts of its contents, evaluated qualitatively and/or quantitatively, for any purposes whatsoever (...)". However, Art. 8(2) provides that "a lawful user of a database which is made available to the public in whatever manner may not perform acts which conflict with normal exploitation of the database or unreasonably prejudice the legitimate interests of the maker of the database." In some situations, anomalies arise in the application of both paragraphs of Art. 8. For instance, if a lawful user re-uses insubstantial parts of a database for a commercial purpose, this may run afoul of Art. 8(2). Hence, it may not be obviously apparent that a lawful user can re-use insubstantial parts without ever infringing the database owner's rights under all circumstances.

Arts.9 of the Software Directive and 15 of the Database Directive are therefore not fully effective. Full imperativeness of some of the provisions of those Directives is not achieved because of the clumsy language of the Directives. It is interesting to note that granting imperative character to a provision is a legislative technique which aims at protecting the contractually weak party against a party considered

---

[108] Directive 96/9/EC of the Council and the Parliament on the legal protection of databases of 11th March 1996, OJ, L 77/20, 27th March 1996.

in a power situation.[109] However, Arts 9 and 15 do not differentiate between classic fully negotiated contracts and adhesion contracts.[110] All contractual clauses will be null and void if they contravene the respective provisions.

The last relevant copyright Directive, the so-called Copyright or InfoSoc Directive[111], which could have addressed the issue of the mandatory character of exceptions, remains however silent.

Apart from those provisions of the Directives and their corresponding implementations into laws by the Member States, there are no provisions in the national copyright acts rendering exceptions imperative, except in Belgium.[112] In 1998, the Belgian legislator rendered all exceptions expressly mandatory (Art. 23 bis of Belgian Copyright Act). This Art. states that "the exceptions provided in Arts. 21, 22, 22 bis and 23(1) and (3) are mandatory". These latter provisions relate to the right to quote, to make reproductions for private use, for news reporting and parodies, the right to make incidental use of the work and the right to lend the work to the public. Similarly to the solution adopted in the Directives, the Belgian lawmaker has made no difference between fully negotiated agreements and contracts of adhesion in respect of the mandatory character of exceptions. It is to be noted that the mandatory nature of exceptions do not confer an access right to users. This access can be subject to conditions such as the conclusion of a licence and the payment of remuneration.[113] There have been very few comments on this change in Belgian law so far.[114]

In conclusion, except where the limitations are expressly declared mandatory, the silence of the national laws can be interpreted in two ways: the exceptions are overridable or they are not. According to one interpretation, since exceptions are an integral part of the copyright balance, if the legislator has deemed it appropriate to carve exceptions in the law, this means that it is not possible to derogate

---

[109] *Dubuisson*, Le régime des exceptions au droit d'auteur après la loi du 31 août 1998 concernant la protection juridique des bases de données ", 2 A&M 200, at 213, fn. 70 (2001), citing M. *Fontaine*, "La protection de la partie faible dans les rapports contractuels (rapport de synthèse)", in Ghestin (ed.), La protection de la partie faible dans les rapports contractuels (Paris 1996), 632.

[110] See also *Heide*, The approach to innovation under the proposed Copyright Directive: time for mandatory exceptions, IPQ, 215, at 228 (2000).

[111] Directive 20001/29/EC of the European Parliament and of the Council of 22 May 2001 on the harmonisation of certain aspects of copyright and related rights in the information society, OJ L 167/10, 22nd June 2001.

[112] It is worth mentioning in a broader perspective, that the exceptions are considered mandatory not only in Belgium, but also in Denmark, Japan and Mexico. *Spoor*, above fn. 1, point 6 General report.

[113] *Dubuisson*, above fn. 109, 214.

[114] See *Strowel*, La loi du 31 août 1998 concernant la protection des bases de données, Journal des Tribunaux, 297, n. 24 (1999); *Dubuisson*, above fn. 109. This latter author is surprised that the legislator has given an imperative character indistinctly to all exceptions, character that supposes the protection of individual interests whereas certain exceptions pursue a general interest. The legislator, in his logic to erect exceptions in rights, could have given to this latter category of exceptions a character of public order (see his fn. 86).

from them by contract.[115] On the other hand, if the more naturalist approach (which prevails in France) is taken, the silence of the law would mean that unless the legislator has declared exceptions mandatory, they are overridable.[116]

c) Conclusion

In the United States, exceptions are overridable in light of the *ProCD* and *Bowers* cases, although it seems a correct application of the pre-emption doctrine would result in the opposite being true. In Europe, some exceptions (the right to make a back-up copy of a computer program and to test, study and observe a computer program as well as the right to make restricted acts in order to access and use a database normally) have been expressly stated by the Directives to be imperative whilst some exceptions due to the ambiguous use of language are not clearly mandatory (decompilation exception and right to use insubstantial parts of a database). In Belgium, all exceptions are clearly overridable but it is pure speculation whether other exceptions are overridable in the other European countries.

II. Should Restrictive Copyright Contracts be valid? A tentative solution within copyright law itself

1. Solutions outside copyright law are not satisfactory

L. Guibault has opined that since copyright law has not provided an acceptable answer to the question of whether copyright limitations can be overridden by standard contracts, we should then look to other branches of law. These include civil law (abuse of rights), consumer protection law, competition law and constitutional law. However, her thesis has brought to light that even these other branches of law cannot provide a definitive answer to the issue due to a lack of case law.

So far there have been no competition law decisions in either Europe or the U.S. to give guidance on this issue. At the end of her thesis, L. Guibault concluded that the principles of antitrust or competition law in these two continents are limited and strictly applied; as such they do not always provide a basis to invalidate a restrictive copyright licence.[117]

In European countries, consumer protection is embodied in the Unfair Contract Terms Directive (or in the corresponding national implementation laws)

---

[115] In Germany, *L. Guibault* has argued that some limitations should be seen as mandatory. Because the German Copyright Act is subjected to the principle of Sozialbindung (article 14(2) of the Constitution), the Constitutional court has held that while the legislator can safeguard the reward the copyright holder gets from exploiting his copyright, he must also allow reasonable use of the work "in compliance with the nature and the social component of the right". See *Guibault*, above fn. 16, 168, citing *Bundesverfassungsgericht*, 31, 229, 7 July 1990 (Kirchen- und Schulgebrauch), GRUR 1972/08, 481.

[116] In this regard, *Spoor*, above fn. 1, at point 6, notes that in most countries contracting out is allowed: this is the case in Australia, Canada, Finland, France, Germany, Greece, Italy, the Netherlands, Sweden, the United Kingdom and the U.S..

[117] For developments on this issue see *Guibault*, above fn. 6, 245 et seq.

and there have been no judicial decisions in which the fairness of a copyright licence term has been challenged on the basis of abusive clauses or on the general principle of good faith. Whether a contract which circumvents exceptions would be invalid is thus moot[118] though L. Guibault thinks that French courts would be reluctant to invalidate such a contract but the German courts would be more willing to do so. In the U.S., it is very difficult to invalidate contract terms under the American unconscionability doctrine.[119] The fact that a clause in a standard form contract deviates from the limitations recognised under American copyright law would not appear to be a factor for consideration under this doctrine.

Under the U.S. copyright misuse doctrine, practices which preclude others from developing and creating new works would in L. Guibault's view, be abusive (for example, a clause restricting reverse engineering or terms precluding the possibility to quote or parody a work). On the other hand, clauses preventing libraries and educational institutions from making copies of works would probably not be considered abusive since such types of uses would be duplicative (they do not create new works). The same finding applies to limitations aimed at reducing or eliminating transaction costs.[120] She nevertheless notes that even if there are now more cases applying the misuse doctrine, it remains an exceptional remedy whose scope, in addition, is vague.[121] While the application of the misuse doctrine might provide some solution to the use of copyright restrictive contracts, such solution seems ruled out under the French theory of abuse of rights. There is no case law directly on point i.e. stating that it is an abuse of right to contract out of a copyright limitation but speculatively, L. Guibault thinks a French court would not hold such clause abusive.

There are no decisions either under American or European constitutional law which relate to the use of restrictive copyright contracts and which would declare such contract invalid because it contravenes a user's fundamental right. L. Guibault's comments are again speculative. She thinks it is difficult to conclude in the abstract for partial waivers but that a total waiver of the exercise of a limitation would probably be held invalid.[122] In the U.S., the application of constitutional rights to contracts is even more uncertain although she thinks that in certain cases, a standard form contract could be held invalid because it restricts freedom of speech.[123]

In conclusion, resorting to other branches of law has not provided a clear and complete answer to the issue. L. Guibault herself has concluded that legislature should take note of this unsatisfactory state of the law and unambiguously make some exceptions imperative.[124]

---

118 See *Guibault*, above fn. 6, 256 et seq.
119 See *Guibault*, above fn. 6, 261.
120 *Guibault*, above fn. 6, 285–286.
121 *Guibault*, above fn. 6, 194.
122 *Guibault*, above fn. 6, 265.
123 *Guibault*, above fn. 6, 275.
124 *Guibault*, above fn. 6, 304.

American academics have also looked into doctrines outside copyright law to try and invalidate restrictive licences. Some have even proposed their own novel doctrines.[125] It is impossible to review these doctrines in this book and neither is it our goal. On the contrary, I propose that copyright law itself can provide a more definitive answer to the problem. On the basis of copyright policy alone, at least some exceptions are already imperative in all countries. Many commentators seem also to prefer the copyright solution rather than the consumer law one.[126] However, none has developed this assertion. Only a rather small number of European commentators have discussed the relationship between restrictive contracts and copyright works and an even smaller number has done it in detail.[127] This is hardly surprising since this a new issue for copyright law. Some have argued that the exceptions should be imperative on the basis of four grounds: (i) the rationale underlying the exceptions; (ii) the exceptions' legal nature; (iii) the wording used in the acts and copyright goals. An overwhelming majority of those authors also think more or less intuitively that copyright should in certain circumstances prevail over contract.[128] Since no systematic analysis of all the possible arguments based on copyright has been made, I propose to do so hereafter.

2. *Satisfactory solutions may be found within copyright law*

a) Historical Arguments

The first historical argument is that some exceptions are by their nature mandatory so that when legislation was enacted which made them mandatory, legislation was merely stating the obvious. Examples of these are the various Directives referred to subsequently, and the Belgian Copyright Act.

---

[125] See *Reichman & Franklin*, Privately legislated intellectual property rights: reconciling freedom of contract with public good uses of information, 147 U. Pa. L. Rev. 875 (1999) (the public-interest unconscionability doctrine).

[126] "Existing legislation on standard form contracts and consumer protection should not be applicable, because they do not secure the copyright balance between interests of authors and users. Therefore copyright regulation is preferable." See the participants views at Imprimatur Legal SIG Workshop, 1 November 1997, reported in *Guibault/IVIR*, Contracts and copyright exemptions, (Amsterdam 1997), 43. See also *Vinje*, Copyright Imperilled, EIPR, 192, at 195 (1999): "But relying on such doctrines [abuses of right, consumer protection] is cumbersome and the results of doing so are likely to be rather haphazard. Indeed, the results of applying non-copyright doctrines would seem unlikely fully to reflect the balance contained in copyright law." See also *Wiese*, The Justification Of The Copyright System In The Digital Age, 387, at 394 (2002): "Generally, however, copyright law should not be any less capable of dealing with such problems than other areas of law such as consumer protection laws."

[127] See esp. *Buydens & Dusollier*, Les exceptions au droit d'auteur: évolutions dangereuses, CCE, 13 (2001) and *Heide*, above, fn. 110.

[128] See e.g. *Goldstein*, Copyright and its substitutes, Wisconsin LR, 865 (1997) (only implicitly); *Nimmer, Brown & Frischling*, above fn. 103; *Lemley*, above fn. 101; *Vinje*, above fn. 126; *Hugenholtz*, above fn. 1; *Heide*, above fn. 110, 215; *Guibault*, above, fn. 6; *Buydens & Dusollier*, above fn. 127; *Dalcq*, La protection des banques de données et le droit des contrats, 9 Rev. dr. ULB 87 (1994); *Geiger*, Droit d'auteur et accès du public à l'information, Approche de droit comparé (Paris, 2004).

The practice of agreeing to the distribution of copyrighted works with an adhesion contract or licence started only in the 1980's so that the issue of overridability of exceptions was not an issue until then.[129] The advent of the shrink-wrap software licences triggered such practice. Not surprisingly therefore, the phenomenon of making exceptions imperative started with the Software Directive, and continued with the Database Directive. Recently, when Belgium began implementation of the Database Directive into its law, Belgium made all its exceptions mandatory. Hence, we observe an emergence of a practice which seems to be a reaction to abuses in software end-user licences and an anticipation of such similar abuses in database licences. Taking the Belgian legislature as an example, it foresaw that the abuse of adhesion contracts will not be confined to software and databases,[130] but will be extended to the delivery of all sorts of works on the Internet in digital form through click-wrap licences; and legislature counteracted such abuse by making all exceptions imperative. Of course this first argument in isolation is insufficient to support my proposition that (some) exceptions are by their nature mandatory.

Another argument is based on comparative legal history. Copyright law, because of its internal balance, has already taken into consideration possible abuses by copyright owners; in contrast to contract and competition laws.

At the end of the 19th century, the doctrine of laissez-faire had unleashed such liberties to parties to determine the terms of contract and competition that it lead to such great abuses against the party with less bargaining power that the state had to intervene with regulations though new laws (antitrust law and consumer protection law or modifications in contract laws prohibiting abusive clauses). In the area of copyright, no such additional regulation has been necessary since copyright acts already embody from the outset limits to such abuses of freedom by copyright owners. This point supports my proposition that exceptions and limits have always in nature been mandatory.

However, because of recent practice (i.e. the growing use adhesion contracts), lawmakers would be well advised to prohibit such contracts explicitly in the copyright acts. If this is done so that the regulation of abuses is already enshrined in copyright laws, we do not need to look at other laws (such as consumer law, competition law etc.) for additional regulation.

b) Superiority of Copyright Law: Copyright as a Norm of Public Order

In the U.S., apart from arguing pre-emption, the non-overridability of copyright limits can be based on the Constitution's Intellectual Property clause (Art. I, section 8, clause 8). As was intuitively stated by one author, shrink-wrap and click-wrap licences are not enforceable because they take copyright outside "its

---

129 This seems to be suggested by *Vinje*, above fn. 126, 195 as well: "Because direct electronic contracting with consumers of copyright works has never occurred on a wide scale before, neither European legislators nor courts have really been faced with the question of the mandatory nature of copyright limits and exceptions."

130 *Guibault*, above fn. 16, 166.

constitutionally permissible bounds".[131] The Intellectual Property clause states: "The Congress shall have power to promote the progress of science and useful arts, by securing for limited times to authors and inventors the exclusive right to their respective writings and discoveries." Clearly it would be unconstitutional if federal copyright law, and *a fortiori* a state law and a contract entered into by private parties would provide that copyright lasts for ever. This is a power left exclusively to Congress. Similarly, a federal law, state law or a clause of a contract which does not "promote the progress of science and useful arts" would be anti-constitutional. Of course whether a provision does not promote progress is more difficult to ascertain since it is more vague than the "limited times". However arguably, the definition of the promotion of the progress of science and useful arts has been set out in federal copyright law. Arguably, all the limits set out in the Copyright Act embody this promotion of the progress of science. Contravening the federal copyright statute would thus by domino effect be contravening constitutional law. In other words, if the states cannot legislate in contravention to Congress's laws, then *a fortiori* private parties cannot do it either. The recourse for the private party to a contract overriding copyright limits would risk challenging the constitutionality of the federal Copyright Act. In at least two famous cases[132], two limits (originality and duration) of copyright have been affirmed by the Supreme Court. It seems doubtful that the Supreme Court would hold that the exceptions and other limits (such as the idea/expression dichotomy) do not participate in the promotion of the progress of science. Therefore, it would seemingly hold at least some of them non-overridable. A similar consideration has been expressed by a famous copyright scholar: "In the U.S., both the purpose for which copyrights are granted, i.e. to promote science and useful arts, and the *Feist* decision reflect the public order considerations built into the copyright regime. (…) A majority of scholars believe that this emphasis on public order implies that copyright exemptions cannot be overridden."[133] The referral of a case similar to *ProCD* to the Supreme Court is still awaited to clarify the issue.

This argument is not only valid in the U.S. In the U.S., the promotion of progress is a superior norm since it is embodied in the federal Constitution. A similar principle exists in Germany. L. Guibault believes that because of Art. 14(2) of the Constitution (principle of *Sozialbindung*), limits and exceptions should be seen as imperative. In Germany, the author's economic rights are generally construed as property rights protected under Art. 14(1) of the Constitution. But Art. 14(2) further provides that the right to private property recognised by the constitution must also serve the public interest.[134] Not every form of exploitation is thus possible. "The legislator has received the task

---

[131] *Maher*, The shrink-wrap license: old problem in a new wrapper, Journal of the Copyright society of the U.S., 292, at 298 (1986–87).

[132] See *Feist*, above fn. 106 and Supreme Court, 15 January 2003, 537 U.S. 186, 123 S.Ct. 769 (*Eldred v Ashcroft*).

[133] *Guibault/IVIR*, above, fn. 126, 35 reporting views of Samuelson.

[134] *Guibault*, above fn. 6, 224.

under the Constitution to weigh the interests of the right owners against those of the users in order to define the contours of the copyright protection and its limitations".[135] It has been argued in support of the "social character of the right owner's exclusive right" that first the author is an individual who relies on the public domain to create and second, that the work, when the author decides to publish it, is meant to be communicated to the public to allow as many people as possible to enjoy it. Therefore the public should have the possibility to have as much as possible the unhindered dissemination of works. If the German legislature had taken into account this public interest there should therefore not be a possibility for private parties to derogate from exceptions.

Case law has confirmed this view. Authors have tried to circumvent the exhaustion doctrine and some exceptions. One of the decisions concerned a notice preventing persons from renting a sound recording.[136] The court of first instance ruled that the copyright owner cannot prevent the renting of a work s/he put on the market. However right holders under Art. 27(1) of the Copyright Act are entitled to receive remuneration for the rental. The Supreme Court opined that if a rights holder was able to prevent the further distribution of the works, it would impede the free circulation of goods in an unacceptable manner. The Explanatory Memorandum to the bill on the German Copyright Act of 1965 stated that the legislator had not intended to allow restrictions on the distribution right. The distribution right did not allow the rights holder to monitor the use of the work once lawfully put on the market. In addition, the right of remuneration for rental and public lending would not have been necessary if the rights holder could prevent rental and public lending of the work. The reasons given in the three instances of this case point at the fact that the limitations can by analogy reasonably be held to be imperative. This has also been confirmed in the *Elektronischer Pressespiegel* case.[137] According to this decision, neither the owners nor the users can restrict or extend the scope of the limitations to their own advantage. "In other words, the copyright balance must be respected and no one may derogate from the legislator's intent one way or the other."[138]

The above argument will not hold in those countries whose constitutions do not give the same weight to their copyright law. Nevertheless, an analogous argument can be made and applied to both European and American legal systems, even internationally. The argument is that copyright law is superior to the law made by private parties, i.e. contracts[139] since it is a law made in interest of the public, its goal is encouraging creation and promotion of the development of

---

135 Ibid.

136 *Landgericht* Munich, 9 June 1983, 12 GRUR 1983, 763 (Vermietung von Tontraegern). This decision was confirmed by the Supreme Court and the Constitutional court.

137 Oberlandsgericht Hamburg, 6 April 2000, 3 AfP 303 (2000).

138 *Guibault*, above fn. 6, 229.

139 See also *Vinje*, above fn. 126, 195 referring to "the private law of contract and the public law of copyright" even if this author does not develop this idea.

culture and science[140]. In other words, copyright incorporates superior values in a democratic society. The public interest element in copyright law lies in the promotion of the progress of science and the arts which have been embodied in the limits set out by copyright law. Instances of such limits may be found in those provisions in any copyright law which legislate that public order provisions shall override contractual provisions which contravene them.[141] On the other hand, private agreements further private interests which are inferior to public interest. In addition, most contract law rules are default rules. Since the freedom of the parties is above all, the rules in the statutes are generally subject to a contrary provision of the parties.[142] Private agreements should not be allowed to contravene copyright's important aims. If a private agreement goes against the promotion of this principle, it goes against the public's interest—against public policy or the public order ("ordre public")[143], and the public's interest should supersede any contrary provisions in a contract.

c) Rationale Behind the Exceptions

When the discussion on this issue of the mandatory character of gained momentum in the 1990's, some rightly felt that "[p]erhaps it would be too blunt simply to provide that all copyright limits and exceptions are mandatory[144], but it was also equally unwise to do the opposite. Perhaps each limit and exception should

---

140 As shall be seen below (see section II.5, fn. 181), even in continental Europe where originally copyright laws were rather based on the protection and promotion of author's private interests (the reward for his labour), exceptions similar to those of the American copyright act exist and therefore the underlying goal of promoting progress is also present in continental laws, even if less apparent. Surprisingly, it is in Europe that some exceptions have been made imperative despite this traditional prevalence of the authors' interests whereas in the United States no such initiative has been taken by the legislator.

141 In the UK, an author does not address this question directly but seems to believe that exceptions are public policy overriding copyright's exclusive rights. See *Bradshaw*, Copyright, Fair Dealing and The Mandy Allwood Case: The Court of Appeal Gets the Max Out of a Multiple Pregnancy Opportunity, Ent. L.R., 125 (1999).

142 *Guibault*, above fn. 6, 116.

143 The public policy or "ordre public" has been defined in different ways but a constant is that the public policy is the social or public interest. See *Malaurie*, L'ordre public et le contrat (Reims, 1953), 261 citing a number of definitions given by experts and courts: e.g. *Duguit*, L'Etat, le Droit objectif et la Loi positive I, 566; *Hemard*, Précis élémentaire I, n. 188: "l'ordre public consiste dans l'ensemble des règles établies par le législateur dans l'intérêt vital de la société"; *Planiol*: Une disposition est d'ordre public "toutes les fois qu'elle est inspirée par une considération d'intérêt général qui se trouverait compromise si les particuliers étaient libres d'empêcher l'application de la loi"; *Portalis*: la loi est d'ordre public quand elle intéresse plus directement la société que les particuliers. The American and English case law also define public policy as being the reflection of the general interest. See Supreme Court, 4 May 1931, 51 S. Ct 476 (*Twin City Line v Harding Glass*) (le principe de droit qui affirme que personne ne peut juridiquement faire ce qui a tendance à porter préjudice au public ou ce qui est contraire au bien commun); Tindal C. J. in *Horner v Graves*, 7 Bing 735 (tout ce qui porte préjudice aux intérêts du public est contraire à la public policy).

144 *Vinje*, above fn. 126, 195. See also *Heide*, above fn. 110, 230.

be evaluated on its own merits to determine whether it should be mandatory or not, bearing in mind the underlying public policy considerations of each limit or exception."[145]

Recently, other European commentators have proposed that after examination of supporting arguments, there can be several categories of exceptions[146],[147]. The first category would be made up of those exceptions which guarantee fundamental freedoms such as freedom of expression and information, freedom of the press and the right of privacy. Examples are parody, quotation, criticism, news reporting and private uses of works[148]. The second category is justified by needs of public interests[149] or dissemination of knowledge[150] or in other words, those exceptions are "intended mainly to facilitate public access to information and culture".[151] These are the exceptions concerning uses by educational institutions,

---

[145] *Vinje*, above fn. 126, 195. See also *Wiese*, above fn. 126, 394.

[146] *Guibault*, above fn. 6, 27 et seq. distinguishes four categories (exceptions based on constitutional rights, on the regulation of industry practice and free competition, on dissemination of knowledge and on market failure); *Buydens & Dusollier*, above fn. 127, citing *Sirinelli*, Exceptions aux droit d'auteur et droits voisins: Atelier sur la mise en oeuvre du Traité OMPI sur le droit d'auteur, Genève, 6–7 December 1999, available on the WIPO web site; *Hugenholtz*, Fierce Creatures, Copyright exemptions: Towards extinction?, in Rights, Limitations and exceptions: Striking a proper balance, Conference IFLA/Imprimatur, Amsterdam, 30–31 October 1997, available on www.ivir.nl/; *Spoor*, above fn. 1, point 4 of the report, distinguish only three categories (exceptions based on constitutional rights, on public interests and on market failure). However Guibault does not make the analysis made by Buydens & Dusollier as regards the imperativity of exceptions based on their rationale. She only concludes that exceptions based on freedom of speech should be made imperative at least in relation to standard form contracts, see p. 304.

[147] Some authors are also in favour of the non-overridability of some limits but without giving a justification. *Dalcq*, above fn. 128, while discussing the relationship between contracts and databases, seems to be in favour of the mandatory character not only of limitations but also of the general limits of copyright, e.g. idea/expression dichotomy and originality. In her opinion, a clause which designates the rights holder of a database prejudges of the quality of 'work' of the database and of the information contained in it. Such clauses are without value. Either one recognises to the producer a protection by author's right and the reference in the contract is just declarative of right, the only utility of such clause being to attract the parties' attention on this point, or the database cannot be protected by copyright because it is not a work, and thus the clause cannot have the effect to create a intellectual property right for the producer. See *Dalcq*, 75–76, citing Denis, Poullet & Theunis, Banques de données: quelle protection juridique?, Cahiers du CRID 1988, n. 2, 84, n. 146 and Lamy Informatique, 1993, n. 1730. The same author believed that it should not be possible to derogate by contract to the then article 11(6) of the Draft Database Directive which provided the user's right to extract substantial parts for his or her own private use.

[148] In France for instance, the private use exception is an exception to the reproduction and communication rights. "The use must be restricted to personal or private purposes, there must be no motive for profit and the copies must not be made by a remunerated third party". *Guibault*, above fn. 6, 50.

[149] Words used by *Buydens & Dusollier*.

[150] Words used by *Guibault*, above fn. 6.

[151] *Vinje*, above fn. 126, 193.

libraries, archives[152], museums, persons suffering from a handicap and exceptions for the needs of justice and of the state. Thirdly, there are exceptions based on regulation of industry practice and competition.[153] They aim either at facilitating trade or regulating competition in any given sector. The exemption for broadcasting organisations to make ephemeral recordings and the exception allowing the reproductions of artistic works in catalogues or exhibitions, auctions and fairs which facilitate trade will fall within this category as would compulsory licences for the broadcasting and recording of musical works. Other exemptions regulating industry practice and competition are press reviews[154] and reproduction of computer programs.

Finally certain exceptions have been introduced as a remedy to market failure. Market failure arises in situations when authors can neither control the use of the works nor forbid certain uses; in other words when they cannot enforce their copyright. It is the case of private copying and reprography exceptions. Since the authors cannot control the making of private copies by machines (video recorders, copy machines, tape recorders etc.) an exception has been granted to the users as long as some remuneration is paid.[155] These exceptions are a protection against the practical impossibility of copyright enforcement. However, current technological developments have removed this impossibility. The author can now prevent the digital copying of works. Encryption helps reduce market failure which exists in the analogue world, so that copyright can be enforced. For some commentators the relevance of the privacy argument is gone. There is no more threat of an invasion on the individual's private sphere. This is true for anti-copying devices but not for some devices which can record the duration of a use and how many uses of a work are made by the user. Now what is at stake is the person's informational right to privacy (i.e. the collection treatment and storage of the individual's personal data).[156] For such uses, the private use exception is not exclusively based on market failure. There remains an important constitutional right to protect.

The private interests of authors should not be allowed to take precedence over those exceptions which reflect values and collective interests. Instead the underlying rationale behind the exceptions should be consulted to determine the status of the exceptions.[157] As regards the first group of exceptions (i.e. parody,

---

152 Note that contrary to s. 108 of the US Copyright act, at least in France and Germany, there are no specific limitations for libraries and archives. They are covered by private use exemption, the reprography regime and the public lending against remuneration. The reproduction of a work for preservation or archiving purposes by a library would fall under the reprography regime in France, Germany and the Netherlands. See *Guibault*, above fn. 6, 74–75.

153 *Guibault*, above fn. 6, 56 et seq.

154 Press reviews or news reporting (which allows the reproduction not only of news but also of articles by other newspapers) falls therefore in two categories.

155 See for instance the German Copyright Act of 1965 which introduced the first right to equitable remuneration for authors, performers and phonogram producers for home taping in the form of the imposition of levy on the sale of sound recording equipment. See *Guibault*, above fn. 6, 51.

156 See *Guibault*, above fn. 6, 55–56.

157 *Buydens & Dusollier*, above fn. 127, 13–14.

citation, private copying, criticism, news reporting), which safeguard the fundamental freedoms within copyright, some believe that a character of "ordre public" (public policy) underlies these exceptions.[158] Hence, such exceptions should not be limited or else it would put to question the principles from which they derive, i.e. it would annihilate freedom of speech or of the press[159] and as such runs against the grain of a democratic society. Consequently, a contract cannot restrict or prevent a user in the exercise of his freedom of speech. Contracts cannot override norms of public policy.

The second set of exceptions is founded on general interest. The same authors believe that private contract cannot supplant general interest.[160] These exceptions must also be safeguarded.[161] However, since copyright also serves general interest, a balance between the interests of the users and those of the authors should be targeted, for instance by way of an equitable remuneration to the authors.[162] This implies that the exception does not touch fundamental principles of society and is therefore simply an imperative rule, rather than of "ordre public".

The rationale underlying the exceptions based on regulation of industry practice or the facilitation of trade is less strong as those above. Exceptions based on regulatory practice could therefore be left overridable. On the other hand, those exceptions which regulate competition such as decompilation have already been made mandatory in Europe. It is in the public's interest that compatible computer programs can be created to enhance public welfare and this can only be achieved through a mandatory exception to the exclusive right of reproduction of the holder of a copyright on a computer program.

The underlying support for exceptions exclusively founded on market failure, do not reflect a fundamental value to society nor to general interest. It disappears since authors can now prevent the digital copying of works and enforce their copyright. Examples of such exceptions are: the exception relating to the ephemeral recordings of works made by broadcasting organisations (Art. 5.2(d) Copyright Directive)[163]; and the incidental inclusion of a work or other subject-matter in other material (art. 5.3(i)) and use in connection with the demonstration or repair

---

[158] *Buydens & Dusollier*, above fn. 127, 13–14.

[159] It might be objected that it is always possible to not borrow the expression of an author to express oneself. It is enough to convey the same ideas in different expression. Therefore overriding the exceptions for quotation, criticism or parody are not preventing freedom of speech. However, sometimes the reproduction of the author's expression is necessary to report or criticise efficiently this person's work. A reporter may have to reproduce the mood, tone or nuances of a work and this may not be possible without reproducing the expression. See *Guibault*, above fn. 6, 30. The quotation is sometimes as has been pointed out, even "demanded by intellectual honesty, for fear that the author is suspected of deforming the challenged opinions." See *Kéréver*, Note—*Vladimir Jirinovski c. Didier Daeninckx*, Tribunal de Grande Instance de Paris, 3e chambre, 10 mai 1996, 170 RIDA 315, at 323 (1996).

[160] *Buydens & Dusollier*, above fn. 127, 14.

[161] *Buydens & Dusollier*, above fn. 127, 14; Vinje, above fn. 126, 193.

[162] *Buydens & Dusollier*, above fn. 127, 14.

[163] Note that this exception is classified differently by L. Guibault, as an exception made to regulate industry practice.

of equipment (art. 5.3(1)).[164] In the opinion of some commentators, each Member State can be allowed to attribute to these exceptions a default character.[165]

Can such classification be discovered from the reading of these Directives? And if so, can it be implied that the Community lawmaker intended a number of exceptions to be considered imperative?

The Software and Database Directives contain some mandatory exceptions. This shows that the European legislature recognises fundamental interests which cannot be overridden by contract. But the fact that the Community lawmaker only made some exceptions imperative also proves, so it seems, that not all of them are by definition imperative. The Directives could therefore be interpreted in two ways. On the one hand, the exceptions other than those made expressly imperative can be overridden by contract. On the other hand, it could be argued that exceptions close in nature to those made imperative in the Directives should by analogy be imperative as well. The imperative exceptions of the two Directives could serve as models to determine which other exceptions, similar in rationale, are imperative in Europe. But can the Directives be interpreted one way or the other?

The exceptions made imperative in the Software Directive are namely: the right to make a back-up copy, the right to observe, study or test the functioning of the program in order to determine the ideas and principles which underlie any element of the program and the right to decompile also to the same aim. The exceptions made imperative in the Database Directive are the right to perform a restricted act if it is necessary to access to the database and to use the database normally and the right to extract and re-use insubstantial parts of a database's content, for any purposes whatsoever. The most important exception is decompilation, from that exception it seems rather clear that ideas must be left free. The decompilation exception was seemingly made imperative because unrestricted access to ideas is a fundamental principle of copyright law which cannot be overridden. It is absolutely necessary to provide an exception because unlike other works, ideas are not readily seen in a computer program and it is necessary to translate the object code, and therefore perform a restricted act, in order to discover them. Thus enforcing a prohibition to use ideas would not only restrict freedom of expression problems but also prevent the making of compatible computer programs and in addition create patent-like protection for a much longer period.[166] A contract preventing a user to use ideas is necessarily unenforceable. This exception clearly falls into the first category and is the prime embodiment of the freedom of speech.

The right to make a back-up copy falls into the second category as an archival right. The other exceptions are at the same time extremely important and rather minimalist. The right to observe is not an exception to a restricted right but simply an application of the idea/expression dichotomy. The right to perform a restricted act in order to access and use a database is a necessary act if the database

[164] *Buydens & Dusollier*, above fn. 127, 14.
[165] *Buydens & Dusollier*, above fn. 127, 14.
[166] See *Vinje*, above fn. 126, 195.

is digital (a reproduction will always be made in the RAM of the computer when the database is accessed). The database may also be have to be adapted or modified in order to be used on a certain computer or with a specific computer program. Finally, the right to use insubstantial parts is again not a restricted act since the rights of extraction and reutilisation are defined in the Database Directive as the rights to prevent the use of substantial parts. This latter exception can be compared to the right to use ideas safeguarded in the Software Directive. Therefore, these imperative exceptions safeguard important values (freedom of speech (decompilation, right to test, right to use insubstantial parts of a database), access to information (back-up copy) and right of privacy (make a restricted act to use the database normally)). These values are those proposed by some authors to be recognised as conferring an imperative character to exceptions.

The Software Directive did not contain one more exception, the exception contained in Art. 5(1). This is exception is similar to the exception to perform restricted acts for using the database normally in the Database Directive and provides that "*in the absence of specific contractual provisions*, the acts referred to in Art. 4 (a) and (b) shall not require authorization by the rightholder where they are necessary for the use of the computer program by the lawful acquirer in accordance with its intended purpose, including for error correction." (Emphasis added). The Software Directive makes clear that this exception can be overridden by contract. It is in contradiction to a similar exception in the Database Directive which was made imperative. The Database Directive contained other exceptions to restricted acts but they were all optional. It is perhaps therefore not surprising that they were not made imperative. Those exceptions all pertain to the first and second categories as identified above. Finally, the Copyright Directive did not make any exception mandatory although it could have. The fact that the Software Directive allows the overridability of the exception contained in Art. 5(1) combined with the silence of the Copyright Directive shows that the intention of European legislator is confused in this area. All that can be said with some certainty is that the overridability of the general and most fundamental limits of copyright and the *sui generis* right (ideas and insubstantial parts of databases)[167] in addition to an archival right are in principle forbidden. It is difficult to say that the intent of the European legislator is that other exceptions are also mandatory by analogy.

"In the U.S., both the purpose for which copyrights are granted, i.e. to promote science and useful arts, and the *Feist* decision reflect the public order considerations built into the copyright regime. Copyright can be seen as a social bargain to promote knowledge and public access. A majority of scholars believe that this emphasis on public order implies that copyright exemptions cannot be overridden. As a result, there has traditionally not been any interest in distinguishing between public interest based and other types of copyright exemptions."[168] This perhaps explains the dearth of American commentaries on the imperative nature

---

[167] This was at least the lawmaker's intention. As has been seen above (section I.2.b), the use of clumsy language of the Directives results in inefficient provisions which finally allow overridability is most cases.

[168] *Guibault/IVIR*, above fn. 126, 35, reporting the views of Samuelson.

of exceptions. Their focus is on the application of the pre-emption doctrine to contracts restricting exceptions since this is where the copyright act and the constitution specifically regulate the conflict between state contract law and federal copyright law. However some commentators have argued that some less fundamental exceptions in the U.S. Copyright Act could be overridable.[169]

A final and important point must be stressed. The question whether exceptions should be imperative only for a class of persons is hardly touched by any of the authors.[170] Those authors discuss in the abstract and believe that some exceptions are imperative notwithstanding the status of the contractual parties.[171] It has been observed however that making or consideration of rules imperative generally purports to protect the weak party to a contract.[172] Perhaps this absence of distinction is not surprising since the Directives did not make this distinction either. In her thesis, L. Guibault distinguishes between standard form contracts and fully-negotiated contracts while discussing the mandatory character of exceptions. We insist once more that the analysis developed in this Art. is valid only for standard form contracts since we have restricted it at the beginning to those contracts only.

This analysis of the justification of exceptions provides a conclusion for exceptions to copyright. Beyond this field, there is even greater dearth of commentaries on the possibility to override more generally any of the limits of copyright[173] although there are some, albeit rare, decisions. By limits of copyright, we refer to idea/expression dichotomy, the originality requirement, the copyright term and the exhaustion doctrine. Should a contract purporting to restrict the use of ideas be enforceable?[174] The answer should be in the negative. We have seen that the non-overridability of ideas is the implicit foundation of the decompilation and 'observation, study and test' exceptions in the Software Directive. These exceptions have been expressly made mandatory. By analogy, any contract restraining the use of ideas must be unenforceable.[175] The same reasoning should apply to unoriginal expressions. The rationale behind the free use of unoriginal expression is again freedom of speech.

---

[169] *Vinje*, above fn. 126, 196 referring to the exception for performances of musical works at horticultural fairs.

[170] Some have also suggested that some exceptions be mandatory in some circumstances and not in others but they have not carried out their analysis further. See *Vinje*, above fn. 126, 196.

[171] However, see the reactions of participants to the Imprimatur Congress in 1997. Participants think that the criterion of the status of the parties is important in determining the waivability of exceptions. "The distinction between negotiated and non-negotiated contracts and the regulations of standard form contracts are recommended as criteria for establishing waivability." See *Guibault/IVIR*, above fn. 126, 41–43.

[172] See *Dubuisson*, above fn. 109.

[173] One rare author to consider this is *Vinje*, above fn. 126, 195. See also *Dalcq*, above fn. 128.

[174] This leaves untouched the protection of (non) original ideas by trade secrets and confidentiality agreements. Such contracts are valid. But for those contracts to be valid they must pertain to secret information. The information must not have been otherwise disclosed.

[175] *Vinje*, above fn. 126, 193 also thinks that the idea/expression dichotomy and originality are fundamental limits of copyright. Ibid., 195.

One U.S. case has declared a contract void on the basis that it had meant to put an end to the use of an idea for an excessive duration. In *Lasercomb*[176], a licence prevented the licensee from developing any kind of computer-assisted die-making software. The restraint lasted for 99 years. Lasercomb not only attempted to control competition in an area outside of copyright (the idea of computer-assisted die manufacture), but for a duration which could go far beyond the legal duration of protection.[177] This decision was not based on the copyright rationale but on the doctrine of copyright misuse. Nevertheless it could be argued that behind limiting the copyright term, there is again a free speech consideration and that such contracts extending copyright's term should, on the basis of the rationale of the limit, be unenforceable.

Some courts have also held that it was not possible to override the principle of exhaustion either. Twice the Dutch Supreme Court ruled that a restriction preventing the redistribution of a work in contradiction with the exhaustion principle was ineffective.[178] As has been explained above[179], the German courts have also ruled in the same direction but their decisions were based directly on a higher principle established in the Constitution rather than on the rationale of the limits. No doubt the principle of exhaustion is also one of the most fundamental principles of copyright law. Preventing its application through standard form contracts would mean a standstill of the economy. If persons were barred from transferring copies, the freedom of commerce would be deeply affected. It would mean the end of second hand bookshops, the prohibition of making gifts and more importantly even the end of commercial deals (just think of the market of sculptures and paintings). In addition, it seems that restrictions concerning exhaustion would run afoul of the principle of free movement of goods and services as established in Arts. 28 and 29 ECT.

In conclusion, in view of their rationale (freedom of speech and free circulation of goods), no circumvention of copyright limits should be permitted.

d) The Legal Nature of Exceptions

There is some degree of overlap between the arguments which have been put forward for the rationales behind the exceptions and those set out hereunder. A fundamental question here is—are these exceptions *rights* or simple *interests*? If they (at least some of them) are rights, then they are of the same level of importance as the author's rights and as such cannot be overridden by something of equivalent level of importance. Whilst, if they are only simple interests of users,

---

[176] Court of Appeals of the 4th Circuit, 16 August 1990, 911 F.2d 970, *Lasercomb America, Inc. v. Reynolds*.

[177] *Guibault*, above fn. 6, 284.

[178] Hoge Raad, 25 January 1952, 1952 Nederlandse Jurisprudentie 95 (*De N.V. Drukkerij "de Spaarnestad" v Leesinrichting 'Favoriet'*—the *Leesportefeuille* case); Hoge Raad, 20 November 1987, 1988 Nederlandse Jurisprudentie, 280 (*Stemar v Free Record Shop*—the CD cover had a notice which forbade purchasers to further transfer it to others). See *Guibault*, above fn. 6, 222–223.

[179] See section II.2.b

they are on a lower level as the authors' rights and thus may be overridden. The legal nature of exceptions has been scarcely studied.[180] The majority view of the academics in France for instance is that exceptions are only interests rather than rights.[181] There is a minority of French academics who oppose that point of view using the philosophy of Anglo-American countries where a balance is explicitly sought between authors' rights and users' interests. It is consistent then in those countries to speak of user's *rights*.[182] However, it is doubtful whether just merely pointing to the wide gap in the philosophy between the two traditional copyright systems is sufficient. Even in an author's rights systems, humanistic or naturalist justifications are intermingled with utilitarian ones.[183] As a matter of fact, why then would it be necessary to enact any exceptions in naturalist systems if the author is (absolute) king? It is clear that even continental systems take into account the public's interest when exceptions are enacted.

If copyright is a fundamental human right, then it must be on the same level as other fundamental human rights such as freedom of speech and the right to privacy.[184] For instance, French academics use the term "right" when speaking of exceptions for parody, citation and decompilation.[185] The Software Directive also uses the words "[the user] shall be entitled" in Art. 5(3). Thus it is arguable that exceptions based on those human rights have the same force as an author's exclusive rights, leading one to conclude that those exceptions can be properly seen as rights of users.[186] The other limits which were enacted based on economic or practical considerations as opposed to fundamental human rights thus

---

[180] See *Geiger*, above fn. 128, at n. 216 et seq. The two main authors who discuss it at some length are *Guibault*, above fn. 6 and *Geiger*, above fn. 128.

[181] See *Geiger*, above fn. 129, at n. 216, citing e.g. *Lucas*, Droit d'auteur et numérique, n. 338 (1998); *Sirinelli*, Synthèse des Journées de l'ALAI, in *Baulch, Green & Wyburn* (eds.), above fn. 1, 121 & 135 ff; *Goutal*, L'environnement de la Directive droit d'auteur et droits voisins dans la société de l'information en droit international et comparé, Communication Commerce Electronique, 10 (2002) but contra: *Huet*, Quelle culture dans le "cyberspace" et quels droits intellectuels pour cette "cyberculture"?, Dalloz, 1998, Chron., p. 190 & et seq.; *Gautier*, Propriété littéraire et artistique (4e ed. 2001), n. 192.

[182] *Geiger*, above fn. 128, at n. 216, citing several publications by A. *Lucas*. *Nimmer* et al., above fn. 103, at 23 for instance speak of users' rights.

[183] *Geiger*, above fn. 128, n. 216. See also *Guibault/IVIR*, above fn. 126, 12 who reminds us that the two systems are not that far apart, citing *Strowel*, Droit d'auteur et copyright, Divergences et convergences (Paris, 1993); *Ginsburg*, A Tale of Two Copyrights: Literary Property in Revolutionary France and America, 147 RIDA 125, at 131 (1991) so that an instrumentalist undercurrent can be found in French law as well. "Nowadays French courts not only apply natural law principles when rendering decisions in copyright matters but are also preoccupied with considerations of economic efficiency and public interest". *Guibault/IVIR*, above fn. 126, 12. In addition, through international harmonisation, both systems have had to accept one another's philosophy (e.g. moral rights for copyright countries and provisions on computer programs for civil law countries) therefore all countries recognise exceptions although they may vary in nature and scope form country to country.

[184] *Geiger*, above fn. 128, n. 217.

[185] *Geiger*, above fn. 128, n. 217.

[186] *Geiger*, above fn. 128, n. 217 and n. 219.

reflect interests only. It is interesting to note that the Copyright Directive considers private copying and reprography as rights for users. The Directive has followed the view that those exceptions are no longer viewed only as compensation for the inefficiency of exclusive rights in certain circumstances. The development of new means to control uses of works especially in the digital environment could justify reverting to a system of preliminary authorisation. The Copyright Directive encourages the use of technological measures but forces member states to ensure that users benefit from certain exceptions including private copying if users and right holders have not entered into private arrangements. (Art. 6 (4)).[187]

L. Guibault in her thesis also seeks to determine the legal nature of exceptions.[188] She concludes that they are privileges (in American legal jargon) or objective rights (in continental legal jargon), but not subjective rights. Thus they are at a lower level than author's rights which are subjective rights. For the American analysis of exceptions, she follows Hohfeld's theory of rights. At the end of her analysis, she concludes that "the usual analysis of the fair use doctrine is that it is a privilege in others than the owner of a copyright to use the copyrighted material in a reasonable manner without his consent notwithstanding the monopoly granted to the owner". This in Hohfeld's model is the equivalent of saying that users do not have a duty to "stay off the land"—there is no duty to refrain from using the protected works. Furthermore, the "no-right" corollary of the user's "privilege" implies with regard to the limitations on copyright that right-owners have "no-right" to prevent users from making use of the protected works in the particular circumstances defined in the Copyright Act."[189] Unfortunately, L. Guibault did not take her analysis further. Since in practice copyright holders 'lose' their right to users, this clearly indicates that the exceptions have been accorded equal importance as author's rights. It could therefore be said that exceptions cannot be overridden by contract since the copyright owners have no right (at all either under copyright law or contract law and even no right to use technological measures) to prevent the users from exercising them. This analysis does not take into account the justifications under the exceptions however since this would mean that all exceptions whatever the nature of their justifications may be.

Later, Guibault discusses if and how the justification behind an exception influences the latter's nature.[190] First, the justification has an influence on the exception's nature. For instance, a European state is obligated by law to protect fundamental freedoms.[191] Therefore, similar obligation should be imposed upon

---

[187] *Dubuisson*, above fn. 109, 215.

[188] *Guibault*, above fn. 6, 90 et seq.

[189] *Guibault*, above fn. 6, 98–99. For Hohfeld's theory see: *Hohfeld*, Fundamental legal conceptions as applied in judicial reasoning, in Cook (ed.) (New Haven, 1966).

[190] *Guibault*, above fn. 6, 103 et seq.

[191] See art. 1 of the European Convention for Human Rights which states that the contracting parties must secure the freedoms provided in the convention to everyone within their jurisdiction. In France the constitution forces the legislator to implement rules to protect freedom of expression. A similar obligation exists in German law.

the state in relation to copyright matters. It follows that the authorisation to make parodies, quotations, news reports and private uses are different expressions of the state's obligation to protect the user's fundamental rights and freedoms. This might explain why it is often referred to those uses as rights of users.[192] The state intervention to protect the legitimate interests behind other limitations is more arbitrary and depends on national policy. Limitations based on fundamental freedoms should weigh more on the scale than e.g. limitations based on industry practice. Thus the user's objective right or privilege is as strong as the legitimate interest or public policy objective behind it.[193]

The legal nature of exceptions will affect the outcome of whether they may be circumvented by contract. Those exceptions which are rights of users, i.e. those justified by fundamental rights should be imperative—contracts should not be allowed to derogate from them.[194] *A contrario*, those exceptions based on other considerations should be seen as default rules and can be overridable by contract. Thus, the analysis of the legal nature of exceptions meets the analysis of their rationale. A major difference however is that the analysis based on the exceptions' rationale is more refined since it makes further distinctions between exceptions. Those based on the general interest cannot be overridden but as it has been suggested, remuneration should instead be paid. As rightly pointed out by Guibault, "the classification of a norm as imperative is intimately linked with the notion of public interest" and what is in the public's interest in one country might not be in another country.[195] Since there is no international notion of public interest, these imperative copyright exceptions must be identified individually in each country.[196] It is difficult then to determine with certainty the fate of those exceptions which are not justified by fundamental rights—some commentators have considered those exceptions in favour of educational institutions, libraries, museums and archives to be in the public's interest[197] whilst others have not.[198]

---

[192] *Guibault*, above fn. 6, 106.

[193] *Guibault*, above fn. 6, 107–108.

[194] See *Geiger*, above fn. 128, n. 228, citing *Hugenholtz*, above fn. 1; *Vinje*, above fn. 126; *Wiese* above fn. 126; *Guibault*, Pre-Emption Issues In The Digital Environment : Can Copyright Limtiations Be Overriden By Contractual Agreements Under European Law ?, in F. *Grosheide & K. Boele-Woelki*, Europees Privaatrecht, Molengrafica 1998 (Lelystad, 1998), 258; Gautier, above fn. 182, n. 203.

[195] *Guibault/IVIR*, above fn. 126, 24.

[196] *Guibault/IVIR*, above fn. 126, 27.

[197] See *Buydens & Dusollier*; above fn. 127.

[198] *Guibault/IVIR*, above fn. 126, 27: "Education, research and learning contribute to the general welfare. But, in our opinion, limitations of this type do not pursue objectives so fundamental to the defence of individual freedoms and the free flow of information that they should be considered imperative rules which parties may not deviate by contract, under any circumstances. (. . .) Library, archives and museum exemptions do not constitute imperative copyright rules." *Hugenholtz*, Copyright, contract and code : what will remain of the public domain, 26 Brooklin J. of International law 77, at 82 (2000) also notes that "Copyright limitations not serving a clearly defined social function, such as statutory licenses enabling photocopying in government institutions or the broadcasting of musical works, may well be set aside by contractual arrangements."

In conclusion, there seems to be general consensus among scholars that at least the exceptions grounded on fundamental rights (research, study, criticism, parody and news reporting) should be imperative.[199] Generally, these exceptions exist in all European countries with the exception that one for parody does not in the UK, [200] where the exception must be based on the right of criticism or review.[201] Hence, in the UK, parody is held in lower regard and this turn is evidence of the difference in treatment from country to country.

e) The Wording of the Copyright Acts

Support for the view of non overridability of exceptions by contracts may be drawn from the interpretation of the wording used in each copyright act. Dusollier has pointed out that many European copyright acts formulate exceptions as "the author is not entitled to prohibit".[202] In her view, this means that "the author does not have the power to interfere with the legitimate exercise of an exception, be it by enforcement of her rights before a court, by contract or with a technical device." The author's exclusive rights end where the exception begins.[203] This wording is also used in some exceptions in the Software and Database Directives.[204] The difference with national copyright acts is that the Directives make the exceptions expressly imperative. However it could be argued on this basis that exceptions formulated in this way in national acts should also be seen as mandatory.

We have seen that the Copyright Directive has not made any exceptions expressly mandatory. However the wording of the Directive may imply that some exceptions are imperative. The first argument to support the view that exceptions are imperative can be found in Art. 6(4). This provision states that if no agreement is reached between users and copyright holders, Member

---

199 *Geiger*, above fn. 128; *Guibault/IVIR*, above fn. 126, 27; *Guibault*, above fn. 194, 257; *Wiese*, above fn. 126, 394; *Buydens & Dusollier*, above fn. 127; *Hugenholtz*, above fn. 1; *Hugenholtz*, above fn. 198, 82. See also *Guibault/IVIR*, above fn. 126, 41 reporting that there is consensus among the participants to the congress that at least parody and news reporting are exemptions that should not be waived. See also *Vinje*, p. 195, who also includes use by disabled persons.

200 Chancery Division, High Court, 29 November 1983, [1984] FSR 210, *Schweppes v Wellingtons* and Chancery Division, High Court, 29 July 1986, [1987] FSR 97,*Williamson Music v Pearson*.

201 Section 29 Copyright, Designs and Patents Act 1988.

202 *Dusollier*, Exceptions and technological measures in the European Copyright Directive of 2001—an empty promise, IIC 62, at 73 (2003). It can be noted here in passing that it is equivalent to the words "the right owner has no right to prevent" which are the words used under the Hohfeldian analysis above (section II.5). Thus at least one author agrees implicitly with our analysis of the consequences of Hohfeld's theory applied to exceptions.

203 *Dusollier*, above fn. 202, at 73.

204 Article 5(2) of the Software Directive states that "the making of back-up copy" (...) "may not be prevented by contract". Article 8(1) of the Database Directive similarly states that the maker of database "may not prevent" a user to extract or reutilise insubstantial parts.

States must intervene to allow users to benefit from a number of exceptions when they are prevented to do so by technological measures.[205] Consequently, some authors have admitted that users here have an embryonic form of subjective right.[206] There is hence only one more little step to make to conclude that those exceptions mentioned in Art. 6(4) are imperative. Contracts and technological measures have the same effect: they prevent users from benefiting from exceptions. Thus why distinguish between contracts and technological measures? Art. 6(4) of the Copyright Directive allows users to benefit from certain exceptions when technological measures prevent them from exercising them. This solution could be applied by analogy for contracts having the same effect.

Recital 31 could also be seen as an indication that exceptions should be seen as mandatory. It states "a *fair balance* of *rights* and *interests* between the different categories of rightholders, as well as between the different categories of rightholders and users of protected subject-matter *must* be *safeguarded*." (Emphasis added) But it would perhaps stretch the Directive's interpretation a bit far. The fact that the Directive speaks of interests of users could well signify that those interests can be overridden since they are not rights.

On the other hand, recital 45 of the Directive states that "the exceptions and limitations referred to in Art. 5(2), (3) and (4) should not, however, prevent the definition of contractual relations designed to ensure fair compensation for the rightholders insofar as permitted by national law". This seems to mean simply that financial reward for the exercise of some exceptions must be possible, for example through contracts. However some have argued that this recital makes clear that the exceptions are default rules.[207] This is reinforced by the fact that the Directive does not expressly declare any of the exceptions mandatory while it was in previous Directives.

In conclusion, the status of exceptions in the Directive is totally unclear. There are more arguments against than for their implicit mandatory character.

The U.S. Copyright Act is arguably worded in an even more peremptory way than the European copyright acts. Many sections on limitations are worded "it is not an infringement". This means that the limitations are not exceptions to the rights but rather are outside the scope of the exclusive rights in the first place. Thus there are even more reasons to argue that they are imperative.

---

205 Article 6(4) provides: "Notwithstanding the legal protection provided for in paragraph 1, in the absence of voluntary measures taken by rightholders, including agreements between rightholders and other parties concerned, Member States shall take appropriate measures to ensure that rightholders make available to the beneficiary of an exception or limitation provided for in national law in accordance with Article 5(2)(a), (2)(c), (2)(d), (2)(e), (3)(a), (3)(b) or (3)(e) the means of benefiting from that exception or limitation, to the extent necessary to benefit from that exception or limitation and where that beneficiary has legal access to the protected work or subject-matter concerned (...)."

206 *Goutal*, above fn. 181; see also *Geiger*, above fn. 128, 218.

207 *Buydens & Dusollier*, above fn. 127; *Heide*, above fn. 110, 223.

f) Copyright's Aims

In common law countries at least[208], copyright has always been seen by a majority of authors and courts as pursuing mainly economic efficiency and public interest functions.[209] The American Constitution is a prime example of this. Art. I, Clause 8, Section 8 states that Congress shall have the "power to *promote the progress* of science and useful arts, by securing for limited times to authors and inventors the exclusive right to their respective writings and discoveries" (emphasis added). Copyright's aim is to benefit the public by encouraging the production and dissemination of new works.[210] The whole copyright system has been built to promote innovation.[211]

How is innovation possible? Not only do the author's exclusive rights promote innovation but the limits as well. Copyright limits greatly contribute to this aim. The author is enticed to create because he receives protection for his work (in the form of exclusive rights) against similar and identical copies. With his exclusive rights he can reap the reward for his creative endeavours. On the other hand, limits on copyright leave room for other authors to build upon unprotected parts of works to create new works.[212] Unprotected parts of works are not only ideas, but

---

208 As has been exposed above, this is originally less true for continental countries which put the emphasis on the protection of the author. But with the cross-fertilisation of both systems of common law and civil law and the fact that continental systems also recognise limits on copyright, the argument developed here can be extrapolated to most countries. Also for instance German case law interprets the citation exception rather broadly. See *Guibault*, above fn. 6, 39–40.

209 *Guibault/IVIR*, above fn. 126, 11. The colonies' statutes in the US were modelled on the first English copyright statute, the statute of Anne of 1709 ("An act for the encouragement of learning, by vesting the copies of printed books in the authors… during the times therein mentioned"). The federal Copyright Act 1790 was entitled "An act for the encouragement of learning by securing the copies of maps, charts and books to the authors and proprietors of such copies, during the times therein mentioned." Ibid. see also *Samuelson*, cite by *Guibault/IVIR*, above fn. 126. The US Supreme Court case law shows that the primary objective of copyright law is to "promote the public welfare by enhancing the public's access to an increasing number of works, implemented by Congress through an elaborate scheme of economic incentives". *Guibault*, above fn. 6, 286 citing Supreme Court, 3 December 1953, 347 U.S. 201, 219, *Mazer v Stein*; *Feist*, above fn. 106, at 349–350.

210 *Guibault/IVIR*, above fn. 126, 11 citing *Kreiss*, Accessibility and commercialization in copyright theory, 43 UCLA L.R. 1, at 2 (1995). See also *Rowland & Campbell*, above fn. 5, 24.

211 *Heide*, above fn. 110, 216. Recital 3 of the copyright Directive also acknowledges this role of copyright. Recital 3 provides: "Whereas a harmonised legal framework on copyright and related rights, through increased legal certainty and while providing for a high level of protection of intellectual property, will foster substantial investment in creativity and innovation, including network infrastructure, and lead in turn to growth and increased competitiveness of European industry, both in the area of content provision and information technology and more generally across a wide range of industrial and cultural sectors; whereas this will safeguard employment and encourage new job creation." See *Heide*, above fn. 110, 218. However whether the promotion of innovation is actually fostered by the Directive is uncertain. As Heide notes, the Directive rather reinforces protection and restricts free uses. Despite its declaration in recital 3, the aim of fostering competitiveness might not be achieved because the level of protection granted in the Directive is too high. See *Heide*, above fn. 110, 218–219.

212 See also *Heide*, above fn. 110, 216–217.

also unoriginal expressions and bits of protected expressions which can be used in certain defined cases. As a result, copyright ignites innovation and promotes competition. Since copyright limits allow some substitution between works, some competition is promoted as well. Of course this competition is not without boundaries. Competition by making infringing copies is not permitted.[213]

If this balance is tipped by the cancellation of copyright limits, downstream, creation will be reduced or even halted. Perhaps isolated instances where limits are overridden in some contracts such as fully negotiated contracts may not be damaging but the overall use of standard form contracts by many copyright holders severely restricts innovation. Such restrictive contracts restrain the competition which copyright law had meant to leave intact in order to give an incentive to newcomers to create. Those contracts create complete monopolies and annihilate the possibility of new creation. Moreover, if such practice is not halted, those who draft restrictive contracts might themselves fall victims to the very practices they had tried to enforce

What happens in practice when restrictive standard form licences are enforced *en masse*? Private standard form contracts will replace copyright legislation and its intended effects (innovation and competition). For instance, a contract prohibiting resale or any type of redistribution of copies of works (such as through inheritance) would impede the freedom of commerce and movement of goods. If works cannot circulate, access is reduced and the possibility downstream to create derivative works is annihilated—the public is worse off. This contravenes the goal of copyright: promote progress to the public's benefit. In passing, it can be noted that this meets the argument above based on the constitutional supremacy of copyright in the U.S. Contracts preventing the exercise of copyright limits directly conflict with the wording and the intention of the copyright constitutional clause. This halt to progress which is allowed to be achieved by such contracts lasts until works fall in the public domain—progress can be stopped for over a century![214] Should society wait a hundred years or more?

Can this reasoning which applies clearly to the copyright's limits (idea/expression dichotomy, originality, first sale doctrine and term) apply equally to copyright's exceptions to exclusive rights? Is progress prevented if users cannot quote or parody a work? If one argues that a parody or a quote results in a new work which promotes progress, then yes. However, it seems that criticism, review, news reporting, parody and quotation are based on freedom of speech.[215] Similarly, private copying is not based on this progress promotion but rather on the need to preserve users' privacy, another constitutionally guaranteed right. Other exceptions for libraries, museums and educational establishments cannot be said to directly promote progress. Generally the copies made are not made for creating new works. They are made to conserve the past or to promote the spread of knowledge. It can be argued that at least the educational establishments' reproduction exception

---

213 *Heide*, above fn. 110, 217.

214 Assuming the average age of creation of an author is 40 and that he dies at 70, then copyright lasts for more than a century.

215 See above section II.2.c.

indirectly promotes progress, since by disseminating knowledge, the persons receiving instruction are able to further create. The rationale for making exceptions imperative could thus be the distinction between the uses which kill innovation and those which (directly or indirectly) foster it. Therefore, the libraries, archives and museums exceptions and similar reproductive exceptions would be the only ones which could be restrained. This would mean that those institutions would have to purchase original copies of works rather than making copies of works. Arguably, if the copy cannot be purchased anymore (e.g. because it is out of stock), the right to make the copy should remain.

It is clear therefore that innovation-promoting exceptions should be made clearly imperative in the copyright acts.[216] Overriding limits and exceptions is contrary to copyright's goal as it kills innovation and competition. If only innovation-promoting exceptions are made mandatory, only some users can invoke exceptions, those whose aim is to create and not those who purely substitute and second, "compensation to the rights holder of an already created work is involved as any creator or innovator must be a lawful user to invoke any exception."[217] It is nonetheless submitted that the innovation-promoting aim of copyright should be combined with the free speech and right of privacy overriding principles which apply to the other (even if duplicative) exceptions to render the exceptions based on both justifications (the promotion of innovation and on fundamental freedoms) imperative.

g) Economics of Copyright

The economic analysis of copyright law shows that the possibility of overriding copyright limits goes against economic efficiency and maximisation of economic welfare. The argument based on the economics of copyright leads to similar results as the previous one. Contracting out of copyright limits considerably reduces creation, in other words, the number of works produced decreases. This effect is felt when any of the copyright limits and exceptions are put into jeopardy.

Landes and Posner, in their seminal article[218], did not explain the effect of contracting out of copyright limits but explained why those limits make economic sense and the effects if those limits do not exist. They had also illustrated why without copyright limits, social welfare decreases. Their analysis can be summarised as follows. Monopolies on ideas create welfare loss. If every new author has to come up with an original idea of his own because he cannot use the idea of others, it takes more time and effort to create a work, hence the number of works is reduced.[219] This reduces social welfare.[220] In general, if any

---

216 See *Heide*, above fn. 110, 230.

217 Ibid.

218 The main economic analysis of copyright remains the analysis by *Landes & Posner*, XVIII Journal of Legal Studies, 325–363 (1989).

219 *Landes & Posner*, above fn. 218, 348.

220 They think this is what happens rather than an increase in price like in monopolies where both effects occur (reduction in the number of goods and increase in price). They note that in a more complex model, the price of works would raise if ideas were protected.

borrowing of the expression of a work is completely forbidden, the number of works will decrease.[221] Book reviews quoting brief passages of a work, should be allowed. Even if publishers would be better off if they could act against unfavourable reviews, this would be to the detriment of consumers of books.[222] For other applications of the fair use doctrine, they distinguish between *productive* and *reproductive* uses. Productive fair use lowers the cost of expression[223] which reduces the cost of creating new works, thereby increasing the total number of works. Reproductive uses reduce the demand for the protected work. For instance, if a parody reduces the demand for the original work, then it should be infringing and not fair use.[224] It is uncertain whether the law has struck the right balance but it recognises the problem, since ideas are not protectable and substantial rather than simple similarity is required for infringement.[225] Finally, the economic rationale for limiting the duration of copyright—to reduce both monopoly profits and tracing costs. The longer the term, the fewer the works in the public domain and thus the higher the cost of expression which spirals into the production of even less works.[226] Again, social welfare is not enhanced.

Landes and Posner did not make an economic analysis of the remaining copyright limits, i.e. originality, the first sale doctrine nor of the exceptions other than fair use and neither do we. A simple analysis of the effects of the overriding of these limits has been made above in section 2(f) and we refer the reader to it.

An application of their economic conclusions has lead to the following results in relation to the restriction of limits and exceptions by adhesion contracts:

(i) anyone should be able to use ideas and unoriginal expressions without restraint;[227] authors should not be able to prevent fair uses of their works nor extend the term of copyright perpetually;
(ii) if authors could, creation would be considerably reduced and the whole world (not only users but subsequent creators) would be worse off;
(iii) if ideas were protected, authors would have to create new ideas which is very time-consuming and very difficult and perhaps in some cases impossible or would have to seek licences from other authors and, provided they grant them, this would increase the costs of works dramatically;
(iv) the size of the public domain would be extremely small, made up only of ideas and expressions which in due course come into the public domain

---

221 *Landes & Posner*, 360.

222 *Landes & Posner*, above fn. 218, 359.

223 The costs of expression are opposed to the costs of production. The former include the cost of creating the work (the author's time and effort) "plus the cost of the publisher of soliciting and editing the manuscript and setting it in type". *Landes & Posner*, above fn. 218, 327. The costs of production are the costs of printing, binding and distributing individual copies. Ibid.

224 *Landes & Posner*, above fn. 218, 360.

225 *Landes & Posner*, above fn. 218, 361.

226 *Landes & Posner*, above fn. 218, 362.

227 It seems that the explanation they gave for ideas could be extrapolated to unoriginal expressions.

on expiry of copyright term. If copyright is not allowed to end, the size of the public domain would never grow but would only be constituted of ideas and fair uses.

A combination of all these effects (the use of ideas is restricted, fair use is not possible and copyright lasts perpetually) would mean that public domain will disappear and use of copyright works would be only possible under licence. The price of works will be increased (entering into licences engenders transaction costs in addition to the price of the licence) and the number of works will be dramatically reduced. The world is worse off. Pushed to the extreme, users might not even be able to buy the works because they are priced so high, making it in turn totally economically inefficient to produce works in the first place... In such scenario we would live in a world frozen at a certain period of time when creation has ceased to occur, and be left to live for ever with the same books to read, the same films to watch, the same music to listen to, the same computer programs to use. The entire world would be at a complete standstill.[228] This scenario resembles a science-fiction plot or perhaps, with a bit more hope, to the story of Sleeping Beauty, the kiss of the prince being the legislative initiative to make limits imperative...

Some additional comments on fair use and other exceptions should be made. It can seemingly be implied from Landes & Posner's analysis that the fourth factor of fair use (the impact of the use on the market for the copyright work) is the decisive criteria for determining when a use should not be permitted. The criteria—whether the demand for the original work decreases. Reproductive uses, those which substitute works in the market and diminish the sales of the original work, should therefore not be allowed. Their analysis stops short at fair use. Other exceptions in the U.S. Copyright Act however allow reproductive uses to occur even without the payment of a fee.[229] It is not clear whether Landes & Posner would agree that such exceptions relating to reproductive uses could be overridden because they decrease the demand for the original work and thus decrease the incentives to create. However, it would seem also to derive implicitly from their analysis that when transaction costs are low, fair uses exclusively based on high transaction costs should not be considered fair anymore.[230] Since a licence can be sought at low cost, payment should occur. However this should be nuanced. Their previous analysis should be added to this one. This means that in cases, where transaction costs are low but the use is transformative, the use should still be considered fair since the market for the work is not diminished. On the contrary, because of quotation, it is enhanced. Users might want to access the quoted work in full. The brief quote of works, like in a book review, is free advertising for

---

[228] We insist once more that such scenario would occur by the cumulative use of adhesion contracts. We do not here extrapolate these conclusions to fully negotiated contracts.

[229] See sections 108 to 121 of the US Copyright Act, e.g. section 117 (archival copy for computer programs) and section 108 (reproduction by libraries and archives). In the US, educational institutions can make use of copyright material under a range of limitations none of which require the payment of remuneration.

[230] *Landes & Posner*, above fn. 218, 357.

the author of the work. As regards the other uses, which are reproductive and involve low transaction costs, it can be implied from their relatively short analysis that there is no reason to leave the copyright holder without royalties.[231]

Should this mean that the copyright holder can prevent the work's use? An answer cannot be derived from Landes and Posner's analysis. The analysis made above which is based on copyright's aims may provide an answer. If the use directly or indirectly promotes progress, then it should be allowed and not prevented. The analysis of the rationale of exceptions (free speech and right of privacy) should also be added for non (at least always) innovation-promoting exceptions (criticism, review, news reporting, parody, quotation and private copying). Whether such uses should be allowed for free or only upon payment is a question best left to policy makers.[232] However it still remains that such uses should not prevented, i.e. overridden by contract, because of the strong rationale of promotion of progress, free speech or right of privacy behind the exception.

Finally, there is also a more general argument to be made against the extension of copyright's scope, be it by standard form contracts or by law. Economists generally warn of the potential dangerous effects of extending the scope of copyright. Throughout the history of research and analysis by economists, economic historians and lawyers, on the role of patents and copyright in stimulating innovation and creation, no firm conclusions have been reached about the need for those intellectual property rights to support new industries. No one can say with conviction that intellectual property rights in general, and copyright law in particular, stimulate creativity. And there is still very little empirical evidence of copyright's effects.[233] That is no argument for not having copyright but it should sound loud notes of caution about increasing its scope.

h) Conclusion

Under contract law, restrictive shrink and click-wrap licences are generally upheld. However under copyright law, such copyright contracts should not be enforced. It has been argued that copyright does not provide an answer to the question whether copyright limits are or should be imperative. Furthermore, others have shown that resort to outside policies such as abuse of rights and copyright misuse, consumer protection and competition law has not yielded satisfactory solutions. This article has attempted to show that copyright law itself proves that some of its limits and exceptions should be mandatory.

"Market forces may ultimately discourage the use of overly restrictive [...] contractual provisions".[234] In other words, "competition among vendors, not judicial

---

[231] *Guibault*, above fn. 6, 86–87 thinks however that asking payment in the digital world for uses which were in the analogue world considered fair may actually be counter-productive. The greater excludability of a public good does not necessarily result in greater social benefit because it may lead to under-utilisation of the good (here the copyright work). Therefore no or less new works are created due to the prices charged.

[232] As a matter of fact, some countries provide for a system of remuneration (compulsory or statutory licence) while others, like the US, do not. See above fn. 230.

[233] See e.g. *Towse*, Creativity, incentive and reward (Cheltenham, 2001), 21.

[234] *Heide*, above fn. 110, 230.

revision of a package's contents, is how consumers are protected in a market economy."[235] But so far this does not seem to be happening.[236] On the contrary, history has shown that when freedom of contract is unrestricted, market conditions deteriorate, monopolies are formed.[237] Several devices have been used to regulate freedom of contract (competition law, theory of abuse of rights, consumer protection). In the area of copyright, the devices are already written in the statutory law. They just need to be declared clearly mandatory. In view of the growing use of restrictive copyright adhesion contracts, there is a need to address the issue of whether exceptions should be imperative, lest the values of our democratic societies deteriorates and the progress of the world comes to a standstill. In view of new practices, legislators around the world, should be advised to clarify the situation and make explicit in the copyright acts that at least the exceptions based on fundamental rights and those promoting innovation are imperative while it would be left to them to decide whether the others such as so-called "public interest" exceptions and exceptions based on industry practice or market failure are overridable or not. While in the U.S., a simple sentence in the Copyright Act would suffice to solve the problem, in Europe, for a harmonised and thus better result, the mandatory effect of exceptions should be addressed directly at Community level.[238]

B. Country Reports

Note: The contributors to the country reports are listed in the introductory preface.

I. China

1. Neither the Copyright Law of the People's Republic of China nor the Regulation on the Implementation of the Copyright Law of the People's Republic of China contain many special provisions regarding copyright contracts. The basic principles of contract law as set forth in the Contract Act (1999) such as the freedom of contract, and to act in good faith should nonetheless be applicable.
2. Sec. 7 Contract Act provides, "In concluding and performing a contract, the parties shall abide by the laws and administrative regulations, and observe social ethics. Neither party may disrupt the socio-economic order or damage the public interests." Sec. 329 of the same Act provides that a contract that monopolizes a technology or impedes technological progress shall be null and void. Although most copyright contracts are not affected by the latter section since such contracts do not relate to technology, that section still plays a role in respect of some copyright contracts, for example, those dealing with computer software.

---

235 J. Easterbrook in *ProCD*, above fn. 18, at 1453.
236 *Lemley*, above fn. 101, stating that the use of many standard form contracts is growing and their content is very similar.
237 *Guibault*, above fn. 6, 195.
238 *Heide*, above fn. 110, 229.

The amendment bill to the Foreign Trade Act (1994) was adopted on 4 June 2004, and it has several articles relating directly to intellectual property rights. According to the Article 30 of the amended law, the competent authority may take measures against any intellectual property licensing contracts which contain conditions preventing challenges to validity, coercive package licensing or exclusive grant back conditions; or which have an adverse effect on fair competition in the country's foreign trade.

3. At present in Mainland China, there is an absence of a complete codified collection of anti-trust laws. The debate on the creation of such an antitrust act has been on-going for the past several years.

In recent years the business practices of the intellectual property owners who are usually the large corporations, indicate a great tendency to abuse their rights. This unfortunate situation has caught the attention of the academics and stirred much discussion amongst them o what mechanisms outside of the IP arena—such as the various arms of anti-trust laws—are available to limit the power of intellectual property right holders.

II. Hong Kong

1. *Licence*

A licence granted by the copyright owner is obviously the most common defence to an infringement action. The word 'licence' can be found in many provisions throughout the Copyright Ordinance. Section 22(2) of the Copyright Ordinance provides that copyright in a work is infringed by a person who without the licence of the copyright owner does or authorizes another to do any of the acts restricted by the copyright.[239] An exclusive licence is defined in section 103 of the Copyright Ordinance as:-

> *"a licence in writing signed by or on behalf of the copyright owner authorizing the licencee to the exclusion of all other persons, including the person granting the licence, to exercise a right which would otherwise be exercisable exclusively by the copyright owner."*[240]

a) Shrink-Wrap and Click-Wrap Agreements

Normally, contracts for the sale of goods are entered into on the basis of express terms agreed between the parties or implied by law. In the case of consumer sales, there are generally no express conditions of sale, but the law imposes implied terms, including various warranties as to the title, quality, fitness for purpose and

---

[239] Acts restricted by copyright in a work:
to copy the work (section 23)
to issue copes of the work to the public (section 24)
where the work is a computer program or sound recording, to rent copies of the work to the public (section 25)
to make available copes of the work in public (section 26)
to perform, show or play the work in public (section 27)
to broadcast the work or include it in a cable programme service (section 28)
to make an adaptation of the work or do any of the above in relation to an adaptation (section 29)
and those acts are referred to in this Part as the "acts restricted by the copyright."

[240] Applies to Division V of the Copyright Ordinance.

safety of the goods sold, as well as an implied right to keep and use the goods without interference from the seller. Otherwise, it is said, the seller would be in derogation of his grant to the purchaser.

The above is subject to any intellectual property rights which may be reserved to the seller and have not been exhausted by the original sale. Generally speaking, intellectual property rights are exhausted once goods have been put on the market without an express restriction on further sale or use. Such restrictions are only enforceable if the purchaser has notice.

In the case of computer software, the right to use is necessarily curtailed by the fact that any reproduction of the software may amount to an infringement of copyright. Whilst there may be an implied right for the purchaser to use software, how far does this extend? It obviously does not extend to making large numbers of copies for commercial re-sale. The purchaser therefore needs a licence, express or implied, to do these things. In the case of a shrink-wrap agreement, the terms and restrictions of the licence are contained in a document which the purchaser only sees after purchase, after the product has been unwrapped or accessed, for example by breaking a seal. In the case of a click-wrap agreement, the terms and restrictions may be contained either on a homepage by hyperlink leading to it or after scrolling through until reaching the "I accept" or "I agree" button at the bottom of the page.

b) Contracting Online

Computers and the Internet have fundamentally reshaped our way of life as well as how we conduct business transactions. The Electronic Transactions Ordinance (Cap 5653) was introduced by the Hong Kong government in early 2000 to facilitate and regulate electronic transactions in Hong Kong. Electronic transactions conducted through the Internet are regarded as valid and enforceable. Section 17 of the Electronic Transactions Ordinance provides that offer and acceptance may be expressed by electronic means. Common law principles on the formation of contract still apply, namely, the essential elements of offer, acceptance, consideration and an intention to be legally bound need to be satisfied in order to form a valid online contract.

c) Case Law

The validity of shrink-wrap as well as click-wrap licences was commented on in a Court of First Instance case[241]. Although the case was not concerned with shrink wrap or click wrap licences the comment offers a hint as to the approach a Hong Kong Court would take in respect of such licences. Deputy Judge Cheung commented[242]:-

> *"...generally speaking when a person buys a mass-marketed computer software from a retailer these days, he must know or be taken to know that he can only make use of the software he so "buys" in accordance with the terms of a licence imposed by the developer or the proprietary owner of the software which comes together with the physical software package. Sometimes the terms of the licence are apparent from the outside of the box containing the software; sometimes they are not and can only be read after the box is opened or the CD-ROM is*

241 *Ho Lai Chuen v Xerox (Hong Kong) Limited_[2002] HKEC 70*
242 At para 62

inserted into and run on the computer. This is so in the case of a consumer... In my judgment, if the buyer chooses to "buy blind", i.e. without finding out the terms of the licence first before he purchases it from the retailer, he does so at his own risk in that if subsequently he does not find the terms of the licence agreeable to himself, which in most consumer cases are non-negotiable, he will risk not being able to use the software, at least legitimately."

2. *Antitrust*

There is no antitrust law in Hong Kong.

III. Taiwan

The recent amendment to Taiwan's Copyright Act (2003) introduced provisions regulating new types of copyright infringements but those provisions dealing with copyright contracts still follows the existing rules of the Civil Code. Shrink-wrap and click-wrap licences have been widely used for transactions of computer software, whether they have been sold through real, brick-and-mortar shops, or through the internet. The current debate centres on issues brought about by rapid technical improvement and the need to ensure that consumer protection has not been eroded thereby. Recent court cases have not given clear directions which reflect these concerns.

This report discuses these issues against the background of the Civil Code, Copyright Act, Consumer Protection Act and Fair Trade Act.

1. *The Structure of Civil Code and Consumer Protection Act*

The "shrink-wrap" licence contracts usually may be read from the outside of the software package and its terms run along such lines as—"By opening this box, you agree to the terms and conditions of the licence."[243]Similarly, software available on-line specifies that clicking on an "accept " button has the same effect: the so-called "click-wrap" contract. Such EULA gives the purchaser one of two options: (1) he agrees and is bound by all of the terms in the licence, or (2) he rejects the licence and refrains from using the software. Obviously, the second option is meaningless to a consumer, as it negates the whole purpose of purchasing the software. In other words, a consumer in reality has no choice but to agree to all terms of the licence, after purchase but before use. Such transactions convert a sale with some aspect of implied licence into one of a pure licence.

Under contract law, both parties must agree to key terms of the contract (Sec.153 Civil Code) before a contract is deemed concluded. The status and obligations of both parties and validity of such a contract are also regulated by the Civil Code. In the above situation the consumer, being the less savvy and powerful party, has to passively accept these standard-form contracts having had little time for contemplation, let alone negotiation.[244] This clearly indicates that

---

[243] *David Callan*, "How is click-wrap contract better than shrink-wrap contract?", from http://www.akamarketing.com/click-wrap-shrink-wrap-contracts.html

[244] Ibid., and also see *Robert A. Hillman & Jeffrey J. Rachlinski*, Standard Form Contracting in the Electronic Age, 77 N.Y.U.L. REV. 429 (2002).

such contracts have been subjected to little public scrutiny. The consumer has come to accept such "shrink-wrap" or "click-wrap" licences as standard and has accepted his position of non-negotiation with the copyright holder. Such being the case, then Sec. 247-1 of Civil Code, Sec. 11 to 12 of the Consumer Protection Act (CPA and Sec. 14 of the Implementation Regulations of the CPA should be applicable.

If the terms of the contract include a "shrink-wrap" or "click-wrap" licence that require consumers to waive their legal rights without prior consultation these terms are obviously unfair and the licence should be declared invalid. Similar literature is presented in the Consumer Protection Act. (Sec.12 of CPA)

2. *The Collision of Copyright and Contract Law*

Bearing in mind the limits of intellectual property rights, one might ask whether such limitations often rooted in social policy should be compromised by the software industry's method of licensing through non-negotiable "shrink-wrap" or via "click-wrap" agreements. In other words, should the law aid copyright holders and exploiters who inequitably force an individual to "waive" his or her freedom to use an intellectual property in a manner outside of the owner's exclusive right? If such restrictions on consumers are allowed, what special requirements, if any, must exist for such a waiver to be valid? Just as important a consideration is the frequency of such clauses.

Secs. 44 to 65 Copyright Act concern matters of fair use and restrictions of copyright. It is usual that shrink wrap and click warp licences contain terms and conditions which in essence require the purchaser to waive the defence of fair use or the limitation of exhaustion as an ancillary part of the transaction. Is such a waiver valid? According to Sec. 12 Consumer Protection Act, if the terms and conditions of standard contracts are "obviously contradictory to the legislative purport of the discretionary provisions, it may be excluded by such terms and conditions", therefore, they shall be presumed unfair. So it is very important to appropriately explain the limitations of copyright under Sec. 44–65. In our opinion, since the legislative purpose of these statutory limitations is to protect fundamental rights, they should not be so easily waived by mere contractual terms. Sec. 52 Copyright Act which is based on the fundamental right of the freedom of speech and which grants users the freedom to quote publicly released works for reports, comment, teaching, research, or other legitimate purposes, should not be excluded by standard contract. The same can be said for Sec. 51 Copyright Act, which grants similar rights of use in private or non-commercial purposes.

Some other statutory limitations have been implemented for public interest purposes, such as legislative or administrative purposes (Sec. 44), judicial purposes (Sec. 45), library, museum or cultural institutions for preserve materials (Sec. 48, 48-1), etc. If they would be excluded by standard contracts, the legislative purposes will not be fulfilled. The other statutory limitations include the condition, which require "within the reasonable scope of use". In our opinion, the copyright owner could arrange some terms and conditions for the reasonable scope of use, but they must not be unjust.

The decision of the US court *ProCD, Inc. v. Zeidenberg*,[245] considered the issue of the enforceability of a "shrink-wrap" licence for a telephone directory computer database. There are no similar cases in Taiwan. We hope to see judicial opinions in this regard in the future.

3. *Standard Contracts, Copyright and Fair Trade Act*

Some standard software contracts include terms which forbid the licencee from decompiling computer programs (reverse engineering). Since such decompiling is vital in order to achieve interoperability of different computer programs, we do not consider such terms to be consistent with the fair competition doctrine. If business operators try to adopt the principle of freedom of contract to limit the legal right granted by copyright law, it could be deemed to violate Sec. 45 Fair Trade Act, abuse of intellectual property right. When the business operator (copyright owner) ties in the copyrighted work with another product, the reason for the tie-in should be investigated. Each party's bargaining power should also be taken into account by the Fair Trade Commission (FTC) or the court. If the FTC or the court regards any arrangements as unsupported by any legitimate reasons, the terms of the standard contract should be held to contravene Sec. 19 Fair Trade Act.

4. *Conclusion*

Although copyright contracts, public policy and antitrust are still emerging issues in Taiwan, due to the phenomenal growth of Internet use, these issues are now drawing more attention than ever. The academic and professional communities have just moved their attention to this ambiguous but critical area. Actually, foreign cases, such as *ProCD, Inc. v. Zeidenberg* or *Mallinckrodt, Inc. v. Medipart, Inc.*,[246] have all been eagerly discussed amongst local practioners and academics. We believe that copyright contracts, public policy and antitrust will soon become main concerns of our country. More judicial decisions on this issue are needed to shape our discourse, which in turn will provide a direction for future modification and amendment of the Copyright Act.

IV. Japan

1. *Copyright and Contract prior to the Digital Age*

Secs. 17 and 59 Copyright Act provide for copyright to be transferred in *toto*, with the exception of moral rights. As a protection to the copyright owner, some jurisdictions have introduced a so-called "purpose-of-transfer" rule whereby the copyright owner transfers only such rights as the other party requires for that specific purpose. Future and unknown forms of use cannot be transferred. Such a rule exists in Germany under Sec. 31(5) Copyright Act. The Japanese Copyright Act has no mandatory provisions that would limit contractual freedom, though some

---

[245] 86 F.3d 1477 (7th Cir. 1996).
[246] 967 F.2d 700 (Fed. Cir. 1992).

academics have advocated the introduction of a purpose of transfer rule.[247] In the legislative process, the 1966 draft contained the provision that a contract that transfers the whole copyright of the work both for the present and future unknown uses, was void (Sec. 54 of the draft). The draft also stipulated that the right to exploit a work in an unforeseeable manner at the time of contract should be vested in the author (Sec. 55 of the draft).[248] This presumption was to apply to rights of translation or adaptation (Sec. 27) and to the exploitation of a derivative work (Sec. 28) (Sec. 61 (2)). These proposals did not become law. Apparently the cause was too much opposition from the industry. However, there was some academic opposition to the introduction of more equitable rules into this aspect of copyright law[249].

2. *Copyright Contracts in the Digital World*

In a good many countries, clauses introduced by click wrap or shrink wrap licences have to pass the threshold of consumer protection laws in order to be deemed valid. This is not the case in Japan, where neither specific legislation nor court rulings have imposed measurable limits on the validity of such clauses[250]. Doubts about the validity of shrink wrap or click wrap clauses thus have to be based either on copyright or anti-trust law.

In the legislative process, copyright limitations were categorised as follows:

(a) an exploitation to which copyright should not extend in nature;
(b) an exploitation to which copyright should be limited by public interest;
(c) an exploitation in which copyright should be restricted to accommodate other rights; and
(d) an exploitation as social custom, in which the limitations of copyright are not unreasonably detrimental to the economic interests of the copyright owner.[251]

At least those limitations that fall under (b) would not be enforceable. There is not much case law on this matter. However, any limitations overriding the exhaustion of copyrighted works would be deemed void[252] and even contravening the

---

247 O. *Watanabe*, *Chosakuken keiyaku no kaishaku* (The Construction of Copyright Contract) in Festschrift für F.K.Beier, Japanese edition, *Chiteki zaisan to kyôsôhô no riron* (Theory of Intellectual Property Law and Competition Law) (1996), 323; *H. Shiomi*, Chosakukenhô ni okeru sôsakusha shugi no hensen katei—shokumu chosaku seido no bunseki wo chûshin to shite (The Development of the "Creator Doctrine" in Copyright Law: the Case of "Works Made in Employment" in Japan), 119-9 Hôgaku Kyôkai Zasshi 1799, 1868 et seq.

248 Monbushô (Ministry of Education), Chosakuken seido shingikai tôshin setsumeishô (Explanation of the Report of the Council about Copyright Legislation) (1966), 77–78.

249 *H. Shiomi*, 119-6 Hôgaku kyôkai Zasshi 1006 et seq.

250 A. *Ômura*, Shôhisha keiyakuhô (Consumer Contract Law), 2nd ed. Tokyo 2003; idem, Keiyakuhô kara shôhishahô he (From Contract to Consumer Law), Tokyo 1999.

251 M. *Katô*, Chosakukenhô chikujô kôgi, (Commentary on the Copyright Act), 4th ed. 2003, 222.

252 This view is taken by MITI's Study Group on Copyright Law (Chosakuken hôrei kenkyûkai), Chosakukenhô fusei kyôsô boshihô kaisetsu (Explanations on copyright and unfair competition), Tokyo 1999, 115.

Antimonopoly Act. In the Fair Trade Commission's (FTC) "Nihon Record II" decision[253], certain manufacturers of audio discs had tried to prevent shops from renting out these discs to customers. Since the Copyright Act at that time did not provide for any specific rights of rental and lending, the obligation was unenforceable, as the rights over these audio discs were exhausted by the first sale. It was anti-competitive to try to enforce the restriction by way of a boycott against these shops. The FTC, at least when reviewing licensing agreements, generally finds clauses that contractually limit the licencee beyond the scope of the IP right in question, void. Yet most shrink wrap and click wrap contracts are made between the manufacturer and the end user rather than an entrepreneur, making it more difficult for the FTC to intervene. It is thus open to question to what extent limits on the private use (Sec. 30 Copyright Act) of copyrighted works are enforceable, particularly after legislature already allowed limitations on private use by digital means (Sec. 30(2) Copyright Act). One academic thus finds private-use restrictions by contract enforceable[254].

Outside the limitation of exhaustion, no clear case law exists on this matter

V. Korea

The recent rapid development and diffusion of information technology are dramatically changing not only the methods which process an enterprise's internal tasks, but also modes of trading and even the businesses themselves. Further, the use of intellectual property (IPR) licensing agreements in electronic commerce has been on the increase. The general legal issues relating to e-commerce and licensing apply accordingly to licensing of IPR in e-commerce. A variant of the shrink-wrap licence has emerged in information transactions. It is called an "on-line licence" or "click-wrap licence."

Copyright law aims to balance the right of the copyright holder to control the use of his work with the public's interest for its widespread dissemination. However, contractually individual parties are free to negotiate and agree on terms of use which may be more or less stringent than those which would be implied under copyright law. Nonetheless, such mutually agreed terms may allow the supplier to exert much more control over the future use of the software than would otherwise have been the case if only copyright law was applicable.[255]

A major fair-access issue has arisen regarding situations where a copyright holder attempts to restrict a reverse engineering right by copyright infringement litigation, contractual shrink-wrap licences or a protective system that defeats the reverse engineering permissible under the "fair-use" doctrine. Reverse engineering computer software is defined as the process of studying a computer program to obtain useful and detailed insight into the functional mechanisms of the work.

---

[253] FTC, 15 December 1983, 389 Kôsei Torihiki 34—"Nihon Record II".

[254] *N. Koizumi*, Chosakuken to seigenkitei to keiyaku, gijutsuteki hogo shûdan no interface (Interface between Copyright Limitations Provisions and Contract, Technological Protection Measures), Copyright (July 2003), 5.

[255] *Rowland/Campbell*, Supply of Software: Copyright and Contract Issues, Int. Journal of Law and Information Technology, Vol. 10 No.1, at. 23.

Reverse engineering commonly involves copying an original program without the permission of a copyright owner. Indeed, the owners seek to prevent reverse engineering by bringing infringement suits, imposing contractual limitations or installing technological impediments. In the United States, the Digital Millennium Copyright Act ("DMCA") provides a software vendor with extra protection for its protective system, and allows reverse engineering only for the purpose of interoperability. The Uniform Computer Information Transactions Act ("UCITA") makes a shrink-wrap licence enforceable even if it contains a term prohibiting reverse engineering. These protectionist measures ensure that a copyright holder can dominate the computer software industry by restricting reverse engineering. Although the Computer Program Protection Act in Korea allows a reverse engineering purporting to achieve interoperability as an exception, this is still not enough to strike a balance between the copyright holder's interests and the public right of access to a copyrighted work. The current trend toward copyright protectionism undermines that balance; thus, the critical question regarding clarification of the right to conduct reverse engineering should be answered by policymakers in terms of reconciliation between copyright, contract and competition policy.[256]

The principal purpose of transferring software products to consumers via a shrink wrap licence rather than via a sale transaction is to negate the copyright "doctrine of first sale", which provides that the copyright holder's rights in the particular copy are exhausted upon the sale of the copy. Under the Copyright Act,[257] a purchaser of copyrighted work may freely resell, lease, lend, or otherwise dispose of the purchased copy. By hiding under the guise of a licence rather than an outright sale as the means of transferring the use computer programs, the industry has succeeded in avoiding the exhaustion of copyright by first sale doctrine.[258]

What have the courts decided about the enforceability of such under Korean law? Despite the apparent importance of this issue there do not appear to be any reported cases. It would be interesting to see whether the Korean judiciary would be swayed by similar policy consideration.[259] Contract and copyright laws and various other laws governing digital information do not differ largely irrespective of whether a physical or an electronic distribution takes places. The legal issues that do arise concerning questions such as, validity of contract, enforceability of contract, identification of parties, underlying copyright protection, and remedies against infringements.

Another reason why software supplied via a shrink-wrap licence cause contractual difficulties in Korea is the failure to incorporate proper terms and conditions into the sale or licence. Assuming that the Korean courts will enforce all terms of such licences, there will be greater certainty for all parties if such licences are carefully drafted so that the courts would not have to resort to implied terms.

---

256 *Son, Seungwoo*, Can Shrink-wrap Licenses override Software Reverse Engineering? Vol. 13 Journal of Industrial Property Law 193–220 (2003).

257 Sec. 43 (1) of the Copyright Act.

258 *Byung-Il Kim*, Software Licensing, Vol. 2 No.1 Journal of Digital Property Law, 13–138 (2002).

259 *Id.*, at 140.

UCITA expressly provides for the incorporation of the terms and conditions of the contractual licence into the supply contract.[260] Even if the introduction of UCITA has been controversial and has been the subject of a vigorous debate in the US, it does appear to provide a pragmatic approach to the potential problem of the incorporation of terms into shrink wrap licences, and this approach may provide useful guidance for Korea.

Information technology accounts for a huge share of the Korean economy and is rapidly expanding its boundaries. There is a need for new legislation in Korea which will apply to computer software, multimedia products, computer data and databases, online information, and other such products. Such legislation should be drafted to create a uniform commercial contract law for these transactions and to furnish clear, consistent uniform rules for the intangible subject matter involved in digital information transactions over the Internet and elsewhere. Prior to drafting the new legislation, a study of the approach taken in UCITA may be a good starting point. It is vital that any proposed new legislation eradicates existing uncertainties, implements those areas of law which are uncontroversial, and intellectual property doctrines such as fair use and exhaustion by first sale are given their proper role. Furthermore, various terminologies such as "conspicuous", "authenticate", "electronic agent", and "digital information transactions" should be more accurately drafted in the new legislation to ensure correct interpretation. Lastly, loopholes in shrink-wrap licences should be addressed, and proper remedy and warranty provisions must be prescribed. [261]

VI. Singapore

Singapore's contract law does not allow the courts to invalidate any contractual term[262] which restricts or excludes the user's right to use the copyright work granted by the Copyright Act, on the basis that it is an attempt to usurp the decision of legislators/policy-makers and therefore against public policy.[263] This concern is addressed within the Copyright Act itself, but only in relation to two particular rights:

a) the right of the owner of a non-infringing copy of a computer program to make a back-up copy thereof, i.e. in the event that the original copy is lost, destroyed or rendered unusable;[264] and

---

260 *Reed/Angel* (Ed.), Computer Law, Fourth Edition, Blackstone Press Limited, 39 (2002.)

261 *Byung-Il Kim*, *Id.*, 143.

262 Note, though, that it is possible for the court to hold that the clause delimiting the licencee's right to use the copyright work is not a term of the contract where, in the view of the court, it was brought to the attention of the licencee after the conclusion of the contract. This has important implications in the supply of software and the accompanying 'shrink-wrap' licence.

263 Singapore has an Unfair Contracts Terms Act. This Act, however, is not relevant to the discussion at hand because it is concerned with contractual terms that attempt to avoid civil liability for breach of contract or for negligence or other breach of duty.

264 See s 39(1) of the Copyright Act.

b) the right of the owner of a computer program or of a compilation to make a copy or adaptation thereof where such copy or adaptation is created as an essential step in the utilization of the computer program or compilation in conjunction with a machine and that it is used in no other manner.[265] The second right holds some significance for reverse engineering of software.[266] These two rights are considered so important by the legislators that they have specifically provided in the Copyright Act that any term or condition in an agreement which purports to prohibit or restrict the scope of these rights is void.[267]

It has been mentioned earlier that Singapore has just enacted The Competition Act 2004.[268] It prohibits conduct which amounts to an 'abuse of a dominant position' and agreements which have as their object or effect the 'restriction or distortion of competition'. To the extent that the behaviour of the copyright owner in using contract to expand his control over the use of his copyright work would be considered anti-competitive within the new regime, it would be regulated therein.

VII. Malaysia

The right of a copyright owner to grant a licence over his copyright is recognised under Malaysian law, subject only to the requirement that it must be in writing.[269] Apart from that formality, the Act does not otherwise prescribe the limits or scope of any licence, except that the term 'licence' itself is defined as 'a lawfully granted licence in writing, permitting the doing of an act controlled by copyright'.[270] Thus, the licence cannot exceed the bounds of the law, for the copyright owner cannot have more rights than what is given to him under the Act.

The rights given under the Act enable the copyright owner to control the following acts in relation to a work:[271]

(a) the reproduction in any material form;
(b) the communication to the public;
(c) the performance, showing or playing to the public;

---

265 See s 39(2) of the Copyright Act.

266 See *Ng-Loy*, "Copyright Protection for Computer Programs in Singapore: *Creative Technology Ltd v Aztech Systems Pte Ltd* [1997] 4 Computer and Telecommunications Law Review 182. Singapore introduced, with effect from 1 January 2005, two other rights which are relevant for reverse engineering of software: the right to decompile a computer program (s 39A) and the right to observe, study or test a computer program (s 39B). It is expressly provided that any contractual term or condition which purports to prohibit or restrict such permitted acts of reverse engineering would be void.

267 See s 39(3) of the Copyright Act. Another instance in the Copyright Act disregarding the effect of a contractual term or condition is where the copyright owner attempts by contract to restrict the exhaustion of rights principle: see s 24(4).

268 This legislation is available at the website of the Singapore Competition Commission which is http://www.ccs.gov.sg/.

269 Copyright Act 1987, s. 27(3).

270 Copyright Act 1987, s. 3.

271 Copyright Act 1987, s. 13(1).

(d) the distribution of copies to the public by sale or other transfer of ownership; and
(e) the commercial rental to the public

A licence purporting to restrict or control acts other than the above, for example acts falling under 'fair use', could be invalid. With shrink-wrap or click-wrap licences, the issue is usually not about the terms and conditions therein; rather it is with the character of the licence itself and whether a person is bound by it. This goes back to basic principles of contract law regarding the formation of a contract. In Malaysia, contracts are governed by the Contracts Act of 1950, which codifies much of the common law. The law here is familiar: a contract is formed when an offer is made and it is accepted with the passing of consideration and an intention to be bound.

Therefore, so long as the terms of a shrink-wrap or click-wrap licence are sufficiently brought to the notice of the purchaser and the purchaser indicates acceptance of it, it will hold. This has led to, for example, a redesign of how websites and software packages process an order or installation. Instead of putting the terms and conditions on another link or page, they are now prominently displayed prior to confirmation and the customer has to actively click an 'I Accept' button in order to proceed. Software packages that used to only have a shrink-wrap licence now supplement that with a click-wrap version that is seen during installation in order to increase the likelihood that a contract has been formed. That said, the point remains that the terms and conditions themselves cannot exceed the scope of rights granted under the Act. Hence, it is arguable whether a term prohibiting the decompilation, disassembly and reverse engineering of a work (which is quite common in software click-wrap licences) is enforceable since the Act in the first place does not give the copyright owner the right to control these activities.

VIII. Thailand

Under Thai law on juristic acts, an agreement is formed and legally binding when an offer is met by an acceptance. This normally does not have anything to do with whether the agreement is done in writing. Nevertheless, in most cases, a deed of agreement is necessary as proof that the offer and the acceptance have met and therefore there exists a legally binding agreement.

It seems that shrink-wrap or click-wrap agreements are used mostly in the computer software industry. In my opinion, there is a problem with shrink-wrap agreements in that the computer program manufacturer (the copyright owner and licensor) may not always be able to obtain clear proof of the "acceptance." A computer program registration card that has been signed by the consumer who has purchased a package of computer program and returned to the manufacturer, for example, is clear proof of the acceptance. The problem is some consumers buy a computer program and use it without bothering to fill out and return the product registration card to the manufacturer, in which case the manufacturer will have no proof that the consumer has "accepted" the terms and conditions of the computer program licence agreement. Nevertheless, this does not mean that the consumer may do anything he likes with the computer program purchased. He is still required by copyright law to respect the basic rights of the copyright owner. He may not make unauthorized copies of, adapt, communicate to the public or rent out the program. In most cases, a shrink-wrap agreement's terms and conditions which the copyright owner wants the consumer to observe are no more than what the copyright law already requires of the consumer. Therefore, even in the absence of a clear "acceptance" of the shrink-wrap agreement by the consumer, the copyright owner's rights remain protected.

So far, this exact issue has not been settled by case law.

It should be noted that Sec. 15 of the Copyright Act provides that copyright licensing agreements may not incorporate conditions which are "unfairly restrictive of competition." What conditions are then to be considered "unfairly restrictive of competition"? We are directed by the Act to the Ministerial Regulations of 1997 issued pursuant to Sec. 15. However, the Ministerial Regulations do not address the issue of shrink-wrap agreements but only the issues involving copyright licensing agreements between copyright owners and manufacturers of copyrighted products.

IX. Philippines

A contract is a meeting of minds between two persons whereby one binds himself, with respect to the other, to give something or to render some service.[272] There is no contract unless there is, among others, consent of the contracting parties.[273] In other words, the parties must have fully understood the terms of the contract and they freely gave their consent to the performance of an obligation either "to give something or to render some service." Shrink-wrap and click wrap licences must possess these features before they can be considered valid contracts under Philippine law.

Shrink-wrap licences occur when a consumer opens the package containing the terms as to the use of the computer program. It is understood that when the consumer opens the package, he arguably contractually accepts the terms of the licence.[274] Click-wrap licences take place when the terms of the licence are flashed and read on-line by a computer-user who arguably contractually accepts the terms as soon as he proceeds to access the software on-line.

Considering that the terms of the licence have already been prepared when offered to the consumer and the latter is simply asked to agree to them, the shrink-wrap and click-wrap licences may be considered a type of contract of adhesion.[275] A contract of adhesion is one in which one of the parties imposes a ready-made form of contract, which the other party may accept or reject, but which the latter cannot modify.[276]

---

[272] New Civil Code Article 1305.

[273] Ibid. Article 1318.

[274] *Gerald Dworkin and Richard Taylor*, Blackstone's Guide to Copyright Designs and Patent Act 1988, (1989), p. 179.

[275] *Arturo Tolentino*, supra. v. IV p 411.

[276] Ibid. p 506.

Below is a comparison of the essential elements of a contract of adhesion, shrink-wrap licence and click-wrap licence:

A contract of adhesion usually contains stipulations that increase the responsibilities of the adherent and reduce the responsibilities of the offeror.[277] While the contract appears to favour the offeror, it cannot be said that there is "such economic inequality between the parties to these contracts" that the will of the offeree (or party adhering to the terms) is suppressed. The party who adheres to the contract is free to reject it entirely. If the party adheres to the contract, then he is deemed to have given his consent.[278]

To constitute a valid contract, it is essential that the offeree in a shrink wrap and click wrap licence has freely given his consent. Under our laws, "consent is manifested by the meeting of the offer and the acceptance upon the thing and the

Contract of Adhesion	Shrink-wrap Licence	Click-wrap Licence
Offeror (such as transportation or insurance company) prepares all the terms and conditions of the contract	The software company prepares all the terms and conditions of the contract	The software company prepares all the terms and conditions of the contract
The other party to whom the contract is presented cannot modify the provisions stated therein	The other party to whom the contract is presented cannot modify the provisions stated therein	The other party to whom the contract is presented cannot modify the provisions stated therein
Contract is usually in written form	Contract is usually in written form, either attached to the cellophane packaging or printed on the box or case containing the software	Contract is flashed on the computer screen, online, via the internet
Consent is give through the signing of the prepared agreement	Consent is indicated by opening the shrink wrap packaging or other packaging of the software, by use of the software, or by some other specified procedure	Consent is indicated by clicking the "I Agree" button, or proceeding to access the software after the user has read the provisions in the contract

[277] Ibid.
[278] Ibid.

cause which are to constitute a contract. The offer must be certain and the acceptance absolute."[279] The acceptance must be known to the offeror and such acceptance may be express or implied.[280]

In a shrink wrap licence, consent is given and the licence terms are deemed accepted when the packaging is opened and the "terms of the licence are set out on the outside of the packaging, visible through clear plastic film."[281] In a click-wrap licence, the computer-user is assumed to have accepted the terms of the licence since he cannot proceed to access the software on-line unless he gave his consent on the licence terms. In both cases, the party adhering to the terms has the opportunity to review the licence and may reject the same in the event the terms thereof are unacceptable.

However, there are software products whose licence terms are not visible from the outside. The offeree is not given an opportunity to review the terms of contract of adhesion prior to accepting them. So long as the conditions of the licence come to the user's attention before he agrees to be bound by its terms, then the contract is valid and enforceable. In this regard, it appears that the contract terms in most shrink-wrap licences are found inside the package and is not visible from the outside. The offeree has no opportunity to review to the terms of the licence prior to breaking the seal of the package. The absence of an opportunity to review the terms prior to acceding or rejecting the terms, will work against upholding the validity of this type of shrink-wrap licence.

A contract of adhesion is already construed strictly against the party who drew the terms of the ready-made agreement[282] as public policy protects the adherent against oppressive and onerous conditions.[283] Under our laws, the consent of a party is vitiated when the other party "takes improper advantage of his power over the will of another, depriving the latter of a reasonable freedom of choice."[284] It would all the more be difficult to sustain the validity of a contract of adhesion where there is an absence of opportunity for the offeree to review or reject the terms. A well respected Filipino jurist has commented as to why contracts of adhesion shall be interpreted strictly against the drafters and may be denied enforcement on grounds of public interest. His comments are as follows:

> "Against monopolies, cartels and great concentrations of capital, the individual is usually helpless to bargain for better terms; and must accept those offered, usually in printed forms. Travellers against transportation monopolies, the insured against insurance combinations, customers against exclusive agencies, are all forced to accept contracts carefully worded by skilled counsels to stack the cards against the lone individual and in favor of the corporations. This situation demands greater corrective remedies than contract law produces by bargaining on equal terms, with power lodged in the Courts to deny enforcement of provisions th are exclusively for the benefit of the stronger party, and cannot be justified by reason of public interest". [285]

---

[279] New Civil Code Article 1319.

[280] New Civil Code Article 1320.

[281] *Graham Smith*, "Software Contracts" in Computer Law, edited by Chris Reed (1990), page 48.

[282] *Eastern Shipping Lines v. Margarine-Verkaufs*, 93 SCRA 257 (1979).

[283] *Villacorta v. Insurance Commission* , 100 SCRA 467 (1980).

[284] New Civil Code Article 1337.

[285] *Justice JBL Reyes*, Lawyers Journal, 31 January 1951, p. 59.

We are aware of the view that, in the event the offeree is given the opportunity to reject the terms of the licence, the validity of the contract should be upheld. It is likely that courts will examine the facts surrounding the existence of such opportunity. The procedure for the return of the software products, if in fact in place, must be reasonable and practicable for the consumer. The law expressly provides that the offeree must be afforded "a reasonable freedom of choice."[286]

Likewise there have been attempts to override the limitations of copyright by incorporating provisions favourable to the copyright owners in a shrink wrap or click wrap licence. Assuming the execution of the contract was in order, that is, the offeree has expressly given his consent to waiving such limitations, it would be interesting for the courts to squarely decide on these issues under Philippine laws. Whilst the validity of shrink-wrap and click wrap licences are strictly construed against the copyright owner-offeror, we cannot overlook the right of the parties to freely enter into an agreement and "establish such stipulations, clauses, terms and conditions as they may deem convenient, provided they are not contrary to law, morals, good customs, public order, or public policy."[287]

It is likely that public policy considerations will work against the validity of such provisions in view of the express limitations under the IP Code. The courts cannot ignore a principle explicitly stated in the new law which states as follows:

> "The State … shall protect and secure the exclusive rights of scientists, inventors, artists and other gifted citizens to their intellectual property and creations, *particularly when beneficial to the people, for such periods as provided in this Act.*

The use of intellectual property bears a social function. To this end, the Sate shall promote the diffusion of knowledge and information for the promotion of national development and progress and the common good. …"[288]

It is submitted that overriding copyright limits is inconsistent with the declared policy of the State of extending exclusive rights to copyright owners when such protection is beneficial to the people and for such periods as provided in the law. To deprive the consumer and the public in general of the copyright limitations may restrict the application of the social function of intellectual properties: promote the diffusion of knowledge and information. The consumers and the general public will be restricted in the lawful use of the licensed software even if such restrictions are beyond the limits provided by the IP Code. This view is supported by the principle that laws restrict the freedom of contract for the good of the public.[289] It is obvious that however broad the freedom of the contracting parties may be, it does not go so far as to countenance disrespect for or failure to observe a legal prescription. The statute thus takes precedence.[290]

---

[286] New Civil Code Article 1337.

[287] New Civil Code Article 1306.

[288] IP Code Section 2.

[289] *Sweet Lines v. Teves*, 83 SCRA 361 (1978).

[290] *Lakas ng Manggagawang Makabayan v. Hon. Carlos Abiera*, 36 SCRA 437 (1970); *Ortigas v. Feati Bank*, 94 SCRA 533 (1979).

6
Contributory and Vicarious Liability for Copyright Infringement

ANDY Y. SUN

Enforcement of copyright infringements often encounters difficulty for many reasons including social stigma when it means taking legal action against private consumers in instances such as the use of music recordings at karaoke bar and downloading of songs or film works for private viewing. Whilst legal action is possible, in many cases it is unrealistic and impractical to do so. A more promising alternative lies in suing the managers of karaoke bars, the manufacturers of machines, the writers of copying programmes or the Internet service providers. Reported prominent cases come from the US (Napster), Japan (File Rogue) and Korea (Soribada). The individual country reports address the applicability of such cases with respect to the laws of their countries and all ancillary legal issues.

A. Introduction - Is it the Gun or the Man who pulls the trigger who is liable —On Secondary Liabilities of Copyright Infringement

I. Introduction

The advancements of technology and law have not always been in harmony. Contrariety seems to be true with each going their own ways, sometimes in total opposition, even to the extent that one is perceived as an obstacle (if not a major one) to the other. This perception and tension is not completely without merit. For example, we have witnessed how the law has treated the technological advancement of computer software in the past 30 years—at least in the patent arena where it has advanced from the position of an outlaw to celebrity status, with some arguing that at present it is overly protected.

It may surprise some to note that the intellectual property system has not been designed primarily for the protection of industry interests; and that industries do not always prevail in getting what they consider "sufficient" intellectual property rights protection over the technologies they have developed and marketed. Courts tend to take a more "conservative" (or "prudent," depending on the beholder's point of view) approach to issues concerning new technologies when its full potential has yet to be fully ascertained. Indeed, we may view the process of delineating the scope of legal protection over the advancement of technology as an act akin to walking a tight rope, always seeking balance between the private interests and the public good. To compound the difficulties and complexities, the rope is not still, but is expanding in unknown directions with the progress of time. As long as there are new innovations as technology keeps rolling out and marching on, there will always be the call for more flexibility in the laws that govern them.

As a result, while technological innovations, provide more conveniences for our daily lives, they ironically pose new and difficult challenges to the existing legal framework, forcing lawyers to use innovative approaches to confront them. It is clearly evident that any solution for such complex issues of today and tomorrow will not be found in just one single discipline but must involve legal, technological, managerial and economic expertise.

Dr. Alan Greenspan, Chairman of the U.S. Federal Reserve Board, observed: "Only in recent decades, as the economic product of the United States has become so predominantly conceptual, have issues related to the protection of intellectual property rights come to be seen as significant sources of legal and business uncertainty. Intellectual property is clearly more difficult to define and ... to protect."[1]

A growing problem which highlights this point is the massive end-user copyright piracy over the Internet.[2] When audio and video industries finally felt enough is enough and began to take strong legal actions against the end users in the United States, they quickly found themselves in a public relations disaster. Similar situations have occurred in Europe and Asia.[3] The image of a twelve-year old honour-roll student being subpoenaed to court for downloading unauthorised, copyrighted music files online does not sit well on the music industry or with the general public.[4] Arguably, no real winner emerges from this legal hot pursuit. Naturally, it elicits immediate queries: Is there a better alternative? Who are the real culprits, the ones who created the technologies which enabled such actions or the end –users who acted on them, or both?

---

[1] See *Alan Greenspan*, Market Economies and Rule of Law, Keynote speech delivered at the Financial Markets Conference of the Federal Reserve Bank of Atlanta, Sea Island, Georgia, 4 April 2003.

[2] Based on the survey statistics of BigChampagne, there are on average 8.5 million individuals engaging in peer-to-peer file share globally at any time (presumably most of which are music files, or MP3). The number has grown from 5.5 million in 2003 to 8.5 million through the first five-and-a-half months of 2005. Two dips occurred. One was when the first wave of publicity hit about the Recording Industry Association of America's intent to sue individual US residents it believed were violating copyrights. The other was when it actually started filing the suits. See 8.5m P2P File Sharers on Average at Any Time, ONLINE REPORTER (USA), Issue 450, June 21, 2005.

[3] Similar incidents occurred in both Mainland China and Taiwan. In 1999, Microsoft (China) sued Beijing Yadu Corporation. Dubbed the very first end-user software infringement case China, the court tossed the case out of the window on the grounds that the defendant lacked proper standing to be sued. This allowed the court to dodge the bullet despite that fact that Microsoft thought it has gotten an iron-proof case. In 2002, Taiwan witnessed its very first end-user copyright infringement incident. Fourteen students from a local, prestigious university were about to be criminally prosecuted after their computers were found to contain hundreds, if not thousands of music files, before a major public outcry broke out against the industry on the island. The incident was eventually settled, but not before both sides would have to deal with their respective image problems. For detailed illustrations, see *Andy Y. Sun*, Reforming the Protection of Intellectual Property: The Case of China and Taiwan in Light of WTO Accession, MARYLAND SERIES IN CONTEMPORARY ASIAN STUDIES, University of Maryland School of Law, No. 4—2001 (165)(2002).

II. Secondary Liability for Copyright Infringement

The US courts have long established, under the realm of torts, a rule that those who assist and facilitate infringement are as equally liable as those who commit actual infringement.[5] This so-called "secondary liability" or third-party liability has a practical purpose as well: it ensures real and effective enforcement against those who are *truly* legally and financially responsible.[6] In other words, it grew out of a need to establish fundamental fairness in infringement cases.[7]

American courts have traditionally distinguished between two categories of secondary liabilities; vicarious and contributory liability. Vicarious liability is imposed "[w]hen the right and ability to supervise coalesced with an obvious and direct financial interest in the exploitation of copyrighted materials... the purpose of copyright law may be best effectuated by the imposition of liability upon the beneficiary of that exploitation."[8] On the other hand, one "who, with the knowledge of infringing activity, induces, causes, or materially contributes to the infringing conduct of another" has been held to be contributorily liable.[9]

Therefore, to establish secondary liability, the ingredient of direct infringement by a primary party must be present. Vicarious liability is proven when the defendant (or third party) had both the right and ability to supervise or control the infringing activity and had acquired direct financial benefit from such infringing activity;[10] whilst contributory liability, requires not only that the defendant had knowledge of the infringement but also that he had made material contribution/s to the infringing activity.[11]

III. Statutory Enactment/Codification

Secondary liability for copyright infringement was formally codified when Congress enacted the Copyright Act of 1976.[12] Section 106 provides, among

---

[4] See Courting Disaster; The RIAA Hurts Its Cause Immeasurably by Targeting A 12-year-old, KANSAS CITY PITCH WEEKLY, vol. 22, Issue 62 (18 September 2003).

[5] The root of secondary liability can be traced as far back to a 1911 case of the U.S. Supreme Court. See *Kalem v. Harper Brothers*, 222 U.S. 55 (1911)(The "Ben Hur" Case). Note that the Copyright Act of 1909 did not expressly address secondary liability. Thus the Court based its decision on logical inference: "In some cases where an ordinary article of commerce is sold, nice questions may arise as to the point at which the seller becomes an accomplice in a subsequent illegal use by the buyer ... If the defendant did not contribute to the infringement, it is impossible to do so except by taking part in the final act. It is liable on principles recognized in every part of the law." Id., at 63.

[6] The term can be somewhat misleading, as the damage awards against those "indirect" infringers normally far exceed the "direct" infringers, a reflection of the "deep pocket" approach or theory.

[7] See *John T. Soma and Natalie A. Norman*, International Take-down Policy: A Proposal for the WTO and WIPO to Establish International Copyright Procedural Guidelines for Internet Service Providers, 22 HASTINGS COMM. & ENT. L.J. 391, 398 (2000).

[8] See Shiparo, Bernstein & Co. v. H. L. Green Co., 316 F.2d 354 (7th Cir. 1929).

[9] See Gershwin Publishing Corp. v. Columbia Artists Management, Inc., 443 F.2d 1159, 1162 (2nd Cir. 1971).

[10] See above note 8. This doctrine thus closely resembles the torts doctrine of *respondeat superior* or enterprise liability.

[11] See above note 9.

[12] Pub. L. No. 94-553, Title I, 90 Stat. 2541 (1976), as codified in 17 U.S.C.§ 101 et seq. This is the so-called "bundle of rights."

other things, "[t]he owner of copyright under this title has the exclusive rights to do *and to authorize* any of the [reproduction, adaptation, publication, performance, and display rights] ..." [emphasis added.] Congress tried to make it clear that "[t]he use of the phrase 'to authorize' is intended to avoid any questions as to the liability of contributory infringers."[13] Congress "recognize[s] the impracticability or futility of a copyright owner suing a multitude of individual infringers... [Thus] the law allows a copyright holder to sue a contributor to the infringement instead, in effect as an aide and abettor."[14] In other words, courts have borrowed from the concept of criminal aiding and abetting to impose civil liabilities in copyright infringement.

Recognising that these rules were created out of equitable considerations and necessity, nevertheless a built-in controversy has been created. Drawing upon the analogy of gun control, was it the gun that committed the crime or was the crime committed by the man who actually pulled the trigger? Where should the blame be placed? If the law were to punish those who have facilitated the illegal copying or distribution of copyrighted works through their designs or manufacture of devices, gadgets, or software, what form, type and manner should the standards take?

To tackle this built-in problem and to maintain a certain degree of flexibility to cope with the ever constant advancement of technological innovation, while statute has allowed direct enforcement against the "middlemen" who encourage, facilitate and benefit from such infringement—especially when it involves large dissemination of the copyrighted works, statute has nonetheless left many details open-ended for the courts are to fill the gaps. The main task of the courts has been to ensure a proper balance between infringement and fair use. The developments of judicial decisions eventually lead to the codification of the same Act in 1976.[15]

IV. The Sony Betamax Case

The first landmark case dealing with these issues was the so-called *Sony Betamax* case.[16] There, the U.S. Supreme Court had to decide whether the manufacturer of videocassette recorders (or VCRs) was liable for the infringing actions of its customers. The court held that the VCR manufacturer was *not* liable because it had at best only constructive and not actual knowledge of the infringing activity for which customers used the device.

The court's dilemma: By the time the case had reached the Supreme Court, VCRs had already gained such tremendous popularity that any decision reached by the court would have a very significant impact on the entertainment and other

---

[13] See H.R. Rep. 94-1476, p. 61. In the report, Congress further illustrated: "For example, a person who lawfully acquires an authorized copy of a motion picture would be an infringer if he or she engages in the business of renting it to others for purposes of unauthorized public performance."

[14] See In re Aimster, 334 F.3d 643, 646 (7th Cir. 2003).

[15] 17 U.S.C.§§ 107-122 (2000, Supp. II).

[16] *Sony Corporation of America v. Universal City Studios, Inc.*, 464 U.S. 417 (1984).

related industries. Recognising the complexity of issues and interests involved, the court first made it clear that the imposition of contributory liability must "rest on the fact that [the defendant] has sold equipment with constructive knowledge of the fact that its customers may use that equipment to make unauthorised copies of copyrighted material."[17]

The court recognised that it had to strike a balance between a copyright holder's legitimate demand for effective—not merely symbolic—protection of the statutory monopoly, and the rights of others to freely engage in substantially unrelated areas of commerce. Hence, the mere sale of copying equipment did not constitute contributory infringement if it was used mainly for legitimate, unobjectionable purposes.

To set the standard for contributory infringement liability and to frame exceptions, the court could not find any guidance from the Copyright Act of 1976. In its stead, the court looked for guidance from patent law, borrowed the "staple article of commerce" doctrine and applied that into the copyright arena, holding that the exception to patent infringement likewise applied in copyright. In other words, the sale of a "staple article or commodity of commerce suitable for substantial non-infringing use" does not constitute contributory infringement.[18] Thus, to avoid contributory liability, the key issue is whether an article of commerce "need merely be capable of substantial non-infringing uses" and such uses are indeed "commercially significant."[19]

Here, the Supreme Court reaffirmed the district court's finding that a significant number of VCR purchasers had used the equipment for "time-shifting" purpose, *i.e.*, the recording of a television program to be viewed at a later, more convenient time, and then erased it, which clearly constituted fair use; and concluded that Sony Corporation, the manufacturer, was not liable for contributory infringement since there was neither actual knowledge of infringement nor were VCRs *incapable commercially of substantial non-infringing uses*, i.e. there was no material contribution to the infringing activity.

V. The Napster Case—The First Peer-to-Peer Challenge

The onset of the widespread use of the Internet spelt the arrival of electronic commerce. Two of the most significant technological developments that have sparked the trend are; the so-called MP3 standard and the subsequent peer-to-peer

---

[17] Id., at 439. Courts do not require actual knowledge; rather, a defendant incurs contributory copyright liability if it has reason to know of the third party's direct infringement (constructive knowledge). See *Cable/Home Communication Corporation v. Network Productions, Inc.*, 902 F.2d 829 (11th Cir. 1990); *Sega Enterprises Ltd. v.* MAPHIA, 948 F. Supp. 923 (N.D. Cal. 1996).

[18] 35 U.S.C.§ 271(c)(2000) states, "[w]hoever offers to sell or sells within the United States or imports into the United States a component of a patented machine, manufacture, combination or composition, or a material or apparatus for use in practicing a patented process, constituting a material part of the invention, knowing the same to be especially made or especially adapted for use in an infringement of such patent, and *not a staple article or commodity of commerce suitable for substantial non-infringing use*, shall be liable as a contributory infringer." [Emphasis added.]

[19] See above note 16, at 442.

file-sharing technology.[20] The convergence of these two has inevitably put the development of technology and content at the very least, on a path of confrontation.

In 2001, the U.S. Court of Appeals for the Ninth Circuit got the first taste of this challenge in *A&M Records v. Napster*, the first known peer-to-peer file-sharing case.[21] Here, the court was asked to reverse the lower court's grant of a preliminary injunction, which, if sustained, would have effectively shut down the entire operation of a highly popular, albeit mostly illegal web file-swapping service. Note that the alleged infringing acts in this case (*i.e.*, the actual file-share or file transfer, which involved both unauthorised duplication and distribution of copyrighted materials) were done by the end-users themselves, not Napster. Napster, however, did maintain a centralised server to work as a master index so that different users were able to identify what files were available and with whom they could exchange files. As a result, the court only needed to deal with the issues of secondary infringement and liability and it eventually affirmed the district court's injunction.[22]

On contributory liability, Napster was found to have actual knowledge of infringing activities; its software and services constituted a material contribution to the infringement. The court specifically stated that "if a computer system operator learns of specific infringing material available on his system and fails to purge such material from the system, the operator knows of and contributes to direct infringement."[23] The Ninth Circuit went on to conclude that "Napster has *actual*

---

[20] MP3 originates from a 1987 research and development project on high quality and low bit-rate audio coding technology code named "EUREKA Project EU 147, Digital Audio Broadcasting (or DAB)" at the Fraunhofer Institut of Integrierte Schaltungen (or Fraunhofer IIS-A, which is part of the prestigious Fraunhofer Gesellschaft) of Germany. Through collaborations between Dr. Karlheinz Brandenburg (who is now often referred to as the father of MP3) of Fraunhofer IIS-A and Professor Dieter Seitzer of the University of Erlangen near Nuremberg, Germany, with subsequent contribution from Professor Heinz Gerhäuser, their team eventually developed a successful compression/decompression algorithm that enables fast transmission of audio files over a computer network while preserving the original sound quality, all within the environment or confine of limited bandwidth and storage space. In 1989, Fraunhofer received a German patent over this technology and in 1991 it submitted the invention for standard certification. The case was taken up and reviewed by the Moving Pictures Expert Group (MPEG, established in 1988 as a subcommittee of the International Standards Organization /International Electrotechnical Commission, ISO/IEC). In 1992, it was first integrated into the MPEG-1 video compression standard (for low bandwidth), with the audio portion being recognised as ISO-MPEG Audio Layer-3, hence the abbreviation "MP3." On 26 November 1999, the U.S. Patent and Trademark Office issued U.S. Patent No. 5,579,430 to MP3 (entitled "Digital Encoding Process"), which listed Bernhard Grill, Karlheinz Brandenburg, Thomas Sporer, Bernd Kurten, and Ernst Eberlein as its co-inventors. In September 1998, Fraunhofer started to enforce its patent rights. All developers of MP3 encoders or rippers and decoders/players now have to pay a licensing fee to Fraunhofer.

[21] 239 F.3d 1004 (9th Cir. 2001). The Ninth Circuit affirmed in part, reversed in part the original injunctive relief and remanded the case to the district court on certain procedural/technical matters.

[22] 284 F.3d 1091 (9th Cir. 2002).

[23] See above note 21, at 1021.

knowledge that *specific* infringing material is available using its system, that it could block access to the system by suppliers of the infringing material, and that it failed to remove the material."[24]

On vicarious liability, Napster was found to have enjoyed financial benefit from the infringement and has the right and ability to police its system, or, to put it differently, to supervise the infringing conduct by blocking end users' access to the Napster service. The Ninth Circuit interpreted *Sony Betamax* to be a defence applicable *only* when the device or software manufacturer has no actual, specific knowledge of infringement in the first place.

Against the defence of "staple article of commerce" brought out by *Sony Betamax*, the court here was "compelled" to distinguish between the architecture of the system itself and Napster's conduct in relation to the operational capacity of that system. This, as it turned out, eventually affected the U.S. Supreme Court's later decision when that court was confronted with an even more difficult technological challenge.

Incidentally, as a tactical manoeuvre, Napster had indeed raised the affirmative defence of fair use. It claimed fair use under the following circumstances: "sampling", where users made temporary copies of a work before purchasing; "space-shifting," where users accessed a sound recording through the Napster system that they already owned in audio CD format; and permissive distribution of recordings by both new and established artists. The Ninth Circuit, however, discounted each of Napster's arguments. In reply to the argument that the music industry had not shown a significant loss of volume of its existing sales (at that time), the court specifically declared that the "lack of harm to an established market cannot deprive the copyright holder of the right to develop alternative markets for the works."[25]

In the face of insurmountable legal hurdles and mounting legal bills and other suits, Napster eventually shut down its entire operations, and went into bankruptcy. Then, its name first was bought by a former rival, the German media conglomerate Bertelsmann AG. Subsequently, it was repurchased, reformed, transformed and its doors were finally reopened as a business for legitimate online music exchange.[26]

---

[24] Id., at 1022.

[25] Id., at 1017.

[26] Napster is now a paid-subscription online music provider publicly traded on the NASDAQ. Since 19 May 2003, it has been under the management of Roxio Corporation, which bought the name brand and virtually all interests of Napster at a bankruptcy auction from Press*play*, a joint venture between Universal Music Group (UMG) and Sony Music Entertainment, restructured as Sony BMG Music Entertainment (SBME) since 5 August 2004 after its merger with BMG. SBME remains wholly owned by Bertelsmann AG. Note that the record label EMI initially joined with UMG to sue Bertelsmann AG and Hummer Winblad Venture Partners (the venture capital firm which once funded Napster) in February 2003 in the federal district court in New York, claiming that by investing US$60 million in Napster, Bertelsmann AG was, in effect, promoting piracy and infringing on the copyright of their music. This case was eventually settled with the formation of the Press*play* joint venture. See *Jeff Leeds*, Music Industry Turns to Napster Creator for Help, NEW YORK TIMES, December 3, 2004, at C1.

VI. The Aimster Case—A twist but no cigar

While the Ninth Circuit was wrestling with the challenges brought on by the Napster phenomenon,, a somewhat different kind of peer-to-peer file-sharing software emerged elsewhere. Less than two years later, the U.S. Court of Appeals for the Seventh Circuit in Chicago, Illinois owns presented with *In re Aimster*, a case that involved end users using a software provider's instant messaging (IM) service to transmit encrypted copyright-infringing attachments.[27] The court only addressed the contributory liability issue here and affirmed the lower court's preliminary injunction. The Seventh Circuit rejected Aimster's argument that the encrypted attachment prevented it from having knowledge of the infringing activity, and concluded, instead, that it was merely an attempt to avoid liability by remaining purposely ignorant of the infringement. "[W]illful blindness is knowledge, in copyright law ... as it is in the law generally"[28] so declared the court. The court tried to make it clear that its decision was not against the use of encryption *per se* ("Encryption fosters privacy, and privacy is a social benefit, though also a source of social costs.")[29] but rather "a service provider that would otherwise be a contributory infringer does not obtain immunity by using encryption to shield itself from actual knowledge of the unlawful purposes for which the service is being used."[30] Given that the software's tutorial showed how it was to be used and that it had only included copyrighted music files; the fact that Aimster did provide a paid service to enable subscribers download copyrighted materials, Aimster was found to have sufficient knowledge.

What makes this case interesting is that the court (*i.e.*, Judge Richard A. Posner in particular) took a swipe at the Ninth Circuit's approach, and hence, the Supreme Court's rationale in the *Sony Betamax* case. Coming from the legal-economic point of view, the court held that it was not enough for a defendant to show that a product or service was physically capable of a non-infringing use. Even if such substantial non-infringing uses could be shown, Aimster would still have to show that it would have been disproportionately costly for it to eliminate or at least reduce substantially the non-infringing uses. Therefore, to raise a successful defence, Aimster had to show that its software "is widely used for legitimate, unobjectionable purposes," and the court needed not give precise content to the question of how much use was commercially significant.[31] Here, the court found that Aimster failed to present evidence that the added encryption capability *effective against the service provider itself* added important value to the service or saved significant costs. Thus, encryption serves were no cover for Aimster to hide behind the *Sony-Betamax* defence.

The Seventh Circuit clearly departed from the Ninth Circuit's interpretation of the *Sony Betamax* defence. Evidence of cost-effectiveness or probability, *i.e.*, how "probable" the non-infringing uses of a product were, had to be introduced

---

[27] 334 F.3d 643 (7th Cir. 2003).
[28] Id., at 650.
[29] Id.
[30] Id., at 650-651.
[31] Id., at 648, 653.

even in light of commercially significant non-infringing use and the lack of actual or specific knowledge of infringing activity. These diverse points of view, in fact, set the stage for the U.S. Supreme Court to revisit its *Sony Betamax* ruling after two decades.

VII. MGM v. Grokster—Decentralised file-sharing and Inducement

I notice a cat and mouse game being played by software developers. As soon as any technological device is struck down by the courts for infringement, a new version is just as quickly innovated to overcome legal objections. Looking at the Napster example, whilst it was in the midst of full-scale legal battles with the music industry, thanks in part to the prevalence of the broad bandwidth of Internet capacity and burgeoning usage, newer and faster peer-to-peer software were already emerging, ready to seize the advantage from Napster's downfall.[32] Two of the most popular of such software names are Grokster and Morpheus. Although the software can be used for any kind of electronic or digital file exchange, it appears most of their users use the software to swap copyrighted audio and/or video files without authorisation. Thus, in *Metro-Goldwyn-Mayer Studios, Inc. v. Grokster, Ltd.*, the American federal courts were once again confronted with the legality of these latest technological developments.[33] From the technological point of view, the most significant difference between these newer software packages and Napster or Aimster was that the newer versions did not require a centralised server to police file exchanges; this both increased the speed and reduced the risk of service disruption should a server fail.[34]

As expected, the defendants used the *Sony Betamax* arguments as their primary defence, arguing that distribution of a commercial product capable of substantial non-infringing uses could not give rise to contributory liability for infringement unless the distributor armed actual knowledge of specific instances of infringement had failed to act on that knowledge. The district court agreed with this

---

[32] *Tom Spring*, Napster Fans Find Lively Alternative—For Now As FastTrack's Popularity Grows, Napster's Old Foes Gear Up For A New Fight, PC World, 12 July 2001, available at http://www.pcworld.com/news/article/0,aid,55006,00.asp.

[33] 125 S.Ct. 2764 (2005).

[34] Grokster uses the so-called FastTrack technology. On its network, the user's request goes to a computer given an indexing capacity by the software and designated a "supernode," or to some other computer with comparable power and capacity to collect temporary indexes of the files available on the computers of users connected to it. The supernode (or indexing computer) searches its own index and may communicate the search request to other supernodes. If the file is found, the supernode discloses its location to the computer requesting it, and the requesting user can download the file directly from the computer located. The copied file is placed in a designated sharing folder on the requesting user's computer, where it is available for other users to download in turn, along with any other file in that folder. On the other hand, Morpheus, developed by another defendant, StreamCast, uses the Gnutella technology, similar in terms of function and structure to FastTrack but with no "supernodes" being used in some versions. In these versions, peer computers using the software protocol communicate directly with each other. When a user enters a search request into the Morpheus software, it sends the request to computers connected with it, which in turn pass the request along to other connected peers. The search results are communicated to the requesting computer, and the user can download desired files directly from peers' computers. See Id., at 125 S.Ct. 2771.

assessment.[35] Apparently impressed by the decentralised architecture software design, the Ninth Circuit also accepted the defendants' argument and affirmed the district court's ruling, holding that they had no actual or constructive knowledge and did not materially contribute to the infringement. On vicarious liability, the Ninth Circuit held that there was no evidence on defendants' right and ability to supervise their users. In fact, the defendants did not operate and design an "integrated service," which they monitored and controlled. Given the lack of a registration and log-in process, the Ninth Circuit held that the defendants had no ability to block or actually terminate access to file sharing functions.[36]

Thinking the Ninth Circuit read too broadly into the *Sony Betamax* defences, the U.S. Supreme Court, however, unanimously vacated the Ninth Circuit's decision and remanded the case back to the district court. To clarify, the Supreme Court held that *Sony Betamax* barred secondary liability based on presuming or imputing intent to cause infringement solely from the design or distribution of a product capable of substantial lawful use, which the distributor knows is in fact used for infringement. This does not mean that whenever a product is capable of substantial lawful use, the producer can never be held to be contributorily liable for third parties' infringing use of it.[37] "Nothing in *Sony* requires courts to ignore evidence of intent if there is such evidence, and the case was never meant to foreclose rules of fault-based liability derived from the common law."[38] Thus, the Supreme Court simply chose not to further elaborate on *Sony Betamax*, especially the "staple articles of commerce" exceptions to contributory and vicarious liability, but focused instead on "intentional inducement" as a separate category of secondary liability, *i.e.*, when one induces commission of infringement by another, or entices or persuades another to infringe.[39] Here the Supreme Court formally adopted the "intentional inducement" doctrine by declaring that "one who distributes a device with the object of promoting its use to infringe copyright, as shown by clear expression or other affirmative steps taken to foster infringement, is liable for the resulting acts of infringement by third parties."[40]

---

[35] 259 F.Supp.2d 1029 (C.D.Cal. 2003).

[36] 380 F.3d 1154 (9th Cir. 2004). The Ninth Circuit made a distinction between centralised and decentralised architecture of defendants' software design, and did not apply its own ruling in the *Napster* case. Nor did it accept the holding from the Seventh Circuit in *Aimster*. As a result, this diversity of opinions provided the opportunity and paved the way for the U.S. Supreme Court to review its *Sony Betamax* decision.

[37] See above note 33, at 2778.

[38] Id. at 2779.

[39] Here, the U.S. Supreme Court attempted to make a clear distinction between *Sony Betamax* and *Grokster*: "*Sony* dealt with a claim of liability based *solely* on distributing a product with alternative lawful and unlawful uses, with knowledge that some users would follow the unlawful course. The case struck a balance between the interests of protection and innovation by holding that the product's capability of substantial lawful employment should bar the imputation of fault and consequent secondary liability for the unlawful acts of others ... Here, evidence of the distributors' words and deeds going beyond distribution as such shows *a purpose to cause and profit from third-party acts of copyright infringement*. If liability for inducing infringement is ultimately found, it will not be on the basis of presuming or imputing fault, but from inferring a patently illegal objective from statements and actions showing what that objective was." [Emphasis added.] Id., at 2782.

[40] Id., at 2780.

The Supreme Court was mindful of the need to keep its ruling from encroaching onto regular commerce or discouraging the development of technologies with lawful and unlawful potential. Accordingly, the court gingerly pointed out: "[M]ere knowledge of infringing potential or of actual infringing uses would not be enough here to subject a distributor to liability. Nor would ordinary acts incident to product distribution, such as offering customers technical support or product updates, support liability in themselves. The inducement rule, instead, premises liability on *purposeful, culpable expression and conduct*, and thus does nothing to compromise legitimate commerce or discourage innovation having a lawful promise."[41] [Emphasis added.]

On this premise, the court framed the key question as: whether it had sufficiently proven by the plaintiffs that the defendants had communicated an inducing message to their software users. The court believed they had. Firstly, each defendant had showed itself to be aiming to satisfy a known source of demand for copyright infringement, the market being former Napster users. Secondly, the evidence of unlawful objective was given added significance by plaintiffs showing that neither defendant attempted to develop filtering tools or other mechanisms to diminish the infringing activity when using their software. Thirdly, there was a further complement, *i.e.*, the profit motive, to the direct evidence of unlawful objective. Infringement by the software distributors was found on the high-volume usage of their software which then brought immense commercial sense to their enterprise.

VIII. The Aftermath of Grokster—The "Induce Act" Now on Hold

In *Grokster*, the U.S. Supreme Court clearly backed away from what a machine or device is capable of and turned its attention, instead, to the act of the developer or distributor of that machine or device. While backing away from *Sony Betamax*, the Supreme Court did not accept the invitation to adopt a more economic or cost-effect probability analysis from the Seventh Circuit, either. It seems that the rationale in *Sony Betamax* and *Aimster* will be secondary in similar types of cases in the future. This means defendants in future civil infringement suits cannot just turn a deaf ear to what is going on around their designed or developed technologies and still rely on the *Sony Betamax* line of defence. In other words, there is now a new "intentional inducement" category independent and separate from the traditional contributory and various liabilities as far as secondary infringement is concerned, and courts are required to first look at whether inducement is present before turning to other issues.

Grokster also trumps what Congress intended to do, at least for now. On 22 June 2004, several influential senators jointly sponsored and introduced a bill entitled "Inducing infringement of Copyrights Act of 2004."[42] The bill sought to

---

[41] Id.

[42] S. 2560, 108th Cong., 2d Sess. (2004). This bill has been commonly referred to as the "Induce Act." The six original co-sponsors of the bill were: Senators William (Bill) H. Frist (R-Tennessee), Senate Majority Leader; Thomas A. Daschle (D-South Dakota), Senate Minority Leader; Orrin G. Hatch (R-Utah), Chairman of the Judiciary Committee; Patrick

create a new type of secondary copyright infringement, *i.e.*, whoever intentionally induces any violation of a copyright owner's enumerated exclusive rights is an infringer and shall be liable accordingly. The bill defined "intentional inducement" as intentionally aiding, abetting, inducing, or procuring. "Intent" may be shown by acts from which a reasonable person would find intent to induce infringement based on *all* relevant information about such acts then reasonably available to the actor, including whether the activity relies on infringement for its commercial viability.[43] Meanwhile, the bill also expressly indicated that the doctrines of contributory and vicarious liability remain the same, *i.e.*, they will *not* be enlarged or diminished. While this bill was supposed to focus only on a defendant's intention and behaviour and remain technology neutral, it was obviously designed to deal with Internet-related types of copyright infringement.

The bill, as expected, was controversial and indeed generated quite a bit of discussion within the copyright circle immediately after its introduction.[44] It nevertheless quickly gained the endorsement from the Register of Copyrights and the copyright industries in general, but the Institute of Electrical and Electronic Engineers (IEEE)—USA raised concerns over its balance with fair use as well as research and development incentives.[45] The IEEE-USA proposed, instead, the outright adoption of patent law's *active inducement* standard, requiring the active inducement conduct instead of mere control, *i.e.*, an affirmative undertaking to induce conduct known to be an infringement.[46] Due to its controversial nature, the 2004 mid-term election, the budgetary process and some other political manoeuvring, the bill never got out of the Senate Judiciary Committee, but the

---

Leahy (D-Vermont), Ranking Member of the Judiciary Committee; Lindsey O. Graham (R-South Carolina) and Barbara Boxer (D-California); subsequently Senators Lamar Alexander (R-Tennessee), Hillary Rodham Clinton (D-New York), Paul S. Sarbanes (D-Maryland), Robert (Bob) Graham (D-Florida) and Debbie Stabenow (D-Missouri) also signed on as co-sponsors, all heavyweight members of the 108th U.S. Senate. It was to demonstrate bi-partisan support of the bill despite the controversies between technology and content providers.

43 Senator Leahy, in fact, tried to assure those who merely provide copying technology that they would not be liable under the bill because they lacked indicators of "intentional inducement," *e.g.*, reliance on infringement for commercial viability, and encouragement of distribution for copyrighted works, among other things. Thus, the mere manufacturing or selling of a portable MP3 player would not be reason to be held liable.

44 *See*, for example, *Declan McCullagh*, Senator Wants to Ban P2P Networks, CNET NEWS, 22 July 2004.

45 The Register of Copyrights, having consulted with various interested parties, eventually proposed amending the language of the original bill on 9 September 2004: "Whoever manufactures, offers to the public, provides, or otherwise traffics in any product or service, such as a computer program, technology, device or component, that is a cause of individuals engaging in infringing public dissemination of copyrighted works shall be liable as an infringer where such activity: (A) relies on infringing public dissemination for its commercial viability; (B) derives a predominant portion of its revenues from infringing public dissemination; or (C) principally relies on infringing public dissemination to attract individuals to the product or service." See Register of Copyrights, Recommendations on Amendments to S. 2560, available at http://www.copyright.gov/docs/S2560.pdf.

46 See 35 U.S.C.§ 271(b); see also *Hewlett-Packard Co. v. Bausch & Lomb, Inc.*, 909 F.2d 1461 (Fed. Cir. 1990).

U.S. Supreme Court apparently adopted, in whole or in part, the concept. While still using the term "intentional inducement," the fact that the court squarely imposed "liability on *purposeful, culpable expression and conduct*" suggests that the rule is now more in line with the patent law "active inducement" principle. It is unclear, however, what exactly constitutes "purposeful, culpable expression and conduct," and this vacuum clearly needs to be filled by later court decisions. Rest assured that in the meantime, there will be uncertainties. Recognising this, the court tried, as did the Congress, to calm the technology industry's concerns by declaring that the inducement rule "does nothing to compromise legitimate commerce or discourage innovation having a lawful promise." It remains to be seen whether this new ruling indeed has a "chilling effect," as claimed by some, on future technological developments.

IX. The Challenge—BitTorrent and Others

Even before the Supreme Court has grasped the full implications of the *Grokster* case, another wave of peer-to-peer type of technology emerged and was quickly gaining popularity. A representative of this new wave of technology is BitTorrent.[47] A significant difference between this latest software and the previous ones is that shared files are divided among many end-user computers rather than having one integral file located on a single server or one other computer. In actual operation, the downloading process involves information being divided into numerous bits while the same information is actually being uploaded to other computers at the same time. As a result, so long as there is a large enough shared computer network existing, this total resource sharing can in theory greatly accelerate the speed of file-sharing. In other words, the files passed on by the largest number of users also become the fastest to download: the faster a user uploads, the faster that user is allowed to download. The appearance of this software greatly increased the usage of online video file-sharing, the piracy of which had not been considered as a serious threat until recently due to the much larger sizes of the files and the time needed to swap.

As of 15 December 2004, just a few days after the Supreme Court decided to accept its appeal petition in *Grokster*, the Motion Pictures Association of America (MPAA) began suing several BitTorrent website owners, although the original creator of BitTorrent has not been targeted.[48] Clearly recognising that

[47] First developed by Bram Cohen in 2001, BitTorrent is clearly gaining significant usage since late 2003, particularly since Kazaa, another highly popular peer-to-peer software, was confirmed to have spyware and perhaps too many unwanted advertisements. See *Roben Farzad*, File Swappers Get Creative as Wheels of Justice Turn, NEW YORK TIMES, 18 June 2005, at C13. In addition to BitTorrent, eDonkey is another example of latest software gaining tremendous popularity.

[48] As of May 2005, the MPAA had sued more than 100 BitTorrent websites. The movie association has yet to disclose how many individuals have been targeted thus far, but BitTorrent's original creator, Bram Cohen, is not on the list. "The target of our actions is not technology," MPAA spokesperson John Malcolm said. "There are many legal Torrent sites ... that are dedicated to the distribution of public domain work and we are taking no action against them whatsoever." See Associate Press, Hollywood Sues File-sharing Servers: Action Aimed at Popular BitTorrent Site, 14 December 2004.

there are websites conducting legitimate file-sharing businesses (for either licensed files or those in the public domain), the MPAA needs to be selective in targeting the specific business owners in its copyright infringement actions. With the *Grokster* ruling, it is safe to say that future plaintiffs will probably be even more selective in picking the potential defendants. Therefore, this may be a factor countering the potential chilling effect on technological developments.

The real difficulties, however, may still lie in the very technology which BitTorrent or other similar software employs. By definition, the technology is content neutral. It is designed to facilitate the transmission of zeros and ones over the network. Therefore, assuming that there are no indexing or tracking devices involved, an owner of a website engaging in transactions using BitTorrent as the underlying technology may indeed be facing uncertainties. Does *Grokster* mean that as long as the website owner(s) does not expressly engage in piracy-encouraging activities or at least is discreet about its operations, *Sony Betamax* defences may once again be available, especially given that BitTorrent arguably involves both "time" and "space" shifting. Furthermore, whether or not a website owner may qualify as an Internet Service Provider (ISP), take shelter under the "safe harbour" rule and be exempted from any infringement liability, direct or secondary, is also questionable.[49]

In summary, while the introduction of "intentional inducement" helps the legal enforcement in tackling network-related piracy, it certainly does not resolve all the issues. While courts will continue to seek a careful balance between the right of content owners and the development of technology, technology developers should be mindful that their acts to promote a new technology may well be the determinative factor in infringement suits regardless of what the technology itself is truly capable or not capable of.

X. The International Developments

From the international perspective, on the surface there is no consensus yet concerning secondary liability of copyright infringement: None of the major international conventions or treaties, such as the TRIPS Agreement,[50] the Berne Convention,[51] the Rome Convention[52] or the so called "WIPO Internet Treaties" (WCT and WPPT),[53] contain any specific provisions on this issue.

---

[49] 17 U.S.C.§ 512 (a), (b)(2)(B)(2000, Supp. II).

[50] Agreement on Trade-Related Aspects of Intellectual Property Rights, as Annex 1C of the Final Act Embodying the Results of the Uruguay Round of Multilateral Trade Negotiations (Marrakesh, 15 April 1994)(*Final Act*), MTN/FA-A1C, 1869 U.N.T.S. 299, 33 I.L.M. 1125 (1994).

[51] Berne Convention for the Protection of Literary and Artistic Works (1971 Paris Text), 828 U.N.T.S. 223 (1972), as amended on 28 Sept. 1979, WIPO Document AB/X/32 (1979).

[52] International Convention for the Protection of Performers, Producers of Phonograms and Broadcasting Organizations, done at Rome on 26 October 1961, entered into force on 18 May 1964, 496 U.N.T.S. 43 (1964).

[53] World Intellectual Property Organization (WIPO) Copyright Treaty (WCT), adopted in Geneva on 20 December 1996, 36 I.L.M. 65 (1997); WIPO Performances and Phonograms Treaty (WPPT), adopted in Geneva on 20 December 1996, 36 I.L.M. 76 (1997). Note that WCT entered into force on 6 March 2002, *see* WIPO Copyright Treaty Notification No. 32 (6 December 2001); whereas WPPT entered into force on 20 May 2002, *see* WIPO Performances and Phonograms Treaty Notification No. 32 (20 February 2002).

However, a closer and more in-depth look reveals a very different picture: Secondary liability for copyright infringement has become not only a common, but indeed one of the most critical issues that international community both individually and collectively must deal with, regardless of the legal tradition of a given nation, be it continental (civil) or common law. There is clearly an international trend emerging, treating secondary liability just as seriously as, if not more than, direct infringers.

For instance, in Japan, the Tokyo High Court on 31 March 2005 affirmed the Tokyo District Court's decision in *Nippon Columbia, Co., Ltd., et al. v. Yugen Kaishia Nippon* MMO, holding that both the defendant company (which provided the so called "file rogue" peer-to-peer services) and its president Michihito Matsuda were liable for secondary copyright infringement and that the Limited Liability Law of Internet Intermediary Services does not apply.[54] Using the concept of "expanded scope of users," the High Court held that the defendants amounted to users in fact, and their act rendered the defendants "indirect joint tortfeasors." See also the country report on Japan in part B of this chapter.

In Korea, the Seoul High Court recently in *Asia Media, Inc. et al. v. Yang, et al.* (commonly referred to as the *Soribada* case) affirmed its Suwon District Court's decision that the peer-to-peer service had indirectly infringed on the copyrights of members of the Recording Industry Association of Korea.[55] See also the country report on Korea in part B of this chapter.

In South Africa, Section 23 of its Copyright Act of 1978 specifically provides secondary infringement liabilities, although it is necessary to demonstrate the knowledge of guilt on the part of the infringer.[56]

In Australia, the Copyright Act clearly recognises secondary infringement liability, and the federal courts have confirmed that as well.[57] With regard to peer-to-peer services, the Federal Court in Australia in its very first such case, *Universal Music Australia Pty Ltd. v. Sharman License Holdings Ltd.*, which involves the popular peer-to-peer software known as KaZaA (or Kazaa), held that

---

[54] 2004 (Ne (ネ)) No. 446 on Copyright Infringement and Damages (31 March 2005). The citation for the district court judgment is 2002 (Wa (ワ)) Case No. 4249 (Tokyo District Court, 29th Civil Division, interlocutory judgment of 29 January 2003, 35 IIC 354 [2004]).

[55] No. (2002) KAHAP77 (Suwon District Court, Seongnam Branch, First Civil Department, 9 July 2002). In a separate decision, the Seoul High Court held that the two founding members of the service, Yang Jung-hwan and Yang Il-hwan (brothers), were held not criminally and personally liable for the infringement. This case has been referred to as Korea's Napster case (although technically the two do not work the same) and received widespread attention in the copyright community of the Asian region and elsewhere. The Korean word소리바다(*soribada*) means "sea of sound."

[56] *Frank and Hirsch (Propriety) Ltd. V. A. Roopanand Brothers (Propriety) Ltd.*, 1993 (4) SA 279 (A).

[57] Copyright Act of 1968, Act No. 63 (27 June 1968), as amended by the Copyright Amendment (Digital Agenda) Act of 2000, Secs. 100, 101(1)(A), and 112(E). For the most recent decision on peer-to-peer problems, see also *Universal Music v. Cooper*, [2005] FCA 972 (14 July 2005). Here the Federal court held that the proprietor of the website (Cooper) was held liable for authorising infringement by knowingly allowing others to place on his website hyperlinks to infringing material and encouraging website users to access infringing files via the links.

Kazaa's owners and distributors (altogether six of the ten defendants), led by defendant Sharman License Networks, Ltd., took no action to rein in illegal file-sharing despite posted warnings on their website urging Kazaa users not to swap copyrighted materials.[58] The court found that each of the defendants was aware that a major use of the Kazaa system was the transmission of copyrighted material, and none of them had an interest to prevent or curtail that predominant use; if anything, the contrary had occurred. Each of the respondents was at least acquiescent in the use of Kazaa for copyright-infringing activities. Interestingly, in addition to holding that the defendants' action (or the lack thereof) constituted copyright infringement, the court imposed a duty on the part of the defendants (despite their claim that the backbone of Kazaa's "FastTrack" technology carried no centralized server, hence they had no control over their users) to employ technical measures (such as a filtering mechanism) to ensure no copyrighted work would not be infringed.

In the People's Republic of China (PRC), the Beijing First Intermediate People's Court (BFIPC) got its first taste of online copyright infringement in *Wang Meng, et al. v. Beijing Cenpok Intercom Technology Co., Ltd.* (also known as the *Beijing Online* case) in 1999.[59] Here the court affirmed the lower court's ruling that the defendant's unauthorised posting of plaintiffs' works on the Internet constituted copyright infringement and the damage relief ordered by the lower court was appropriate. This was the third known copyright infringement lawsuit in the PRC concerning the liability of an Internet service provider. Yet it gained national prominence from the outset. The plaintiffs were all celebrity writers, the defendant was the leading Internet firm, and the outcome would no doubt have a profound impact on the future of e-commerce in the PRC.[60] Instead of simply applying Article 2(1) Berne Convention (of which PRC is a member and such application would automatically supersede the PRC's domestic law), the court took a more creative approach and literally stretched the meaning of the existing statute to its limits (or, arguably exceeding its limits) to encompass online publication within the scope of copyright protection.[61] On 30 May 2005, the PRC

58 [2005] FCA 1242 (5 September 2005).

59 [1999) First Intermediate Zhong No. 185 Civil Judgment (17 December 1999). It needs to be pointed out that this case dealt only with direct infringement, albeit in the network environment.

60 For example, the lead plaintiff, Mr. Wang Meng, was one of best-known writers/novelists in the PRC. The case gained more attention by the official Chinese Central Television's national live broadcast of the entire trial on 18 September 1999. The names of the other five plaintiffs are: Zhang Jie, Bi Shumin, Zhang Kangkang, Zhang Zhi and Liu Zhenyu.

61 Article 2(1) provides, "The expression 'literary and artistic works' shall include every production in the literary, scientific and artistic domain, whatever may be the mode or form of its expression ...." Therefore, online publication can easily fit into this category as long as it meets other criteria for being copyrightable. Note that in later domain name disputes, recognising the insufficiency of existing trade mark statutes, the Beijing court did go ahead with the application of Articles 6*bis* (concerning well-known marks) and 10*bis* (concerning unfair competition) Paris Convention as well as the PRC's own Unfair Competition Prevention Act as primary authority in resolving the disputes. The court did not stretch any provision of the Trade mark Act to cover domain names as a protectable subject matter.

began to implement Regulations on Internet Copyright Administrative Protection, a new set of rules designed to clarify the liabilities of online services and/or content providers. Article 11 of this Regulation grants the governing administrative agencies, *i.e.*, the National Copyright Administration and the Ministry of Information Industry, the authority to impose administrative penalties on the service providers if and when they knowingly keep copyright infringing materials on their services. While the Chinese Copyright Law has yet to formally address this issue, and this latest Regulation only covers administrative proceedings, the overall trend nevertheless suggests that China is inching towards recognition of secondary liability, particularly infringement in the online or network environment.

In Germany, while the German Copyright Act (*Urheberrechtsgesetz*, or UrhG) does not specifically touch on this issue, the Federal Supreme Court has repeatedly held that the organizer or promoter of a public performance of musical or literary works, or the proprietor or manager of a dance hall or a restaurant may be subject to copyright infringement liability for another party's direct infringement, even though they themselves did not engage in such infringing activities.[62] Both contributory and vicarious liabilities are principles well established by the German courts.[63]

A court in the Netherlands, however, has held otherwise. In *Kazaa B.V. v. Buma-Stemra*, the Amsterdam Court of Appeals stated that it was not correct to assume that Kazaa had violated the relevant copyright laws simply by providing free and unlicensed software that can also be used for the illegal exchange of copyrighted works. Using photocopiers, tape recorders and CD-writers as analogy, the court held that Kazaa simply could not be held liable for infringements committed by malicious or ignorant users of its virtual copying device.[64]

In the European Union, Article 8(1) EU Copyright Directive requires *all* Member States to "provide appropriate sanctions and remedies in respect of infringement of the rights and obligations set out in this Directive and shall take all the measures necessary to ensure that those sanctions and remedies are applied. The sanctions thus provided for shall be effective, proportionate and dissuasive."[65] Article 13(1) EU Intellectual Property Rights Enforcement Directive further declares: "Member States shall ensure that the competent judicial authorities, on application of the injured party, order the infringer who knowingly, or with

---

[62] RGSt 12, 34 and RGZ 78, 84 and 86; BGHZ 42, 118, 127—Tonbandgerätehersteller. For a detailed analysis, see *Alexander Liegl, Andreas Leupold and Peter Bräutigam*, Copyright Infringement in Germany, contained in Dennis Campbell and Susan Cotter, ed., COPYRIGHT INFRINGEMENT-COMPARATIVE LAW YEARBOOK OF INTERNATIONAL BUSINESS, Special Issue 1997, at 162–164 (1997).

[63] See also the Federal Supreme Court's Video Licensing Agreement Decision, 1987 GRUR 37, 39.

[64] *Kazaa B.V. v. Buma-Stemra*, Court of Appeal Amsterdam, 28 March 2002, no. 1370/01skg.

[65] Council Directive 2001/29/EC, Harmonization of Certain Aspects of Copyright and Related Rights in the Information Society, 2001 O.J. (L 167) 10 (EC). This Directive is commonly known as the EU Copyright Directive (EUCD), and serves as EU's compliance/harmonisation effort with the two WIPO Internet Treaties.

reasonable grounds to know, engaged in an infringing activity, to pay the rightholder damages appropriate to the actual prejudice suffered by him/her as a result of the infringement."[66] In addition, Article 13(2) states that "[w]here the infringer did not knowingly, or with reasonable grounds know, engage in infringing activity, Member States may lay down that the judicial authorities may order the recovery of profits or the payment of damages, which may be pre-established." That "knowledge" is used to differentiate between two types of infringing activities strongly suggests that the EU recognises secondary liability for copyright infringement, at least with regard to contributory and vicarious types of indirect infringement.[67]

On 12 July 2005, in the wake of the U.S. Supreme Court decision on *Grokster*, the European Commission issued a proposal for the European Council and Parliament to adopt yet another *Directive on Criminal Measures Aimed at Ensuring the Enforcement of Intellectual Property Rights* and a *Council Framework Decision to Strengthen the Criminal Law Framework to Combat Intellectual Property Offences.*[68] If both the EU Council and Parliament should agree with the current proposed text, the EU would have gone far beyond the United States by making *all* intentional infringements of an intellectual property right *on a commercial scale* (in conformity with Article 61 of TRIPS Agreement), and *attempting, aiding or abetting and inciting* such infringements as *criminal* offences. Furthermore, when such offences are committed under the aegis of a criminal organization, the defendants may be punishable by a maximum sentence of at least four years' imprisonment.[69]

It is not surprising that this proposal immediately generated controversies across both sides of the Atlantic Ocean, with discussions mostly centred on the vague language of the proposed statute, such as what exactly constitutes "inciting" and what amounts to "a commercial scale".[70] What is not being challenged, it seems, is the fundamental concept that there is a need to level the playing field for secondary liabilities among EU Member States. Obviously only time will tell whether there is indeed a consensus forged to put forth a directive as proposed.

---

[66] Council Directive 2004/48/EC, Enforcement of Intellectual Property Rights, 2004 O.J. (L 195) 16 (EC).

[67] For detailed analysis, see *Rosa Julià-Barceló*, On-Line Intermediary Liability Issues: Comparing EU and U.S. Legal Frameworks, ESPRIT PROJECT 27018 OF THE ELECTRONIC COMMERCE LEGAL ISSUES PLATFORM (December 1999), available at http://europa.eu.int/ISPO/legal/en/lab/991216/liability.doc.

[68] COM (2005) 276 final (12 July 2005).

[69] This approach is quite similar to the U.S. where the Anticounterfeiting Consumer Protection Act of 1996 made copyright counterfeiting a racketeering activity under the Racketeer Influenced and Corrupt Organizations Act (or *RICO*), 18 U.S.C.§§. 1961-1968 (2000, Supp. II), originally designed to crack down on Mafia-type of organized crimes. *See* Pub. L. No. 104-153, Sec. 3, 110 Stat. 1386 (1996) (amending 18 U.S.C. §. 1961(1)(B) to include criminal copyright infringement to the list of RICO predicate offenses). See also *Phillip Stuller*, Note, How the RIAA Can Stop Worrying and Learn to Love the RICO Act: Exploiting Civil RICO to Battle Peer-to-Peer Copyright Infringement, 24 LOY. L.A. ENT. L. REV. 521 (2004).

[70] See *Bruce Gain*, Europe Follows Grokster's Lead, WIRED, 5 August 2005, available at http://www.wired.com/news/politics/0,1283,68418,00.html. See also *Kevin J. O'Brien*, U.S. Ruling to Echo in Europe Despite Differences in National Laws, Case to Have Chilling Effect, INT'L HERALD TRIBUNE, 28 June 2005, at 15.

On 30 June 2005, the Shih-lin District Court in Taiwan issued a judgment on the *ezPeer* case, holding that the co-defendants ezPeer and Yi-da Wu, its legal representative, are not *criminally* liable for copyright infringement under the existing Copyright Law.[71] Facing its very first peer-to-peer case in Taiwan, the court used the culpability analysis to determine whether the prosecutor's evidence was sufficient to show that the defendants either directly engage in the infringing act (unauthorized duplication or distribution of copyrighted materials) themselves or aided or abetted other parties (its members) to engage in such an act.[72] The court answered in the negative in both instances, holding that the development of peer-to-per software did not create the risk prohibited by law, either the Copyright Act or other statutes; that the software was not created specifically for the purpose of infringing others' copyright; and that there was sufficient ground for fair use. Furthermore, using an analogy similar to "capable of substantial non-infringing use," the court held that the ezPeer was just a new platform or tool of e-commerce making file-sharing more convenient. The case is now under appeal before the Taiwan High Court.

Separately, the Taipei District Court issued its judgment on the so-called *Kuro* case on 9 September 2005, another *criminal* peer-to-peer litigation in Taiwan.[73] Unlike *ezPeer*, the court in this case found all the defendants (the Kuro Corporation, three of its legal representatives and an end user) liable for copyright infringement and imposed various criminal penalties against each of them, with the highest penalty of three years imprisonment plus NT$3 million dollars fines (equivalent to approximately US$8.7 million). The court held, among other things, that while there was no issue over the legality of the peer-to-peer technology itself, its provider, however, could be criminally liable at least as an "indirect culprit" if the provider, knowing that the technology could be used as a tool to commit criminal offences, nevertheless drew on the particular illegitimate functions or features to promote and induce others to use the technology in order to receive financial gain. The defendants have vowed to appeal to the Taiwan High Court as well. For details, see the country report on Taiwan in part B of this chapter.

There seems to be at least three critical factors that have lead to the different outcomes between *Kuro* and *ezPeer*: (1) unlike *ezPeer*, the *Kuro* court did not distinguish between technology that had a centralised server from the one that did not nor was this distinction used to treat the cases differently (in fact, the judgment seems to premise on the ground that Kuro *did* have a centralised system to check on the identity or membership of its users and what may be contained in each user's computer files); (2) records showed that Kuro actually had its employees directly engaged in the uploading and downloading of copyrighted works to

---

[71] (2003) Su No. 728 Criminal Judgment, Shih-lin District Court, Taiwan (30 June 2005).

[72] Note, however, that ezPeer does charge a monthly subscription fee (equivalent to approximately US$3) to allow its members engage in unlimited file-sharing (primarily downloading of music files). Records shows that none of the copyrighted music files on the defendants' website are licensed.

[73] (2003) Su No. 2146 Criminal Judgment, Taipei District Court (9 September 2005), opinion issued on 14 September 2005.

enlarge the content of its online music database; and (3) strategically, the prosecutor in *Kuro* sued both the peer-to-peer service provider and a larger-scale end-user, and was clearly confident of a favourable finding for the prosecution. As the end-user was virtually assured to be convicted, a ruling in favour of the peer-to-peer service provider at the same time would be quite absurd if the court should adopt the *ezPeer* line of rationale—how could an end-user paying a monthly fee be guilty, yet the provider who had profited be scot-free? In all likelihood, the Taiwan High Court may well be the forum that has the final say.[74]

While many nations and regions are weighing their respective approach in dealing with the secondary infringement and liability issues, WIPO is also gearing up its efforts on this and other related matters, such as the intermediary liabilities of Internet access and/or service providers (IAPs/ISPs). While there seems to be a consensus among the participants that something eventually has to be done to harmonise the copyright liability issues, especially the standards concerning the IAPs/ISPs, at the present time, however, different opinions and approaches are simply too diverse to be digested into a single and simple format.[75]

XI. Conclusion

The legal issues and challenges brought forth by the prevalent usage of the Internet seem to put the advancement of technology and the right of artistic and literary creation on a collision course. Yet history has demonstrated that this clearly is not the first time such a conflict has ensued between content and technology. In the United States, the advent of cameras, radios, telephones, photocopiers, video cassette recorders, compact discs, computer software, and cable television had each generated significant impact on the evolution of the copyright law, both in terms of legislature and judicial developments.[76] Ironically, experience suggests that the best solution may lie not in the competition between technology and content, but cooperation and harmonisation of the two.[77] This requires at least the fusion of successful management, law enforcement, and an

---

[74] Sec. 376 (1) of Taiwan's Code of Criminal Procedure provides that no criminal cases having the base penalty of less than three years imprisonment may receive the second appeal. Since both *ezPeer* and *Kuro* were based on Sec. 91 of the Copyright Act, which expressly limits the base criminal penalty to more than three years imprisonment for unauthorised duplication of copyrighted works, it follows that the two cases cannot be appealed to the Supreme Court.

[75] See conference materials on WIPO SEMINAR ON COPYRIGHT AND INTERNET INTERMEDIARIES, WIPO/IIS/05, Geneva, Switzerland, available at http://www.wipo.int/meetings/2005/wipo_iis/.

[76] For a detailed illustration of copyright's evolution, see Paul Goldstein, Copyright's Highway: From Gutenberg to Celestial Jukebox (1994); see also *Jessica Litman*, Copyright Legislation and Technological Change, 68 OREGON L. R. 275 (1989).

[77] "Competition is not only the life of trade, it is the trade of life ... we co-operate in our group—our family, community, club, church, party, "race," or nation—in order to strengthen our group in its competition with other groups. [Cooperation] is the ultimate form of competition." *Will and Ariel Durant, The Lessons of History*, at 19 (1968). Thus, whoever can find ways to effectively bring what appears to be competition elements together in harmony is destined to be the winner. See below.

acceptable technological platform. For example, growth in the video rental businesses quickly took off after the Supreme Court's *Sony Betamax* ruling. Instead of being obliterated by the video cassettes and their recording devices, the movie studios turned out to be the biggest benefactor from this technology. While the record industry once again chose to confront or even deny the peer-to-peer technology and the perceived threat that comes with it, Apple Corporation's *iTunes* Music Store and the *iPod* product lines have choosen to embrace both instead turning a crisis into great opportunities for the music industry.[78] In a very short space of time since the inception of iPods and iTunes, this combination has not only transformed the company from a computer maker to a music and entertainment powerhouse but it has also added a major new vehicle for dissemination of pop culture around the world. Even online music piracy has dropped significantly in the United States owing to the gaining popularity of this product.[79]

There are certainly other factors that contribute to the effective curtailment of unauthorised copying and distribution of copyrighted works online: more flexible and ingenious licensing (such as "open source" license as an alternative mechanism and collective license by many universities), effective digital rights management (such as built-in anti-circumvention devices or software), and public awareness (education programmes). But it does show, time and time again, that a strategy encompassing both carrot and stick will probably carry the most significant weight and be the most effective. On the other hand, experiences suggest that by going after end-users with heavy-handed legal means, especially when not doing so at the early stage or when an industry is already created around a new technology, the plaintiffs run the high risk of turning the entire situation into a scorched-earth scenario and no one comes out as winners. Therefore, the introduction of secondary liability of copyright infringement, at least as far as civil liability is concerned, makes economic, logical and practical sense to achieve adequate and effective protection of intellectual property rights.

---

[78] Apple first launched the iPod in October 2003 with the hope to capture the existing MP3 listening market. In light of the fact that most downloaded MP3 music files were probably not authorised, the initial version of iPod did not contain any digital rights management (DRM) device, so that its potential market share would not be jeopardized. See *Leander Kahney*, Inside Look at Birth of the IPod, WIRED, 21 July 2004, available at http://www.wired.com/news/print/0,1294,64286,00.html. See also *Steven Levy*, iPod Nation—In Just Three Years, Apple's Adorable Mini Music Player Has Gone from Gizmo to Life-changing Cultural Icon, NEWSWEEK, July 26, 2005, available at http://msnbc.msn.com/id/5457432 /site/newsweek. On 28 April 2003, Apple launched its iTune Music Store after successfully persuading several major music content providers to license their songs to Apple, which in turn may sell each song for US 99 cents over the Internet. As of 12 July 2004, Apple has sold its 100 millionth song (Apple's CEO, Steve Jobs, originally predicted that this goal could be achieved within a year). Apple is currently migrating iTunes to the MPEG-4 AAC (Advanced Audio Coding) standard and introduced DRM into its newer iPod, which has since generated some controversies over iTunes' compatibility with traditional MP3 and other music portable players.

[79] See *Mary Madden*, Artists, Musicians and the Internet, PEW INTERNET & AMERICAN LIFE PROJECT, 5 December 2004; see also *Mary Madden and Lee Rainie*, Music and Video Downloading Moves Beyond P2P, PEW INTERNET & AMERICAN LIFE PROJECT DATA MEMO, 5 March 2005.

In light of the U.S. Supreme Court's formal recognition of a new "intentional inducement" category in addition to the contributory and vicarious liabilities in terms of secondary liability of copyright infringement, it is safe to say that when dealing with peer-to-peer type infringement cases, the U.S. federal courts will first examine the acts of the defendant and determine whether there is any indication or evidence that "purposeful, culpable expression and conduct" is present, regardless of whether the defendant has knowledge or control over another party's infringing act. Only when no inducement is present will the court revert back to the traditional contributory and vicarious type of analyses, which include the *Sony Betamax* "staple article of commerce" defences, *i.e.*, whether the sale or distribution of a device is commercially capable of substantial non-infringing use.

In summary, while there are still many unanswered questions concerning the future of technological development in the wake of *Grokster*, at least it is clear now that courts in the United States will be paying attention to the act of the alleged infringer, rather than the device or technology being employed. To draw from the analogy of gun-related problems, is it the gun manufacturer or the man who pulls the trigger that is liable for the offence? The U.S. Supreme Court seems to suggest that as long as someone has indeed pulled the trigger, if that is under the guidance, encouragement or inducement from the manufacturer, regardless of whether the manufacturer has benefited from such act, it will nevertheless be held liable, in both civil and criminal terms. Obviously this case will not solve all the problems derived from peer-to-peer file-sharing. Undoubtedly, more cases will come forth to challenge the courts to fine-tune the Supreme Court's rationale in *Sony Betamax* and *Grokster*. Courts in other countries are also taking hints from the *Grokster* rationale. While there is still no consensus over how secondary liability issues should be treated, the majority of courts seem to be more or less following the American approach. Regardless of what is happening on the legal front, with technology and content development not necessarily on a collision course, it is important to note that one way or another, it is the market, not the courts, which will ultimately decide what will be for our future.

B. Country Reports

Note: The contributors to the country reports are listed in the introductory preface.

I. China

Sec. 130 of the General Principles of Civil Law states "Two or more persons that jointly commit infringement and cause damages to others, shall bear joint liability." Joint liability imposes on each individual infringer the obligation to compensate in full all damages incurred by the rightsowner. Rights owners find the legal basis of their protection against indirect infringement on this provision.

In a Judicial Interpretation issued in January 1988, the Supreme People's Court clarified that "One who abets others in committing an infringing act, is a joint-infringer and shall bear joint civil liabilities" (Sec. 148).

In the "A Northern River" case before the People's Courts in Beijing, the judge granted judgment in favour of the plaintiff. The defendant, an internet service provider, had operated a website for literature and allowed users to upload text files and documents onto that website. The plaintiff, Mr. Zhang, had found his novel "A Northern River" there. The courts held that the defendant had failed to meet its obligation of monitoring the contents that were disseminated through its website.[80] This judgment was made in 1999, before the amendment of the Copyright Act.

A more recent infringement dispute concerns the use of music files in karaoke bars. In the spring of 2004, several local law firms in Mainland China, on behalf of some foreign music companies, sent warning letters to over 12,000 karaoke bars requesting them to cease the unauthorised use of their music and to pay damages. Pending judgment, the results are anxiously awaited by the music industry and the public.[81]

In an attempt to give a clearer understanding of a highly controversial area of copyright law, the Supreme People's Court in November 2000 issued a Judicial Interpretation on Internet Copyright which rule was subsequently amended in January 2004. It is now evident from the following provisions that both contributory and vicarious liability are accepted forms of liability under Chinese copyright law.

Sec. 4 of the Judicial Interpretation states, "An internet service provider who participates in any act of another person to infringe copyright, or aids or abets ... others to carry out any act of copyright infringement, shall bear the joint liability together with the others who directly infringe copyright." whilst Sec. 7 stipulates that "an internet service provider who uploads, disseminates or provides means, equipments or materials, knowing that they are exclusively used for circumventing or destroying copyright owner's technological protection measures ... shall bear the civil infringement liability."

II. Hong Kong

1. General

Under the Copyright Ordinance, the commission of various secondary acts in relation to an "infringing copy" are considered as infringements. An "infringing copy" is defined by Sec. 35 as a copy of a work, the making of which infringed copyright, or where imported would have infringed copyright or breached an exclusive license agreement relating to the work if made in Hong Kong.

In Hong Kong, certain forms of contributory liabilities relating to copyright infringement are expressly provided in the Copyright Ordinance.

a) Relevant Sections

Sec. 32—The provision of the means for the making of infringing copies amounts to an infringement of the copyright in a work

Sec. 33—Anyone who gives permission for use of a place of public entertainment for an infringing performance is deemed to be equally liable for infringement of

---

[80] See *Zhang Chengzhi v. Century Intercommunication Technology Co. Ltd.*, Gazette of the Supreme People's Court of the PRC, 2000, pp. 28–31.

[81] See *Xiao Hai*, Rumpus about Karaoke Use Fee, China Patents & Trademarks, 2004 No. 3, pp. 59–63.

the copyright in that work and the section also defines 'place of public entertainment' to include premises which are occupied mainly for other purposes but are from time to time made available for hire for the purposes of public entertainment.

Sec. 34—Anyone who provides an apparatus for infringing performances, any occupier of premises who gave permission for use of the apparatus and anyone who supplied the sound recording or film as also deemed liable for infringement of the copyright in a work.

Under all these sections, the test that is applied is an objective of knowledge i.e., a person has knowledge when the person knows or has reasons to know that the act of provding, giving or permitting will lead to an infringement of the copyright in a work.

Sec. 22(2) of the Copyright Ordinance is also relevant, as it provides that copyright may be infringed by authorizing another, without the licence of the copyright owner, to do any of the infringing acts and Sec. 22(3) makes the extent of that even clearer by specifying that it is immaterial whether the doing of the restricted act relates to the whole or a substantial part of it.

b) Who Will Be Liable?

An example of who falls within this class of persons may be liable under Division II the Copyright Ordinance are managers of karaoke bars. It has to be proven that they had knowledge or ought to have known that certain discs played in the karaoke bars are infringing copies, such as counterfeit discs, if their liability is to come under Sec. 33 as they would be permitting use of the premises for infringing performances or alternatively their liability may fall under Sec. 34 if they had provided the apparatus, i.e. karaoke machine and sound system, for infringing performances.

2. *Internet Service Providers*

a) Introduction

Hong Kong does not have any legislation specifically dealing with Internet Service Providers (ISPs). However, it may be argued that ISPs are governed by Secs. 32 and 34. For instance, Sec. 34 imputes liability on anyone who provides the "apparatus" for infringement and it may well be that ISPs fall within that ambit where the transmission of a work over the internet using certain software on the internet enables users to listen to or to view infringing musical audio-visual recordings. Sec. 26 of the Copyright Ordinance provides that making copies of works available through the Internet counts as an act restricted by copyright. However, Sec. 26(4) provides that the mere provision of physical facilities for enabling the making available of copies of works to the public does not of itself constitute an act of making available copies of work to the public. The issue then lies in what is construed as mere provision of physical facilities by the ISPs.

b) Hong Kong ISP Association[82]

Although there is no express law regulating the conduct of ISPs in Hong Kong, members of the Hong Kong Internet Service Providers Association (HKISPA)

---

[82] http://www.hkispa.org.hk

are expected to comply with the rules and regulations issued by HKISPA. As a self-regulating body, HKISPA formulates and promulgates policies in respect of regulatory and governmental issues involving the internet industry, and represents the internet industry in its interface with governmental bodies and the public at large. HKISPA adopted a general code of practice[83] on 12 April 1997 as guidance for ISPs' conduct in Hong Kong[84]. Regarding quality of services, it provides that "members are committed to quality of service to customers and to serving the interest of the public, including public education on issues related to the Internet." The Code of Practice's rules on illegal content or activities of ISPs provides that members shall not knowingly host any illegal content or facilitate any illegal activities, and shall cooperate with other internet service providers, users and authorities with respect to illegal content and activities.

Currently, there are no reported cases in Hong Kong where internet service providers have been sued for copyright infringement.

3. *Company Directors*

a) Introduction

Under certain circumstances, the courts will allow the lifting of the corporate veil by drawing a distinction between the personal liabilities of directors of a company—the actual ones who control the company's activities - and the liability of the company itself. In the event that a company makes a profit from engaging in activities that infringe copyrights, should the corporate veil be lifted so that the director is held personally liable? One of the legal propositions in support of lifting the corporate veil is that it is against public policy to allow company directors to use a limited company as a vehicle to make personal profits from infringements of copyrights. After all, it has been accepted that a director who commits a tortuous act in the course of his employment is a joint tortfeasor with the company.

b) Joint Tortfeasors

In the Sony and Nintendo cases, the directors' personal liabilities for the infringement acts were also discussed by the court. In the Sony case, the directors were held personally liable for a company's tortious acts since the directors had directed performance of acts with the knowledge that they were likely to be tortious. The facts had showed that the directors' active involvement in the business of the company, and their knowledge that the company was dealing in the illegitimate products that infringed the plaintiffs' rights. In the Nintendo case, the court held that the directors were the 'alter ego' of the company, and every act done by the company was really an act of the directors through the vehicle of the company.

---

[83] It is not mandatory that all members of HKISPA must adopt the code of practice.

[84] Other codes of practice include Anti-spam code of practice and Practice Statement on Regulation of Obscene and Indecent Materials.

In Hong Kong, company directors are commonly prosecuted for copyright infringement by the government.[85]

III. Taiwan

Contributory and vicarious liabilities for copyright infringement are brand new topics in Taiwan. As of May 2005, there had only been two criminal cases relating to these subject matters, the Kuro case and the EZPeer case. While the former is still pending, the latter has been recently adjudicated by the district court. In both these cases, the plaintiffs were the main music companies in Taiwan who had claimed that Kuro and EZPeer had infringed their copyrights.

1. The Taiwanese Copyright Act and the File-sharing Cases

The Taiwanese Copyright Act was originally promulgated in 1929. Since then, there have been 12 amendments, the latest being made in September 2004.[86] The Taiwanese Copyright Act has followed and is parallel to the developments and trends of international copyright protection. Both moral rights and economic rights of a work are protected, and the infringement of the above-mentioned rights is, as in other countries, subject to criminal and civil liabilities.

Under the present Taiwanese Copyright Act, there are no explicit provisions that would address the concepts of contributory or vicarious liability. Offenders are generally indicted for being directly liable. In some cases, there might be accessories to the same offence, but this is an application of principles established under criminal law. In the Kuro and EZPeer cases, Kuro and EZPeer were indicted as accomplices, not accessories, of the users who had engaged in the illegal downloading of MP3 files.

Both the Kuro and EZPeer companies were intermediate services for peer-to-peer MP3 transformation. They provided servers with file name search and IP address transformation services. The peer-to-peer users could download peer-to-peer software from the company's server to his/her local PC. After installation and connecting to the Internet, the users through the above-mentioned file name search and IP address transmission services offered by Kuro or EZPeer, could trace and access the other users' local PC hard disks, which contained MP3 files for download. Through Kuro's or EZPeer's servers, a large number of users via peer-to-peer file-sharing transmitted and downloaded tremendous amounts of MP3s. The companies were accordingly prosecuted for copyright infringement.

a) The Prosecutor's Arguments

The Prosecutor relied on three provisions of the Taiwanese Copyright Act to support his argument that Kuro/EZPeer and the direct users committed crimes.

---

[85] *HKSAR v Mega Laser Products(HK) Limited* [1999] 3 HKC 161.

[86] The latest version of Taiwanese Copyright Act can be accessed on http://www.tipo.gov.tw/eng/laws/e1-4-1an93.asp

According to Sec. 22[87] and Sec. 26-1[88] of the Taiwanese Copyright Act, the right of reproduction and of public transmission of a copyrighted work belongs exclusively to the copyright owner. Sec. 26-1 was a new addition to the Copyright Act, as of July 2003. The purpose of this new provision is to try to regulate the act of public transmission through the internet, and corresponds to Article 8 WCT and Articles 10 and 14 WPPT. Additionally, Sec. 91 Taiwanese Copyright Act provides that infringement of copyrights by reproduction is a criminal offence. The latter provision is a protection of traditional copyright works, and prohibits their unauthorised reproduction.

b) The Liability of the Direct Users

The users, by downloading files, were accused of having infringed the copyright owner's exclusive right of public transmission. The prosecutor based his case of infringement on Sec. 26-1 Copyright Act and claimed that the users, through Kuro's server, had rendered their own files (MP3) open and accessible to an undefined public.

The Prosecutor emphasised that even though peer-to-peer technology in itself is not disallowed in Taiwan by the Copyright Act, the act of downloading from another user's hard disk to one's own local hard disk in itself amounted to "reproduction" within the meaning of Sec 26-1; and since such "reproductions" had not been authorised by the copyrights owner—, the music companies—their exclusive rights had been violated. He also argued that the behaviour of the users (downloader) could not be deemed "fair use" by giving factual evidence that one of the users reproduced 970 copies of MP3s, which flagrantly exceeded the ceiling of five copies, set by Sec. 91 Copyright Act.

c) The Liability of Kuro and EZPeer

Kuro and EZPeer were also prosecuted. The Prosecutor alleged that not only could Kuro and EZPeer have predicted and expected the infringement of the peer-to-peer MP3 transmission, they were directly and critically involved and rendered assistance in such transmission and infringement. The director and the managers of Kuro and EZPeer were accused as accomplices to the infringement of copyrights.[89]

---

[87] Sec. 22 Copyright Act provides that: Except as otherwise provided in this Act, authors have the exclusive right to reproduce their works. Performers have the exclusive right to reproduce their performances by means of sound recording, video recording, or photography.

The provisions of the preceding two paragraphs do not apply to temporary reproduction that is transient, incidental, an essential part of a technology process, and without independent economic significance, where solely for the purpose of lawful network relay transmission, or for the lawful use of a work; provided, this shall not apply to computer programs.

In the preceding paragraph, the phrase "temporary reproduction... for the purpose of lawful network relay transmission" includes technically unavoidable phenomena of the computer or machine occurring in network browsing, caching, or other processes for enhancing transmission efficiency.

[88] Sec. 26-1 Copyright Act provides that: Except as otherwise provided in this Act, authors of works have the exclusive right of public transmission of their works.

Performers have the exclusive right of public transmission of their performances reproduced in sound recordings.

[89] Sec. 28, Criminal Code provides that: "Each of two or more persons acting jointly in the commission of an offence is a principal offender".

d) The District Court's Decision on EZPeer

On 30 June 2005, the Shih-Lin District Court passed judgment on the EZPeer case and EZPeer was found not guilty. The Court reasoned that EZPeer itself was not involved in any MP3 reproduction or public transmission and emphasised that since criminal law is the *ultima ratio* of the state to regulate the social order, criminal punishment should be meted out strictly in accordance with all the established criminal law doctrines. The Court suggested that the case (EZPeer) be brought before the civil courts.

2. Legal Analysis

a) Loading back-up CD music to MP3 File(s)?

It is controversial and disputable whether backing up CD music to MP3 file(s) is illegal or not. Generally, unless undertaken with the consent of the copyright owner, it is considered unlawful to back up music from a CD. The backing up of CD music to MP3 files has been identified as a kind of "reproduction". The Copyright Act allows one copy for computer software backup as fair use. However, the backup of CD music is not regulated in the Copyright Act. A Taiwan High Court case has established that using a home video recorder to make one copy of a copyrighted film for personal use—instead of for profit—should be considered fair use. There two points of view in the academic circles—for and against, on whether backing up CD music to MP3 files is within the realm of fair use.

b) Downloading MP3 files

It is the generally accepted view of both academics and practitioners that downloading MP3 files from a server or another user's hard disk is "reproduction" of copyrighted works. Such reproduction may possibly infringe the copyright of the owner(s), and may thus constitute a crime.

c) Intermediate Platform

At present, the Copyright Act has not regulated on the legality of the provision of an intermediate platform or service for MP3 transmission, In the Kuro case, the service provider did not offer its users any MP3 files, so the provisons of Sec 26-1, which was introduced by the 2003 amendment to the Coyright Act, are not applicable. It is currently an open issue whether similar types of ISPs may fall within the realm of "public transmission".

d) The Fair Use Exemption

The current legal issues regarding the MP3 technology confronting the legal community concern the scope of the fair use exemption under Sec. 65 Copyright Act. According to that section, fair use of a copyrighted work shall not be an infringement or crime. Sec. 65 also provides four tests to evaluate whether the exploitation of a copyrighted work is fair use:

1. The purposes and nature of the exploitation, including whether such exploitation is of a commercial nature or is for non-profit educational purposes.
2. The nature of the work.
3. The amount and substantiality of the portion exploited in relation to the work as a whole.

4. The effect of the exploitation on the work's current and potential market value.

Difficulties and contentions over the menaing of "fair use" arise when these specified tests are applied to real situations.

3. Related Issues

a) Internet Service Providers (ISPs)

Their possible liability has been the subject of much discussion in the local legal community. In the opinion of some experts, since ISPs have both the financial means and capacity to utilise technological devices to prevent MP3 transmission through the internet,, one possible solution to the current maze of legal issues may lie in the imposition of a greater duty of care on ISPs . However, no consensus has been reached.

b) Writers of Copying Programs

The possible liability of the writers of copying programs has also been mentioned in Taiwan. The cases in the United States, such as Napster or Grokster/Morpheus, might influence or even lead the opinions in Taiwan.

c) Manufacturers of Machines

The Taiwanese IP community has not given much of their attention to this other possible avenue of liability - should the manufacturers of machines be held responsible and the extent of their responsibility. Academic papers from other countries have been published introducing this concept, and their expositions would definitely be a good reference point should this topic become a real issue in Taiwan.

4. Conclusion

Contributory and vicarious liabilities for copyright infringements are emerging legal issues in Taiwan and these ambiguous issues though critical have only recently caught the attention of the academic and professional IP community. Reflecting on foreign judicial decisions on these issues that have come to light so far within this decade—the Napster case, the Grokster/Morpheus case, the MMO case (Japan), the Soribada.com case (Korea), and the KaZaA case (Netherlands)- and the stir they had caused not only with the local IP community but also amongst members of the public; and further, bearing in mind the Kuro and EZPeer cases, the author believes that these emerging issues will quickly become major concerns in Taiwan. More judicial decisions will be needed to shape the course, which may, in the future, even lead to modifications and amendments to the Copyright Act.

IV. Japan

There are no provisions in the Japanese Copyright Act containing rules on indirect, contributory or joint liability for copyright infringement. Case law in this respect has developed along lines that relate to managing a favourite pastime in Japan—the use of music in Karaoke bars.

1. The Karaoke Cases

Modern-day Karaoke machines allow for a wide selection of songs. The replay and "performance" of songs by visitors in an establishment with individual Karaoke boxes qualifies as "public performance"[90]. Until a Supreme Court decision of 15 March 1988[91], barkeepers' responsibility, and its extent, to the collecting societies for obtaining their permission to use their music and for it to be replayed at their guests' discretion had not been decided. This Supreme Court decision held barkeepers responsible for the necessary copyright authorisations given that they themselves set up the Karaoke machines for the use of guests and held further that their liability is joint in the event their guests infringed any copyrights. Subsequently, the collecting society, JASRAC, started to sue the lessors of Karaoke machines. The Osaka High Court[92] gave a detailed exposition on why commercial lessors of Karaoke equipment should be held liable:

> "Certainly, the Karaoke machines are not directly used or operated by the lessor. However, already the installation of such machines creates the danger that copyrights administered by the plaintiff would be infringed by users of Karaoke machines through public performances. Neither has the lessor terminated the lease agreement once it became known that the plaintiff was indeed suing for damages by the above-mentioned decision in 1988 because the users of the Karaoke machines acted without the plaintiff's consent and used Karaoke machines for public performances. Granted that the lessor did not positively know about an infringement of the copyrights administered by the plaintiff through public performances, the lessor nonetheless could have easily found out. The lessor knew or should have known that the lessee had not obtained proper permission of the plaintiff for public performances of guests in the Karaoke bar run by the lessee. Despite being aware of such infringement, the lessor did not terminate the lease agreement and the joint administration of the Karaoke machines. This results in aiding and abetting a copyright infringement by the lessee. Even if the lessor did not favour any copyright infringement, it has created the danger thereof by installing the Karaoke machines on the basis of the lease agreement. Thus, three points deserve mention in this respect:
>
> (a) The installation of the Karaoke machines on the basis of the contract of lease led to guests performing Karaoke by using the machines without the plaintiff's consent, resulting in an infringement of the performance rights of the copyrights administered by the plaintiff. For a proper use of the machine, it would have been necessary for the lessor to jointly agree with the lessee on an agreement with the plaintiff concerning the use of copyrighted works. The lessor was well aware of this.
>
> (b) At least sometime after the conclusion of the lease contract, the lessor should have made sure that a contract on the use of copyrights had indeed been concluded and if not, would have had the obligation to insist on the conclusion of such a contract.
>
> (c) Finally, had the lessee not complied with such request, it would have been the lessor's duty to terminate the lease agreement and take back possession of the Karaoke equipment.
>
> Due to the fact that the lessor took no measures to comply with the obligation to prevent copyright infringement as a consequence of the installation of Karaoke machines, and did not terminate the lease agreement despite repeated copyright infringements by the lessees, and also because the Karaoke

---

[90] Osaka District Court, 12 December 1997,—"Karaoke Box". Also Tokyo District Court, 27 August 1998, 1654 Hanrei Jihô 34—"Laser Disc Karaoke".

[91] Supreme Court, 15 March 1988, 1270 Hanrei Jihô 34, comment by Y. *Someno* in 1288 Hanrei Jihô 216—"Club Cat's Eye III". Previous instance, Fukuoka High Court, 5 July 1984, 528 Hanrei Times 308.

[92] Osaka High Court, 27 February 1997,—"Karaoke Snack Bar II".

machines were jointly administered, the lessor is jointly liable. The lessor has acted at least negligently in aiding the lessee in conducting copyright infringements. To that extent, both are joint tortfeasors according to Sec. 719(2) Civil Code."

The Supreme Court Decision on this matter affirmed such joint liability in principle and imposed an obligation on the lessor of Karaoke equipment to ensure that the lessee has obtained permission to use copyrighted material. In contrast to the Osaka High Court, the Supreme Court[93] limited the lessor's obligations to the point in time when the contract was concluded. Thus, there is no obligation to monitor the lessee's subsequent behaviour.

2. The File Rogue Cases

The File Rogue cases were all decided by the Tokyo District Court[94] and basically held that providing an Internet server platform that can be accessed by individual users in order to exchange copyrighted works infringes the distribution and transmission rights of the authors of such copyrighted works, and the transmission rights of phonogram producers.

The plaintiff in the first case was the Japanese Association of Authors (JASRAC), in the second case, 19 phonogram producers. The defendant was a company that operated a server in Canada. From this server, the defendant offered the following service: users could access the server from their computers via the Internet and download software necessary for swapping files that could then be installed on the computers of the individual users. Users had to register and obtain a password. Their identity was not verified. With the downloaded software, users could prepare their files to be transferred to the plaintiff's server to be stored in a common folder. The plaintiff's software then enabled users logged on to the plaintiff's server to tap into the common folder and select files they would like to transfer to their own computer. The files in the common folder were given names by the senders of such files. The common folder contained information on the name of the file, the name of the folder, the size of the file, and the name of the user. The defendant thus ran a sort of database on files that could be downloaded. The common folder contained not only files in the MP3 format, but also other files of films and music. The number of registered users was around 42,000, and the average number of people concurrently using the server, 340. The number of MP3 files offered in the common folder was about 80,000. The service was free of charge and financed by advertisements. The defendant thus offered a platform for the copying activities of its users, yet did not engage in these activities itself. According to the court, while the defendant did not physically engage in any copying activities, it was not a disinterested third party, either, and rather derived a profit therefrom in the widest sense. Providing the necessary software and running the server qualified as an infringement of the right of public transmission under Sec. 23 Copyright Act. "Transmission" under Sec. 2(1)(ix^{quinquies}) also included the interactive transmission as "to connect with telecommunication networks for the use by the public of an interactive transmission

93 Supreme Court, 2 March 2001, "Karaoke Lease III".

94 Tokyo District Court, 9 April and 11 April 2002, 1780 Hanrei Jihô 25—"File Rogue I"; 29 January 2003, 1810 Hanrei Jihô 29—"File Rogue II".

server which records information on its public transmission memory or which inputs information to itself". In addition, the court found the defendant liable for contributory copyright infringement in view of the acts committed by users of the service. In respect of contributory infringement, the court applied the principles as established by the 1988 Supreme Court for liability of managers of karaoke bars in respect of performances of their guests as above.

V. Korea

There have been several decisions around the world about the legitimacy of P2P file sharing. In the US, the Ninth District Court of Appeals upheld a preliminary injunction issued by District Court for the Northern District of California shutting down Napster's peer-to-peer file swapping system. In Korea, a Korean court has held that the operator of P2P file sharing system, Soribada, had violated copyright law.[95] These decisions are all about exchanging music files in the MP3 format via a peer-to-peer network with a central server. As a general rule, the operator of the central server seems to be liable for the operation of the network.

On 25 April 2003, a US District Court held that Internet software distributors (1) were not liable for contributory infringement since it could not be established that they had material involvement in users' conduct, and neither were they (2) liable for vicarious infringement since it was not established that they had any right or ability to supervise users' conduct. This case dealt with the liability of the software distributor to enable P2P file sharing without the central server: Grokster and Morpheus. Both platforms operated in a manner conceptually analogous to the Napster system. In both cases, the software can be transferred to the user's computer, or downloaded, from servers operated by the Defendants. Once installed, a user may elect to share certain files located on the user's computer. Both the Morpheus and Grokster software provided a range of means through which a user may search through the respective pool of shared files. While this US case is the first case to deal with the liability of the software distributor for P2P file sharing with the central server, it will have much impact on the same issue in another country such as Korea.

The US Napster case itself was not against the users; it was brought against Napster (a contributory infringer). As the Napster court noted, [t]raditionally, "one who, **with knowledge of** the infringing activity, induces, causes or materially contributes to the infringing conduct of another, may be held liable as a 'contributory' infringer."[96] Napster facilitated the music copying by its customers, thereby contributing to the infringement of the copyrighted performances.

Criminal liability for contributory infringement is imposed under Sec. 32 Korean Criminal Code. Here, if the contributory infringement was of an assisting

---

[95] Suwon District Court (Sungnam branch), 2002.7.9, 2002kahab77 decision—"Soribada. However, after 22 months and hearings before three different judges, the case was dismissed in May 2003 on the grounds that the charges were defective (an appeal of the dismissal is pending). Private enforcement is similarly hampered. An appeal by the plaintiff to the Supreme Court was finally withdrawn after Soribada had agreed to pay 8.5 billion Won (8 million Euro) to the music producers in compensation. As of April 2006, Soribada has become a pay-per-download service.

[96] *A&M Records, Inc. v. Napster, Inc.*, 239 F.3d 1004, 1025 (9th Cir.2001).

nature to direct infringement, then knowingly aiding the principal offender amounts to committing a crime as an accessory to the crime.[97] Consequently, if in fact direct infringement had occurred and the subjective requisites of accessory liability were fulfilled, the contributory infringer could be punished as an accessory to the crime of copyright infringement under US law. In comparison, the contributory infringement provision in the Republic of Korea's Patent Act, unlike other national statutes, does not provide for subjective requisites of accessory liability, so it cannot be said that all contributory infringers are accessories to the crime of copyright infringement.[98]

P2P service providers like Soribada provide a service that allows their members to search for and download specific music works through their server. Most music works exchanged through a P2P service have not been authorised by the rights owners and a P2P service provider provides their service knowing this. For this reason, the provider participates in an indirect infringement of copyright. Therefore, in the case of a Soribada operator, the liability of a joint violator (contributor) can be imposed according to Sec. 760 (3) Korean Civil Code.

There is, however, a case to be made in respect of a P2P service provider who may not know about works that are unlawfully exchanged through its service. It is absurd that such services are cursorily dealt with just because there is a mere hint of an infringement of copyright. The imposition of too high a degree of responsibility on an online service provider might lead to shrinking of the industry itself, and such consequence conflicts with the general public's interest. With this in mind, the 2003 Copyright Amendment has provided for certain limitations on an online service provider's liability. An online service provider is "the one who provides the service that allows the copying and transmitting of works, performances, records, broadcasting, or databases of others through wire or wireless communications" (Bill Sec. 2 No. 22). Therefore, the operator of Soribada falls under the category of an online service provider. According to Sec. 77 of the 2003 Copyright Amendment, in order for this kind of online service provider to be exempted from or to have a lesser degree of liability regarding infringements of the copyright and related rights, the provider should fulfil at least one of the following requirements: the provider knows copyrights and related rights could be infringed through the reproduction and transmission of others' works, and (1) prevents or interferes the concerned reproduction and transmission[99]; (2) tries to prevent or interfere with the concerned reproduction and transmission, but it is impossible in a technical way[100]; or (3) and tries to prevent or interfere with the concerned reproduction and transmission, but generally and reasonably it is difficult to do so in terms of time or financial matters.[101,102]

---

[97] Criminal Act, Sec. 32 (1997).

[98] *Sang-Jo Jong*, Patent Law and Policy Symposium: Re-engineering Patent Law: The Challenge of New Technologies: Part III: International and Comparative Law Issues: Contributory Patent Infringement in Korea, 2 Wash. U. J.L. & Pol'y 287 n39.

[99] Sec. 77(1) of the Copyright Act.

[100] Sec. 77(2) of the Copyright Act.

[101] Sec. 77(3) of the Copyright Act.

[102] *Hyo-Jil Ahn*, Legal Aspects of File-Sharing System, Vol. 2 No.1 Journal of Digital Property Law 285–287 (2002).

VI. Singapore

In Singapore, contributory or vicarious liability for copyright infringement takes the form of a copyright action against a defendant for 'authorizing' the infringement[103] and a common law action called 'joint tortfeasorship'. These concepts of 'authorizing' copyright infringement and joint tortfeasorship have a narrow scope, as the case of *Ong Seow Pheng v Lotus Development Corp*[104] illustrates.

The defendant's business was in making pirated copies of manuals relating to the use of software, and selling them to one Lur, a software pirate. There was evidence that the defendant would hand one pirated copy of software to Lur, telling him to make as many copies as he (Lur) would require. In a raid, the defendant was found to be in possession of about 6,700 pirated copies of manuals. He was held liable for infringing the copyright in the manual and ordered to pay damages for these 6,700 pirated copies amounting to US$173,000 to the plaintiff, the owner of copyright in the manual. The plaintiffs were also the copyright owner of the software, and urged the court to find the defendant liable for infringing the copyright in the software, that is, for the 6,700 copies of pirated software which Lur must have made pursuant to the defendant's instructions. In essence, the plaintiffs' argument was that the defendant had *authorized* Lur's infringement of the copyright in the software. If this argument had succeeded, the plaintiffs would have received another US$1.5 million in damages.

The Court of Appeal of Singapore did not agree that the defendant had authorized Lur's making of 6,700 pirated copies of the software. It held that the defendant's supply of one pirated copy and suggestion to Lur to make as many copies as Lur required "might well have facilitated, and even incited, Lur's infringements...but that was not the same thing as authorization";[105] after all, the defendant had no control over what Lur would do. In coming to this conclusion, the court observed that Lur was a software pirate himself who "clearly knew that [the defendant] was in no position to grant the right to make infringing copies".[106] The court was clearly influenced by the fact that Lur knew that the defendant had no authority to grant him the right to make copies of the software. If so, the concept of 'authorizing' copyright infringement in Singapore may well be dependent upon the state of mind of the person committing the infringing act itself. This appears to be the approach taken by the English courts, too, which have held that "an authorization can only come from someone having or purporting to have authority to grant" the right to do the act complained of,[107] and that there was no such grant or purported grant when the party committing the infringing act could not reasonably deduce that the defendant

---

103 See Sec. 31 (authors' works) and s 103 (entrepreneurial works) of the Copyright Act.

104 [1997] 3 SLR 137.

105 Ibid, at p 148. The Court was following two English decisions, *CBS Inc v Ames Records and Tapes Ltd* [1982] Ch 91 [whether renting out sound recordings amounted to authorizing 'home taping' of the recordings] and *CBS Songs Ltd v Amstrad Consumer Electronic plc* [1988] AC 1013 [whether manufacture and sale of hi-fi systems which permitted recording amounted to authorizing the making of copies of sound recordings].

106 This was a finding made by the Registrar, and it was a finding that the Court of Appeal was entirely in agreement with: ibid, at 149.

107 *CBS Inc. v Ames Records and Tapes Ltd*, supra, note 26, at 106.

possessed or purported to possess any such authority.[108] Knowledge on the part of the defendant of the specific act of infringement (for which the defendant is alleged to have authorized) appears to have little or less effect on the question of whether the defendant has authorized that act of infringement.[109]

The plaintiffs also had another claim against the defendant based on joint tortfeasorship. Such a claim requires proof that the defendant has acted in concert with the primary tortfeasor (in this case, Lur) pursuant to a common design to commit the tort (in this case, the copyright infringement). The Court of Appeal held that these elements did not exist in the facts before it, when the defendant had no interest in Lur's business.

The *Ong Seow Pheng* case, by focusing the question of 'authorization' on the perception or belief of the primary infringer, may have implications for right-owners who are looking to use the concept of 'authorizing' copyright infringement to control providers of P2P file sharing technology in Singapore.[110]

In the case of libraries and archives which provide photocopying facilities, they also have the comfort of Sec. 34 of the Copyright Act: they will not be taken as having authorized any infringing act made on their machines if they affix a notice in a prescribed form[111] to, or in close proximity to, the photocopying machines in a place readily visible to persons using the machines.[112]

---

108 *CBS Songs Ltd. v Amstrad Consumer Electronic plc, above*, note 26, where the House of Lords held that Amstrad, the manufacturer of hi-fi recording systems which permitted recording, could not be said to be authorizing any copyright infringement because "no purchaser of an Amstrad model could reasonably deduce from the facilities incorporated in the model or from Amstrad's advertisement that Amstrad possessed or purported to possess the authority to grant any required permission for a record to be copied" (at 1053).

109 It should be noted that in the *Ong Seow Pheng* case, there was no clear evidence that Lur had made the 6,700 pirated copies of software pursuant to the defendant's alleged authorization. This was alluded to in the Court of Appeal's judgment: "There was no evidence of how many packages were sold by Lur..." (at p 149). Did this fact influence the Court of Appeal in finding for the defendant? After all, if there was no conclusive proof of the primary infringing act, how could the defendant be said to have authorized such commission? If this was indeed the case, the Court of Appeal's interpretation of the concept of 'authorization' is *obiter*. Nevertheless, this is the only judicial decision on this issue, and it is submitted that the Court of Appeal's interpretation will be followed in Singapore.

110 Compare with *A&M Records Inc v Napster Inc* 239 F 3d 1004 (9th Cir 2001) where Napster was held liable under the US concept of contributory infringement because it was found to have actual knowledge of specific acts of infringement by the end users of its file sharing technology, and had provided a server to support the technology. See also the continuing battle in the US between right-owners and providers of file sharing technology in *Metro-Goldwyn-Mayer Studios Inc v Grokster Ltd* USPQ 2d 1579 (on appeal). In Canada, see *BMG v John Doe* 2004 FC 488 (31 March 2004), where the Federal Court, following the Supreme Court's decision in *CCH Canadian Ltd v Law Society of Upper Canada* 2004 SCC 13, held that a computer user who places a personal copy of music file in a shared directory linked to a P2P service is not authorizing infringement.

111 The prescribed form of the notice is set out in Rule 5 of the Copyright Regulations.

112 Contrast with the Australian position where the High Court in *Moorhouse v University of New South Wales* [1976] RPC 151, found the university liable for authorizing the unlawful copying that took place on the photocopying machines provided in its library. For the Canadian position, see the recent Supreme Court decision in *CCH Canadian Ltd v Law Society of Upper Canada, ibid*, holding that the provision of photocopying machines by the law society in its library did not amount to authorizing copyright infringement in respect of the books in the library.

The exemption from copyright liability of ISPs is also dealt with by statutory provisions. Even before 1999, the Electronic Transactions Act 1998 already provided exemption from any civil or criminal liability for a network service provider (NSP) in respect of third party material in the form of electronic records to which it merely 'provides access'.[113] In 1999, provisions were inserted into the Copyright Act which exempt NSPs from liability for copyright infringement.[114] These 'safe harbour' provisions have been criticized in the following terms:[115]

"Singapore has fashioned a system which provides blanket exemptions from liability for service providers unless and until the provider is notified by the copyright owner that infringing material is being transmitted over its network. Such a system permits the service provider to turn a 'blind eye' to whatever is occurring over its network and apparently where it has actual knowledge that an infringement is occurring over its network. Even in this case the service provider has no obligation, because there is no infringement liability encouraging action, to take down that material expeditiously... Everything is left to the right holder; there are none of the incentives to cooperate in dealing with piracy..."

Under the US-Singapore FTA, Singapore is required to provide legal incentives for service providers to cooperate with right-owners in deterring the unauthorized storage and transmission of copyrighted materials etc.[116]

The extent to which third parties should be made liable for the primary infringing act is a controversial issue. But just as Singapore is about to make changes to require ISPs to 'cooperate with right-owners'—or, as the critics will say, enforce the rights on behalf of these right-owners—right-owners appear to have come round to accept that more effective enforcement of their rights may well lie in taking action against those who bear squarely the responsibility for the infringement, namely, the private users and consumers themselves. In the US, for example, the Recording Industry Association of America has turned its focus on the individuals involved in illegal downloading or online distribution of music. In Singapore, the Association of American Publishers (AAP) has warned the public that it would soon go after the individuals who bring books to be photocopied at the commercial photocopying shops. AAP revealed that it could track down

---

[113] See s 10 of the Electronic Transactions Act 1998. The terms 'provides access', in relation to third-party material, means the provision of the necessary technical means by which third-party material may be accessed and includes the automatic and temporary storage of the third-party material for the purpose of providing access; while 'third-party', in relation to a network service provider, means a person over whom the provider has no effective control.

[114] See s 193B (exemption from copyright liability when enabling access), s 193C (exemption from copyright liability when acting at direction of another) and s 193D (exemption from civil or criminal liability for removal of material from the network or disabling access pursuant to a statutory declaration from the copyright owner notifying alleged infringement).

[115] *Ficsor and Schlesinger*, "WIPO Treaties Implementation Globally: The Key Issues", *supra*, note 1. See also IIPA's criticisms of these provisions in their 2000 Special 301 report/recommendation on Singapore, *supra*, note 37.

[116] Art 16.9.22. See also the Side Letter on Enforcement. The Copyright (Amendment) Act 2004, which came into force on 1 January 2005, and the Copyright (Amendment) Act 2005, which came into force on 15 August 2005, have made significant changes to the 'safe harbour' protection for NSPs.

the individuals because most borrow the original books from libraries and their identities could be checked against the records of the libraries after AAP raids the photocopying shops and gets possession of these original books. The lawyer acting for AAP is reported to have made this statement to the media,[117] "Their [the individuals] first punishment is to pay the overdue library fines of books that have been seized. The next time, they might not get off so easy." It is reassuring to know that the challenges that technology has thrown up for right-owners have made them (or their lawyers) more creative in one aspect, at least—their enforcement tactics.

VII. Malaysia

Under Malaysian copyright law, 'copyright is infringed by any person who does, or causes any other person to do, without the licence of the owner of the copyright, an act the doing of which is controlled by copyright'.[118] In the context of contributory and vicarious liability, the operative word in determining infringement is 'causes', since Malaysian law requires a causal link between a person and the act of infringement in order to find that person guilty where he himself did not perform the act of infringement.

The Malaysian Copyright Act itself does not define the meaning of 'causes', and there have been no Malaysian copyright cases on point. Turning to the Commonwealth, older English statutes, such as the Dramatic Copyright Act 1833 and the Copyright Act 1842, also speak of causation in using words such as 'printed or caused to be printed'. The English Courts, in the cases brought on these statutes, decided that there was only a violation if the act complained of was done by the person himself or his agent. In other words, the relationship between the alleged infringer and the person doing the infringement is decisive; if the latter was an agent of the former, then the former could be said to have caused the infringement. In the case of *Kelly's Directories Ltd v Gavin and Lloyds*,[119] Gavin intended to publish a directory and entered into an agreement with Lloyds, whereby Lloyds would assist in gathering names for the directory, print it and lend their name to the book. Due to certain circumstances Lloyds could not complete the printing in time and Gavin arranged to have another printer print the portion that could not be completed by Lloyds. In this other portion, pirated matter was incorporated (unknown to Lloyds). The two portions were eventually joined and bound in the one book. The question at trial was whether Lloyds were liable for the printing of the pirated portion. The judge held that the agreement did not constitute a partnership between Gavin and Lloyds, even though Lloyds received profit share from the publication and lent their name as some sort of authority for the book. Furthermore, the printing of the pirated portion by the third party, who was engaged and paid for by Gavin, was held not to be an act done by an agent of Lloyds.

The later English Copyright Act 1911 does not use the word 'cause' and has substituted it with 'authorise'. Subsequent cases have demonstrated that the word

---

117 The Straits Times, 20 April 2004.
118 Copyright Act 1987, Sec. 36(1).
119 [1901] 1 Ch 374.

'authorise' carries a wider meaning than 'cause', and that the relationship of agency is no longer the main determinant of liability. In *Performing Right Society Ltd v Ciryl Theatrical Syndicate Ltd*,[120] Bankes LJ said:

I agree ... that the Court may infer an authorization or permission from acts which fall short of being direct and positive; I go so far as to say that indifference, exhibited by acts of commission or omission, may reach a degree from which authorization or permission may be inferred.

Thus, elements of knowledge or awareness now come into play and a person could authorise an act if he did 'sanction, approve and countenance' the act even without the doer being an agent or servant.[121] The word 'authorise' similarly appears in the more recent UK Copyright, Designs and Patents Act 1988 where 'copyright in a work is infringed by a person who without the licence of the copyright owner does, or authorises another to do, any of the acts restricted by the copyright'[122] and cases based on this 1988 Act continue to hold that where a person commissioned or approved the doing of an act (say of manufacturing) he would be seen as 'sanctioning and impliedly purporting to grant the right' to do the act and this would amount to an act of authorising.[123] It remains to be seen whether the Malaysian courts would adopt this wider interpretation, since the language of the Act has not changed accordingly.

VIII. The Philippines

A contributory infringer is "a party who, with knowledge of the infringing activity, induces, causes, or materially contributes to the infringing conduct of another."[124] On the other hand, a person may be held vicariously liable for infringement if he possesses the right and ability to supervise the infringing conduct yet he did not prevent the same, and he has an obvious and direct financial interest in the exploitation of copyrighted materials.[125]

The IP Code effectively penalises persons found guilty of contributory infringement when it provides in Sec. 217.1 that:

"Any person infringing any right secured by the provisions of Part IV of this Act or aiding or abetting such infringement shall be guilty of a crime ..."(underscoring supplied)[126]

Sec. 177 of Part IV explicitly states "copyright or economic rights shall consist of the exclusive right to carry out, authorise or prevent" the infringing acts enumerated in the section. In other words, any person knowingly "aiding or abetting" the infringing acts shall be held criminally liable under the IP Code. Thus, contributory infringement may arise in a situation where the owner or manager of a karaoke bar contracts a professional singer and the latter interprets musical compositions without the appropriate licenses from the right-owners. As the provision

---

[120] [1924] 1 KB 1.
[121] *Falcon v Famous Players Film Company* [1926] 2 KB 474.
[122] Copyright, Designs and Patents Act 1988, Sec. 16(2).
[123] *Pensher Security Door Co Ltd v Sunderland City Council* [2000] RPC 249.
[124] 3 Melville *Nimmer and David Nimmer*, Nimmer on Copyright (1997), Sec. 12.04 [A][2][a].
[125] Ibid. 12.04 [A][1].
[126] IP Code Sec. 217.1.

penalizes a criminal act, the owner or manager will be liable when he knowingly aids or abets the unauthorised rendition of songs.

In addition, the IP Code attaches criminal liability to:

"Any person who at the time when copyright subsists in a work has in his possession an article which he knows, or ought to know, to be an infringing copy of the work for the purpose of:

(a) Selling, letting for hire, or by way of trade offering or exposing for sale, or hire, the article;
(b) Distributing the article for purposes of trade, or for any other purpose to an extent that will prejudice the rights of the copyright owner in the work; or
(c) Trade exhibit of the article in public, shall be guilty of an offence and shall be liable on conviction to imprisonment and fine as above mentioned."[127]

It is interesting to note that Sec. 217.3 (b) may be applied in the case of companies providing peer-to-peer file sharing services. The fact that these companies keep files of unauthorised copies of copyrighted materials in their servers may already be considered as "possession" of infringing materials falling under the IP Code. These companies provide an avenue to obtain and distribute more infringing materials to various persons. The act constitutes distribution of the infringing article "for any other purpose to an extent that will prejudice the rights of the copyright owner" and the service provider may thus be held liable under same Sec. 217.3 (b). Similarly, those who obtain bootleg tapes, compact discs, and DVD for re-sale or rental purposes may be penalized based on the same provision.

In the case of *Habana v. Robles*,[128] there appeared to be an attempt on the part of the complainants to hold the publisher Goodwill Trading Co., Inc. liable as a contributory infringer. The complainants Ms. Habana, et al. were the authors of the book entitled "College English for Today". Respondent Ms. Robles was the author of the book entitled "Developing English Proficiency" ("DEP"), which, according to the complainants, was strikingly similar to the contents, scheme of presentation, illustrations and illustrative examples of their book. The complainants filed an infringement suit against Ms. Robles and against Goodwill Trading Co., Inc. as the publisher and joint co-owner of the copyright covering DEP. Goodwill Trading Co., Inc. attempted to avoid the applicability of Subsection 217.3 (which was then Sec. 29 of PD 49) by claiming lack of knowledge of the infringing character of the article. The Supreme Court found Ms. Robles liable for direct infringement. It was silent on the extent and nature of the publisher's liability, if any. The case was remanded to the lower court to ascertain the damages sustained and recoverable by the complainant based on the evidence submitted.

In some foreign jurisdictions, the concept of vicarious liability has been made to apply in copyright infringement cases[129]. In the Philippines, the concept of vicarious liability is more commonly used in torts or quasi-delicts. Sec. 2180 of the Civil Code provides for instances when a person may be held liable for damages for the acts or omissions of another:

"The obligation imposed by Sec. 2176 is demandable not only for one's own acts or omissions, but also for those of persons for whom one is responsible.

---

[127] IP Code Sec. 217.3.
[128] 310 SCRA 511 (1999).
[129] *Nimmer*, above footnote 45 12.04 [A][1].

The father and, in case of his death or incapacity, the mother, are responsible for the damages caused by the minor children who live in their company.

Guardians are liable for the damages caused by the minors or incapacitated persons who are under their authority and live in their company.

The owners and managers of an establishment or enterprise are likewise responsible for damages caused by their employees in the service of the branches in which the latter are employed or on the occasion of their functions.

Employers shall be liable for the damages caused by their employees and household helpers acting within the scope of their assigned tasks, even though the former are not engaged in any business or industry.

The State is responsible in like manner when it acts through a special agent; but not when the damage has been caused by the official to whom the task done properly pertains, in which case what is provided in Sec. 2176 shall be applicable.

Lastly, teachers or heads of establishments of arts and trades shall be liable for damages caused by their pupils and students or apprentices, so long as they remain in their custody.

The responsibility treated of in this article shall cease when the persons herein mentioned prove that they observed all the diligence of a good father of the family."

There may be difficulty in applying Sec. 2180 in copyright infringement, since the cases where Sec. 2180 had been applied involved negligence. Even if it is possible to successfully argue the application of Sec. 2180 in copyright infringement cases, persons may still be able to overcome this liability by proof that the "diligence of a good father of the family" had been observed.

Moreover, the application of Sec. 2180 is limited as it presupposes a degree of familiarity between the direct infringer and the party sought to be held vicariously liable; that is, "for those persons for whom one is responsible." This section may be applicable in cases where employees sell infringing goods or where hired performers make use of copyrighted compositions without authority. However, its application may be defeated by the fact that the performer is merely an independent contractor and there is no employer-employee relationship between karaoke owner/manager and the performer.

The Supreme Court has yet to clarify the applicability of vicarious liability in copyright infringement cases. In the FILSCAP[130] case cited earlier, the proprietor of the restaurant was sued when he refused to pay the necessary license fee for the playing and singing of musical compositions in his establishment. Since the Supreme Court found no acts of infringement, it did not hold the the respondent vicariously or contributorily liable for infringement. In *20th Century Fox Film Corp. v. Court of Appeals*,[131] the Supreme Court took the view that "television sets, video cassette recorders, rewinders and tape cleaners" found in a commercial establishment engaged in the legitimate business of lending or renting video tapes and, per se there is no involvement in piracy or infringement of copyright laws.

Unlike contributory infringement, the applicability of vicarious liability in copyright infringement cases remains uncertain. Without any existing precedent on the applicability of Sec. 2180 in copyright infringement cases, it would be difficult to foresee whether the courts would be willing to apply the said provision as basis

---

130 148 SCRA 461 (1987).

131 164 SCRA 655, 665 (1988).

for finding vicarious liability in copyright infringement. To illustrate, and even assuming Sec. 2180 is applicable, a strict interpretation of the provision will exclude lessors of bazaars from the coverage of the provision. The infringing acts of a tenant will not hold the lessor vicariously liable since a lessor-lessee relationship is not covered by Sec. 2180. In the end, the applicability and scope of vicarious liability in copyright infringement cases could only be clarified by the Supreme Court, by giving a more definitive ruling on the matter, or by Congress, by enacting a law specifically providing for vicarious liability in copyright infringement cases.

7
Looking Forward: Contemporary Trends of the Copyright Economics Research in the Digital Era

WAYNE FU

I. Introduction

Copyrightable goods are characterised as public goods by economists[1]. The public good property refers to the condition of non-rivalrous consumption, i.e. one's consumption of the good does not reduce its availability to others. The content of an intellectual creation can be accessed by anyone who so attempts if there is no effective exclusion mechanism. Free riders, i.e. those who do not duly pay for their access, unjustly cause costs (opportunity or actual costs) to the creator, and copyright is aimed to abridge the potential for this free-riding situation. To be explicit, copyright is a legal apparatus to prevent non-payment or unauthorised parties from consuming an intellectual creation.

As will be explained later, from an economic perspective, the enforcement of copyright is neither desirable nor detrimental in all circumstances regardless of the scope and context. Rather, from an economic basis, the optimal implementation of any given legal measure, including copyright, requires a careful calculation (at least, consideration) of all trade-off factors. What economic pros and cons should be known about copyright? How can the optimal terms and practice of copyright be determined, given a technological environment and commercial structure? Last but not least, how would the evolutions of the technological and business ecologies shift the optimality of the scope of copyright enforcement?

These questions are of paramount significance to scholars pondering the broad theme of whether and how copyright law and practice can contribute to the economy, domestic and international, as well as the overall welfare of our lives. Undoubtedly, the economic understanding of copyright and its current state is crucial. This article seeks to reaffirm the role and logic of economic analysis of copyright and shed some light on the common understanding of copyright economics. In order to do so, the author first would like to review the underpinning economic arguments about copyright.

II. Economic Rationales For and Against Copyright Law

Explaining the analytical framework of economics is very instructive. The objective of an economic study is to maximise "economic efficiency." In a nutshell, the efficiency of a good transaction is embodied in the realisation of the total net

---

[1] Landes, W.M. & Posner, R.A. (1989). An economic analysis of copyright law. 38 *Journal of Legal studies* 325-363.

benefits accrued to all involved parties over their combined costs. In the context of copyright, the parties involved can be categorised into copyright creators and holders, copyright users (legitimate or not), and end-consumers (legitimate or not).

Once an intellectual asset is created, the benefits that can arise immediately include the profit that the creator earns from selling the creation, the profits that all copyright users earn, and the utility that individual consumers receive from a lawful or unlawful consumption of the creation. The pivotal departure of the economic analysis from the pure legal deliberation is that only efficiency variables are considered, but not other dimensions which lawmakers or legal experts would be concerned about. These aspects comprise static efficiency, i.e. the maximal benefit that can be generated once a creation exists. Yet, the static benefit cannot capture the entire picture by itself. The entire long-term benefit of any intellectual asset further includes "dynamic efficiency", i.e. the payoff that a creator can expect to appropriate.

The static efficiency deals with the matter of how the actual benefit of an intellectual creation can be *optimally distributed* across those different transaction groups. On the other hand, the dynamic efficiency concerns whether there exists a sufficient remunerative incentive for encouraging creative production. As a rule of thumb, a large anticipated reward induces resilient innovation, while a weak one dampens the drive for such costly and painstaking endeavours. Taken together, the economic goal of copyright is (or should be) to achieve the maximum of the combined benefit minus all costs including transaction costs. All economic research analysing optimal copyright follows this conceptual paradigm[2].

Copyright inherently creates a legal monopoly. Textbook theory tells that the monopoly condition impedes the attainment of best efficiency, as monopoly is traditionally associated with limiting output and high price. But it may also be true that high monopoly rewards bring about the best intellectual creation. Conversely, with a creation whose right is monopolised, it may be that too little of the creation will be used[3].

Copyrighters suffer financial losses when their assets are pirated, and copyright law aims to protect creators from such costs. On the other hand, copyright protection increases the costs of users and thus hinders free spread and use of the creation. Therefore, in principle, copyright law is expected to reach an optimal balance between the two opposing interests.

Based on this, the scholarly undertaking concerning "this optimal balance" has borne fruit in various aspects of copyright and piracy: royalty contract, royalty fee, protection scope and length, risk sharing, fair use, copyright collectives, copyright and competition, copyright and antitrust, etc. In their analyses, academics do not assume that copyright violation is economically deleterious by default; instead they base the calculation on comparing its costs and benefits. Bluntly speaking, tolerating a certain level of "private copying" may be socially advantageous, especially if

---

[2] See Watt, R. (2000). *Copyright and Economic Theory: Friends or Foes?* UK, Cheltenham: Edward Elgar Publishing, p. 16.

[3] Cooter, R. & Ulen, T. (1988). Law and Economics. London: Glenview.

the transaction costs of policing and administering copyright-use activities overshadows the gains[4]. It is proposed that neither over- nor under-protection is desirable: the former leads to inefficient consumption and allocation of the creation, and the latter results in disruption of innovation incentives. Efforts for economists in structuring and implementing copyright law are, or should be, to find the best trade-off between the above two considerations. One important ramification is that the greatest payoff to society of an intellectual creation, no matter by whom, may come not necessarily from copyright protection, but from the lack of it.

Moreover, to economists the efficiency criterion predominates the equity one—that is, equity can be compromised in return for an improvement in efficiency. For economists, the beauty of equity is in the eye of the beholder; it is much less quantifiable and is hardly considered as a factor in the welfare equation. As Watt[5] briskly articulated,

> "The law and the legal profession is primarily concerned with equity or 'justice', in defining and attempting to protect personal property and rights, and in establishing individual obligations in such a way that the underlying society members live together in peace and harmony. It is notoriously frequent that the establishment of equity is only possible if a certain amount of efficiency is sacrificed."

These paradigmatic differences set apart the arguments of economists and lawyers, and underlie the disagreement between the economic view and the legal perspective in treating copyright issues. Arguably, either the creator's interest or rights users' can attract disproportionately larger attention or even emphasis in the public forum, depending on the political or business climate of a particular time. This is so when one party's gain or loss becomes easier to quantify (or to make a case for) than the other's. Still, in an economic welfare analysis, no side's interest should be prioritised over that of other stakeholders.

III. The Ignored Corner of Copyright Research: Is Piracy Always so Evil?

Media portrayal of copyright holders' loss allegations has preponderantly put unauthorised copyright use under a hideous light. Copyright-holding companies roll out far-reaching publicity efforts blaming the unpaid usage behaviours as the culprit for their sale loss and typecasting them as theft of property or, at least, unjust business activity. The public impression is spawned that "private copying" and "pirated sales" disrupt market order and sabotage legitimate sales, causing inexorable revenue damages to the copyrighters[6]. Side-stepping the issue about how unauthorized rights access is immoral or lawful, the revenue loss to rights holders as an overall outcome remains an unproven assertion.

All too often, the true scene is left undisclosed, which makes the public debate about piracy a one-sided story. As mentioned, a copyright product is a public

---

[4] Coase, R. (1960). The problem of social cost. 3 *Journal of Law and Economics* 1–44.

[5] Watt, R. (2000). *Copyright and Economic Theory: Friends or Foes?* UK, Cheltenham: Edward Elgar Publishing, p. 16.

[6] E.g. Counterfeiting is out of Control, The Herald Tribune, 13 May 2005: "The theft of intellectual property has become as serious for society as the theft of physical property...$600 billion per year in counterfeit goods...". Tellingly, the author, Maria Livanos Cattaui, is secretary general of the International Chamber of Commerce.

good, and by and large is characterized as an experience or network good too. As "experience" products, the copyright commodities like music, movies, other forms of media content, and/or software live on serious promotion and marketing efforts to survive and thrive. Word of mouth, reviews, purchase referrals, and the like are very critical for products of this kind to penetrate the market[7]. Diffusion through illegitimate duplication/sale acts as an "alternative" distribution channel and, in effect, fuels the awareness and, the adoption of the product and can stimulate legitimate market demand for it as well.

Private downloading and sharing of a popular music song helps spread word of mouth among listeners, and accordingly promotes the frequency of play in radio stations, which in turn propagates its popularity among the legitimate CD buyers. In a very recent study, Oberholzer-Gee and Strumpf[8] found that there is no discernible adverse effect of online downloads on CD sales and downloads; on the contrary, they may even boost the music sales in general. As another example, the value of sophisticated graphics software such as Photoshop is enhanced by the availability of a vast array of online tutorials donated to the public domain by private users. However, many of these users cannot afford the very steep price of a legal copy of Photoshop. Their possession of unauthorised copies, leading to their contribution of tutorials, increases the value of Photoshop to the paying customer, and therefore, in theory at least, should help support legitimate product sales. The empirical study of Hui and Png[9] also confirmed that the "beneficial demand-stimulation effect" substantially mediates the business theft effect of piracy.

It is worth noting that the advent of inexpensive and convenient copying technologies has fostered consumer demand for original creations and increased incomes more than it has injured the producers' long-run earnings. Some prominent examples illustrate this well: The availability of photocopiers in universities and libraries enhances the merit of a book collection and so boosts the demand for publication orders. Videocassettes for VCR playback, prior to DVD, once claimed more than half of Hollywood movie makers' total revenue gross, as more people watched movies at home, even though initially industry people regarded these as a big threat, worrying about private copying of their movies.

Consider an international case. The Chinese market has long been short-listed among the top pirate countries for American copyrighted products. Products "plundered" the most are Hollywood movies and computer software. Needless to say, the rampant circulation of illegal copies deflects many potential sales from the authorised businesses *for now*.

A curious question, nevertheless, is what would have been the case now if the piracy had been blocked altogether in the first place. Would the Chinese audience have become so fond of Hollywood pictures as they are now? Ironically, the

---

[7] De Vany, A., & W. D. Walls (1997). The market for motion pictures: Rank, revenue, and survival. 35(4) *Economic Inquiry* 783–97.

[8] Oberholzer-Gee, F. & Strumpf, K. (2004). The effect of file sharing on record sales. Working Paper. Harvard Business School.

[9] Hui, K.L & Png, I. (2003). Piracy and the legitimate demand for recorded music. 2 *Contributions to Economic Analysis and Policy* 1.

widespread availability of the cheap pirate VCDs and DVDs has effectively allowed Hollywood to infiltrate this market, despite the government's ban on general film imports and the scant quota for foreign film screenings. The illegal circulation has successfully "cultivated" a strong appetite among the Chinese masses for American productions. If not for this piracy, the demand would not have been nurtured and Hollywood would not occupy such an invincible share in the most promising market of the world.

Coming back to *Microsoft*, computer software is a robust network product. The value, or say, market strength, of a software product heavily derives from the size of its user base, which is the very notion of network externality. Computer users find a piece of widely-adopted software more attractive since various sources of benefits can be enjoyed, such as interoperability, compatibility, technical support, know-how and, of course, convenience[10]. Thus, even though the use of MS *Office* in China may not paid directly to the company, MS's worldwide user network is being enlarged with the person's recruitment, and hence the overall value of this software is enhanced, as commentators have observed[11]. At least theoretically, *Microsoft* becomes able to charge a higher price in all markets beyond China, as opposed to its rivals. In this sense, piracy can be, more or less, deemed a form of penetration or introductory pricing—a low or zero price during a trial/promotion period, which is quite common among software firms.[12]

Furthermore, history has told us of the wisdom that "piracy" is often a gateway for entering some counties' markets and is a prelude to the collection of huge dues, albeit somewhat late. When the market share is firmly secured, the program yield significant gains once copyright can be enforced, even at a minimal level, and some users start paying. This is increasingly likely to happen as disposable incomes in China rise, and consumers begin demanding the higher quality of original recordings.

As Liebowitz[13] pointed out, the new copyright economics literature has turned its focus to these "benign" effects that moderate the ostensible damage of copyright infringement. The research along this line will be a focal point in the copyright economics domain and will continue to flourish.

IV. Legal Copyright Protection or Self-help Piracy Control?

The fast-moving technological advances have made the task of maintaining and reinforcing copyright a very daunting if not impossible mission in the digital age. Copyright law can only try not to lag too far behind the pace of technological innovation in relevance and applicability. In light of the volatility of the technology and

---

[10] See Rohlfs, J. (2001). *Bandwagon effects in high-technology industries*. Cambridge, MA: The MIT Press for the latest survey on network externality.

[11] Png, I. & Wu, C. (1996). Piracy helps. Asian Wall Street Journal. 9-10 February 10.

[12] King, S.P. & Lampe, R. (2003). Network externalities, price discrimination and profitable piracy. 15(3) *Information Economics and Policy* 271–290.

[13] Liebowitz, S. (2003). Back to the future: Can copyright owners appropriate revenues in the face of new copying technologies? in Gordon, W. & Watt, R. ed. *The Economics of Copyright: Developments in Research and Analysis*. UK, Cheltenham: Edward Elgar Publishing.

business environments, copyright-holding enterprises have been increasingly educated about the advantage of self-control of their rights over the mere passive reliance on legal protection. Shapiro and Varian[14] in their seminal volume discuss a broad range of rights management strategies and tactics that businesses can leverage to reap the most from digitalisation while minimising the impact of the Internet on control of their products.

All sorts of pricing, packaging, and marketing tools enable the business to turn the elusive game of technology to their favour: Software makers can incorporate advertising functions in their applications, which still stream in revenues even if the program has been unofficially obtained and installed (e.g. Eudora). Shapiro and Varian [15] advocated the benefits for information sellers to tier up or version their product line. That is, the same generic product (or content) can be packaged into an array of different versions, each with a disparate price, quality and sales term. Within a line-up, some "economy" packages can be made available free of charge for the market. The low-end give-away pack, with modest functions and requiring some obligations (registration with personal information), can not only curtail the room for piracy but also stimulate consumer interest or even lock in customers in the long run. Premium or deluxe versions tap into the markets of institutional and high-end users and can rake in the bulk of the revenues.

Another powerful strategy to defy piracy is to bundle content or information which is vulnerable to copying with some complementary but unduplicable hardware or to make the software only operable on the machine. Thereby, the mere possession of the software copy is useless without the platform. The software can even be given away while the equipment is sold for a premium price[16]. This practice can convert peer-to-peer downloading and file sharing into a pot-of-gold opportunity.

Shy[17] observed that the software industry has gradually removed copy protection, which used to be the norm before, from its products over the past years. Program developers are now opting for less restrictive mechanisms for copy control on their products. The core reason for this was explained earlier—the gain from the value of an expanded user base is likely to outweigh the loss due to some degree of piracy. In developed countries, software or information vendors earn most of their income from institutional, but not individual, users, who rely on added-value support and service. Site-licensing has proven itself a lucrative and effective anti-piracy method to release software.

Of course, it would be not be realistic to think that self-management on copying control can outright replace the role of copyright law in levelling the playing

---

[14] Shapiro, C. & Varian, H. (1999). *Information Rules: A Strategic Guide to the Network Economy*. Boston, MA: Harvard Business School Press.

[15] Shapiro, C. & Varian, H. (1999). *Information Rules: A Strategic Guide to the Network Economy*. Boston, MA: Harvard Business School Press.

[16] Shy, O. & Thisse, J.F. (1999). A strategic approach to software protection. *Journal of Economics and Management Strategy*, 8, pp. 163–190.

[17] Shy, O. (2000). The economics of copy protection in software and other media. In *Internet Publishing and Beyond: The Economics of Digital Information and Intellectual Property*. Ed. Brian Kahin & Hal R. Varian. Cambridge, MA: MIT Press.

ground. Also, grave anticompetitive situations could arise from overtly lifting copyright protection, since players are in unequal positions (in terms of pricing power and technological feasibility) to execute the rights management[18]. With that said, if businesses can better administer by themselves the intellectual property of their products, it will alleviate the burden of incessantly revamping copyright law and its enforcement. Experience seems to suggest that *de facto* forces which develop themselves in the marketplace usually pave a more stable and sustainable path than choices made *de jure*, which sometimes risk disrupting the market by artificially selecting winners and losers.

In the emerging network economy, exploitation of the premium of copyright property in the information business centrally hinges on proactive value creation and smart customer community building. Opportunities of value creation will surface when products are made exposed to the market as widely, though smartly, as possible, and not kept exclusive to certain user groups. Think about this question: Does it facilitate or harm the publisher's sales when some part of a book is posted on Amazon.com for shoppers to sample?

In sum, the "rights-restrictive" approach in copyrights management seems to have become a historic vestige and is increasingly giving way to the "market-nurturing" approach.[19] The new mantra is: "If you don't give something, you won't get great things back." It can be anticipated that while the industry is embracing this regime, there will be less and less reliance on copyright law.

V. Indirect Revenue Appropriation

As copy prevention is ineffective and costly, copyright holding companies are seeking alternative ways of getting compensated for their creative effort. Right owners have demanded the levying of mandatory charges on manufacturers of copy-capable equipment, by which users can make unauthorised copies. Should makers of CD burners or MP3 players pay record companies for their users' (possible) unlawful reproduction and consumption of the songs? Should PC makers pay software developers for their users' (possible) software duplication? Should photocopy machine makers pay authors for potential losses from illicit book copying?

This latest industry development has engendered a flurry of controversial debates and spurred a fresh strand of research in copyright economics[20]. Pragmatically, this indirect revenue collection can at least overcome the plight of how to compensate the right holder, which has vexed policymakers. In some

---

[18] Farchy, J. & Rochelandet, F. (2003). Self-help systems: Good substitutes for copyright or new barriers to competition? in Gordon, W. & Watt, R. ed. *The Economics of Copyright: Developments in Research and Analysis*. UK, Cheltenham: Edward Elgar Publishing.

[19] Conner, K. & Rumelt, R. (1991). Software piracy: an analysis of protection strategies. 37 *Management Science* 125–139.

[20] See Landes, W. & Lichtman, D. (2003). Indirect liability for copyright infringement: Napster and beyond. 17(2) *Journal of Economic Perspectives* 113-24 for their synthesised review on this topic; Besen, S. & Kirby, S. (1989). Private copying, appropriability and optimal copying royalties. 32 *Journal of Law and Economics* 255–280 for a general economic model and analysis of this issue.

countries, indirect compensation has been adopted in the media equipment industry. For instance, television set makers are levied a fee for each unit produced, which is used to receive and show television programs. Nonetheless, the proposal is far from foolproof yet, and the levied party is sure to oppose to this.

As a general economic principle, non-targeted pricing leads to inefficiency. Additional costs imposed on hardware vendors will be passed on to the end-customers across the board. Whether one engages in private copying or not and, if so, regardless of the copying level, he or she will have to bear the (same) extra cost. The increase in price will cause what economists call "deadweight loss." As a consequence, the consumption of the technology will be diminished. Of course, the extent of the consumption reduction is an empirical question to study, among others.

VI. Concluding Remarks

As ICT technologies have rendered the duplication and transmission of information and content increasingly cheaper and easier, copyright law stakeholders will always be confronted with newer and greater challenges. Understanding and even incorporating the basic logic of it will positively contribute toward the making of a better integrated approach to copyright.

www.ingramcontent.com/pod-product-compliance
Ingram Content Group UK Ltd.
Pitfield, Milton Keynes, MK11 3LW, UK
UKHW020117290926
15471UKWH00003B/196

9 781841 136547